A DELACORTE PRESS BOOK
DISTRIBUTED BY THE DIAL PRESS, NEW YORK

A
TREASURY
OF AMERICAN
POLITICAL
HUMOR

EDITED BY LEONARD C. LEWIN

Acknowledgments: Grateful acknowledgment is made to the authors, publishers and agents listed below for their permission to use the material reprinted in this anthology:

CHARLES ALVERSON, "Every Neighborhood Needs One," from Vol. 1, No. 42 of *Outsider's Newsletter*. Reprinted by permission of the author.

ROGER ANGELL, "The Great Starch Debate," from *The New Yorker*, May 19, 1962. Reprinted by permission; Copyright © 1962 by The New Yorker Magazine, Inc.

M. J. ARLEN, "The Space Race," from *The New Yorker*. Copyright © 1962 by The New Yorker Magazine, Inc. Reprinted by permission of the author. "Who Wants to Know?" Copyright © 1962 by Esquire, Inc. Reprinted by permission of the author.

HERBERT ASBURY, "The Noble Experiment of Izzy and Moe." Reprinted by permission of Edith Evans Asbury, copyright owner.

RUSSELL BAKER, "How Congress Ended," from *The New York Times*, November 7, 1963; "Security Test," from *The New York Times*, December 5, 1963; "Tax Day," from *The New York Times*, April 15, 1963. Copyright © 1963 by The New York Times Company. "The Enemy Moon," from *The New York Times*, February 4, 1964. Copyright © 1964 by The New York Times Company. "The Vast Wasteland of Hard-Nosed Multi-Gigaton Words," from *The New York Times*, September 17, 1961. Copyright © 1961 by The New York Times Company. Reprinted by permission of The New York Times Company. "The President's 2,500,000 Right Arms," from *An American in Washington*. Copyright © 1961 by Russell Baker. Reprinted by permission of Alfred A. Knopf, Inc.

ROBERT BENDINER, "The 1952 Campaign," from several *Once Over Lightly* columns in *The New York Post*. Reprinted by permission of the author. "How to Listen to Campaign Oratory If You Have To," from *Look* Magazine, October 11, 1960. Copyright © 1960 by Cowles Magazine & Broadcasting, Inc. Reprinted by permission of the author and of Cowles Magazine and Broadcasting, Inc.

SAMUEL C. BRIGHTMAN, "Self-Interview," from *Monocle*. Reprinted by permission of the author and of Monocle Periodicals, Inc.

HEYWOOD BROUN, "Hints to the Epicure." Copyright © 1938, 1941 by Heywood Hale Broun. Reprinted by permission of Heywood Hale Broun and of Constance Broun.

ART BUCHWALD, "I Have a Lady in the Balcony." Reprinted from syndicated column *Art Buchwald at Home, New York Herald Tribune* by permission of the author. Copyright © 1963. "The Perils of Informing," from *I Chose Capitol Punishment*, by Art Buchwald. Reprinted by permission of the author. Copyright © 1962. "Conversation on a Plane," from *How Much Is That in Dollars?*, by Art Buchwald. Reprinted by permission of the author. Copyright © 1960. "Talk, Talk, Talk, Talk," from *Is It Safe to Drink the Water?*, by Art Buchwald. Reprinted by permission of the author. Copyright © 1962. "P.S. from NATO." Reprinted by permission of the author. Copyright © 1957.

WILLIAM F. BUCKLEY, JR., "A Fortnight with Murray Kempton," from *Monocle* and from *Rumbles Left and Right*. Reprinted by permission of the author and of Monocle Periodicals, Inc.

AL CAPP, "I Can Give You Anything But Love, Baby," from *Monocle*, Vol. 5, No. 1. Reprinted by permission of the author.

WHITTAKER CHAMBERS, "Letter from Afar." Copyright © 1958. Reprinted by permission of *National Review*.

JOHN CROSBY, "The Pangs of Utopia" from *The New York Herald Tribune*. Copyright © 1963 by New York Herald Tribune, Inc. Reprinted by permission of New York Herald Tribune, Inc.

GUY DANIELS, "A Biologist Looks at the Civil Service," from *Poems and Translations*. Copyright © 1959 by Guy Daniels (Inferno Press Editions); originally published in A *Houyhnhnm's Scrapbook*.

GEORGE DIXON, "Romney," published by King Features Syndicate, May 26, 1963. Copyright © by King Features Syndicate. Reprinted by permission of King Features Syndicate.

F. P. DUNNE, "Reform Administration," from *Observations by Mr. Dooley*. Copyright 1902 by Harper & Brothers. "The Negro Problem," from *Mr. Dooley's Philosophy*. Copyright 1900 by Harper & Brothers. "The Vice-President," from *Dissertations by Mr. Dooley*. Copyright 1906 by Harper & Brothers. Reprinted by permission of Harper & Row, Publishers, Inc.

ROGER EDDY, "Why I Won't Be Governor of Connecticut." Copyright © 1962 by *Harper's* Magazine. Reprinted by permission of A. Watkins, Inc.

RALPH ELLISON, "The Political Nigra." Copyright © 1963 by Ralph Ellison. Reprinted by permission of Random House, Inc.

JULES FEIFFER, "Corruption," "The Dogs," "Civil Defense," "Bureau of Images." Reprinted by permission of the author.

JOHN T. FLYNN, "Von Pleesemall of Schlumpberg," from *The New Republic*, July 15, 1935. Reprinted by permission of the Committee for John T. Flynn.

ROBERT FORSYTHE, "Redder Than the Rose," from the collection of the same name. Reprinted by permission of Robert Crichton.

SENATOR J. W. FULBRIGHT, "Seagull Wisdom," "On 'Liberalism' and 'Coexistence,'" from *United States Senate Speeches*. Reprinted by permission of Senator Fulbright.

WOLCOTT GIBBS, "Glorious Calvin," from *The New Yorker*, February 9, 1929. Copyright © 1929, 1957 by The New Yorker Magazine, Inc. "The Candidate from New York" (excerpt from "St. George and the Dragnet") from *The New Yorker*, May 25, 1940. Copyright © 1940 by The New Yorker Magazine, Inc. Reprinted by permission of The New Yorker Magazine, Inc.

HARRY GOLDEN, "The Vertical Negro Plan," from *Only in America*. Copyright © 1958 by Harry Golden. Reprinted by permission of The World Publishing Company.

SENATOR BARRY GOLDWATER, excerpts from his "Alfalfa Club Speech" of January 20, 1962. Reprinted by permission of Senator Goldwater.

PHILIP HAMBURGER, "Hq.," "Sculling on the Schuylkill," from *Our Man Stanley*. Copyright © 1963 by Philip Hamburger. Reprinted by permission of The Bobbs-Merrill Company, Inc. and of The New Yorker Magazine, Inc.

JOSEPH HELLER, "Milo," from *Catch-22*. Copyright © 1955, 1961 by Joseph Heller. Reprinted by permission of Simon & Schuster, Inc.

ARTHUR HOPPE, "White Moderates Are a Bit Limited." Reprinted by permission of the *San Francisco Chronicle*. "Interesting Native Customs in Washington and Other Savage Lands," "Dammit, Steve, You Forgot Modest," "Abundance Is a Four-Letter Word," "Everybody Loves a Party," from *The Love Everybody Crusade*. Copyright © 1963 by Arthur Hoppe. Reprinted by permission of Doubleday & Co., Inc.

LANGSTON HUGHES, "There Ought To Be a Law," from *The Best of Simple*. Copyright © 1961 by Langston Hughes. Reprinted by permission of Hill and Wang, Inc.

OLIVER JENSEN, "Gettysburg Address in Eisenhowerese." Reprinted by permission of the author.

JOSEPH KASELOW, "P. R. Brains in Birmingham." Copyright © 1963 by New York Herald Tribune, Inc. Reprinted by permission of New York Herald Tribune, Inc.

SENATOR KENNETH KEATING, "Mine Enemy—The Folk Singer" from a United States Senate speech. Reprinted by permission of Senator Keating.

EMERY KELEN, "Press Gallery," from *Platypus at Large* by Emery Kelen. Copyright © 1960 by Emery Kelen. Reprinted by permission of E. P. Dutton & Co., Inc., and of the author.

MURRAY KEMPTON, "The Sorehead," from *America Comes of Middle Age*. Copyright © 1952 by The New York Post Corporation. Reprinted by permission of Little, Brown and Company.

GEORGE G. KIRSTEIN, "Non-Survivability Plus," from *The Nation*, March 5, 1960. Reprinted by permission of *The Nation*.

MARVIN KITMAN, "Confessions of an Ex-Anti-Communist," from *The Outsider's Newsletter*. Copyright © 1962 by Monocle Periodicals, Inc. Reprinted by permission of Marvin Kitman and of The Sterling Lord Agency.

6 Acknowledgments

FLETCHER KNEBEL, excerpts from *Potomac Fever* columns dealing with the 1960 Kennedy-Nixon campaign. Copyright © by the Register and Tribune Syndicate. Reprinted by permission of the author and of the Register and Tribune Syndicate.

KARLA KUSKIN, "The Rocky Road Upward." Reprinted by permission of the author.

RING LARDNER, SR., "On Prohibition," from *First and Last*. Copyright 1923 by International Magazine Co. Copyright renewal 1951 by Ellis A. Lardner. Reprinted by permission of Ring Lardner, Jr.

J. B. LEE, JR., "Letter from a West Texas Constituent." Reprinted by permission of Representative Ed Foreman, 16th District, Texas.

CHARLES LEVY, "Statute of Liberty," from *Monocle*, Vol. 2, No. 1. Copyright © 1958 by Monocle Periodicals, Inc. Reprinted by permission of the author and of Monocle Periodicals, Inc.

A. J. LIEBLING, "The Alderman," from *Chicago: The Second City*. Copyright © 1952 by A. J. Liebling. Reprinted by permission of the author and of James Brown Associates, Inc. "Governor Long Speaks," from *The Earl of Louisiana*. Copyright © 1958 by A. J. Liebling. Reprinted by permission of Simon & Schuster, Inc., of W. H. Allen, of the author and of his agent, James Brown Associates, Inc.

RICHARD R. LINGEMAN, "The Fleeced Land," "Automation Fear Hits D.C.," "Moon Shot Eclipsed by Sun." Reprinted from *Monocle* by permission of the author.

DWIGHT MACDONALD, "A Note on Wallese." Reprinted from *Memoirs of a Revolutionist* by Dwight Macdonald, by permission of Farrar, Straus & Co., Inc., and of the author. Copyright © 1957 by Dwight Macdonald.

NORMAN MAILER, "Some Notes from the 1960 Democratic Convention," "Newspapers and Politics," from *The Presidential Papers*. Copyright © 1963 by Norman Mailer. Reprinted by permission of the author and of G. P. Putnam's Sons, Inc.

DONALD MALCOLM, "Dooley Redivivus." Copyright © 1957 Harrison-Blaine, Inc., Publishers, *The New Republic*. Reprinted by permission of *The New Republic*.

RUSSELL MALONEY, "Short-Wave Propaganda Program Suitable for Jamming by an Axis Power," from *It's Still Maloney*. Copyright © 1945 by Russell Maloney. Reprinted by permission of William Morris Agency, Inc. and of The Dial Press, Inc.

MARYA MANNES, "Sales Campaign," "Postmaster vs. Poet," "You're a Big Boy Now," from *Subverse*. Copyright © 1959 by Marya Mannes. Reprinted by permission of the author and of the publisher, George Braziller, Inc.

H. L. MENCKEN, "Gamalielese," "Imperial Purple," from *The Baltimore Sun*. Reprinted by permission of *The Baltimore Sun*.

EVE MERRIAM, text of "Fashions in Candidates" (with drawings by Robert Osborn) from *The New Republic*, July 11, 1960. Reprinted by permission of the author, Eve Merriam, and of *The New Republic*.

KARL E. MEYER, "That Image in the White House," from *The New America* by Karl E. Meyer, Basic Books, Inc., New York, 1961. Reprinted by permission of Basic Books, Inc. "J.F.K.'s Pressmanship," from *Monocle*. Reprinted by permission of the author and of Monocle Periodicals, Inc.

RICHARD B. MORRIS, "A Presidential Sense of Humor," from *The New York Times*, April 30, 1961. Copyright © 1961 by The New York Times Company. Reprinted by permission of The New York Times Company and the author.

OGDEN NASH, "Invocation," from *Verses from 1929 On* by Ogden Nash. Copyright 1931 by Ogden Nash. Reprinted by permission of Little, Brown and Company and of J. M. Dent & Sons.

EDWARD K. NELLOR, "Office Memo on Expense Accounts." Reprinted by permission of the author.

The New York Times, "No Clear Reply at Foggy Bottom," from *The New York Times*, May 11, 1963. Copyright © 1963 by The New York Times Company. Reprinted by permission of The New York Times Company.

ROBERT OSBORN, drawings for "Fashions in Candidates" (with text by Eve Merriam), from *The New Republic*, July 11, 1960. Reprinted by permission of the artist, Robert Osborn, and of *The New Republic*.

WESTBROOK PEGLER, "Promoting Fight of the Century," "Little Words of Big Men,"

"His Day," "Myriad-Minded Us," "Those Were the Days." Reprinted by permission of the author.

S. J. PERELMAN, "Thunder Over Alma Mater." Copyright © 1964 by S. J. Perelman. Reprinted by permission of the author.

CHARLES J. PRENTISS, "Remembrance of Past Things," from *Monocle*, Vol. 2, No. 1. Copyright © 1958 by Charles J. Prentiss. Reprinted by permission of the author.

ROGER PRICE, "J. G. Meets the Candidate," from *J. G., The Upright Ape*. Copyright © 1960 by Roger Price. Reprinted by permission of the author.

JOHN FRANCIS PUTNAM, "A Plan for Surrender," from *The Realist*, Summer 1962. Reprinted by permission of *The Realist*.

"Mike Quin," "The Mugity Wumpus," from *On the Drumhead* and *The People's World*. Copyright 1948 by the Pacific Publishing Foundation, Inc. Reprinted by permission of the Pacific Publishing Foundation, Inc.

JAMES RESTON, "To Ingemar Johannson, With Love" from *The New York Times*, June 29, 1960. Copyright © 1960 by The New York Times Company. Reprinted by permission of The New York Times Company.

WILL ROGERS, "The Capitol Comedy," "Some Presidential Nominating Conventions," "Chamber of Commerce," "Sick Hogs," "The War of Washington," "Recognizing Russia," from *The Autiobiography of Will Rogers* and *How We Elect Our Presidents* by Donald Day. Reprinted by permission of Donald Day.

LEO ROSTEN, "An Open Letter to the Mayor of New York," from *Look* Magazine, February 12, 1963. Copyright © 1963 by Cowles Magazines and Broadcasting, Inc. Reprinted by permission of Cowles Magazines and Broadcasting, Inc. and of Madeline Rosten Lee.

RICHARD ROVERE, "I've Got a Paper Here," from *The New Yorker*. Reprinted by permission; Copyright © 1954 by The New Yorker Magazine, Inc.

MORRIE RYSKIND, "The Rover Boys in Los Angeles." Copyright © 1960. Reprinted by permission of *National Review*.

MARION K. SANDERS, "Meet the Boys," from *The Lady and the Vote*. Copyright © 1955, 1956 by Marion K. Sanders. Reprinted by permission of the author.

REUBEN SHIP, "St. Peter Takes the Stand," from *The Investigator* by Reuben Ship (Sidgwick & Jackson, London: 1956). Copyright © 1956 by Reuben Ship. Reprinted by permission of Hope Leresche & Steele and of the author.

MERRIMAN SMITH, "Hair by Sealyham, Shoulders by God," from *The Good New Days*. Copyright © 1962 by Merriman Smith. Reprinted by permission of The Bobbs-Merrill Company, Inc., and of Curtis Brown, Ltd.

TERRY SOUTHERN, "Cuba Libre," from "How I signed Up at $250 a Month for the Big Parade Through Havana Bla-Bla-Bla and Wound Up in Guatemala with the CIA," from *Esquire*, June, 1963. Copyright © June, 1963, by *Esquire*. Reprinted by permission of *Esquire* and of The Sterling Lord Agency.

DONALD OGDEN STEWART, "The Whisky Rebellion," from *A Parody Outline of History* by Donald Ogden Stewart. Copyright 1921 by George H. Doran Company. Reprinted by permission of Doubleday & Company, Inc.

CASKIE STINNETT, "And If Elected, and I Think I Will Be . . . ," "Only in America," from *Back to Normal*. Copyright © 1963 by Caskie Stinnett. Reprinted by permission of Bernard Geis Associates.

FRANK SULLIVAN, "The Cliché Expert Testifies on the Atom," from *The New Yorker*, November 17, 1945. Reprinted by permission; copyright © 1945, The New Yorker Magazine, Inc.

CONGRESSMAN FRANK THOMPSON, JR., "A Modest Proposal for the Return to Conservatism Through Decentralization." Reprinted by permission of Congressman Thompson.

JAMES THURBER, "The Dewey, Dewey Fog," from *The New Yorker*, February 14, 1948. Copyright © 1948 by James Thurber. Reprinted by permission of Mrs. Helen Thurber and of the New Yorker Magazine, Inc. "The Very Proper Gander," from *The New Yorker*, February 4, 1939. Reprinted by permission; Copyright © 1939 The New Yorker Magazine, Inc. "The Rabbits Who Caused All the Trouble," from *The New Yorker*, August 26, 1939. Reprinted by permission; Copyright © 1939 The New Yorker Magazine, Inc. "The Tiger

8 Acknowledgments

Who Would Be King," originally from *The New Yorker* and from *Further Fables for Our Time*, published by Simon and Schuster, Inc. Copyright © 1956 by James Thurber. Reprinted by permission of The New Yorker Magazine, Inc. and of Mrs. Helen Thurber.

JOHN UPDIKE, "Mr. Ex-Resident," from *The New Yorker*, August 5, 1961. Reprinted by permission; Copyright © 1961 by The New Yorker Magazine, Inc.

DAN WAKEFIELD, "Wags and the West," from *The New York Pest*, December 1962, published by Monocle Publications, Inc. Copyright © 1962 by Dan Wakefield. Reprinted by permission of the author and of his agent, James Brown Associates, Inc.

GERALD WALKER, "The Racial Inferiority of the White Southerner," from *Cavalier*, April, 1963, and *The Negro Digest*, June, 1963. Copyright © 1963 by Fawcett Publications, Inc. Reprinted by permission of the author.

JAMES A. WECHSLER, "Rocky & Dick," from *The New York Post*, March 13, 1963, "Dry Spell" from *The New York Post*, October 28, 1963. Copyright © 1963 by *The New York Post*. Reprinted by permission of The Sterling Lord Agency.

CONGRESSMAN JIM WRIGHT, "Hot Line." Reprinted by permission of Representative Wright.

CONTENTS

10　*Contents*

4. WHAT DO THEY MEAN?

12 Contents

14　*Contents*

PREFACE

Unlike the distinguished speaker "who needs no introduction to the people of this community," but gets one just the same—ten pages' worth—this anthology does in fact need an introduction, it seems to me, primarily because "American political humor" means different things to different people, including politicians, humorists, and librarians. I'll try here to provide the reader, if not with a precise definition of the subject, at least with a reasonably clear notion of what he can expect to find in this book, largely by indicating some of the practices and prejudices that influenced the selection of the 160-odd pieces that follow.

"American political," as used here, covers a wide variety of themes, but the issues and personalities dealt with, whether factual or fictional, are all recognizably part of the United States political scene. The range extends, for example, from the appointment of a postmaster in Laramie, Wyoming, in 1882, to a satire of American-Soviet relations in outer space in the future; the issue under discussion may be the qualifications of a precinct captain in Chicago or the semantics of atomic warfare. I have not included general "social" or "cultural" satire except where the subject has lent itself to political expression; there is no satirical comment on such matters as fashion, Madison Avenue, automation, or supermarket culture—*as such*. Look at the section and subsection headings.

What constitutes the humor—and the word is used loosely—has been arrived at by way of the customary subjective judgment. (If you look for this introduction to contain a novel and interesting psycho-sociological theory of humor you will be disappointed.) All but a dozen or so of the pieces here are "funny," to me, without qualification or explication; the remaining handful, however, I simply recognize as funny in the context of the circumstances in which they were written. Since the selections were deliberately eclectic, it is hard for me to imagine that any single reader will be amused by everything he finds here. Anyone who does has a dangerously permissive sense of humor, and may need help.

What about chronological range? The table of contents will reveal selections that date as far back as the American Revolution. But I have not used the subtitle "from the Revolution to the 1960s," or some such, because I think this might imply a certain claim to "complete" historical coverage, which is not being made. The pieces in this collection were chosen to be enjoyed for their own values, not to be revered for their historical significance. Although the principal political humorists of the nineteenth century are represented, the emphasis is on the writings of our own times. Most political humor is topical, and therefore perishable; not much of the older material can come through to us as humor without long and destructive explanation. The vogue, almost a convention in humorous writing, of dialect, phonetic, or illiterate spelling, which began in the early 1800s and lasted nearly a century, creates another problem. Struggling with it rarely seems worth the reader's effort today; the only general exception, as far as I'm concerned, is the work of Finley Peter Dunne, the creator of "Mr. Dooley."

The transience of political humor explains more than its low survival rate. It explains, for example, why so much first-class writing in this field is, like first-class journalism, so undervalued in the world of letters. It explains why there are so few collections that are even first cousins to this one. Not until I began to assemble it did I have a full appreciation of how extremely perishable this material usually is, nor did I have an adequate regard for those samples of the older writing that still look good. Even as I type these lines I cannot blink off the vision of obsolescence. Since I look forward to seeing this book around for a few years, the estimated longevity of prospective inclusions eventually carried more weight with me than I had anticipated. Nevertheless, by 1975, perhaps earlier, a quarter of these pieces will probably require footnotes. Sic transit.

Oddly enough, this intimation of mortality has a bearing on my decision to risk explaining too little rather than too much; it reminds me that I have no crystal ball that will tell me which references are the ones that will eventually need explanation. Also, the book was designed to be opened to almost any page and to be read for pleasure; it is not offered as a work of definitive scholarship. (One does not preclude the other, but I have elected to intrude with editorial comment only where it seems absolutely necessary, or where the temptation is irresistible.) Most of the rather limited commentary will appear at the beginnings of sections. There will be virtually no biographical data furnished, for example; although this kind of information can be very useful, it rarely earns its space in a general anthology. Not enough can be said to satisfy more than a casual curiosity, and writers still in business won't stay quietly in their assigned pigeonholes.

The selections have been organized topically, for convenience and comparatively easy reading. The "topics," however, are necessarily arbitrary, as is, occasionally, the placement of a selection in one section rather than in another. Within the subsections the order is usually, but not always, chronological; I've seen no compelling reason to follow a rigidly consistent rule in this. It's possible that some readers may find ten consecutive pieces dealing with the same general subject an overly concentrated diet, but I don't expect many people to consume the book seriatim from soup to nuts, and it's handy to have things together when you want to taste how different writers have cooked up the same ingredients.

This is a book of written humor—to be read. With negligible exceptions (a few political speeches, Gridiron Club songs, etc.), it contains no scenes from plays, cabaret skits, comedians' monologues, television or radio scripts, nor anything else that was meant to be performed. It wasn't originally planned that way. Many wild geese were pursued before I realized what a miniscule fraction of even the very best material intended to be spoken or sung amounts to much on the printed page. If you are disappointed, therefore, because you don't find anything here by Dick Gregory, Mort Sahl, or perhaps Fred Allen, consider that you might be more disappointed if you did. The same is true for plays; there is nothing from *Of Thee I Sing, Pins and Needles,* or *The Best Man.*

This is not a picture book. Political cartooning has been a consistent medium of American political humor since the days of Nast, and today's political cartoonists as a group surpass their predecessors, but that's another book, not this one. The apparent exceptions you will find here (by Feiffer, Osborn, Kuskin) are illustrated writing, which is not the same thing.

This is not a collection of jokes or amusing anecdotes. You will find a few one- or two-line epigrams and wisecracks scattered here and there, and a few pages of them grouped together—but that's another book, too. This is why there is so little from our best-known wits in public life, such as Adlai Stevenson, Alben Barkley, and, most notably, Abraham Lincoln. (I have included Richard B. Morris' "A Presidential Sense of Humor" as a kind of sampler of such anecdotes.)

Most of the pieces are expressly satirical; it's the nature of the beast. What may be surprising is how many are not. Some of the most successful are carefully factual accounts of inherently ridiculous or outrageous situations, their comic implications heightened by the treatment afforded by such engaging practitioners as the late A. J. Liebling. Some are straightforward, if malicious, political portraits. Style ranges from heavy-handed sarcasm to brilliant parody, some so subtle it rewards repeated readings. There are specimens of inadvertent humor, but not many; most of the good ones I found were too long (and incompressible), redundant in subject matter, or out of place in this collection for other reasons. Not included, for example, are a Senate debate on the comparative merits of Wisconsin and Oregon cheese, the

Inaugural Address of President Warren G. Harding, or any Eisenhower press conference.

Anthologists are fair game for their sins of omission and commission, chiefly the former. It's a reasonable penalty, I think, for making arbitrary decisions. Explaining the choices that had to be made and remade to assemble what was planned to be a coherent and well-balanced collection of manipulable size thins out to a kind of shop talk, of limited interest. Of such explanations there is no end—one leads to another ad infinitum—so in general, therefore, I won't attempt to rationalize particular inclusions and exclusions. But inquiries, comments, suggestions, and expressions of outrage will be welcomed.

Comment on one choice, however, may be revealing. Mark Twain was a great writer and a great humorist, yet I found very little of his work suitable for inclusion in this anthology. Most of his writing classifiable as *political* humor is badly dated, prolix, or heavy-handed. But does "To the Person Sitting in Darkness," his furious satirical indictment of American policy in the Philippines, really belong in a book of "humor"? I think not—but I have included it. Much of the detailed treatment is "funny," if macabre, and it is a magnificent explosion. The problem exemplified by this exception is that, while the most effective political humor is usually satirical, the most effective political satire is not necessarily funny.

Consider the source. Who said it, and under what circumstances, makes a difference, unfair as this may be to professional humorists. I have in mind politicians, for the most part. It is no reflection on Senator Barry Goldwater, for instance, to note that his Alfalfa Club speech can be considered funny largely because it is attributed to him; it wouldn't be included here if it had a writer's name attached to it. J. Proctor Knott's hilarious rhetoric would lose much of its impact if it were not clear that it had been emitted in the halls of Congress.

Something old, something new. Most of the selections in this book have never been anthologized before; about half of these "newer" entries, in turn, have never been inside the covers of any book. On the other hand, I have included some pieces that can be found in several other collections. I'm glad to assure the reader that he won't come across many twice-told tales, but no prospective selection carried more force because it was "fresh" (or because it was "established").

One of the most cheerful revelations that came my way during the course of assembling this book was that far more political satire is being written these days than I—or anyone else I had talked with about it—suspected. And the prospect, I think, is for more, barring a great and unpleasant change in the political climate. The Forties and the Fifties were a dreary period for political humor in this country; the cloud of political repression and the shadow of unusually far-reaching economic conformities dimmed the wit of even the least intimidated. New and brilliant satirical talents have been emerging during the last five years, some as uncompromising and bitter as Jules Feiffer and Lenny Bruce, some as sensitive to the nonsense of official Washington as Russell Baker and Art Buchwald. You will find at least a few pieces in this book by writers you never heard of before (published in magazines you may have never heard of before); I think you will hear more about them.

The most conspicuous political satire of recent years has been on-stage, in one sense or another, exemplified by the imaginative monologuists already mentioned and by cabaret or stage reviews. The surprising popular success of the BBC's politically free-wheeling *That Was The Week That Was* in 1963 inspired at least two American television "equivalents"; I use quotation marks because I am skeptical. In spite of the bold noises coming from the networks, American commercial broadcasting remains a subdivision of the advertising industry, and is hardly likely to bite the hand that holds its leash more than now and then; I find it hard to visualize a regularly scheduled national program consistently engaged in satirizing important issues or institutions. (Perhaps they order this matter better in England, but that's another discussion.) If I have to eat these words, it will be a pleasure.

The more open political air of the Sixties has so far blown more freely through the composing room than around the transmission tower. Although there are cold business reasons why editors and publishers are, as a class, less cowardly than broadcasters, it is still refreshing to see that even the mass-circulation magazines are breaking many old taboos, including those devolving about political humor. You will find several of them represented here, along with journals of political opinion and such a dependable source as *The New Yorker*. You will also find several selections from the only current American publications devoted entirely to political satire, *Monocle* and its offshoot, the *Outsider's Newsletter*; they have a resourceful editor, a talented staff, and a versatile roster of occasional contributors. Also represented is *The Realist*, a magazine of "freethought criticism and satire."

Anyone who ever tried his own hand in this game has a healthy respect for the growing list of newspaper columnists specializing in one or another sort of political humor. For all their pieces that don't come off, for all their efforts that can only be described as trivial, for all their various limitations of scope, no one who ever faced an opposing daily deadline while holding his typewriter poised over an injunction to be funny will impugn their batting averages. The current sluggers include Arthur Hoppe, of the *San Francisco Chronicle*; the better-known Buchwald and Baker, previously mentioned; and such widely syndicated old hands as George Dixon, Fletcher Knebel, and Bill Vaughan.

In politics, perhaps more than in most activities where interests conflict, what's funny depends on whose sacred cow is gored. This raises the unavoidable questions of taste and of point of view. My own preference, which may already be clear, is for purposeful political satire that reaches successfully for the heart of an issue, that enters its point with precision and malice, and that is basically serious about a matter important to the writer. Nevertheless, a fair part of this book, including some of its funniest pieces, is unsatirical humor of the gentler, it's-all-among-friends sort. I have tried to make the selections in a politically non-partisan or multi-partisan manner; how successfully, I don't know. Because, as a matter of record, there is comparatively little genuine "right-wing" humor to draw upon, I took special pains to seek out what I could; I am so out of tune with its political premises, however, that the discord may be audible in the pages that follow.

The matter of "bad taste" can be even trickier in political humor than the possible failure of an editor to recognize his own political bias and take it adequately into account. This book contains some savage attacks, on institutions and on individuals. I think their "bad taste," for those who might call it that, is defensible. I wouldn't say the same for the sleazy coloring books, sniggering family jokes about political figures, or other examples of the principle that *anything* about a politician is good for a laugh. A fair criterion for this aspect of political humor, I think, is not whether a low blow or personal slur is "offensive" to the victim or his friends, but whether it is germane to a *political* point.

At the beginning of these notes I raised the question of whether any introduction to this anthology was necessary or desirable, and quickly suggested that it was. A more pertinent question might be: Is this *book* necessary? As the politician who introduced the distinguished speaker might say, I'm glad I asked that question. As I listen to the speeches, scan the newspapers and magazines, and peer at the television screen, my answer, voters, now more than ever, is: Yes! Yes!

New York, 1964

1 THE WORLD OF WASHINGTON

LIFE IN THE HOT CENTER

It seems appropriate to introduce this collection with some "inside information" about what goes on where the greatest concentration of American political activity is found. Washington-watchers may or may not be surprised to learn that what goes on today, in Congress, for example, is not so different from what went on a century ago as an outsider might expect.

THE SCENE

ARTHUR HOPPE

Interesting Native Customs
in Washington and Other Savage Lands

When visiting a strange country like Washington, it's incumbent on us responsible ace newsmen to file what we call "a backgrounder." You know, a lengthy review of annual rainfall and grazing conditions with a few paragraphs about quaint native courting customs thrown in to sex things up a little.

Well, Washington is several miles square and about as tall, say, as the Washington Monument, give or take a little. It is surrounded on all four sides by reality. The winters aren't too hot. Neither is the rest of the climate. The natives, in general, are sullen.

While the outside world refers to it as "Washington," the natives call it "the District," short for "District of Columbia." And the natives, of course, do not think of themselves as "natives." They think of themselves as "experts." The population, at the moment, consists of 998,762 experts and two tourists from Camden, Ohio, who, on being interviewed, said they hadn't the foggiest notion of what was wrong with U.S. foreign policy.

The main industries are eating, drinking, and talking. The major import and export—indeed, the staple of the economy—is money. As with many other countries these days, Washington imports more from us than it exports. This creates what we economists call "an unfavorable trade balance." Which, in this case, it certainly is.

The local unit of currency is "the Million Dollar." Usually written "$1 million." Many of these, however, are required to purchase anything. So they are generally referred to in the plural, such as "thus and so many Million Dollars." In recent years, a new denomination, "the Billion Dollar" (written "$1 billion") has come into wide use. And lately one even hears "the Trillion Dollar" mentioned on occasion. But only in referring to the national debt.

It is exceedingly difficult to calculate a rate of exchange between Washington money and our money because the essential characteristic of Washington money is that it's not real. No native, to my knowledge, has ever seen "a Million Dollar," much less "a Billion Dollar," although they remain the chief topic of conversation.

Lesser denominations, such as "the Thousand Dollar" or "the Hundred Dollar" have, like the old French centime, virtually disappeared from circulation. And the only place the natives use real money, such as the dollar, is after office hours. Indeed, any mention of real money tends for some unexplained reason to make the natives restless. Take, for example, the case of the underground garage.

The Solons, a local tribe living on Capitol Hill, recently decided to build an underground garage so their cars wouldn't get sunburned. This would cost only four "million dollars," and everybody was quite content. But then someone, presumably an anthropologist from the real world, announced, after much calculation, that this figure came to somewhere around $25,000 per car. Which sounded like real money. And it was suggested that the Solons might economize by merely buying cheap cars and throwing them away each day on arriving at their meeting place. This talk about real money made the Solons terribly nervous. Not nervous enough, of course, to cancel their plans for the four "Million Dollar" garage. But terribly nervous.

Despite the obvious need for a drastic currency reform, however, the local economy is booming. Everywhere the visitor looks, new buildings are going up. And when you realize that the natives neither manufacture nor produce anything of salable value, this expansion is all the more fantastic.

The new buildings are, of course, all being constructed in the Foursquare Monolithic Style of modern native architecture. The natives, it is believed, pour a solid cube of concrete, hollow out the inside, and stick a flagpole on top. The result, it is generally agreed, is much more permanent than the thatched huts of the Wambeesi. If not as pleasing to the eye.

But it is certainly clear to even the most casual observer that all this activity indicates the natives, due to our help, have at last reached "the economic takeoff point." And while my heart goes out to them in their struggle to better themselves, I feel it is now our grim duty to cut back drastically on our financial-aid program so that they may learn to stand on their own two feet. I feel strongly that we should take this step before April 15 at the latest.

Let us now turn to the social structure of the country. As in many of the new African nations, the natives of Washington belong not to one, but to numerous separate and distinct tribes, each spiritedly warlike and fiercely jealous of its prerogatives. The best known of the local tribes are, of course, the Solons, occupying the strategic heights of Capitol Hill, and the Presidents, who live on the flats perhaps a mile away. . . . Lesser known are the numerous other interesting tribes of the flats, such as "State," "Commerce," "Interior," "NRA" (now extinct), and so forth. While nominally joined by treaty with the Presidents, these lesser tribes devote most of their energies to battling each other. . . .

The young warriors of each tribe are prepared for leadership in these devious wars by a rite known as Shafting—a test similar to the trial-by-fire dance for young Ugulaps in North Borneo. Unlike the fire dance, which is a one-time fling for the young Ugulap, Shafting remains the prime occupation of the Washingtonian from his entry into the tribe until his death or retirement.

The goal in the rites of Shafting is telephone buttons. A telephone without buttons is a symbol of shame, and the native who has one invariably keeps it turned away from his visitors. A phone with two buttons is the symbol of having arrived at manhood, and so forth on up. Status is carefully equated. A six-button native, for instance, would never telephone a four-button native. Except through his secretary. The current scepter of chiefhood in all tribes is a conference phone, a light green model with chromium hooks and no fewer than eighteen plastic buttons, two of them red. With this goes a corner office, a conference table, two flags in standards, and four in-and-out baskets.

Most of the inordinately complex rituals of Shafting are fathomable only by anthropologists. Three of the simpler forms will be discussed here: Leaking, Copy-to-ing and Jack Hornering.

Leaking is practiced only at the highest levels in each tribe. Usually by subchieftains. When a mistake is made, Subchief X announces quickly that no mistake was made. Then he Leaks the inside information to the Columnists (a tribe of local historians of tremendous unimportance) that in reality it was a horrendous mistake. And that Subchief Y made it. When three or more Columnists print the leak, it becomes known as a *fact*. And Subchief Y is stripped of one secretary, his leather couch, and four buttons from his telephone. . . .

Copy-to-ing is practiced on the lower levels. Should Al Z, a young native working under Chief Y, make a minor slip, he will immediately receive fourteen interoffice memos from his fellow tribesmen. Such as: "Al, I was very sorry to see us get in that awful bind. But I did warn you at Staff beforehand. How about talking it over? Perhaps something can still be saved from the wreckage."

At the bottom of each memo is typed: COPY TO CHIEF Y. While no chief could possibly read all the scores of copies of memos he receives each day, the psychological damage on Al Z of those words, COPY TO CHIEF Y, can well be imagined.

I stumbled on Jack Hornering by making friends with a young native barely of the Executive Dining Room level. I found him busily initialing each page of an eight-page report to his chief.

"It cuts the chance of being Jack Hornered," he said.

Jack Hornered? "Sure," he said. "This report's loaded with good ideas. And it's got to pass through a lot of hands on its way to the top. Each hand's got a thumb. Remember? 'So he stuck in his thumb and pulled out a plum and said, "What a good boy am I." ' Sometimes an eight-page report gets to the top saying nothing but: 'Dear Chief; Yrs Truly.' I figure if I initial every page it will be a psychological burglar lock. To tell you the truth, though," he added gloomily, "it never works."

In my forthcoming book, *Interesting Native Customs in Washington and Other Savage Lands,* I've decided to prepare the gentler readers for the bloody accounts of Washington tribal shafting by building up to them gradually. For example, the early chapters will deal with less gruesome customs of more civilized tribes. Like: "Disembowelment Techniques Among the Mau Mau."

With all this intertribal and intratribal warfare, the natives, understandably enough, have little interest in the outside world, except as its events affect their internecine quarrels. Indeed many modern anthropologists feel that if the natives could ever be knit into one homogeneous unit, their skill and deviousness in the arts of warfare would inevitably mean that Washington would soon come to rule the world.

As of now, however, this danger appears extremely remote.

MERRIMAN SMITH

*Hair by Sealyham, Shoulders by God**

. . . The capital bubbles and squeaks in polyglot ritual. It abounds, particularly in these breathless days, with breeds and personalities of such high-octane performance that their contrails must be observed closely and quickly for proper recognition.

Perhaps this era was spied a-coming by one of the nation's pioneer psychiatrists shortly after World War I. This New Frontiersman of his day had a spare moment, in fact he had many spare moments in those early hours of psychiatry, in which he spoke to his son. This was significant in itself because the son didn't understand too clearly what his father did for a living. . . .

This may be irrelevant to the narrative, but there is such a demand in Washington today for *true meaning* and reporting *in depth,* even *omnifocus,* that snippets of history are included primarily as defensive measures.

At any rate, this perceptive doctor said to his boy, who has told the story many times since from the reclining leather comfort of his Jaguar, "Son, I want to open my own mental hospital and I want to pick an area where I know some day there'll be a lot of sick people. And son, that place is Washington."

Were it not for certain obscure medical ethics, this man would be memorialized for vision ranking with that of Alexander Graham Bell, the Wright brothers, and the Heeps who figured out installment credit.

This is not to say that Washington has more than another big city's share of square wheels, but there has been in recent years a noticeable influx of those whose behavior, if not hard to understand, certainly is more interesting than that of some of the dreary folk who used to take up space in our town.

* from *The Good New Days.*

Take, for instance, the government official who works fifteen hours a day at the genuinely needed and onerous chore of combating racial discrimination. As government salaries go, he's paid well but the money doesn't cover as much as it might, because he and his wife are strapped by tuition bills for their children at a private, segregated school.

Not all Washingtonians regarded their station so gravely.

Young men with natural shoulders and Wally Cox haircuts walk briskly to their Hillmans and Volvos at night, speaking earnestly and vibrantly across the nearly empty parking lot about the bully fun of running a government as though it were a spring semester project for Poli Sci 23.

Or, in some of the federal corridors, indelibly stamped products of Radcliffe or Smith in beige loafers, overblouses that tend to blur distracting endowments and Sealyham hair effects which they like to believe are mildly suggestive of Jacqueline. These frequently join forces with the young fellows in Volvos, returning to either his or her castle for marriage, thence back to Georgetown to dismay the disciples of Margaret Sanger. They blessedly thus create openings in government for other Radcliffe and Smith girls. Also, eventually ending up as customers for Rambler station wagons.

. . . .

Probably as much read as the Yellow Pages are society sections of Washington newspapers, which have a language of their own; a language for which there is no Berlitz save experience; a language that the New People know and thereby base their decisions to feel fortunate or left out of things.

An N.P. knows with experience that if a project, a process, or even a meeting is described as *supersecret* or *hush-hush*, in the *patois* of Washington, it means the writer knew something was going on, but not entirely.

If a woman is *attractive*, *vivacious* or *charming*, chances are that she's a wee bit plain, fiftyish but important. To mention her *attractive silvery locks* means that she has one foot in the grave. To say that she has *prematurely gray hair* can be quite catty.

Should a woman be said in print to be *ravishing* or *beautifully tanned*, her dress showed everything. She was half-naked if the gown was *stunningly cut*. Should she have an *athletic figure*, this is a sure Washington sign that she's disgustingly young but built like a Percheron.

If a man is described as *courtly* or having *charming Old World ways* and a *still-erect figure*, watch for an obituary soon. He's on his last legs and with what breath left to him, he's a frightful old bore, he talks endlessly about Senator Borah and how they quit making good cars when they quit making the Reo. Because of Washington's greatest common determinator, seniority, which we will deal with shortly, the man with *charming Old World ways* must be tolerated even though young ladies shudder at the memory of his scraggly hands on their thighs the last time they sat beside him at dinner.

When a social affair is described as *lavish, sumptuous, glittering*, or *breathtaking*, put it down that the food was tasty and plentiful, and the liquor lasted. If the account contains such clues as *unfortunately rainy, mob scene, loud clatter*, or *wedged in*, the canapés were soggy and the whisky was blended, plus the fact that the guests for the most part were second-rate, except one former Supreme Court Justice who went there by mistake.

Where there is reference to guests being a *select few* or *only old friends*, the host and hostess were either out of the current swim entirely, suffering a dollar gap, or merely sore at the society writer.

The experienced Washingtonian, N.P. or O.P., also pays attention to descriptive detail. If the affair was *gay*, it was the sort of thing to which you could take the rector. There was only punch, weak punch. Bananas sliced and floating on top. Imitation cut-glass cups. When the gathering was *très gai*, things are looking up—a few got looped, others went on to finish the job at a quaint gin mill. The hosts were a bit above par.

Occasionally the morning and evening social stock lists display other indices, which might be overlooked by any but true students. *Bubbling gaiety* is a dead giveaway. The writer may have been a shade socked-in. It was fun, though; particularly the handsome military attaché whom the hostess discovered going to the bathroom right beside her boxwood hedge. You can't put this sort of event in the paper, but Barbara did the cutest thing. She ran and got the can of Scat, which she uses to protect the hedge from her dog, and sprayed it all over Tony. . . .

Survival, acceptance, or at least understanding in the Good New Days involves not only social terminology, but knowledge of strangely differing persons, places, and conditions which must be worshiped—or denounced automatically, without question and at all times.

Some of the adorations are nationwide in scope, some peculiar to Washington and the era of New People.

The Irish, for instance. These are the pets of American politics. One may damn the daylights out of the British, the Portuguese, or the Brazilians, but to imply that the Irish or those of Irish extraction are even fractionally short of being mankind's best—past, present and future—is to invite lumps, large ones. This was true in Washington long before the Kennedys. Their arrival only intensified the cultism. . . .

The Proper Washingtonian also must bear awed reverence for Indians. Not American Indians, but Indian Indians. They must be regarded and hailed as invariable examples of gentle, honorable, peaceful, and wise people, despite Goa. This law of wonderful Indian Indians probably dates back to Mahatma Gandhi, but derives its continuing virility from Washington's generally guilty conscience about the years of American neglect of Asia. . . .

If an onyx-eyed Indian Indian comes to town seeking five million dollars for a birth-control clinic in Lower Rastrapati, he and his cause are worthy without question. He's entertained at benefit movies and cocktail parties, although he doesn't drink, himself. But just let an impecunious American Indian creep into town asking for water for his reservation or that his twelve-year-old son with one bad eye be exempt from the draft. He's denounced as a dreadful by-product of the welfare state and drummed back to his boondocks without even a *Congressional Record* to read on the return trip.

It once was *de rigueur* to preconize the poor and humbly begun in national politics and equally *pro forma* to belabor the rich and regard their desire for public office as a forerunner of large-scale larceny. This era apparently is behind us forever. The log-cabin types no longer seem to grow in our forests of presidential timber.

The popular acceptance of such multimillionaires as President Kennedy and New York's Governor Rockefeller has, however, produced some curious changes in public attitude which is reflected to great extent in Washington.

Many Americans now seem to want rich men in high public office, but they want these fellows to act like poor men. This may be called, for purposes of particular study, the riches-to-rags political posture or school of conduct.

Leading up to the 1960 campaigns, Kennedy and Rockefeller competed in raggedness. It was not until after the conventions that we often saw them decently clothed. Prior to that time, they posed for endless pictures in raveling blue jeans and frayed deck sneakers. Rockefeller took to eating in delicatessens. Some political scientists believe Rocke-

RUSSELL BAKER

The President's 2,500,000 Right Arms*

Following is a random sampling of events that occurred within the bureaucracy during the period 1957–9:

1. After a protest from Representative Donald E. Tewes, of Wisconsin, the Department of Justice agreed to revise its handbook *How to Cook in Jail* to include more recipes calling for butter. The decision was reached after Tewes complained that ninety-four recipes in the booklet required oleomargarine while only one mentioned butter, the glory of his native state.

2. The State Department decided against a showing of *South Pacific* at the Brussels Fair on the ground that its subplot, an interracial romance between a white man and an Asian girl, would annoy Southern senators. After several other Broadway successes, including works by Tennessee Williams and Arthur Miller, were rejected on the ground that they would irritate this or that pressure group, one diplomat suggested *Waiting for Godot*. Since no one could understand it, he argued, no one could possibly be offended.

3. In a memorandum, the Defense Department cautioned itself against divulging that monkeys were being shot into space in rocket research. Cannily the military revealed that "primates" were being fired off, but refused to talk when asked if "primates" meant monkeys. A man with a loose tongue revealed that they were monkeys, all right, but that the Pentagon feared the publicity would arouse Asian monkey cultists.

4. After deliberation the National Labor Relations Board refused to act against an employer who had fired a washing-machine repairman for leaving a customer the following note:

> Here is the grinding noise. Had to dismantle the washer to get it out. Machine otherwise okay. Suggest you check thoroughly for bobby pins before washing your hair in this washer. Also keep your mouth closed as the motion of the agitator has been known to dislodge dentures while beating the head back and forth. Also remove your glasses and keep your eyes closed. Your bill will be $6.

* from *An American in Washington.*

5. In the press office at the Pentagon someone posted a sign reading: "If the boss calls, get his name."

6. A veteran employee of the Department of Health, Education, and Welfare revealed that she kept in stock two form letters for replying promptly to the periodic recommendations of business-management consultants for increasing the efficiency of her office. The first read: "To effectuate the recommendations of this report will require an amendment to the Constitution of the United States." The second read: "To effectuate the recommendations of this report will require the repeal or amendment of the law establishing this program."

7. The Office of Civil and Defense Mobilization opened a quiet campaign to persuade the public to quit calling it O.D.C.M. and start calling it O.C.D.M.

8. The Labor Department selected "radiation purple" as the "theme color" for the meeting of the President's Conference on Occupation Safety.

9. The Army issued AR 380-40 (C 1) announcing that AR 380-40 had been amended so that all references to KAG-1/TSEC and KAG-2/TSEC would henceforth read KAG-1A/TSEC and KAG-2A/TSEC, respectively.

10. Reviewing a ghost-written campaign speech that Eisenhower was due to deliver, members of the White House staff split over the question of leaving in a passage denouncing the Democrats as "gloomdogglers." The ghost writer's wife, Mrs. Malcolm Moos, interrupted the conference to call for her husband. Someone asked what she thought of the word. It sounded "cute," she said. The next day in Baltimore the President denounced the Democrats as "gloomdogglers."

11. The State Department, planning its new building, contracted for a $40,000 incinerator for burning "classified trash," waste paper too sensitive to be chanced a passage through janitorial hands. The blueprints included a system of chutes for conveying the "classified trash" from loyalty-screened stenographers directly to the flames.

12. The legend "White House Mess" was ordered removed from matchbook covers distributed in the mess operated by the Navy in the White House.

13. A two-hundred-pound panda residing in Peiping was denied admission to the United States by the State Department. State, disappointing domestic zoo men, invoked its taboo against trade with Communist China, ruling that the panda's admission would imperil the national security.

14. After two senators received complaints that the American Pavilion at the Brussels Fair contained engravings of a semi-nude woman watching a group of savages turn a human carcass on a spit, the Director of the United States Information Agency was flown to Belgium to investigate and report to the President.

15. The State Department accepted informal complaints from Paris after the American press carried reports of a political falling out between President De Gaulle and his cook. State was advised that the cook was actually devoted to De Gaulle and had been terribly upset by the incorrect American reporting, thereby jeopardizing the tranquillity of the General's kitchen.

This catalogue could be expanded, but the samples suffice to convey the flavor of day-to-day life within the government labyrinth. Some will be impressed by the gross triviality of it. Is it not outrageous that men supported by tax revenues should have to spend their hours debating the wisdom of calling Democrats "gloomdogglers," guarding the national security against pandas, and devising tricky synonyms for "monkey"? Why should the taxpayer support such nonsense?

The answer is that the American, though sulking about a profligate bureaucracy, insists upon it. The Wisconsin dairyman, embattled with the oleomargarine interests, demands the government's help. So does the laborer fired for yielding momentarily to picayune impulse. The man who is shocked by an American exhibit in Brussels expects action when he complains to his senator. It requires money and men to get it for him. When Uncle Sam is expected to play big brother to 180,000,000 people, he obviously needs assistants, and plenty of them.

Plenty of them he has. In 1800 the federal payroll consisted of about 130 clerks. The State Department staff was five men. There was not even an office for the Justice Department. The Attorney General paid for his own quarters and staff out of pocket.

From these spare beginnings grew today's federal behemoth, which consists of approximately 2,500,000 employees, exclusive of the armed forces. Concentrated in a single place the bureaucracy would create a metropolis comparable in size to metropolitan Boston, San Francisco, Pittsburgh, or St. Louis. Laid in a straight line, head to toe, its members would form a human bridge extending from the base of the Washington Monument to the Golden Gate.

. . . .

THE BUREAUCRAT'S DUTIES

What do all these people do in their working hours?

They *implement*.

Implementing is whatever anyone on the federal payroll is doing when he is handling paper, which is most of the time. If the President orders troops to Lebanon, the Pentagon implements by preparing a great many papers, some of which instruct soldiers to go to Lebanon. If the Secretary of Agriculture orders a study of American eating habits, his clerks implement by preparing a report showing that in a seventy-year lifetime the average American consumes 6,000 loaves of bread, 4 sheep, 300 chickens, 3 oxen, 12,000 pounds of vegetables, 9,000 pounds of potatoes, 14,000 pounds of fruit, 6,000 quarts of milk, 5,000 eggs, 8,000 pounds of sugar, and 2,000 pounds of cheese. (The statistics are from a Department of Agriculture study of American eating habits.)

When two or more federal employees stop implementing and start talking, they are *co-ordinating*.

Co-ordinating requires a big part of the workday. Its purpose is to find out who is implementing what.

For example, after the Secretary of Agriculture has ordered his survey of eating habits, several deputies must determine which divisions of the Department will handle the work. It will be necessary to keep progress checks on the division studying cheese consumption and on the division studying potato consumption. Someone must take care lest the people studying chicken consumption get bogged down duplicating the work of the people studying oxen consumption. All this is called co-ordinating.

A third consuming duty of the government worker is *formulating*.

Formulating is producing ideas to be implemented.

Usually formulating is a committee operation requiring the collective thinking capacity of thousands. Each January, for instance, the President must report to Congress on the state of the Union and suggest ways for improving it. Dozens of ideas must be formulated for his speech. This ties up a big part of the bureaucracy through late fall and early winter.

All the ideas must, of course, be co-ordinated before they are finally formulated. Once co-ordinated, they are submitted to the President's ghost writers, who sew them together crazy-quilt fashion, co-ordinating among themselves all the while. When their speech is finally implemented, it is *circulated* to the agencies for another round of co-ordinating, then returned to the ghost writers for a final implementing of the co-ordinators' decisions—or, a rewrite. What comes out is, inevitably, an atrocious speech.

From this a fourth important duty of the bureaucrat becomes manifest. He *circulates*.

Circulating is the passing from one office to another of the millions of pieces of paper that hold the government together. An eternal tornado of paper whirls inside the government and, not surprisingly, the circulating system often breaks down. The State Department proposals for the 1959 State of the Union speech were circulated toward the desk of Robert Gray at the White House, but wound up in the circulation system of Gordon Gray at the O.C.D.M., whence it took days to retrieve them.

A fifth activity of the government worker is *referring*.

Referring is usually done on the telephone. When someone telephones the government worker for information or help, the person receiving the call refers him to another government office, preferably in another agency. It is done in a self-assured, no-nonsense manner. "I will refer you to Mr. Clark in the Bureau of Yards and Docks," the referrer says after interrupting the caller's story, and gives him Clark's number.

Clark then refers him to a party in the Federal Power Commission, who refers him to a man in the Pentagon, who refers him to an extension in the Weather Bureau, which refers him to a fellow in the White House. At any moment during the Washington workday, the telephone wires are laden with desperate men being referred from bureaucrat to bureaucrat. Usually the chain breaks when one party is "tied up in conference" and his secretary promises that he will call back. If he does call back, he will then refer the citizen to another office. Sometimes the caller travels full circle and finds himself referred back to Clark.

If the citizen appears in person he may be easily referred into physical collapse, for he can be sent from one side of the building to the other and several times across Washington until spirit and strength are broken.

There are several reasons for referring. The main reason is the bureaucrat's congenital uncertainty about the extent of his own authority. A delicate problem gives him the jellied quivers, for his boss in the next echelon up may be annoyed if he says the wrong thing or angered if burdened with the caller's problem. The boss, of course, has a boss above him, who has a boss above him, with a boss above him, and each confronts the crisis of decision with agony. Their business is not deciding, but implementing, co-ordinating, formulating, and circulating.

They solve the problem by referring, or passing the crisis to someone else in an endless variation on the game of old maid. . . .

THE MEN WHO RULE US

WILLIAM WIRT HOWE

*How Congress Governs**

1859

To the Erudite Abel Ben Hassan:
(Copy to that excellent journal, the *Evening Post*, of New York, a place of some importance in the American Republic.)

My well-beloved, magnanimous, and eminent friend, Keeper of the Green Seal, Superintendent of the Sacks of the Bosphorus, Antelope of my Affections—In the Name of the Prophet, Greetings! I have been to Washington, in my capacity of Rear Admiral of the Turkish Navy, and —ALLAH be praised! I have returned in safety to New York.

I ought to give you a full description of the Capital of the United States of America, but, really, I am at a loss for something to describe.

It has no topography—no commerce—no art—no manufactures—no physical characteristics of a city.

Perhaps it may best be described by saying that it is a large lodging house for the executive, legislative, and judicial representatives of the Sovereign People. While these representatives remain in their lodging house, it flourishes. When they depart, it is like the ruins of Palmyra, and the wild beast and the serpent might wander safely through its desolate halls.

But what you chiefly wish to know, O learned friend, is the manner in which the business of governing is done in Washington. Let me briefly unfold this to your mind.

The representatives of the Sovereign People of the United States are original in their theory, and aboriginal in their practice, of legislation. The theory is that the Best Government is that which governs least.

* from *The Pasha Papers*.

The Members of Congress convene, pledged to support that glorious doctrine. From all parts of the land they assemble, prepared to do as little as possible in the way of governing. They have been carefully selected from the members of those who know nothing about the business of governing. They have studiously avoided any preparation for the task of governing. They carefully shun any associations, affiliations, affinities that might possibly furnish them with any knowledge of the subject of governing. Having assembled in solemn conclave, fully imbued with this original theory, they commence its aboriginal practice.

Like the North American Indians, of whom you have read in history—they have a Big Talk.

Before the session has commenced, however, it is well-known that the Territory of Kickapoo is the subject to be talked about, and every Senator and Representative is fully prepared to talk about Kickapoo. As to the material and moral welfare of Kickapoo, they know nothing and care nothing; but as a subject for a Big Talk, they understand it thoroughly, and soon the talk begins.

Mr. Spreadeagle, Republican Representative in the House from Pennsylvania, gives notice of a Bill to Extend the Free Soil Area by Organizing the Territory of Kickapoo. The Bill goes to the Committee on Territories, whose chairman is hostile to the measure. He combats it from motives of the purest patriotism. Is he not a Democrat, and will not the Territory of Kickapoo send to Congress a Republican delegate, and when she becomes a state, Republican Senators and Representatives? The chairman puts the bill in his pocket and employs his time in driving out with the lovely wife of the gentleman from Arkansas.

Just as the motion is finally about to be put, Mr. Spreadeagle rises to a question of privilege.

—His remarks have been distorted and misinterpreted by the *Metropolitan Tomahawk*—the most ignorant, contemptible, dirty newspaper—

The Member from New York, second cousin of the editor of the *Tomahawk*, expresses the opinion that the Gentleman from Pennsylvania is a villain.

Mr. Spreadeagle gives utterance to his conviction that the Gentleman from New York is a drunken liar.

Sensation! Flashing of bowie knives! A rush from different quarters of the chamber! A lull. The Member from Pennsylvania explains his language by saying that he intended no personal allusion to the Gentleman from New York. The Gentleman from New York avers that the Member from Pennsylvania is the most upright and honorable man on the floor, and that as his remark to the contrary was made under the excitement of sudden exasperation, he withdraws the same.

The question returns to the motion to instruct the Committee on Territories to report on Kickapoo. The motion is debated by twenty-five Members on either side, each speaking not less than three hours.

The Gentleman from Alabama moves as an amendment that the word "not" be inserted in the resolution under discussion, so that it shall read that the Committee on Territories be instructed *not* to report on Kickapoo.

The debate is renewed and continued for a fortnight; during which time the Gentleman from Missouri distinguishes himself by talking three days and a half—the longest speech ever made by any man from the beginning of the world to the date of this letter.

At the expiration of this fortnight, the Gentleman from Vermont moves an amendment that the words "Fejee Islands" be inserted in the resolution, in place and stead of the word "Kickapoo."

The Speaker rules that the amendment is out of order. An appeal is taken from his decision. The Speaker holds that the question of appeal cannot be discussed. Another appeal is taken, and decided against the Speaker.

The question of the first appeal is thereupon discussed for one week— during which period the Gentleman from Connecticut favors the House with an eloquent review of English Parliamentary Law and Jefferson's Manual.

At length, the decision of the Speaker is sustained—when a motion is made to strike out from the resolution everything after the word, "Resolved." More talk. The Gentleman from Wisconsin delivers a speech which fills ten columns of the *Great Western Prairie Hen*, and which, says the editor of that journal, "for profound research and classic elegance, is unequaled in the annals of debate."

As he concludes, and the vote on the last amendment is about to be taken, the Gentleman from Michigan moves that the House adjourn. As that motion is always in order, the vote is taken and the House adjourns.

The friends of the Bill are in despair. The Senate has just passed a Bill to organize the Territory of Kickapoo, with the proviso that no native of Congo or Switzerland shall ever be allowed to set foot upon its soil; and that no one shall vote who cannot with his revolver bring down six men in six seconds at the distance of sixty feet.

Sensation! The Senate produces the sensation. The measure is known as the Six Sixty Bill. It goes to the House, and, after an interesting discussion of four weeks, is referred to a Special Committee. With singular swiftness, the Committee report it in six minutes, without amendment. Greater sensation!

The Lobby—mighty mystery—is too busy for the Special Committee, and when the Report comes in it is ordered to lie on the table. It lies there for one month, and is nearly forgotten; when Mr. Spreadeagle gives notice that he shall call up the Bill—the Senate Bill—next week in the House.

The Bill is called up. The Gentleman from Maine offers an amendment to the effect that all natives of Congo who are whitewashed once a month may enter the territory, and that the Six Sixty Revolvers shall be of the Colt patent.

Debate on this amendment exceeds in length any previous one, occupying six weeks, including the evening sessions. Six of the more prominent members speak two days, each. The Gentleman from Maryland denounces the Colt patent, and asserts that Colt, the patentee, spends all his winters in Washington, dining, wining, and winning the Representatives of the People.

The Gentleman from Florida reviews the Scriptural and Ethnological arguments in favor of refusing any residence to natives of the Congo, whitewashed or unwhitewashed, and proves clearly that they have no business to be natives of the Congo. Fifteen other Gentlemen obtain permission to print speeches, which they have never had a chance to deliver, and so the country is supplied with waste paper at a postal expense of $250,000.

At last the previous question is moved and carried, and the Bill, as amended by the House, is passed. It returns to the Senate, and, by way of instructive variety, is there debated. The Senate orders a Committee of Conference. The House does the same.

The Committee of Conference convene. After due deliberation, they report in favor of the House amendments, provided the House will vote an appropriation of $50,000,000 for the purpose of establishing a line of ferry boats from San Francisco to the Navigator Islands.

A majority of the House are in favor of this simple compromise—their system of legislation being, confessedly, a congeries of compromises—but, unfortunately, only six days of the session remain.

Twenty members of the Opposition speak against time, relieving each other like sentinels, and instructing the country with regard to the prospects of everybody in the next Presidential campaign.

The momentous hour of adjournment arrives. The clock strikes.

The Speaker's hammer falls. Congress has adjourned. THE BILL IS KILLED. At the hour of adjournment, thirty members of the House are on the floor, in a technical sense, and twenty-five, in a literal sense. Spiteful observers say that the supine posture of the latter is to be attributed to the effect of stimulating drink.

But the sublime theory, of which I have spoken, has been realized in practice. The Legislature has disbanded without governing at all. Do you ask what they *have* done? Well—

They have worn a large number of well-cut garments.

They have driven a large number of elegant horses.

They have aided the cause of temperance by destroying a large quantity of alcoholic beverages.

They have played innumerable games of billiards.

They have argued some causes in the Supreme Court.

They have combatted, with more or less success, the great Washington Tiger—faro.

They have aided a deserving Lobby in the prosecution of its shrewd designs.

They have flooded the country with printed documents, which are useful for various purposes.

They have drawn their pay and mileage.

And, with this, I suppose that you and I must be content.

In wonder, Thine,
Mohammed.

FINLEY PETER DUNNE

The Vice-President

1906

"It's sthrange about th' vice-prisidincy," said Mr. Dooley. "Th' prisidincy is th' highest office in th' gift iv th' people. Th' vice-prisidincy is th' next highest an' th' lowest. It isn't a crime exactly. Ye can't be sint to jail f'r it, but it's a kind iv a disgrace. It's like writin' anonymous letters. At a convintion nearly all th' dillygates lave as soon as they've nommynated th' prisidint f'r fear wan iv thim will be nommynated f'r vice-prisidint. They offered it to me frind Joe Cannon, and th' language he used brought th' blush iv shame to th' cheeks iv a naygur dillygate fr'm Allybamy. They thried to hand it to Hinnery Cabin Lodge, an' he wept bitterly. They found a man fr'm Wisconsin, who was in dhrink, an' had almost nommynated him whin his wife came in an' dhragged him away fr'm timptation. Th' way they got Sinitor Fairbanks to accipt was be showin' him a pitcher iv our gr-reat an' noble prisidint thryin' to jump a horse over a six-foot fence. An' they on'y prevailed upon Hinnery Davis to take this almost onequalled honor be tellin' him that th' raison th' Sage iv Esoopus didn't speak earlier was because he has weak lungs.

"Why is it, I wondher, that ivrybody runs away fr'm a nommynation f'r vice-prisidint as if it was an indictment be th' gran' jury? It usen't to be so. I've hollered mesilf black in th' face f'r ol' man Thurman an' Hendricks iv Injyanny. In th' ol' days, whin th' boys had nommynated some unknown man fr'm New York f'r prisidint, they turned in an' nommynated a gr-reat an' well-known man fr'm th' West f'r vice-prisidint. Th' candydate f'r vice-prisidint was all iv th' ticket we iver see durin' a campaign. Th' la-ad they put up f'r prisidint stayed down East an' was niver allowed to open his mouth except in writin' befure witnesses, but th' candydate f'r vice-prisidint wint fr'm wan end iv th' counthry to th' other howlin' again' th' tariff an' other immortal issues, now dead. I niver voted f'r Grover Cleveland. I wudden't vote f'r him anny more thin he'd vote f'r me. I voted f'r old man Thurman an' Tom Hendricks an' Adly Stevenson befure he became a profissional vice-prisidint. They thought it was an honor, but if ye'd read their bio-graphies to-day ye'd find at th' end: 'Th' writer will pass over th' closin' years iv Mr. Thurman's career hurriedly. It is enough to say iv this painful peryod that afther a lifetime iv devoted sarvice to his counthry th' statesman's declinin' days was clouded be a gr-reat sorrow. He become vice-prisidint iv th' United States. Oh, how much betther 'twere that we shud be sawed off arly be th' gr-reat reaper Death thin that a life iv honor shud end in ignomy.' It's a turr'ble thing.

"If ye say about a man that he's good prisidintial timber he'll buy ye a dhrink. If ye say he's good vice-prisidintial timber ye mane that he isn't good enough to be cut up into shingles, an' ye'd betther be careful.

"It's sthrange, too, because it's a good job. I think a man cud put in four years comfortably in th' place if he was a sound sleeper. What ar-re his jooties, says ye? Well, durin' th' campaign he has to do a good deal iv th' rough outside wurruk. Th' candydate f'r prisidint is at home pickin' out th' big wurruds in th' ditchnry an' firin' thim at us fr'm time to time. Th' candydate f'r th' vice-prisidincy is out in Ioway yellin' fr'm th' back iv a car or a dhray. He goes to all th' church affairs an' wakes an' appears at public meetin's between a cornet solo an' a glee club. He ought to be a man good at repartee. Our now honored (be some) prisidint had to retort with th' very hands that since have signed th' Pannyma Canal bill to a Colorado gintleman who accosted him with a scantling. An' I well raymimber another candydate, an' a gr-reat man, too, who replied to a gintleman in Shelbyville who made a rude remark be threatin' him as though he was an open fireplace. It was what Hogan calls a fine-cut an' incisive reply. Yes, sir, th' candydate f'r vice-prisidint has a busy time iv it durin' th' campaign, hoppin' fr'm town to town, speakin', shakin' hands with th' popylace who call him Hal or Charlie, dodgin' bricks, fightin' with his audjeence, an' diggin' up f'r th' fi-nance comity. He has to be an all-round man. He must be a good speaker, a pleasant man with th' ladies, a fair boxer an' rassler, something iv a liar, an' if he's a Ray-publican campaignin' in Texas, an active sprinter. If he has all thim qualities, he may or may not rayceive a majority at th' polls, an' no wan will know whether they voted f'r him or not.

"Well, he's ilicted. Th' ilictors call on th' candydate f'r prisidint an' hand him th' office. They notify th' candydate f'r vice-prisidint through th' personal columns iv th' pa-apers: 'If th' tall, dark gintleman with hazel eyes, black coat an' white vest, who was nommynated at th' convintion f'r vice-prisidint, will call at headquarters he will hear iv something to his advantage.' So he buys a ticket an' hops to Wash'nton, where he gets a good room suited to his station right above th' kitchen an' overlookin' a wood-yard. Th' prisidint has to live where he is put, but th' vice-prisi-dint is free to go annywhere he likes, where they are not particklar. Th' Constitution provides that th' prisidint shall have to put up with darky cookin', but th' vice-prisidint is permitted to eat out. Ivry mornin' it is his business to call at th' White House an' inquire afther th' prisidint's health. Whin told that th' prisidint was niver betther he gives three cheers, an' departs with a heavy heart.

"Th' feelin' iv th' vice-prisidint about th' prisidint's well-bein' is very deep. On rainy days he calls at th' White House an' begs th' prisidint not to go out without his rubbers. He has Mrs. Vice-Prisidint knit him a shawl to protect his throat again' th' night air. If th' prisidint has a touch iv fever th' vice-prisidint gets a touch iv fever himsilf. He has th' doctor on th' 'phone durin' th' night. 'Doc, I hear th' prisidint is onwell,' he says. 'Cud I do annything f'r him,—annything like dhrawin' his salary or appintin' th' postmasther at Injynnapolis?' It is princip'lly, Hinnissy, because iv th' vice-prisidint that most iv our prisidints have enjoyed such rugged health. Th' vice-prisidint guards th' prisidint, an' th' prisidint, afther sizin' up th' vice-prisidint, con-cludes that it wud be betther f'r th' counthry if he shud live yet awhile. 'D'ye know,' says th' prisidint to th' vice-prisidint, 'ivry time I see you I feel tin years younger?' 'Ye'er kind wurruds,' says th' vice-prisidint, 'brings tears to me eyes. My wife was sayin' on'y this mornin' how comfortable we ar-re in our little flat.' Some vice-prisidints have been so anxious f'r th' prisidint's safety that they've had to be warned off th' White House grounds.

"Aside fr'm th' arjoos duties iv lookin' afther th' prisidint's health, it is th' business iv th' vice-prisidint to preside over th' deliberations iv th' Sinit. Ivry mornin' between ten and twelve, he swings his hamock in th' palachial Sinit chamber an' sinks off into dhreamless sleep. He may be awakened by Sinitor Tillman pokin' Sinitor Beveridge in th' eye. This is wan way th' Sinit has iv deliberatin'. If so, th' vice-prisidint rises fr'm his hammock an' says: 'Th' Sinitor will come to ordher.' 'He won't,' says th' Sinitor. 'Oh, very well,' says th' presidin' officer; 'he won't,' an' dhrops off again. It is his jooty to rigorously enforce th' rules iv th' Sinit. There ar-re none. Th' Sinit is ruled be courtesy, like th' longshoreman's union. Th' vice-prisidint is not expected to butt in much. It wud be a breach iv Sinitoryal courtesy f'r him to step down an' part th' Sinitor fr'm Texas an' th' Sinitor fr'm Injyanny in th' middle iv a debate undher a desk on whether Northern gintleman ar-re more gintlemanly thin Southern gintlemen. I shuddent wondher if he thried to do it if he was taught his place with th' leg iv a chair. He isn't even called upon to give a decision. All that his grateful counthry demands fr'm th' man that she has ilivated to this proud position on th' toe iv her boot is that he shall keep his opinyons to himsilf. An' so he whiles away th' pleasant hours in th' beautiful city iv Wash'nton, an' whin he wakes up he is ayether in th' White House or in th' sthreet. I'll niver say annything again' th' vice-prisidincy. It is a good job, an' is richly deserved be ayether iv th' candydates. An' be Hivens, I'll go further an' say it richly desarves ayether iv thim."

WILL ROGERS

The Capitol Comedy

1923

The way to judge a good Comedy is by how long it will last and have people talk about it. Now Congress has turned out some that have lived for years and people are still laughing about them.

Girls win a little State Popularity Contest that is conducted in some Newspaper; then they are put into the Movies to entertain 110 million people who they never saw or know anything about. Now that's the same way with the Capitol Comedy Company of Washington. They win a State Popularity Contest backed by a Newspaper and are sent to Washington to turn out Laws for 110 million people they never saw.

They have what they call Congress, or the Lower House. That compares to what we call the Scenario Department. That's where somebody gets the idea of what he thinks will make a good Comedy Bill or Law, and they argue around and put it into shape.

Then it is passed along, printed, or shot, or Photographed, as we call it; then it reaches the Senate or the Cutting and Titling Department. Now, in our Movie Studios we have what we call Gag Men whose sole business is to just furnish some little Gag, or Amendment as they call it, which will get a laugh or perhaps change the whole thing around.

Now the Senate has what is considered the best and highest-priced Gag men that can be collected anywhere. Why, they put in so many little gags or amendments that the poor Author of the thing don't know his own story.

They consider if a man can sit there in the Studio in Washington and just put in one funny amendment in each Bill, or production, that will change it from what it originally meant, why, he is considered to have earned his pay.

Now, Folks, why patronize California-made Productions? The Capitol Comedy Co. of Washington, D.C. have never made a failure. They are every one, 100 percent funny, or 100 percent sad.

WOLCOTT GIBBS

Glorious Calvin

(*A Critical Appreciation Many Years Later*)

1929

The comic art of Calvin Coolidge was a thing so subtle that it almost defied analysis, for like all great actors, his was the technique of implication. In fact, in his ability to suggest frustration—the bitter futility of all living—by such small things as an eyebrow infinitesimally raised, an incomplete, embarrassed gesture, he was equalled only by the immortal Chaplin, only occasionally approached by Harry Langdon. As I write this it occurs to me to doubt whether this man, who was known and loved by millions of moviegoers, was essentially a comedian. There was more than a hint of tragedy in the shy little figure staring with solemn bafflement on an inexplicable world. There was a great pathos about him as he went awkwardly and unhappily through the gaudy antics which were so hilariously at variance with his appearance. This great sense of the comic value of paradox was never better illustrated than in the magnificent film in which, resplendent in buckskin and feathers, he was created a chieftain of the Blackfeet Indians. While tom-toms beat under a copper sky, naked red bodies circled in a furious dance about a tightmouthed little man with the edge of a stiff white collar showing at the neck of his costume and the toes of sturdy black boots peeping out under the gay fringe at the bottom of his trousers. His expression, which never varied throughout the ceremony, suggested the faintly apprehensive geniality of an elderly gentleman who has been dragooned into a game of Post Office. The effect was irresistible.

This intelligent emphasis on contrast was present in all Coolidge's camera work. I recall happily the film in which, attired in a cowboy suit with "Cal" stenciled across the seat of the trousers (a touch of genius, by the way), he made timid overtures to a faintly derisive steer. Incidentally, an adroit and characteristic touch was added to this picture by a subtitle, reading "COOLIDGE IS AMUSED BY RODEO," which was immediately followed by a glimpse of the comedian, his back turned morosely on the rodeo, staring with horrid dejection at nothing whatever.

Coolidge, ascetic in cap and gown, receiving a degree from the president of a university; Coolidge, in yachting costume with a vague hint of nausea in his expression, standing at the rail of the *Mayflower*; Coolidge, in overalls, thriftily chopping kindling against the bitter Massachusetts winter (the glittering nose of an enormous Packard appearing in a corner of this scene was a note of sheer and beautiful idiocy); Coolidge, the fisherman; Coolidge, the President of the United States—the man's comic sense was unerring and his range apparently infinite.

In passing, it is perhaps worth noting that while, unlike Chaplin, Coolidge varied the major details of his costume with each part, the stiff collar was a constant item. With an unfailing instinct for the incongruous, he chose it as the inevitable label of the urban, the clerkly, the humdrum. Infinitely more subtle than Chaplin's cane, derby, and baggy trousers, it was at the same time far more effective. To take a setting as strange and beautiful as the one used in a picture he made in Georgia— bearded Spanish oaks, oxcarts, the lovely keening of spirituals—and in an instant reduce it to absurdity by the introduction of a stiff collar, that was something very like genius.

While Coolidge depended upon simple incongruity for most of his effects, when he did introduce gags they were incomparable. I have in mind a bit, again in the Georgia picture, in which the comedian entered surrounded by secret-service men in business suits, uneasily raised a gun to his shoulder and fired once into the air. A subtitle was then flashed on the screen—"TRIBUTE TO A STEADY HAND AND A CLEAR EYE"—and the next picture showed us two guides shouldering a long pole, bowed under the weight of a deer, two or three smaller animals which appeared to be raccoons, and several wild ducks. The expression of the comedian's face as he studied this exhibit—wild surmise succeeded by a nervous and deprecating smile—I regard as one of the screen's great comic achievements.

Unlike many cinema favorites, the introduction of the talking picture held no terrors for Coolidge. His voice, happily, was perfectly in keeping with the part he has chosen to portray—dry, nasal, utterly without inflection. The lines, which I am told he made up himself, were miracles of brevity and did much to further the effect of anticlimax upon which his art depended. Again in the Georgia picture there was the moment when the comedian rode onto the scene, seated upon an ancient wooden cart drawn by oxen. His progress through the green tunnel made by the

overhanging trees was attended by the wailing of spirituals, the cracking
of whips, and the muffled clump of the oxen's hooves. It was a moment
of rare, almost intolerable beauty. The cart stopped as it reached the
forefront of the picture and the spirituals died away. There was a sudden
silence, which was broken by Coolidge's companion, who addressed him
in a tone of great deference upon a problem apparently of national importance.—"What is your solution of that, Mr. President?"

The comedian smiled nervously, stared at the oxen, but did not reply.
His companion tried again.

"What would you think of putting a tax on gasoline?"

This was obviously intended to be facetious, but the comedian considered it with perfect solemnity. At last his face brightened.

"Wal," he said, "I don't think I'd be in favor of that."

The spirituals rose again, and the cart drove on.

When Coolidge left the pictures, he was succeeded by Herbert
Hoover, a comedian whose work displayed certain similarities. To the
critical mind, however, it was thin and derivative, a self-conscious echo
of his predecessor's magnificent technique. I doubt if we shall ever see
the Master's like again.

When I was a boy I was told that anyone could become President; I'm beginning to believe it.—*Clarence Darrow*

H. L. MENCKEN

Imperial Purple

1931

Most of the rewards of the Presidency, in these degenerate days, have
come to be very trashy. The President continues, of course, to be an
eminent man, but only in the sense that Jack Dempsey, Lindbergh, Babe
Ruth, and Henry Ford are eminent men. He sees little of the really in-

telligent and amusing people of the country: most of them, in fact, make it a sort of point of honor to scorn him and avoid him. His time is put in mainly with shabby politicians and other such designing fellows—in brief, with rogues and ignoramuses. When he takes a little holiday his customary companions are vermin that no fastidious man would consort with—dry Senators with panting thirsts, the proprietors of bad newspapers in worse towns, grafters preying on the suffering farmers, power and movie magnates, prehensile labor leaders, the more pliable sort of journalists, and so on. They must be pretty dreadful company. Dr. Harding, forced to entertain them, resorted to poteen as an analgesic; Dr. Coolidge loaded them aboard the *Mayflower*, and then fled to his cabin, took off his vest and shirt, and went to sleep; Dr. Hoover hauls them to the Rapidan at 60 miles an hour, and back at 80 or 90.

The honors that are heaped upon a President in this one hundred and fifty-sixth year of the Republic are seldom of a kind to impress and content a civilized man. People send him turkeys, opossums, pieces of wood from the *Constitution*, goldfish, carved peach-kernels, models of the State capitols of Wyoming and Arkansas, and pressed flowers from the Holy Land. His predecessors before 1917 got demijohns of 12-year-old rye, baskets of champagne, and cases of Moselle and Burgundy, but them times ain't no more. Once a year some hunter in Montana or Idaho sends him 20 pounds of bearsteak, usually collect. It arrives in a high state, and has to be fed to the White House dog. He receives 20 or 30 chain-prayer letters every day, and fair copies of 40 or 50 sets of verse. Colored clergymen send him illustrated Bibles, madstones and boxes of lucky powders, usually accompanied by applications for appointment as collectors of customs at New Orleans, or Register of the Treasury.

His public rewards come in the form of LL.D.'s from colleges eager for the publicity—and on the same day others precisely like it are given to a champion lawn-tennis player, a banker known to be without heirs of his body, and a general in the Army. No one ever thinks to give him any other academic honor; he is never made a Litt.D., a D.D., an S.T.D., a D.D.S., or a J.U.D., but always an LL.D. Dr. Hoover, to date, has 30 or 40 such degrees. After he leaves office they will continue to fall upon him. He apparently knows as little about law as a policeman, but he is already more solidly *legum doctor* than Blackstone or Pufendorf, and the end is not yet.

The health of a President is watched very carefully, not only by the Vice-President but also by medical men detailed for the purpose by the Army or Navy. These medical men have high-sounding titles, and perform the duties of their office in full uniform, with swords on one side and stethoscopes on the other. The diet of their imperial patient is rigidly scrutinized. If he eats a few peanuts they make a pother; if he goes in for a dozen steamed hard crabs at night, washed down by what passes in Washington for malt liquor, they complain to the newspapers. Every morning they look at his tongue, take his pulse and temperature, determine his blood pressure, and examine his eyegrounds and his knee-jerks. The instant he shows the slightest sign of being upset they clap him into bed, post Marines to guard him, put him on a regimen fit for a Trappist, and issue bulletins to the newspapers.

When a President goes traveling he never goes alone, but always with a huge staff of secretaries, Secret Service agents, doctors, nurses, and newspaper reporters. Even so stingy a fellow as Dr. Coolidge had to hire two whole Pullman cars to carry his entourage. The cost, to be sure, is borne by the taxpayers, but the President has to put up with the company. As he rolls along thousands of boys rush out to put pennies on the track, and now and then one of them loses a finger or a toe, and the train has to be backed up to comfort his mother, who, it usually turns out, cannot speak English and voted for Al in 1928. When the train arrives anywhere all the town bores and scoundrels gather to greet the Chief Magistrate, and that night he has to eat a bad dinner, with only gingerale to wash it down, and to listen to three hours of bad speeches.

The President has less privacy than any other American. Thousands of persons have the right of access to him, beginning with the British Ambassador and running down to the secretary of the Republican county committee of Ziebach county, South Dakota. Among them are the 96 members of the United States Senate, perhaps the windiest and most tedious group of men in Christendom. If a Senator were denied admission to the White House, even though he were a Progressive, the whole Senate would rise in indignation, even though it were 80% stand-pat Republican. Such is Senatorial courtesy. And if the minister from Albania were kicked out, even the French and German Ambassadors would join in protesting.

Many of these gentlemen drop in, not because they have anything to say, but simply to prove to their employers or customers that they can do it. How long they stay is only partly determined by the President himself. Dr. Coolidge used to get rid of them by falling asleep in their faces, but that device is impossible to Presidents with a more active interest in the visible world. It would not do to have them heaved out by the Secret Service men or by the White House police, or to insult and affront them otherwise, for many of them have wicked tongues. On two occasions within historic times Presidents who were irritable with such bores were reported in Washington to be patronizing the jug, and it took a lot of fine work to put down the scandal.

All day long the right hon. lord of us all sits listening solemnly to quacks who pretend to know what the farmers are thinking about in Nebraska and South Carolina, how the Swedes of Minnesota are taking the German moratorium, and how much it would cost in actual votes to let fall a word for beer and light wines. Anon a secretary rushes in with the news that some eminent movie actor or football coach has died, and the President must seize a pen and write a telegram of condolence to the widow. Once a year he is repaid by receiving a cable on his birthday from King George V. These autographs are cherished by Presidents, and they leave them, *post mortem,* to the Library of Congress.

There comes a day of public ceremonial, and a chance to make a speech. Alas, it must be made at the annual banquet of some organization that is discovered, at the last minute, to be made up mainly of gentlemen under indictment, or at the tomb of some statesman who escaped impeachment by a hair. A million voters with IQ's below 60 have their ears glued to the radio: it takes four days' hard work to concoct a speech with a sensible word in it. Next day a dam must be opened somewhere. Four dry Senators get drunk and make a painful scene. The Presidential automobile runs over a dog. It rains.

The life seems dull and unpleasant. A bootlegger has a better time, in jail or out. Yet it must have its charms, for no man who has experienced it is ever unwilling to endure it again. On the contrary, all ex-Presidents try their level damnedest to get back, even at the expense of their dignity, their sense of humor, and their immortal souls. The struggles of the late Major-General Roosevelt will be recalled by connoisseurs. He was a melancholy spectacle from the moment the White House doors closed upon him, and he passed out of this life a disappointed and even embittered man. You and I can scarcely imagine any such blow as that he suffered in 1912. It shook him profoundly, and left him a wreck.

Long ago I proposed that unsuccessful candidates for the Presidency be quietly hanged, as a matter of public sanitation and decorum. The sight of their grief must have a very evil effect upon the young. We have enough hobgoblins in America without putting up with downright ghosts. Perhaps it might be a good idea to hand over ex-Presidents to the hangman in the same way. As they complete their terms their consciences are clear, and their chances of going to Heaven are excellent.

But a few years of longing and repining are enough to imperil the souls of even the most philosophical of them. I point to Dr. Coolidge. He pretends to like the insurance business, but who really believes it? Who can be unaware that his secret thoughts have to do, not with 20-year endowment policies, but with 1600 Pennsylvania Avenue? Who can fail to mark the tragedy that marks his countenance, otherwise so beautifully smooth and vacant, so virginally bare of signs? If you say that he does not suffer, then you say also that a man with cholera morbus does not suffer.

On second thoughts, I withdraw my suggestion. It is probably illegal, and maybe even immoral. But certainly something ought to be done. Maybe it would be a good idea to make every ex-President a Methodist bishop.

RICHARD B. MORRIS

A Presidential Sense of Humor

1961

In his first few months in the White House, President Kennedy has displayed a subtle and intellectual brand of humor that sets him apart from most of his predecessors. A tradition of solemnity was established in the beginning. George Washington and John Adams conducted themselves with an icy aloofness, quasi-regal in character. Although Jefferson and Jackson democratized the White House, each in his fashion, neither was distinguished for his humor. In fact, not until Abraham Lincoln was the tradition of Presidential earnestness and exhortation broken.

Lincoln exemplified American frontier humor. It drew upon strength, size, exaggeration. It exploited allegory and animal imagery. To illustrate the value of public discussion in ending slavery, he said: "What kills a skunk is the publicity it gives itself." In a debate in Congress on the war with Mexico, he recalled the Illinois farmer who declared, "I ain't greedy about land. I only want what jines mine."

Although President Lincoln's critics denounced him as a clown and a vulgarian, the fact is that humor lightened the unremitting pressures and worries under which he labored. A funny story, like "a good square drink of whisky" for an old toper, he once said, "puts new life into me." During interviews with belligerent politicians and oversolicitous visitors —his "public-opinion baths," he called these contacts—Lincoln fell back on anecdotes to avoid making hasty commitments.

Lincoln's successors, from Andrew Johnson to William McKinley, ran the gamut from ill-temper to high moral exhortation, but, taken as a whole, they were a dull lot.

Theodore Roosevelt brought the second era of Presidential stuffiness to an abrupt end, and it has never been revived. In contrast to the log-cabin-born and largely self-educated Lincoln, T. R. was an affluent, Harvard-educated Easterner with an established social background. Nevertheless, his humor had a Western tinge, reflecting his boyish, Tom Sawyer strain, impulsive, activist and enthusiast temper, and love of travel and outdoor life. He enjoyed nothing better than to tell cowboy stories.

During the Spanish-American War he organized the "Rough Riders," a mélange of cowboys, ex-polo players and ex-convicts. He always considered a "Rough Rider" better qualified for any appointment than any other aspirant, although he was aware of weaknesses in this theory. In 1906, when Secretary of War Taft asked for the nomination of a Yale man to some post in the Southwest, President Roosevelt replied:

"I guess Yale '78 has the call, as there seems to be no Rough Rider available and every individual in the Southern District of the Indian Territory (including every Rough Rider) appears to be either under indictment, convicted, or in a position that renders it imperatively necessary that he should be indicted. Let us, therefore, appoint George Walker, Yale '78, charge to Taft, and see if the Senate (God bless them!) will confirm him."

In the early days of the Spanish-American War, when he was still Assistant Secretary of the Navy, Roosevelt received a frantic request from one of the Atlantic seaboard cities for protection against the Spaniards. He dispatched a Civil War monitor to perform that task.

"It was armed with one smooth-bore gun about as effective as a culverin," he later recounted with glee. "It was manned by twenty-one naval militia, and it was towed by a tug. I sent it out there to that port and it completely satisfied them. It was quite unfit to deal with any foe of modern times, although it might possibly have dealt with the Spanish Armada, though I am not sure."

.   .   .   .

Roosevelt's hand-picked successor, the affable, ponderous William Howard Taft, is perhaps the only American President who thoroughly relished stories at his own expense. One of his favorites concerned a wedding which his party attended during a visit to New England early in his Presidency. His aide, Major Archie Butt, wrapped in gold braid, was the focus of all eyes. A conversation between the hostess and her Irish gardener after the ceremony was repeated to Taft. He frequently recounted it later with an Irish brogue:

"Ah, it was a foine occasion," the gardener said.

"Yes, and it was pleasant to have the President of the United States," his mistress answered.

"Yis, madam, yis it was. He's a foine-looking man; and what a beautiful uniform he had! But who the divil was the fat old man that was following him around?"

Perhaps the best loser in history, Taft, rebounded from his defeat for reelection in 1912 very quickly. Following the election, a sympathizer called to see him and said: "Well, anyway, Mr. Taft, I voted for you." Taft replied: "Sh-h-h, my friend. If I were you I wouldn't boast about it."

Coolidge's taciturn and thrifty type of Yankee humor with its unobtrusive irony was so low-keyed that no one has ever been able to figure out whether Silent Cal was very simple or very deep. "If you don't say anything, you won't be called on to repeat it," Coolidge once observed with his nasal twang. The remark, which epitomized his epigrammatic style, might be paired with his classic description of a clergyman's sermon on sin: "He was against it."

When he was Governor of Massachusetts, a lady asked him at dinner whether he had participated in athletic events as a student at Amherst. "Yes," he answered, munching a nut. "I held the stakes," and lapsed into silence.

During his Vice-Presidency, while presiding over the Senate, Coolidge sent a note by messenger to an exceptionally verbose Senator reminding him that time was running out. The Senator read the note, glared at the messenger, and said, "You go to hell." The messenger returned to Coolidge. "What did he say?" asked the Vice-President. "You go to hell," the boy reported faithfully. Coolidge mused for a while. "Well, there's nothing in the rules that says I have to."

When the animated and gracious Mrs. Coolidge was sitting for a White House portrait by Howard Chandler Christy, the red velvet evening dress she wore seemed a little too blatant to the President. Christy, however, wanted the bright splash of color in the portrait. "Why not paint her in a white dress and paint the dog red?" Coolidge proposed, deadpan.

Toward the end of his Presidency, he joined a Senator in a stroll. As they approached the White House, the Senator asked facetiously: "I wonder who lives there?"

"Nobody," replied the President. "They just come and go."

. . . .

Herbert Hoover was generally considered a solemn President. Although a certain wit spiced his annual talks before the Gridiron Club, his distinctive style of irony was more apparent after he left office. The New Deal was his chief target. "Riotous spending," "joy-riding to bankruptcy," "repudiation on the installment plan," "effervescence of righteousness" were some of the epithets he reserved for the policies of his successor.

. . . .

Franklin D. Roosevelt's humor had a touch of the slapdash and at times the sting of a rapier. To a far greater extent than any of his predecessors he used it as a political weapon—although he seemed to relish ribbing his intimates almost as much as he did the "economic royalists" ranged in battle against him.

He hailed the Daughters of the American Revolution as "fellow immigrants." To a correspondent in May, 1934, he wrote: "You are right about the need for rain, but the fault lies with Wall Street. They watered their stocks so liberally in past years that the Almighty is trying to average up the moisture by withholding rain."

During the 1936 campaign he told this allegorical tale to the New York State Democratic convention at Syracuse:

"In the summer of 1933 a nice old gentleman wearing a silk hat fell off the end of a pier. He was unable to swim. A friend dived overboard and pulled him out; but the silk hat floated off with the tide. After the old gentleman had been revived he was effusive in his thanks. He praised his friend for saving his life. Today, three years later, the old gentleman is berating his friend because the silk hat was lost."

If F.D.R. used a rapier, Harry Truman wielded a cleaver. His humor lacked subtlety but it was devastating in its effectiveness. His whistle-stop campaign of 1948 was punctuated by one "Give 'm hell, Harry," speech after another. The chief target of his jibes was that "do-nothing, good-for-nothing, worst Eightieth Congress."

"Republicans don't like to talk about depressions," he reminded his audiences. "You remember the old saying, 'Don't talk of rope in the house of somebody who has been hanged.' " Recalling that Herbert Hoover had campaigned on the promise of "two cars in every garage," he cracked, "Apparently the Republican candidate is running this year on the slogan, 'two families in every garage.' " . . .

RICHARD R. LINGEMAN

Automation Fear Hits D.C.

Strike Threat In Congress

1962

Although it may be too early to judge, people are already predicting that the 88th Congress will be a "do-nothing" Congress. Recently Senate Majority Leader Mike Mansfield scolded his colleagues for not passing any legislation during the first six weeks of the session.

Naturally, Sen. Mansfield, whose job it is to see that the President's program is passed and who thus represents management, would be the last to know the best-kept secret in Washington: Congress is on strike! The strike hasn't progressed to the stage of picketing and walkouts yet, but the striking Congressmen are applying such well known labor weapons as the slowdown and the secondary boycott to any bill proposed by the Administration.

CAUSE OF THE STRIKE

What are the Congressmen striking for? Not for higher wages, of course, since they can raise their own salaries any time they wish. Fringe benefits? No, again. The Adam Clayton Powell imbroglio has put the lid on all that for the time being. What Congressmen are worried about is what all the other labor unions are worried about these days—automation. They see the tide of automation inexorably creeping into the other branches of government. In the Department of Defense, Secy. McNamara is replacing generals with computers. The Internal Revenue Service is substituting machines for accountants, and the Postal Department has installed an automated post office. Even Congressmen themselves are using machines to answer their mail instead of relatives. The trend is clear; it is but a short step to automated Congressmen.

COMPUTER CONGRESSMAN UNVEILED

Last week, Congressmen's fears were confirmed when the Administration, in a private showing to which only the legislators were invited, unveiled its CX-502 computer capable of performing all the tasks now performed by Congressmen. The Senators and Representatives watched with increasing uneasiness as the machine passed a bill. The bill was coded on tape, then fed into the computer, which could be set for a variety of political viewpoints including Republican–Southern Democrat Coalition, John Bircher, Administration Democrat, and Wayne Morse. They were awed as the machine skillfully cut and amended the bill so that it offended nobody. It was even able to hold committee hearings. A timing device was first set at one of three positions—Delay, More Delay, or Still More Delay—then the coded bill was fed into it. The spectators were told that the machine could sit on a bill for periods ranging from three months to a year.

Although the machine was billed by the Administration as "an experiment," Congressmen, fearful of losing their jobs, have decided to fight it with every means at their command. They were not reassured by a statement by the inventor of CX-502, Earl Poornk, that: "This machine will not do away with Congressmen entirely. All it can do is pass legislation. There are many other jobs performed by Congressmen which the machine can't handle, such as showing constituents around Washington, doing favors for constituents, junketeering, speaking at Lincoln's Birthday dinners, and so on."

RUSSELL BAKER

How Congress Ended

1963

For the first year or two after Congress had come to a full stop, no one could quite believe that it was really beyond repair.

Superficially, everything seemed to be running as normally as ever, and people who pointed out that damp rusty vapors were coming from the cellar were dismissed as Cassandras. Each day, just before the stroke of noon, Speaker John McCormack would appear, as he always had, smoking his beloved cigar, to announce that none of the President's bills could be enacted.

In the Senate, the familiar old routine seemed to be going on with clockwork regularity. Senator Morse continued to declare that vicious attacks by unprincipled enemies of the Republic would never deter him from the fight to save humanity. Senator Russell went on delivering, at periodic intervals, his famous defense of the filibuster.

In the caucus room, Senator McClellan's interrogations of rascals and gorillas continued to amuse national television audiences, as though nothing unusual had really happened. Month after month, as he always had, Chairman Mills declared that medical care for the aged was dead in committee, and Senator Harry F. Byrd went right on announcing that tax revision would have to wait until next year.

Finally, of course, it became impossible to pretend that everything was all right. In 1963, after Congress had sat in the Capitol for the whole year just listening to the hum of the air conditioning, children began snickering and scandalous rumors began circulating.

By the late 1960s, after Congress had sat in continuous session for six years and produced only seven appropriations bills and two resolutions (deploring Communism and fire and depredation in the South), the Lampwick Commission delivered its historic report.

Those old enough to remember that period will recall the public's incredulous response when the commission reported that Congress had long since slipped through a keyhole in the time-space continuum and escaped from the human concept of time. In the typical Senate committee room, they found, years might pass while the committee performed the work of a single day.

When Chairman Mills talked of getting around to medical care for the aged "next year," they concluded, he was quite sincere. But "next year" in Congressional time, they demonstrated, would not come in earth time until the 25th century.

The discovery of the hideous coat of moss that had grown out of the machinery and was beginning to spread through the entire building precipitated the crisis. The President's proposal for a radical moss elimination program—the only request he made in that year's State of the Union message—was doomed from the start.

Speaker McCormack appeared, as he always had, smoking his beloved cigar, to announce that the moss bill could not be enacted. Senator Morse said that he would tie up the Senate for weeks rather than fatten the purse of the moss-killer trust. Senator Byrd said that he had 405 witnesses who wanted to testify in committee on the moss bill and that he couldn't see how he could finish hearings until next year.

The upshot, as every schoolboy knows, was the bitterly controversial Preservation Proclamation, under which Congress was made a branch of the Smithsonian Institution, and the Agriculture Department was put in charge of a crash moss-eradication program.

As a result, this relic of the nation's heritage has been lovingly preserved in its original form. Today's visitor can come and watch these quaint figures behave just as they did in real life. Each day, just before noon, Speaker McCormack still appears, smoking his beloved cigar, to announce that none of the President's bills can be enacted.

On clockwork schedule, Senator Morse still denounces the unprincipled, Senator Byrd still says that taxes must wait until next year, and Chairman Mills still announces that it looks bad for medical care for the aged.

No one can visit it without marveling at the hardiness of these early Americans.

It could probably be shown by facts and figures that there is no distinctly native American criminal class except Congress.

—*Mark Twain*

2 CAMPAIGNS AND CANDIDATES

GETTING THERE IS HALF THE FUN

Since it is the election campaign, more than anything else in American politics, that arouses the active interest of the citizenry—and the satirists —this section of the book is much the longest. Many of the selections that appear elsewhere also deal with candidates and campaign issues, of course, but not as explicitly as these do.

So when he shakes his head, I naterally look out for a tough spell of weather. When I got home from Baltimore, says I, "Well, Uncle Joshua, you got my letter in the Intelligencer, didn't you?" And says he, "Yes."

"Well, didn't we do that business up well?" says I.

"I don't know about that," said Uncle Joshua; "I have my doubts about it."

"Why, don't you think," says I, "the nomination of Gineral Pierce will put the Democratic party on its legs again, and give it a fine start?"

Uncle Joshua looked up to me kind of quizical, and says he, "It *has* gin the party a pretty considerable of a start already, it come so unexpected." And then he sot as much as two minutes drumming his finger on the table, and didn't say nothin'.

And then he looked up again, and says he, "Major, *who is Gineral Pierce?* It ain't a *fictious* name, is it?"

"Why, Uncle Joshua," says I, "how you talk! It is Gineral Franklin Pierce, of New Hampshire."

"Gineral Franklin Pierce, of New Hampshire, is it?" says he. "Well, now, Major, are you sure there *is* such a person, or did somebody play a hoax on the Baltimore Convention?"

"Yes," says I, "Uncle, I'm as sure of it as I am that there is such a person as Uncle Joshua Downing. To make all sure of it and no mistake, I come through New Hampshire, and went to Concord, where they said he lived, and inquired all about it. The neighbors there all knew him perfectly well, and showed me the house he lives in. He wasn't at home, or I should a seen him myself, and should got his promise to keep the Downingville Post-Office for you. But you needn't be afraid but what you'll have it, for I sent a telegraph to him from Baltimore, as soon as he was nominated, to keep it for you."

Here I see by the looks of Uncle Joshua's eyes that he begun to get hold of some new ideas. Says he, "Well, Major, it is a fact, then, is it, that he was nominated in real earnest, and 'twasn't no joke?"

"Upon my word and honor," says I, "there isn't a particle of joke about it—it was all done in real earnest."

"Well, then, if you've really got a candidate," says Uncle Joshua, "I should like to know something about him. Does he belong to the Old Fogy class or Young America class?"

"I guess about half and half," says I, "and he'll be all the stronger for that, because he can draw votes on both sides."

"After all," says he, "I'm afraid it's a bad nomination. Them old pillars of the Democratic party, Gineral Cass, and Mr. Buchanan, and

Governor Marcy, and General Houston, and the rest, will feel so insulted and mortified at being pushed aside for strangers to take the lead, that they'll all be agin the nomination, and their friends, too, and that'll upset the whole kettle of fish."

"Don't you never fear that, Uncle Joshua," says I; "them old pillars that you speak of are all very much tickled with the nomination. Ye see, it broke the nose of Young America, and they was delighted with it. As soon as the nomination was out of the mould, before it had time to cool, they all telegraphed right to Baltimore that nothin' in the world could have happened to suit 'em better; it was a most excellent nomination, and they felt under everlasting obligations to the Baltimore Convention. You needn't have no fears that they'll feel any coldness towards the nomination. They'll turn to and work for it like beavers."

"Well, how is it," said Uncle Joshua, "about that boy candidate for the Presidency that they call Young America? If his nose is knocked out of joint he'll of course oppose the nomination, tooth and nail."

"There's where you are mistaken again, Uncle Joshua," says I. "On the contrary, he goes for it hotter than any of 'em; and he telegraphed back to Baltimore, as quick as lightning could carry it, that the nomination was jest the thing; it couldn't be no better. Ye see, he looks upon it in the light that it chokes off all the Old Fogies, and leaves the field clear for him next time. He thinks so highly of the nomination, and feels so patriotic about it, they say he is going to stump it through all the States, and make speeches in favor of Gineral Pierce's election. You may depend upon it, Uncle Joshua, we've got a very strong nomination—one that'll carry all afore it—and everybody is delighted with it, and everybody's going to go for it. I didn't expect you to hold back a moment. I thought you would have things all cut and dried for a rousin' ratification meeting by the time I got home."

"Well, you know, Major," said Uncle Joshua, "I always follow Colonel Crockett's rule, and never go ahead till I know I'm right. How foolish we should look to call a ratification meeting here in Downingville, and be voted right plump down. You know the Free-Soilers are very strong among us; they are strong in all the Northern States. And you know the Baltimore Convention fixed up a platform to stand on, that's all in favor of the Compromise and the Fugitive law, and is dead set agin the Free-Soilers. Now, Major, you must have more understanding than to think the Free-Soilers will ever swallow that platform; and if they don't, we are dished."

"You are wrong again, Uncle Joshua," says I, "for the biggest Free-

Soiler in all America swallowed it right down, and didn't make a wry face about it."

"Who do you mean?" says he.

"I mean Mr. John Van Buren," says I.

"But you don't mean," says Uncle Joshua, "that Mr. John Van Buren accepts this platform, and is willing to stand on it."

"Yes I do, exactly so," says I, "for he got right up in Tammany Hall and made a speech about it; and he said he would go the nomination, and he'd stand the platform; at all events, he'd stand the platform for *this election*, anyhow. You needn't be at all afraid of the Free-Soilers, Uncle; they ain't so stiff as you think for, and they are as anxious to get the offices as anybody, and will work as hard for 'em. Now let us go to work and get up our ratification, and blow it out straight. The Democracy of the country expects Downingville to do its duty."

"Well, Major," says Uncle Joshua, "you've made out a better case than I thought you could. I'm willing to take hold and see what we can do. But I declare I can't help laughing when I think it's Gineral Franklin Pierce, of New Hampshire, that we've got to ratify. I wish we knew something about him; something that we could make a little flusteration about, and wake up the Democracy."

"Good gracious, Uncle Joshua," says I, "have you been Postmaster of Downingville this twenty years, and always reading the papers, and don't know that Gineral Pierce was one of the heroes of the Mexican war?"

At that, Uncle Joshua hopped out of his chair like a boy, and says he, "Major, is that a fact?"

"Yes," says I, " 'tis a fact. You know Mr. Polk sent me out there as a private ambassador to look after Gineral Scott and Mr. Trist. And Gineral Pierce *was* out there; I knew all about it, and about his getting wounded."

"Good!" says Uncle Joshua, snapping his fingers; "that's lucky, then we've got something to go upon; something that the boys can hoorah about. And if we don't have too strong a team agin us we may carry the day yet. Who do you think the other party will put up?"

"Well," says I, "it's pretty likely to be Mr. Webster or Mr. Fillmore, and they can't either of 'em hold a candle to Gineral Pierce."

"Of course not," says Uncle Joshua, "if he was the hero of the Mexican war. I s'pose it was Gineral Scott's part of the war that he was in, because that's where you was. Which of the battles did he fight the bravest in, and mow down most of the Mexicans? Did he help storm that Gibralta castle at Vera Cruz?"

"No," says I, "that little matter was all over before Gineral Pierce got to Mexico."

"Well, the great battle of Cerro Gordo come next," said Uncle Joshua; "I dare say Gineral Pierce was foremost in marching up that bloody Bunker Hill and driving off Santa Anna and his fifteen thousand troops."

"I'm sure he would a been foremost, if he'd been there," says I, "but he hadn't got into the country yet, and Gineral Scott wouldn't wait for him. It seems as if Gineral Scott is always in a hurry when there is any fightin' to do, and won't wait for nobody."

"Well, the next great battle, if I remember the newspapers right," said Uncle Joshua, "was Contreras; and after that came the bloody and hot times of Cherubusco, and the King's Mill, and Chepultepec, and marching into the City of Mexico. These was the battles, I s'pose, where Gineral Pierce fit like a lion, and became the hero of the Mexican war. But which battle did he shine the brightest in, and cut down most of the enemy?"

"The truth is," says I, "he got wounded at Contreras, and so wasn't able to take a part in them bloody affairs of Cherubusco, King's Mill, and Chepultepec."

"Then he *was* in the battle of Contreras," said Uncle Joshua, "and that can't be disputed?"

"O yes," says I, "he certainly was in the first part of it, when they was getting the battle ready, for there's where he got wounded."

"Good," said Uncle Joshua, "he was in one battle, and got wounded; that's enough to make a handle of, anyhow. Where abouts was his wound?"

"Well, he had several hurts," said I; "I believe in his foot and ancle, and other parts."

"Rifle balls?" said Uncle Joshua, very earnest.

"O no, nothing of that kind," says I.

"What then; sword cuts? Or did the Mexicans stick their bayonets into him?"

"No, no; nothin' of that kind, nother," says I.

"Then it must be grape or bombshells," said Uncle Joshua. "How was it?"

"No, no, 'twasn't none of them things," says I. "The fact was, when they was skirmishing round, getting ready for the battle, his horse fell down with him and lamed him very bad."

Uncle Joshua colored a little, and sot and thought. At last he put on one of his knowing looks, and says he, "Well, Major, a wound is a wound, and we can make a handle of it without being such fools as to go into the particulars of how he came by it. I say let's go ahead and ratify Gineral Pierce, and who knows but what we can make something out of this Mexican business?"

Well, Mr. Gales and Seaton, the thing was done. We ratified on the 21st of June, in the evening, and it was a tall piece of business. When I begun, I meant to give you a full account of it, with some of the speeches and resolutions; but I've made my preamble so long that I can't do it in this letter. *We had a torchlight procession.* Cousin Ephraim took his cart and oxen, and went into the woods and got a whole load of birch bark and pitch-pine knots, and all the boys in Downingville turned out and carried torches. The school-house was illuminated with fifty candles. Uncle Joshua presided, as usual. Banners were hung round the room, with large letters, giving the names of all the great battles in Mexico; and the enthusiasm was immense. When we'd got about through, and was just winding up with three tremendous cheers for the "Hero of Mexico," a message came up to Uncle Joshua from the Post-Office, stating that the telegraph had just brought news that the Whig Convention at Baltimore had nominated Gineral Scott for President. It gin the whole Convention the cold shuggers in a minute. Uncle Joshua looked very serious, and says he, "Feller-Democrats, to prevent any mistakes, I think you had better give them three last cheers over again, and put in the name of Gineral Pierce." So we did, and gin three rousin' cheers for *Gineral Franklin Pierce, of New Hampshire, the Hero of Mexico.*

Downingville is wide awake, and will do her duty in November.

> *So I remain your old friend,*
> Major Jack Downing

The "hero" of the following verses is James A. Garfield, Republican candidate for President; "329" refers to the amount of a dividend he was alleged to have received as a virtual bribe; "Parsons" and "pavements" refer to Garfield's representation of a Washington contractor while he was in Congress.

ANONYMOUS

The Hero of "329"

1880

When I was a boy, to keep me alive,
A canal boat team I was driven to drive;
I traveled on foot and the reins I did yank,
And I held the mule's tail on the boat's gang-plank.
   I clung to that tail with such fixed intent
   That now I'm a candidate for President.

A trade I learned and theology scanned,
And I joined likewise the legal band;
But politics I found was my strongest game,
And so a Congressman I soon became.
   As Congressman I followed such a goodly bent
   That now I'm a candidate for President.

I took my bribery dividend,
But finding that it didn't my credit extend,
With all the solemnity an oath invokes,
I swore that my aims were as upright as oaks.
   I swore so devoutly I never got a cent
   That now I'm a candidate for President.

Next with Dick Parsons I chanced to meet,
Who converted me to pavements, abstract and concrete;
As an attorney I accepted a good fat fee,
For urging before my own commit-tee.
   So convincing did I make that argument
   That now I'm a candidate for President.

Now, Republicans all, whoever you may be,
If you want to rise to the top of the tree,
In your youth get a chance to drive a mule,
And in politics be guided by this golden rule:
    Take whatever you can get, and swear it was lent,
    And you all may be candidates for President.

WOLCOTT GIBBS

*The Candidate from New York**

1940

In a great many ways, Thomas Edmund Dewey is an impressive Presidential candidate. He was born in a typical American town (Owosso, Mich., pop., 14,496) and he came of sound American stock (the hero of Manila Bay was his grandfather's third cousin). In his virtuous youth, he belonged to the Boy Scouts, sang in the choir, and peddled the *Saturday Evening Post*, winning a bicycle. At one time he spent the summer working as a hired hand on a farm, and at another he learned to set type on his father's newspaper. He went to the local public schools and was never late or absent a day in his life. After he was graduated from the University of Michigan and had taken his LL.B. at Columbia, he was admitted to the bar, and presently emerged, at the age of thirty-three, as a fighting prosecutor and the terror of the underworld.

Obviously all this is in the most acceptable tradition—the saga of a more virile and melodious Coolidge, without the snobbish taint of Amherst or the sad comedy of the electric horse. Fortunate as he was in this personal background, however, he was even more fortunate in the times that produced him. Whatever else it accomplished, prohibition got the world ready for the coming of Dewey. The intense melodrama of the twenties accustomed people to the idea of an aristocracy of crime, to a superheated vision of America ruled by an outlaw nobility of vast

* from *St. George and the Dragnet*.

and incalculable powers. Beer barons and vice lords were a dime a dozen; almost every thug was at least a king. In New York, there were kings of vice, poultry, dope, fur, policy, and artichokes, to mention a few, and each of them commanded a band of desperadoes capable of dealing with the United States Marines. It was wonderful. Even more wonderful were the names that some of these monsters and their mates obligingly bore. In addition to such celebrated figures as Lucky, Waxey, Dixie, Legs, and Lepke, there were Spasm Ison, Cokey Flo Brown, Stone-Faced Peggy, Jenny the Factory, Crazy Moe, Abadaba, Gashouse Lil, Six-Bits, and Blue Jaw Magoon.

From almost the beginning of his political career, Dewey tangled with this demoniac royalty, and he made the most of it. If the voters were already inclined to believe that they were taking part in a moving picture, he did little to disillusion them. His private and public conversation always emphasized the menace of the underworld, omnipresent, almost omnipotent, crouched for a leap. "What do *you* know about the Unione Siciliana?" he asked a startled interviewer, and when it turned out that the man knew almost nothing, he described the fate of a prominent writer who offered to sell *Liberty* a story about its machinations and was shot down like a dog for his pains. "Never been in the papers!" whispered the District Attorney, rolling his eyes wildly. "No indictment. A terrific business! If you had seen men blanch as I have at its mere mention—its mere *mention*—you would know what terror it holds." He was no less alarming when addressing millions. "He has a Japanese butler," he said over the radio, referring to the king of something or other, "who —serves—him—well." He has prosecuted few cases in which he was unable to suggest that there were nameless forces at work, and this has sometimes irritated his critics. "No matter if it was only rolling a lush," said one of them in his homely way, "Dewey could always make it look wonderful on the record."

While there are many things in favor of the District Attorney, almost an equal number oppose him. Physically, he is not majestic, or even especially bizarre, which is probably the next best bet. He is five feet eight and a half inches tall and he weighs a hundred and fifty-seven pounds stripped. His teeth, with centre gaps in both the upper and lower sets, are his most unfortunate feature; his eyes, next to the mustache and the voice, his most arresting. These are brown, with small irises surrounded by a relatively immense area of white, and Dewey has a habit of rotating them furiously to punctuate and emphasize his speech, expressing horror and surprise by shooting them upward, cunning by sliding them from side to side behind narrowed lids. At climactic moments, he can pop them, almost audibly. Lloyd Paul Stryker, who has had less occasion to admire them than most, says that they are the only piercing brown eyes he has ever seen.

Dewey has a jutting paw, high cheekbones, a slightly bulbous nose, and thick eyebrows. His face, on the whole, has a compressed appearance, as though someone had squeezed his head in a vise. His suits are custom-made but uninteresting, and always seem a little too tight for him, although the Merchant Tailors and Designers Association of America chose him this year as one of the twenty-five best-dressed men in America. Altogether—smallish, neat, and dark—he looks like a Wall Street clerk on his way to work; unlike the late and magnificent Harding, he is a hard man to imagine in a toga.

Dewey is also unfortunate in the fact that people too close to him are usually either entertained by his supercinema technique or else irritated by his proud, peculiar ways. One crisp hostess has said, "You have to know Mr. Dewey very well in order to dislike him," and the reporters in the Criminal Courts Building usually speak of him lightly as The Boy Scout or, more simply, just The Boy. One man, who frequently boycotts Dewey's press conferences for ten days at a stretch, explains his absence airily. "You got to rap The Boy on the knuckles once in a while," he says.

Lawyers, politicians, and others whose careers are directly affected by Dewey's activities are apt to be more portentous. An attorney for the Civil Liberties Union has compared him with Mayor Hague, though conceding Dewey a good deal more class, and a Republican leader, noting the candidate's petulant behavior at a Party dinner, observed gloomily to Mr. Kenneth Simpson that they seemed to have a problem child on their hands. He has been accused of bullying hostile witnesses and coddling favorable ones, demanding exorbitant bail, wire-tapping, condoning the use of perjured testimony, and even (in the case of Dixie Davis, who was allowed to leave the Tombs some eighty or ninety times in the course of three months to go up to a lady's apartment and change his shirt) of conniving at adultery. In this case, Dewey's answer was frank, if not precisely responsive or even in the best possible taste. "Well, gentlemen," he told the jury, "if Davis did not have . . . desires, he wouldn't be human. . . ."

Some hecklers even go to the length of complaining that the leading contributors to the Dewey campaign fund represent more wealth and special interest than seem quite consistent with his notorious enthusiasm for the underprivileged. . . .

Dewey's most serious handicap, however, is the fact that he was born as recently as March 24, 1902. It is difficult for a great many people to think seriously of a candidate who was sixteen years old at the end of the World War, ten when the Titanic went down, six when William Howard Taft entered the White House, and thirty-one before he could buy a drink legally at any bar in the United States. If he happened to be elected, Dewey, of course, would be the youngest President in history, four years younger than Theodore Roosevelt, thirty years younger than William Henry Harrison, and about sixteen years below the average age of his predecessors at the time of their inauguration. . . .

Critics, in an attempt to make these cold figures a little more picturesque, have pointed out that he is only eight months older than Lucius Beebe, the fashionable pamphleteer, and seven weeks younger than Colonel Charles A. Lindbergh, the aviator—two national phenomena who, although of almost equal prominence, are not generally regarded as quite ready for the Presidency. Dewey's detractors also like to quote Secretary Ickes' comment that the District Attorney of New York had finally thrown his diaper in the ring.

Beyond a slight and comprehensible annoyance, it is doubtful if the candidate pays much attention to these brickbats. Nobody believes that Thomas E. Dewey is better qualified to be President of the United States than Thomas E. Dewey. Last fall many Republican heavy-weights were asked to sign a resolution which read in part:

> Convinced that he possesses above all other leaders in the country today the ability, temperament, training and ideals which the next President of the United States must have, we have determined to cooperate in the movement to elect Thomas E. Dewey President in 1940.
>
> This movement has in every sense originated with the people themselves. Mr. Dewey's record has inspired new efforts on behalf of good government throughout the country. It has evoked a spontaneous demand everywhere for his election to the Presidency. In him the people see a new hope for a better America.
>
> He has experienced judgment on public questions. He has vigor, executive ability, sincerity and devotion to duty. All these qualities have been proved by exceptional performance in the public service. . . .

According to the best authorities, this document was not only circulated by the candidate, who would whip it out of his pocket like an automatic when he had his victim cornered, but was also written by the man of experienced judgment himself.

This version, picturing Mr. Dewey drafting himself almost single-handed, differs a little from the District Attorney's own account of what went on. Shortly after his defeat by Governor Lehman, he says, "they" began to badger him to run for the Presidency. Dr. Gallup made a few soundings and discovered that he was far ahead of all other Republican Presidential possibilities. "It looks like I'm in for it," Dewey recalls saying to himself rather ruefully at the time. "If that many people want me elected, it is my duty to give them a chance." He held out for a while, but when the procession of supplicants began to clog the halls of his office, he saw that it was no good; he shouldered the cross.

The cold fact seems to be that Dewey became the nominal choice of the New York Republican Party for one of those reasons which make practical politics such a fascinating study for the layman. For years the New York delegation had gone to the national convention with its members hopelessly split, some favoring this man, some that. Last year the better minds decided that this was all nonsense and that it would be a good idea if everybody went to Philadelphia agreed on one man. Then, if *he* didn't go over on the first couple of ballots, the state chairman would be in a position to handle his delegation as a solid block in further negotiations. What happened, it seems, was that the dummy candidate decided to run in earnest, on a fine, expansive scale worthy of William Jennings Bryan. "We drafted this monkey," says one humble worker in the vineyard, "and, by Jesus, he took it serious. . . ."

JAMES THURBER

The Dewey Dewey Fog

1948

If 1948 does not mend its political strategies, and quickly, too, it is likely to go down in history as the Presidential Year of the Confused Identities or—and I hate this as much as you do—the Presidential Year of the Dewey Dewey Fog. The latter phrase happens to possess rather more aptness than mischief, and I trust that readers of all parties will excuse it.

I first noticed that there was something oblique about the political situation one night while listening to Quincy Howe's summary of the news over WCBS. He told how he had discovered Governor Dewey in the act of donning certain light and shining political garments that looked very much like those designed by Franklin D. Roosevelt. And Mr. Howe ended his remarks with the sentence "We thus see Dewey trying to out-Truman Truman, which will, of course, lead Truman to out-Dewey Dewey."

I happen to be fairly smart when it comes to political dialectic, but the sudden appearance of three Trumans and three Deweys in one sentence mixed me up. I do not accuse Mr. Howe of trying to out-Crisler Crisler, but there *was* a hint of razzle-dazzle, or Michigan-backfield attack, in this explanation of the new 1948 crisscross political strategy. I lost sight of the point for a moment, the way Southern California lost sight of the ball in the Rose Bowl when they saw what must have looked to them like three Yergeses and three Weisenbergers trying to out-Chappuis Chappuis.

The next day the situation was further complicated by what I can only call a double end-around play. I quote from the *Herald Tribune:* "The shout of 'Wallace-ism' was raised by other Republican senators and representatives in such words as these: Representative Russel V. Mack, Republican, of Washington: 'It looked to me as if President Truman was trying to out-Wallace Wallace . . .' " And the *Times* printed this: "Representative Charles A. Halleck, House majority leader, called the message [Truman's] 'a purely political document designed to out-Wallace Wallace . . .' " The fair-minded critic will not draw the inference that Mack and Halleck are trying to out-Howe Howe. The thing is simply in the air. Everybody's doing it.

Now, it seems to me that Dewey is going to be thrown for a heavy loss, maybe even back of the '44-yard line, if he doesn't change his tactics. For if Dewey is trying to out-Truman Truman and Truman is trying to out-Wallace Wallace, a lot of voters will jump to the conclusion that Dewey Dewey—I mean Dewey—is trying to out-Wallace Wallace. As a matter of fact, he probably intends only to out-Truman the Truman who is trying to out-Roosevelt Roosevelt, and not the Truman who is trying to out-Wallace Wallace, but this may not be clear to the Frightened Fringe, that formidable body of voters who are afraid they may inadvertently cast their ballots for a man who wants to out-Stalin Stalin.

It seems to me that Dewey must reverse his field and try to out-somebody somebody else. The question then arises: out-who whom? Taft is the only man who can successfully out-Taft Taft, and it would scarcely be advisable to out-Eisenhower Eisenhower now that Eisenhower has decided not to Eisenhower. This doesn't seem to leave Dewey much choice in the present field of candidates, and he may find himself in the end with nothing better to do than out-Coolidge Coolidge.

Political historians will tell you that the Out Strategy has been used before in Presidential campaigns, but never, of course, to such a bewildering extent. Harding, for example, set out to out-McKinley McKinley but succeeded only in out-Granting Grant. In 1944, when Bricker was campaigning for first place on the Republican ticket, he also tried to out-McKinley McKinley. McKinley's one contribution to political maneuvering was the conceit of speaking from his front porch, a rostrum designed to enhance the homey and wholesome white carnation. Bricker actually did out-McKinley McKinley, by installing a front porch inside an auditorium, so that his listeners could sit down. McKinley's audiences had had to stand up on the front lawn of the McKinley home. Bricker's achievement in out-McKinleying McKinley got him nowhere, because, almost fifty years after McKinley's death, the people had forgot what it was to McKinley, let alone to out-McKinley McKinley, and the practice of out-McKinleying McKinley fell into high disfavor. Many observers thought, when Bricker mucked up the Out Trend by moving the McKinley porch indoors, that this bewildering strategy was gone forever, and its sudden revival this year, after the brilliant Rooseveling of Roosevelt, has alarmed the shrewder counsellors of both major political parties. The followers of Wallace do not worry, because they know that their leader will go all the way to Election Day crying simply "Look, Mama, I'm Wallacing."

What this Presidential Year needs, I think, is some bright symbol or other in the grand old tradition of the log cabin and the whiskey barrel, the white plume of Henry of Navarre, the shining sword at Armageddon, and the brown derby of the Happy Warrior. Personally, in preference to the monstrous mechanism of identification, I would settle, God help me, for a dark whisper, a little mud, or the grass in the streets.

ROBERT BENDINER

The 1952 Campaign*

What Harold Stassen and Adlai Stevenson have in common is that people don't take them seriously—Stassen when he says he's running and Stevenson when he says he isn't.

The most recent poll of Harry Truman shows that 36 percent of him wants to run, 34 percent does not, 18 percent doesn't know, and 12 percent knows but won't tell.

One top Republican has coined the phrase "Fear Deal" and another proposes the war cry, "Pink, Mink, and Stink." Naturally we can't expect the campaign to stay on this high a plane when the going really gets tough.

They call these contests "preferential" primaries because you can interpret them any way you prefer. If you get the most votes in a primary, you win; if you aren't soundly trounced, you've scored a moral victory; and if you're thoroughly whipped, you weren't really running in the first place.

This is the last week for Republicans to insult each other publicly until Nov. 5.

The gap between Gov. Stevenson and Gen. Sherman is getting noticeable. Stevenson's position now is that he "couldn't accept" the nomination for President and if they offer it to him, by George, he'll think it over.

Some people here can still remember the unforgettable address delivered two days ago by Gen. MacArthur.

* Excerpts from some "Once Over Lightly" columns in the *New York Post*.

Pins are being devised for Taft people here reading: "I don't like Ike yet but I'm working on it."

I've had enough, says Mr. Truman—and that's how Elder Statesmen are born.

The lines of the Presidential campaign are becoming clear. Each candidate will declare his opponent a brilliant, patriotic, upstanding man who unaccountably lacks the sense to steer clear of wicked company.

WESTBROOK PEGLER

Promoting Fight of the Century

1956

Straight telegram, paid to Harry S (for what?) Truman, Independence, Mo.:

Offer you flat guarantee one million dollars, win or lose, for finish fight with Vice-President Richard Nixon, possibly Franklin Field, Philadelphia, possibly one of the big California stadia, or Soldier Field, Chicago, absolutely free style, catchweights, with or without gloves. Such details subject to negotiation and agreement with Nixon. Am wiring him similar proposition simultaneously and hope eye can get you two tough, willing boys together to talk business soon, preferably in Madison Square Garden with television.

We could pack the joint just for the signing of articles in view of your threat to paste Nixon in the snoot on sight. This be terrific attraction, we could sell worldwide movie and broadcast rights and negotiations be wonderful buildup for main event come summer. Would plan charge $1,000 ringside, $50 minimum for gallery for signing, and $5,000 first twenty rows for main event, scaling back to $500 minimum steerage trade.

First thing is to agree on general proposition thereafter eye will call press conference in U.S. Senate Chamber which Dick can place at our disposal as presiding officer. You can help along this phase of the ballyhoo by invoking some right which you undoubtedly do not possess as former Vice-President and presiding officer and former President but to hell with that, we will invoke it anyway and if anyone tries uplouse deal you can call the bum dirty S.O.B.

PROMOTIONAL BUILDUP

Should be easy to give this opposition sensational promotional buildup through papers, magazines, and radio chains, awful saps for such plants and impact of press conference in Senate Chamber be terrific, sensational, colossal. You could write the rats opposing use of Senate Chamber letter like the one to Barney Baruch and the one to that concert reporter who said Maggie sang like screech-owl.

Eye would plan keep you under cover in some mop closet until climax press conference then spring you down center aisle shadowboxing yelling quote Wait till I get that bum in ring, eye will feint with left, pull him out of position, cross right hook left to chin, kick the bum in pelvis, stand back let him fall, kick him under jaw, stomp on face the dirty fourflushing false-alarm. Unquote.

Note what you said about Nixon calling you traitor, that is terrific sock material we can count on enormous traitor trade with tremendous initial boxoffice because traitors practically all rich bums they all be there yelling like crazy so please play down those denials. What do we care? Deny nothing, just say Nixon is a dirty bum, quote, I will knock Bum's brains out unquote. If you insist it might not hurt gate to say you are not traitor but as practical showmen you and eye realize no percentage in alienating enormous traitor element, lets get their dough.

STARTING FIGURE

Please understand million guarantee proposition herein is mere starting figure probably insignificant in prospective total from television of scene in Garden at signing articles and actual fight itself. Also dolls, novelties leading manufacturer whom outsounded tentatively smorning hollered why its sensation of all time eye offer million for right to Truman talking doll saying, quote, S.O.B., S.O.B., unquote also plans Truman miniature sitting desk writing letter with liberal royalty proposition.

With mutual cooperation we could sell terrific sock phonograph record probably gross billion repeat billion by Nixon saying, quote, so Truman says eye called him traitor, hey? Well so what? Unquote or something along those lines. He could also rib you for promoting Harry Dexter White twice after official information showing Soviet spy connections, you could express self unrestrained in answers, profanity soforth because FCC undare interfere your freedom expression such circumstances.

FLETCHER KNEBEL

The Kennedy–Nixon Campaign*

Before:

Nixon theme: Things are wonderful and if something isn't done quickly, they'll get even worse.

Kennedy theme: The country's in such poor shape that even a Democratic administration couldn't hurt it.

Kennedy has a new strategy. When his campaign sags in Nebraska, Iowa, or Minnesota, he rushes back East and beats Nixon all over again in New York City.

Republicans contend we did not lie about the U-2 flights. Absolutely not. We merely told the truth inside out.

Both candidates are leery of corruption charges. In a close election, neither man can take a chance on losing the sinner vote.

Ike tries a last-minute rescue of Nixon. Funny campaign. The Democrats send a boy to do a man's job—and the Republicans send a man to undo a boy's job.

After:

All we ask of the new president is that he stand up to Khrushchev, keep the peace—and stay off TV for two months.

* Excerpts from some 1960 "Potomac Fever" columns.

Jack Kennedy won by a dust slide.

Nixon finally wins California. This is like the thundering arrival of the U.S. cavalry—two hours after the Comanches have scalped everybody in the wagon train.

Statisticians say Nixon ran ahead of his party—but not enough to avoid suspicion of guilt by association.

Republicans press for vote fraud investigations without fear. They say Nixon was not the type for whom people clamored to vote twice in the same day.

The presidential campaign was loud enough to wake the dead, some of whom turned over in their graves—and mailed in absentee ballots.

Ike appoints Nixon as leader of the Republican party. That part's easy. Now the trick is to appoint Goldwater and Rockefeller as followers.

EVE MERRIAM: TEXT

ROBERT OSBORN: DRAWINGS

Fashion Forecast—1960

The Stevenson natural shoulder line: do not overlook this in placing advance orders. The old-fashioned, over-padded arms look is beginning to pall in some influential quarters, and this easier, more relaxed style—although not new, and although displayed without success in previous showings —could yet make a distinguished comeback. Requires forceful presentation, however, to persuade buyers that this natural line will not descend to a baggy, saggy look after first Los Angeles showing. When properly tailored, welfare pleats can take up the slack. This model must be believed in before it can be seen.

The Symington silhouette: artful draping, cut on the bias, achieves an accommodation to all shapes. Adaptable, multi-purpose; seams can be let in or out; undefined waistline can be accented, if need be, with military-type belt later on (that can be removed later on). A triumph of illusionist slimming design that camouflages an extensive rearguard. Comes with union label.

The boyish bang of the youthful Jackie bob is out. Newly in: the sophisticated, more worldly Mr. John coiffure—sweeping high and clear to reveal a thoughtful Galbraith-Commager-Schlesinger brow. Extremely becoming when tinted with a streak of Silver Statesman Gray at the temples. Requires constant spray to hold intact, and color needs retouching from time to time; nevertheless, pre-tests in Wisconsin, West Virginia and other areas show that this hairdo is highly flattering to wearer and helps hide figure faults below the hairline. Needs little further promotion; could be a major style-setter.

The dashing haberdasher look: featuring ties that bind for party, state and all-occasion wear. Available in an extensive range of patterns including almost every variety except coexistence configurations. Displayed most effectively on suits with high hold-'em-harry lapels that are sturdily machine-stitched, thereby furnishing the wearer with durable gripping power. Guaranteed through many washouts, although tending to fade in California sun.

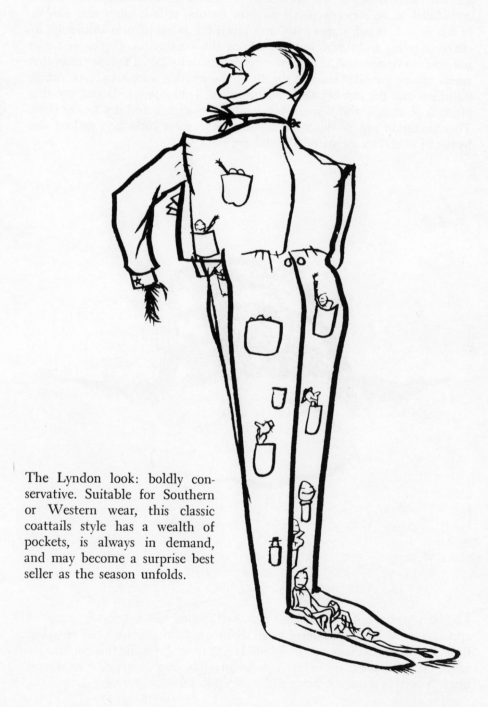

The Lyndon look: boldly conservative. Suitable for Southern or Western wear, this classic coattails style has a wealth of pockets, is always in demand, and may become a surprise best seller as the season unfolds.

On the fabric front: a new miracle fiber, nixon, has been developed that is considered to be superior in all ways to dacron, nylon, orlon and banlon. Nixon is waterproof, impervious, and reversible in midstream. Although inclined to piling and shedding of principles, the weather-proofing process does not seem to be affected. Makes up most dramatically into a military cape that covers up the outdated summit sheath. If the weather warms up, cape can be discarded and the summit sheath refurbished. Laboratory tests indicate that nixon is practically shrinkproof, but inclined to stretch and dip to the right. This limitation can be offset by bulking with center tucks and gathers and by use of liberal fringe material to distract the eye.

The Nelson chapeau: sponsoring a rich, well-sheltered look with top executive appeal. Pliable brim is designed to go sportingly from gubernatorial breakfast through convention cocktails to White House hosting. While this double-play effect may not catch on in mass popularity this year, it might take second place in current wardrobe plans and work up to primacy at a later date.

Colors to watch for: High moral tones. Religious overcasts. California Brown, a novelty shade, favored for quick one-time window display; little staying power. Campaign Gold, a sunny vibrant color that will be sought out more and more, especially for television channeling; a beautifully basic shade, it creates a grand-go-with-everything ensemble effect; enhances every type of complexion; a flattering wearwithall no wardrobe should be without. Bait Red remains as an accessory highlight, but it is not nearly so important a color note as in former seasons. To be seen on all fronts: Republican Rose, a warm, richly glowing hue, clotted with peachy cream. In some lights, appears slightly jaundiced, and could be ousted in popularity by Democratic Blue—but at present this shade is handicapped by too much envy green in the paint pot and by blots of supremacy white that tend to pale the true blue.

SAMUEL C. BRIGHTMAN*

Self-Interview

1962

Q: Mr. Brightman, you have participated in some great Democratic victories—in 1948, in 1954, in 1958, and in 1960. To what do you attribute these Democratic victories?

A: To the Republicans.

Q: I don't believe I get the point.

A: Well, in pro football there's the Washington Redskins and in pro baseball there's the Washington Nats. And in pro politics there's the Republican Party. And in politics, we get to play the same team every game.

Q: Then maybe you can explain to us why you got your brains beaten out in 1952 and 1956.

A: Circumstances beyond our control.

Q: You mean—

A: I mean our candidate. We had insurmountable handicaps. In the first place Stevenson was trained for public service. Not only that, but he promised to talk sense to the American people.

Q: Well—

A: It was all right to promise to talk sense, but Stevenson kept his promise.

Q: But I still don't understand—

A: This poor misguided man was talking to an audience conditioned by TV commercials. People who won't buy a ball-point pen unless it will write on butter and who insist upon a shaving cream that will soften sandpaper are unable to accept a believable proposition. Our opponent's promise to cut taxes and provide more government services was as unbelievable as a TV commercial and the voters flocked right down to their corner voting booth and bought the giant economy size.

* Deputy Chairman for Public Affairs, Democratic National Committee.

We tried, I can tell you, we tried. If we told him once we told him a thousand times, warm them up, boy, warm them up. And muddy up those sentences.

Q: Let's change the subject a little, Mr. Brightman. Our readership is more interested in contemporary politics than in the past generation. Could you tell us who is the most valuable political personality in the Democratic Party today?

A: Certainly, it's Arthur Schlesinger, Jr.

Q: Not John F. Kennedy, not Caroline, not Bobby— Why Arthur?

A: Arthur makes the Republicans see red. I don't know why, but he does. He makes them see red; he makes them sputter with anger; he makes them froth at the mouth. When we have Arthur come out for mother love, or social security, or strong defenses, or better schools, anything like that, the Republicans automatically come out against them. It's a real good mousetrap play. Ken Galbraith used to be pretty good for the same play, but he went off to some foreign country and nobody has heard of him since, so now we got to rely on Arthur.

Q: Mr. Brightman, have you ever tried satire in politics?

A: Yes.

Q: What happened?

A: Ike won.

Q: You think satire is no good as a political weapon?

A: Look, there are some things you can't parody—like the *Reader's Digest* and the Republican Party.

Q: How do you know? Did you ever try?

A: Yes. We tried to do a soap opera bit in the old *Democratic Digest* and it wouldn't come off. We thought we would take a typical Republican—shifty-eyed, ambitious, full of false humility, hungry for the big chance. We were way ahead of *How to Succeed in Business Without Really Trying*. But events knocked this one in the head.

Q: What's the point?

A: The point is that Richard M. Nixon made his Checkers speech on television before we printed our parody. And how could anyone parody the Checkers broadcast?

Q: Let's change the subject again. FCC Chairman Minow describes television as a "vast wasteland." Do you agree?

A: It's not vast to me. I have a ten-inch screen.

Q: Mr. Brightman, that may be a real knee-slapper among your generation, but we young people are looking for some answers of substance. What is your favorite—and please don't ramble—TV show?

A: The Ev and Charlie show.

Q: Tell us why.

A: I am a normal home-loving American citizen and I enjoy the situation comedies on television just like the research fellows told Mr. Minow—he's kind of an egghead anyhow, isn't he?

Q: (*Coldly*) Those are serious charges, Mr. Brightman, and I would hope that you are prepared to prove them. Now, you call that show a situation comedy—

A: Certainly. It brings on to your screen an attractive old codger and an attractive young codger—and they have an answer to every problem. You hardly see things like that on TV anymore except with Walter Brennan on "The Real McCoys." I find it very wholesome. And if you will permit me to make an unsophisticated observation, when it comes to bringing the Republican Party into your living room, the Ev and Charlie show is the real McCoy.

Q: Let's turn now to some specifics. I am sure you have read the Bliss Report, which says that all the Republicans have to do to win elections is to send their organizers into every metropolitan home. I don't mean to step upon any sensitive corns on the Democratic backwardness in using the modern tools of communication, but the Bliss Report was put out with plastic ring binders and was given a presentation with slides! What's your answer to that?

A: Well, we welcome the Bliss Report, and we hope the Republicans carry it out. You see, a lot of Democratic voters are so underprivileged that they have never seen a real, live Republican. They live on the wrong side of town. We want the voters to hear from the Republicans themselves what they hear over TV on the Ev and Charlie show.

Q: Do you find anything amusing in the Republican faith in advertising experts and image makers?

A: I find it more pathetic than funny. It's a little like a buggy manufacturer thinking that advertising is the answer to his lagging sales.

The other day somebody came up with an idea for a sequel to the best-selling "Buttondown Mind of Bob Newhart" record, entitled "The Celluloid-Collar Mind of Ev and Charlie." I know, it's not funny. You can't really get your heart into poking fun at Ev and Charlie. After all, they are so sincere and they really believe what they say. And they are so devastatingly representative of the Republican Party.

Q: I guess this isn't your day to be funny.

A: Try me on some other subject. Shall we have a shot at Abraham Lincoln appearing on the Jack Paar show? Or how about Calvin Coolidge, with David Susskind on "Open End"?

Q: Thank you for coming here today, Mr. Brightman.

A: Not at all. Always happy to have a chance to give young people a clearer insight into American politics.

SENATOR BARRY GOLDWATER

Excerpts from a Speech Before the Alfalfa Club

Washington, D.C., January 20, 1962

Mr. President, fellow members of this convention, guests. . . . This is the most exciting thing that has happened to me since Reuther made me an honorary Auto Worker. Frankly, I feel that I am long overdue for this nomination. But in my modesty I can't believe that there are not others better qualified. Personally I think Nelson Rockefeller would make a wonderful president. Although I don't know how the White House would look with those gas pumps out in front. . . .

Emotion chokes me when I think that you have chosen a bare-foot boy from the Arizona "valley of fear" to lead this underprivileged, undernourished, underhoused, underclothed and over-Kennedied nation of under one hundred and ninety million underlings back to the Old Frontier of McKinley's day. The UNDERtaking, naturally, overwhelms me. It takes my breath away even though I feel the White House is ready for me since Jacqueline remodeled it in an Eighteenth Century decor, and I feel this is a double honor since I've never even been to Harvard. . . .

Now right at the beginning let me scotch one bit of campaign slander the opposition has come up with. It is perfectly true that during the heat of the pre-convention maneuvering, I said that if nominated I would not accept, and if elected, I would not serve. But that statement was lifted out of context and deliberately distorted.

In the first place, when I said it, things didn't look so good. But do they tell you that? Of course not. They claim that I meant it. What I really said was that Sherman had said it first, Eisenhower had said it in 1948, Adlai had said it in 1952 (and wishes to God he'd stuck to it), and Nixon is saying it now. It beats me how they can take a clear-cut sentence like that and distort it. Why even *Pravda* garbled it in translation, and they usually get things right. . . .

Now I must take note of the fact that my opponents call me a conservative. If I understand the word correctly, it means to "conserve"— well, then, I'm just trying to live up to my name and conserve two things that most need conserving in this country—gold and water.

I don't apologize for being a conservative, I can remember when "conservative" and "mother" were clean words.

Now let me turn to my campaign platform. As you all know, I have argued for some time that we should do away with the cumbersome and lengthy, unmeaningful and platitudinous promises that the platforms of both parties have become. We need bold, brief statements that all Americans can understand. . . .

The first plank fits neatly on one page, but I think it's basically sound and honest. It will mean the same thing to you whether you live in the North or the South, whether you're a farmer in Maine or an industrial worker in California. It says, and I ask you to pay close attention: ELECT GOLDWATER. . . .

The other two planks deal with labor, education, foreign policy, and the farm problem. Here's Plank Number Two—ELECT GOLDWATER. Now you may notice a certain similarity between the first plank and the second, and I want you to know that that was deliberate. It has been my experience that the public is confused if you offer too many issues. The thing to do is to get hold of one good one and stick to it. Hammer it home. Repetition is the way Madison Avenue sells toothpaste and soap, and it's the way the New Frontier stays in the limelight. But when repetition occurs at the White House—and it has since 1932— it's not a sales pitch, it's a giveaway. You don't even have to guess the price.

And now for the final plank—Plank Number Three. This is the bell-ringer and it's even shorter. It just says DITTO.

.   .   .   .

Now I think you're entitled to know something about the caliber of men I will have in my cabinet. In presenting the list, I'd like it understood that it is confidential. Also, all the men on this list have already leaked the information to the press, and I have promised to respect the priority of their leaks.

For Secretary of the Treasury, I think I can do no better than to keep Mr. Dillon. Primarily because he has demonstrated that he possesses the one quality so badly needed in these days when we are being pulled one way by the extremists of the left and the other way by extremists of the right. Mr. Dillon is flexible. In fact, you might call him an extreme middle-of-the-roader.

My hat is off to any man who can argue under Eisenhower that we must beware of the inflationary tug of the mounting national debt and then make a rebuttal under Kennedy by saying a mere seven billion dollars added to the debt won't hurt us a bit. I believe that Secretary Dillon belongs in government—I don't think private industry could afford him. . . .

I haven't picked a Secretary of Agriculture yet. I'm waiting to see what governors are unemployed. . . .

I don't claim to have all the answers, but since this Administration took over, I don't even understand the questions.

And another thing. How is it that our government did better against General Electric than they did against Cuba?

I don't want to seem critical. But our first ambassador in space was a chimp. And so far he's the only one in the State Department who hasn't made a mistake.

.   .   .   .

Now, I suppose no acceptance speech would be complete without a reference to the candidate's background. Very simply, I think I'm in the American tradition. I was born in a log cabin, which I had moved to Phoenix, and except for some air conditioning, a swimming pool, a bowling alley, a bar, a shooting range, and a golf course, it remains the simple log cabin it always was.

I have nothing against millionaire Presidents. I'd just like to see the day return when people other than Presidents can be millionaires, too.

I've never hesitated with an answer. When anyone asks me how I stand on integration I've only got one answer—where are you from?

Now, gentlemen, I have told you the story. The rest is up to you. Go out and work from now to election day and fulfill our campaign pledge —ELECT GOLDWATER. Find more of those districts such as the one the New Frontier turned up in Cook County—the one that had twenty-two residents but came up with seventy-seven votes. That's the sort of stuff I mean.

Gentlemen, I'm flattered that you thought first of my name. I have every confidence that with all of you behind me, I could be another Alf Landon. . . .

JAMES A. WECHSLER

Rocky & Dick

March, 1963

(*In the absence of any authoritative accounts of what took place when Gov. Rockefeller recently conferred with Richard Nixon, the following fictional transcript is offered. It is accompanied by certain mental asides, in deference to the revival of* Strange Interlude.)

*   *   *

Rockefeller: H'ya, fellah.

Nixon: Good to see you, Nelson. You're looking well. (*Well! He looks like the lonely long-distance runner.*)

R: It must be great to be out of this political rat-race for a while.

N: (*He couldn't help using the word "rat," could he?*) Well, it is a relief in a way.

R: (*He looks as if he may die of this relief.*) But I'll bet you'll be back soon; a fellah like you can't get it out of his blood.

N: I stand on my statement—

R: (*Boy, here comes another press release.*) Oh, I know, but circumstances can change anybody's mind.

N: Nope, at least not for a long time. The way I see it, you're way out in front for the next shot. I've had my chance.

R: (*Guess he just saw the latest Gallup poll on Kennedy.*) It's nice of you to say so, fellah. But you know I haven't said yet that I'm a candidate.

N: (*If he's not a candidate, I'm an atomic physicist.*) Oh, I understand, of course. But that's the way I size it up.

R: Well, nice of you to say so, but there are quite a lot of other fellahs in the picture.

N: (*Boy, this modest act turns my stomach.*) I can only call it the way I see it. And I want you to know that, if it happens, I'm right behind you.

R: (*In that case I better stand close to the wall.*) Fellah, that's very generous of you, and I won't forget it.

N: (*He doesn't forget anything.*) You know, we could have taken it last time if you'd been on my team. Confidentially, my running mate wasn't much help.

R: (*He doesn't forget anything.*) You could be right, but we'll never know, will we? Hey, who was your running mate?

N: Well, I'll be damned, let's see, oh yeah—Lodge, you remember, Hank Lodge.

R: Oh, of course. Nice fellah, Hank Lodge.

N: (*Yeah, he was a big help.*) By the way, how's the wife—oh, sorry.

R: (*He's a real nice fellah.*) Everything OK with Pat and the kids?

N: Just great. It's good to be able to be a full-time husband again—Sorry—(*That really wasn't a nice crack.*) You're not letting Goldwater worry you, are you?

R: Well, he's got a lot on the ball. Intelligent fellah, in his way. You can't write him off.

N: I do. You know what they say about a shortstop; he's got to know how to go to his left sometimes. Barry just can't.

R: Say, that's not a bad line— So you really think we have a chance.

N: I sure do. I think you can make it.

R: (*He must know something bad.*) Damn decent of you to say so. That was tough luck in California.

N: (*I'll bet it broke his heart.*) It might have been better if we'd had a newspaper strike out there.

R: Those fellahs gave you a rough time, didn't they?

N: (*Now he is giving me the sympathy act.*) Yeah, pretty bad. But I guess I shouldn't have said so. There's no sense looking back.

R: (*Boy, this guy is a phrase maker.*) Well, right now I've got this state to worry about, so there's no sense trying to look too far ahead either.

N: (*Boy, this guy is a statesman.*) Oh, of course, I understand.

R: Tell me privately, though, what do you think about these Ev and Charley shows—are they helping us?

N: They'll never top Jack Paar, as Pat said the other day.

R: You're not kidding.

N: Well, anyway, I just wanted you to know how I see things now, and I hope it all works out.

R: (*I wonder if he still thinks I'd take the Vice-Presidential nomination with him.*) It was fine of you to take the trouble. Real fine.

N: (*I wonder if he thinks I'd run for Vice-President with him—you can't figure some guys.*) Well, I'm trying to think of the party, and I think you're it.

R: (*I keep forgetting, how old will this guy be in '68?*) You're darn nice, but I appreciate it. The main thing is, we have to think about the country, and what's best for it.

N: (*Does he think this is a TV show?*) I couldn't agree with you more— Well, it's been good talking things out.

R: (*Come to think of it, he might make a good Secretary of Commerce.*) It sure has. Thanks again, fellah.

GEORGE DIXON

Romney

May, 1963

Unless he's the slickest sleight-of-mouth artist since William Jennings Bryan, the immediate ambition of Gov. George Romney of Michigan is to remain Gov. George Romney of Michigan. If he's in the Presidential race, he's certainly erecting a lot of obstacles in his course.

We had him to a combination lunch–news conference in the National Press Club where he did the untraditional thing of going on without a pre-luncheon snort to stoke himself against the impending ordeal. Stone-cold sober, he alienated the affections of the pivotal states of the nation.

The man who is touted favorite for the Republican Presidential nomination in the event that Gov. Nelson A. Rockefeller is ditched for being overmarried, Senator Barry Goldwater for being overconservative, and Gov. William Scranton of Pennsylvania for being overeager, went heartily about the task of blowing his chances in one section of the country after the other.

He blew the sunny Southland by declaring he preferred the four-seasonal climate of Michigan to the "monotonous sunny climate" of the South. In one whooshing blast this blew Florida, Alabama, Mississippi, and all of Dixie. Cracks about monotonous sunshine and balmy nights are not tolerated in Louisiana, the Carolinas, Arkansas, Georgia, or even in our neighboring Virginia.

If I were Romney I would think twice about visiting Puerto Rico and Hawaii even as a tourist, much less a candidate for President. Puerto Ricans—especially those who have put in a couple of years up north before being attracted back home again by Operation Bootstrap—would grow livid at hearing the island's sunny days denounced as monotonous.

But Gov. Romney unendeared himself to our Southland more than climatically. To make doubly certain of alienating all Dixie, he extolled civil rights over states rights.

I sat there, sated with the most Lucullan viands that money didn't buy, staring in petrified fascination as Romney blew New England by declaring that Michigan was discovered before Plymouth Rock. My weatherbeaten face blanched from the wind as he blew New York and California by proclaiming Michigan to be the leading State in the Union.

To this blowup, he added an extra blast. He blew Illinois, Pennsylvania, Ohio, and Texas by stating that Michigan shows the way.

Then he proceeded to blow New Mexico by describing Michigan as the real state of enchantment. He blew the rest of the Rocky Mountain empire by calling Michigan the most scenic state; and blasted the upper Midwest and the Pacific Northwest by lauding Michigan as the country's true water wonderland.

In fact, when you come right down to it, the only state whose proudest boast he didn't assail was Rhode Island. He blew a possible commercial tie-up for a former product by failing to claim Michigan as the most compact state in the nation.

The Governor of Michigan succeeded in convincing me he isn't seeking the Presidential nomination. I don't mean he won't accept it; he just isn't seeking it. Of course, if it gets in his way—

I was by no means the only one at our question-and-answer seminar to be deeply impressed. When Romney reached the heights of lyricism in touting Michigan as the most desirable paradise, except presumably Heaven, a political pundit back of me muttered worshipfully:

"He's a combination almanac and salesman!"

Gov. Romney was not abashed in attributing every known virtue to Michigan, even when asked about a meeting then taking place between former President Eisenhower, former Vice-President Nixon, and Gov. Scranton. The author of the question, obviously a sly one, asked:

"Do you think those three met merely to discuss the virtues of Pennsylvania?"

Romney replied blithely, if not responsively, that he had invited Gov. Rockefeller and Senator Goldwater to Michigan.

I don't remember ever hearing a politician as convincing as Romney. He convinced me beyond peradventure that he will not go after the GOP nomination unless he thinks there is an outside chance of getting it.

ARTHUR HOPPE

Dammit, Steve, You Forgot "Modest"

1962

Have you had a chance to read this new book about Mr. Goldwater? It's great. On the front it says: BARRY GOLDWATER—FREEDOM IS HIS FLIGHT PLAN—BY STEPHEN SHADEGG.

Inside, it says Mr. Goldwater is brilliant, courageous, dignified, honest, frank, charming, wise, loyal, patriotic, hardworking, valiant, handsome, and humble. Humble? Humble.

On the back jacket it says:

This is the most accurate and complete story of my life I have ever seen recorded. This is not surprising, however, since Steve Shadegg knows more about me than any other writer in the country.

(*signed*)
BARRY GOLDWATER

Nor is this surprising. Because, as I understand it, Mr. Shadegg is Mr. Goldwater's press agent.

Personally, I feel this is an excellent solution to the whole problem of biographies. After considerable research I've found that there is nobody who better comprehends the real you more completely and accurately than your press agent. Press agents have a knack for analyzing the complexities of your character that other, more casual observers sadly lack.

Indeed, I've engaged my press agent, Mr. Caveat Caviar, to write a book about me. Mr. Caviar knows more about me than any other writer in the country. Firsthand. But we've run into trouble already.

You see, before joining Mr. Goldwater's employ, Mr. Shadegg was a writer of Grade B Western scenarios in Hollywood. This qualified him admirably to compile a biography of Mr. Goldwater, who always wears a white hat. But Mr. Caviar's last two works (both paperbacks) were *Strange Lusts of Teen-Age Coeds* and *Rape Is a Way of Life*. And I'm not sure that his particular style enables him to capture the real me.

In fact, I spoke to him rather sharply about this when he submitted the first draft last week. "Mr. Caviar," I said, "about this opening scene where I'm being born in a log cabin. The log cabin is nice, but—"

"Real socko, eh, baby?" said Mr. Caviar, flicking cigar ashes from his tattersall vest. "Listen to this: 'And the comely young midwife bent over the bed, her low-cut gown revealing her dot, dot, dot.' You remember different, kid?"

"Well, no. And I must say you have accurately described my charm, wit, wisdom, strength, loyalty, courage, reverence, cleanliness and obedience. But this part on page 87— Do you really think I look like Gregory Peck?"

"Who knows you best, baby? Me. So maybe we blur your picture on the jacket a little. Soft focus, that's the stuff."

"I see. One other thing. Take this scene that runs from page 102 to page 376 describing Ava Gardner and me in this bedroom overlooking the Riviera. For the life of me I can't recall—"

"Look, kiddo, leave us not be squaresville. I talked to M-G-M about the Ava bit. They say a plug's a plug. When the book's out, they'll deny. We'll retract. Big fight. That makes it box office. Like the new title."

"New title? I thought we'd agreed to use my name followed by '—Wisdom for the Ages.'"

"That's a great one, baby. Real boffola. But how many slobs know your name? You could count them on the thumbs of one hand. So we're changing it a little like."

"A little like what?"

"Like: *I Was a Teen-Age Sex Maniac.* Now, baby, just sign this blurb for the back jacket: 'This is the best book about me I ever read—' "

I'm giving up the project. I guess I'm just too humble to have my press agent write a book about me. Humble like Mr. Goldwater. Which reminds me of a question I've been meaning to ask him:

How do you stand it, sir?

SENATOR J. W. FULBRIGHT

On "Liberalism" and "Coexistence"

1963

It is a welcome relief, Mr. President, during these muggy, sticky, frustrating summer days, to be diverted even momentarily from the serious problems of government and public policy. We are indebted to the junior Senator from Arizona [Mr. Goldwater] for providing us with such a diversion in his recent remarks to the Human Events Conference here in Washington.

I read the Senator's speech with interest and enjoyment. It is indeed a remarkable speech. At no point does it burden the reader with the complexities of current foreign and domestic problems.

The Senator has a rare gift of clarity. So lucid is his discourse that he makes us wonder what all the fuss has been over nuclear weapons and international tensions and unemployment and all the other stubborn problems that perplex the American people. In the Senator's penetrating analysis, all these problems can be made to evaporate if we will only *declare* a "bold" and "courageous" policy abroad and return to "fundamentals" at home. It is regrettable that, for whatever excellent reasons, the Senator did not see fit to elaborate on his noble sentiments or to spell out how and where and by what means he proposes to take "bold" action abroad or to explain to us which precise "fundamentals" he would have us return to in our domestic life.

Undoubtedly, the Senator from Arizona intends to do these things in some future pronouncement. I think it only proper to assume that he will and, as a Democrat, I think I can assure the Senator that we on the majority side are prepared to wait patiently for the time when he will see fit to translate his brave theories into prescriptions for public policy. . . .

We owe the Senator this forbearance because of his own gracious and generous attitude toward the Democratic Party. In his speech the Senator unequivocally expressed his opinion that Democrats are not Communists and that the Communist Party has not captured control of the Democratic Party—even though, in the view of the Senator from Arizona, the program of the Democratic Administration is viewed with favor by the Communists.

I thank the Senator for his generous—I hesitate to say "liberal"—view of the Democratic Party. In return, I am prepared to state my own unequivocal opinion that the Senator from Arizona is not a Communist either—despite the similarity of some of his views to those of the rulers of Communist China. I am sure this is purely coincidental.

The Senator from Arizona is opposed to "coexistence"; so are the Chinese Communists. The Senator is opposed to the nuclear test ban treaty; so are the Chinese Communists. The Senator thinks it is cowardly to try to avoid nuclear war; so do the Chinese Communists.

I am confident that no fair-minded American will misinterpret the interesting parallel between the Senator's views on these matters and those of the Chinese Communists. The Senator, without doubt, is a loyal and patriotic American.

I was particularly interested in two themes that run through the Senator's remarks: his views on "liberalism" and on "coexistence."

The Senator is four-square in his opposition to "liberalism," which he regards as feeble and exhausted and at the same time—somehow—dangerously aggressive and predatory. "Liberalism," in the Senator's view, represents a whole category of evils that the Democratic Administrations of the last thirty years have invented to destroy the "freedom" of the American people. "Liberalism" stands for such wickedness as social security, which has destroyed the "freedom" of the aged to be destitute or dependent; rural electrification and farm price supports, which have destroyed the "freedom" of the farmer to live in poverty and deprivation by candlelight; public housing and urban renewal, which have destroyed the "freedom" of many of our people to live in rural shacks and urban slums; public works and government fiscal policy, which have destroyed the "freedom" of most—but not all—of our people to be blissfully unemployed; and federal aid to education—the most diabolical plot of all— which threatens to destroy our "freedom" to be ignorant and unemployable.

The Senator is opposed to all these incursions on the "freedom" of the American people. He opposes them for many reasons, but most of all because they violate certain unspecified ethical "fundamentals." No doubt, in the fullness of time, the Senator will spell out these "fundamentals. . . ."

I, for one, am prepared to wait. It is rumored that the Senator from Arizona may be prevailed upon to seek higher office. Should that prove to be the case, he will undoubtedly spell out a dynamic program of national action under some stirring title like "The Fundamentals of Illiberalism" or "Let's Get the Government Out of the Business of Government."

As intriguing as the Senator's opinion of "liberalism" are his views on "coexistence." "To coexist," according to Webster, is "to exist together or at the same time." The Senator, as we all know, is unalterably opposed to such an arrangement between the communist countries and the free world. It would seem to follow that the Senator considers it essential for one side or the other—presumably the communist side—to stop existing at once.

The problem of course—which the Senator has not yet seen fit to comment on—is precisely how the Communists can be persuaded or coerced to terminate their existence. It seems reasonable to suppose that they will not do so voluntarily, so the problem is really one of compulsion. It is precisely at this interesting point that the Senator leaves us in suspense.

He is absolutely clear, however, in his conviction that "coexistence" is craven, cowardly, and un-American. It is, in fact, a communist idea, based on Khrushchev's apparent confidence that if the two sides engage in peaceful competition for the allegiance of mankind, his side will win. For an American to favor "coexistence," he would have to believe that democracy is far stronger than communism, that a free society can create a far better life for the individual than a totalitarian society, that freedom has a magnetism and promise for mankind that communism can never hope to match.

Of this heresy no one can accuse the junior Senator from Arizona. He has stated unequivocally that he favors "boldness and courage and determination" over craven "coexistence." These words, of course, are a bit vague and the Senator has not yet seen fit to translate them into specific proposals for a "bold" and "courageous" foreign policy.

But perhaps we can speculate. Both the United States and the Soviet Union possess hydrogen bombs and intercontinental missiles with which to destroy each other's societies. Neither has the means of preventing the other from doing so. Under these circumstances the only alternative to "coexistence" is mutual destruction. This, perhaps, is the key to the foreign policy favored by the Senator from Arizona—a "bold," "courageous," and "determined" policy of "coannihilation."

This, of course, is speculation because the Senator has not yet chosen to reveal his foreign policy proposals. It may be some time before he does so. In the meantime, there is nothing for us to do but restrain our eagerness and contemplate the delay with equanimity.

AMBROSE BIERCE

*The Plaudits of the People**

A Man who had been mentioned for high political preferment explained through the newspapers that he was "not a candidate." Thereupon he was lustily cheered by the populace.

"Why do you not cheer?" someone asked a Silent Person standing moodily apart.

"Because," answered the Silent Person, "I understand these plaudits to be given for his humility. Whenever you raise the shout for this knowledge of the English language you can count on the assistance of both my lungs."

"Why, how is that?" asked those who stood nearest.

"A candidate is one who has been nominated," said the Silent Person. "He has not succeeded, as yet, in moving Heaven and Earth sufficiently to procure that distinction."

* from *Fantastic Fables*, 1899.

L. L. CASE

Behind the Capital Curtain

1963

In still another thoughtful article, Richard Nixon—private citizen, successful lawyer, world traveler, and prolific magazine writer—says we can lift it, and tells us how.

Since I had made it perfectly clear that I was returning to Washington purely as a private, non-political citizen, I was not surprised to find that there was no official welcoming committee waiting for me at the station. I had decided earlier to arrive by train, so that adequate shelter from possible inclement weather would be available to protect the thousands of loyal Americans I had learned to expect would greet me, as they had in such capitals as Berlin, Warsaw, Budapest, and Sacramento. It was a source of no little satisfaction to me, nevertheless, to observe that the government, fearing a possible uncontrollable mass demonstration in my behalf, had cleared the terminal of ordinary travelers and replaced them with poorly-disguised secret police and a handful of carefully chosen stooge newsmen. For this was the first unmistakable clue to the underlying weakness felt by the Democrat rulers beneath their public posture of vigor and confidence.

The streets were abnormally crowded with pedestrians, pathetically pretending to be going about such ordinary business as shopping and returning to work. Their hurried, over-the-shoulder glances at our inconspicuous procession of open cars made the true reason for their presence obvious, however, at least to anyone with wide experience in world affairs. Furtive gestures and eyebrow-raising were as much as they dared express of their hopes for liberation; the turnout was all the more remarkable since my route and arrival time had not been publicly announced, except for small front-page newspaper stories.

I could see that it would be impossible to ascertain the feelings of the typical man in the street under such forbidding circumstances. I waited, therefore, until nightfall to make my move. "I think," I announced loudly in the lobby of my hotel (to throw the secret police off guard), "that I'll take a walk and see if I can find some of those excellent non-Cuban cigars I used to favor, when I was Vice-President of the United States, from 1953 to 1960, inclusive." The stratagem was successful; I was not followed. Within a few minutes a typical man in the street approached me cautiously, with outstretched hand. "We typical men in the street are glad you came to Washington," he said. "The Republicans, especially those with experience as Presidential candidates, are our only hope." I placed a half-dollar in his palm, so that he could obtain a bottle of the grape medicine he explained he needed.

I had just seen the difference between day and night under Democrat rule.

During my short stay in the oppressed capital I found it impossible not to be reminded of the happy and prosperous days before the dark cloud of despotism descended in November, 1960; if this were not a nonpolitical report by a private citizen, I would be tempted to draw invidious comparisons. Even a far less experienced observer of public affairs than I could hardly fail to note, for example, that comparatively few residents of this once-proud city can any longer afford such a modest article of apparel as a Homburg hat. My lifelong study of (American) economics leads me to attribute this depressing condition to an insidious, two-gaited blend of galloping inflation and creeping socialism—but more of this in a later nonpolitical article. (As I stated in *U.S. News & World Report,* I shall not be a candidate in '64—and that answers all questions of that type.)

Personal reminiscence is a luxury in these critical times, however, and I do not intend to indulge in it. Our nation is in the grip of a tyranny, and our people are clamoring for liberation. It is the first obligation of every far-seeing statesman, in his capacity of private citizen, to point the way to freedom, and I humbly accept this obligation. In this spirit I will reveal my findings.

The government is afraid of being overthrown! Every sign points to this startling, but inescapable, conclusion. The President and his henchmen are secretly, but feverishly, traveling around the country soliciting votes for his re-election in 1964! His public statements and legislative proposals are often outright, unconcealed bids for popular approval and support. Could this be the attitude of a leader who is sure of his hold on the people?

Discontent is becoming more openly expressed! Let me recount a small, but significant, incident. I was standing in Lafayette Park, in the very shadow of the White House, when hundreds of people boldly converged upon me, to shake my hand. Even with policemen in plain view, they courageously stated: "Had we but known in 1960 what we know now, we certainly might have voted for you."

The people are becoming skeptical of Democrat promises! A student told me this amusing, but pointed, story, which had been given clandestine circulation among clandestine student groups. "The Democrat donkey is at its most dangerous when it is nearest," he said. "If you get too close, you may get a kick in the teeth." Such a story is hardly consistent with the uncritical acceptance of the regime pictured by its propagandists.

These disclosures, it seems to me, point the way to a positive, effective program for liberation. The time has come for a complete re-examination of Republican policy toward Democrat rule. To achieve this program, we must take a new hard cold fresh look at the alternatives available to us.

1) The soft, or Eastern, line. We are hearing far too much, these days, about "accommodation," "coexistence," "disengagement," and the like. It is unquestionably a simpler, and temporarily safer, approach to ignore the plight of the millions of Americans gallantly making the best of it under the tyranny of the "New Frontier" by participating in a bipartisan *détente* on such issues as foreign aid, civil rights, tax cuts, and the rest. In the long run, however, this sacrifice of principle to expediency will be disastrous, as my lifelong study of (American) history has shown. An example of this "liberal" thinking is the apparent acquiescence of a New York governor to the Administration's proposed public-opinion-poll moratorium. Now we all can certainly agree on the desirability of minimizing the exposure of the upcoming generation of American newspaper readers to the hazards of statistical fallout. But we must take a longer view. For after the votes are counted next November *it may be too late!*

2) The hard, or Western, line. Even a simpler approach is that taken by a certain Arizona senator: firm opposition to the Administration on all issues. The great appeal of this "reactionary" policy, of course, is that

it relieves us of the time-consuming problem of developing affirmative solutions of our own, and thus makes for more efficient campaigning. The danger of this very popular program, however, is that too many voters may be unnecessarily confused about what we may, or may not, do after we are elected. Our principles must *never* be compromised, but they must be made compatible with (American) public opinion!

3) Riding the dark horse. Americans are traditionally sympathetic to the underdog, but this rarely applies in politics. Many Republicans, especially in Michigan and Pennsylvania, have pointed out the undeniable advantages of a campaign led by a candidate unembarrassed by previous experience in world and national affairs, since such experience so often requires the taking of positions, which can be misunderstood. This advantage, however, is more than offset by the handicap of insufficient pre-conditioning of the voters to the candidate's image, and we must therefore set aside this option for technical reasons.

Now that we have ruled out the more obvious choices that have been suggested, we must next ask ourselves: What, then, should be our positive program for liberation? And where should we look for a candidate to lead us most effectively to implement such a program? (I shall not be a candidate in '64—and that answers all questions of that type.)

First of all, we should make clear to the voters the strong, uncompromising, affirmative program I have outlined. This means that we must eschew any soft "liberal" *compromises* with the Democrats, such as being party to a dishonorable poll-ban agreement. But it also means that we must not let ourselves be trapped in the position of "reactionary" *opposition* to anything the Democrats put forth, such as a reasonable poll-ban agreement, which might be helpful to us. We must set forth our independent program at all times, without consideration of expediency, except where a certain flexibility might be expected to advance our cause.

Second, we must in no way lend ourselves to any program that may serve the interests of the Democrats, unless such a program will at the same time help the people throw off the yoke of Democrat rule. By way of analogy, let me point to my recent foreign-policy proposals in the *Saturday Evening Post*. There I made clear the necessity of finding positive, peaceful methods of helping those living under communist governments overthrow their Red oppressors, but in a responsible manner that would obviate the risk of world war that might be entailed if we were to follow the adventurist policy of calling for the overthrow of the governments of communist-dominated states. The same analogy holds in such domestic issues as civil rights. Just as I have pointed out that our devotion to the cause of world freedom should not lead us into the immature mistake of causing unnecessary embarrassment to the governments of South Africa and Portugal, so I say now that we must not permit our unswerving support of the principle of full citizenship for all Americans to embarrass our friendly relations with the governors and electors of Alabama, Mississippi, and Arkansas. We must have a *single* standard of freedom in the United States as elsewhere.

Finally, we must have a candidate who can unite our party, as well as the masses of enslaved, uncommitted voters, around our program. He should be a man identified neither with the "soft" Eastern wing of the party, nor with the "hard" Western line. He should not be a dark horse; ideally, he should be a man who can be associated both with an important western state, such as California, and an industrial eastern state, such as New York. He should be a man of experienced, mature judgment in public affairs, with the proved capability of handling himself in one or more crises; it would be best if he had previous experience as President, or at least as Vice-President. He should have had legislative experience in Congress, and although he should be known as a political "winner" he should have the common touch of one who knows what it means to lose a close election or two. He should be versatile enough to express his views clearly and forcefully, whether in debate, say with a Russian premier, or in endless magazine articles and interviews.

Skeptics may say: "You are asking too much, Mr. Nixon. Where can we find such a perfect candidate? A natural leader, with such ideal qualities to unite the nation in the fight to overthrow Democrat despotism, would certainly be too good to be true!" I would answer him, and others of little faith, with the Biblical injunction: "Seek, and ye shall find."

Washington's Gridiron Club occupies so special a place as an institution of political satire that I am making it an exception to the general exclusion of "performed" humor in this book. Its annual dinners, with their elaborate skits and songs lampooning current political issues and politicians, date from 1885; the first guest of honor was President Benjamin Harrison, and each succeeding President (except Grover Cleveland) has accepted this designation ever since, however uncomfortably. Those attending constitute as politically influential an audience, pound for pound, as can be found at any quasi-public function in the United States at any time. The club's 50 active members are drawn chiefly from the Washington press corps, but all remarks made at the dinners, however newsworthy, are off the record.

ANONYMOUS

Songs from Gridiron Club Dinners

1912   *This song, part of a "Robin Hood" skit, deals with Theodore Roosevelt's attempt to get the Republican presidential nomination without appearing to seek it. The tune is "The Old Cross Bow."*

> A statesman who dwelt on the Outlook's edge
> Was deft with his old big stick.
> A dove of peace lit on his window ledge;
> He hit it an awful lick.
> He stopped awhile, and to sigh began;
> They heard him both near and far.
> If you wait for the office to seek the man,
> The office says, "Stay where you are."

1924   *This song was part of a* Mikado-*type skit, sung to the tune of "Nanki Poo and Yum Yum."*

Solo—Were it not for prohibition,
I would take a drink with you,
But as I'm a politician
I suggest that you take this cue.
I will make it my vocation
To imbibe upon the sly,
And secure the nomination
On a platform wet and dry.

Chorus—Though it sounds to us amusing
And is also quite confusing
Now some wisdom he is using
Not a vote would he be using. . . .
You are, you are, you are a really model candidate.

1940   *The contenders for the Republican nomination included Senators Taft and Vandenberg.*

Taft: I want a job just like a job
They gave to dear old dad.
Let precedent make me President,
Ohio ain't so bad.
After a Roosevelt you need a Taft.
Close the window on the third-term draft.
I want a job, just like the job
They gave to dear old dad.

Vandenberg: He flies through the air with the greatest of ease,
The Michigan man on the flying trapeze.
He's doing his best all the voters to please,
While the office is seeking the man.

1948   *Democratic national chairman Edward J. Flynn is represented as trying to woo back third-party candidate Henry Wallace, to the tune of "Bill Bailey."*

Won't you come back, Oh Henry,
Won't you come home?
Bring back Glen Taylor, too.
We need his cowboy singing.
Your crystal ball.
You know you done us wrong.
'Member that stormy day that we drove you out

With nothing but a fine-tooth comb?
You know you're to blame,
Well, ain't that a shame?
But Henry, won't you please come home?

1959 *Father Joseph P. Kennedy introduces his son John, to the tune of "All of Me," as the first candidate for President on the "family plan."*

All of us
Why not take all of us?
Fabulous
You can't live without us.
My son John
Heads the procession,
Then comes Bob,
Groomed for succession.

We're the most,
We stretch from coast to coast.
Kennedys
Just go on forever.
I've got the dough;
You might as well know
With one—
You get all of us.

1963 *Nelson Rockefeller and Barry Goldwater enter arm in arm; Rockefeller sings to the tune of "Why Do I Love You?"*

Could I run with you?
Could you run with me?
Could we win with two
Different as we?
We're a ticket they will care for
We're a slate they'd say a prayer for.

You are on the right,
On the left I'll be.
With the two of us,
Hopes bright will be.
Robert Welch will surely love you,
Liberals will go for me.

CONVENTIONS

WILL ROGERS

Some Presidential Nominating Conventions

June 2, 1920 [*before the conventions*]
I'm giving these conventions the absence treatment since I am out in California making a movie, *Cupid, the Cowpuncher*. But you don't have to hear somebody say a thing to know it. Why, I'll bet the typewriter—the machine, not the blond that runs it—which has lived through a convention or two just automatically run off all the speeches including the "applause" and "wild cheering for twenty minutes."

President Wilson says the Old Testament stayed as it was written and he thinks the League of Nations had just as good authors as it did.

It will be considered an honor this year to be nominated by the Republicans but with the Democrats it will be considered a duty. They will meet this year through force of habit.

When Hoover decided to be elected on the Republican Ticket he picked the wrong party. He should have stayed with the Democrats where the opposition was not so keen. I guess he figured that it was better to be defeated for the nomination than to be a Democrat and then get defeated in the election.

Pres. Wilson is going to retire to Princeton University. He says the pay may not be as plentiful but neither is the advice.

June 4, 1920

Congress wants to abolish Slush Funds. Why, that distributes more money among the needy delegates than anything. Imagine a Congress that squandered 30 Billions trying to find out where some candidate spent a few thousand!

I have been asked to cover the Republican Convention, to write something funny. All you have to do to write something funny about a Republican Convention is just tell what happens.

The Convention is held in Chicago. Chicago is located just North of the U.S. I am well acquainted with the American Consul there. Chicago holds the record for Murders and robberies and Republican Conventions.

The Convention started off with a setback. A carload of wine billed for Chicago for "Medical Purposes" got held up.

The Democrats are investigating slush funds. If they can find where it come from they want theirs.

June 9, 1920

I know who will be nominated but the Republican leaders have asked me not to tip it off as the hotels and other crooks in Chicago want to keep the suckers there a few days till they are thoroughly renovated.

They called in a Professional pray-er as none of the Politicians present knew how. Of course Bill Hays [*Republican National Chairman*] has told him what to pray for. A great many of the leading Republicans were against having the Prayer as they didn't think it necessary this year but, to add variety to an otherwise monotonous show, they decided to leave it in.

Bill Hays seemed quite relieved at the end of the Prayer when he heard no applause as he said, "You can never tell what a Republican will do."

Senator Lodge next asked the Lord to bless everybody but Wilson. I got Bill Hays on the phone and asked him, "Bill why has Lodge got it in so for Woodrow?" He said, "Well, Lodge is sore because he took Mrs. Wilson to Europe instead of him." I said, "But why didn't he pray for something terrible to happen to Bryan?" He said, "Something terrible has already happened to him."

June 10, 1920

This is not a Convention; it is a Chatauqua.

I phoned Bill Hays, "Who is praying today?" He told me, "The audience."

I said, "What do you think of the Slush Fund?" He said, "I think it is great."

I said, "How can you tell who bought delegates and who didn't?"

"Why," he said, "that's easy to tell. The fellows who haven't got any delegates haven't bought any."

June 11, 1920

I phoned Bill Hays, "Why don't some of them say something?" He said, "Well, I guess they have told all they know about Wilson."

I said, "Why surely some of all these thousands of Republicans must know of him poisoning a well or dynamiting an orphan asylum or something."

Bryan attended the Republican Convention. He wanted to see how they nominate a President.

Prohibition has raised the price of votes. Votes that used to cost a dozen 5-cent beers are now selling for a four dollar bottle of hair tonic. And the tough part of it is they are no better votes.

[*The Republicans nominated Senator Warren G. Harding of Ohio for its Presidential candidate and Governor Calvin Coolidge of Massachusetts for his running mate.*]

June 14, 1920

Only two detrimental things have come out since Nomination in Harding's whole record. One was his middle name, Gamaliel, and the other he used to play a slide trombone in a country band. Musical circles in Washington are now looking towards a big revival.

Ohio claims they are due a President as they haven't had one since Taft. Look at the United States, they haven't had one since Lincoln.

My idea of an honest man is a fellow who will pay income tax on money he sold his vote for. Politicians who buy votes with Wood Alcohol will have to be very careful to not deliver the drink till after the party has voted.

Chicago crooks say it was the poorest convention on record as all the Delegates had were their badges.

.   .   .   .

June 27, 1924

We have heard nothing since 10 o'clock this morning until 6 tonight but "The man I am going to name." Then they talk for another thirty minutes and then, "The man I am going to name." There have been guys going to name men all day, and all we ever got named were about six out of a possible 200.

Franklin Roosevelt started in early this morning with the "Man I am about to name." He had the opportunity of a lifetime to make a name for himself comparable with the Republican end of the Roosevelt family. But no, he must say, "Man I am about to name" for ten pages.

But when he did get to the end and named Al Smith you would have thought somebody had thrown a wildcat in your face. The galleries went wild and about ten State delegations marched and hollered for an hour. Talk about our civilization! Why, if they ever took a sanity test at a political convention 98 percent would be removed to an asylum.

Oh, yes, a woman from Oregon seconded McAdoo for the ninth time. She didn't have to come. She could have stood on the banks of the Columbia River in Oregon and we could have heard her perfectly. I bet she busted every radio east of the Mississippi.

Talk about Presidential Timber, why, Man, they had whole Lumber Yards of it here. There was so many being Nominated that some of the men making the nominating Speeches had never even met the men they were nominating. I know they had not from the way they talked about them.

A guy from Utah talked so long and loud that all of us couldn't see how it could be anybody in the world he was nominating but Brigham Young—"that matchless father"—but he crossed everybody by seconding McAdoo's nomination.

July 9, 1924

Well, it was 6:30 and they had just read the platform. I had it before me, forty-five pages. If it had come out in the open on every question and told just where they stood, they could have saved themselves, not only forty-two pages of paper, but perhaps their election in November.

When you straddle a thing it takes a long time to explain it.

It favors fixing everything the Republicans have ruined, keeping everything that they haven't, right up to its present standard. In the Republican platform at Cleveland they promised to do better.

I don't think they have done so bad this time. Everybody's broke but them.

July 10, 1924

Who said miracles don't happen? Didn't the Democratic National Convention nominate a man at last?

That should bring more people back to religion than any other one thing. It has been a demonstration of faith, because, after all, God is good.

This convention wound up in a personal triumph for William Jennings Bryan. My old friend W. J. is the greatest character we have in this country today. He is a very unique man. Most of us only attract attention twice on earth. One is when we are born and the other is when we die.

But Mr. Bryan even improves on a bear; a bear hibernates all Winter, but Bryan hibernates for four years, and then emerges, and has a celebration every four years at every Democratic Convention.

In the meantime, he lectures in tents, shooting galleries, grain elevators, snow sheds or any place that he can find a bunch of people that haven't got a radio.

.   .   .   .

August 12, 1928

I didn't think Hoover would accept but he did. He says every man has the right to ask the following question: "Is the United States a better place for the average man to live in because the Republican Party has conducted the Government eight years?" If we are privileged to ask the question, I will be the first one to bite. *Is it?*

August 12, 1928

According to the Republican press of the country, Hoover's speech ranks right along with Washington's after-dinner effusions and some of Lincoln's monologues, but according to the Democratic press it was just another Republican press clipping and is in a "Class with all Presidential seconding speeches."

But as an independent I could see much truth and novelty in it. He was against poverty and favored education, even if you couldn't get into a fraternity. He said prohibition was a noble experiment, and he believed in noble things, even if they were only experiments.

August 17, 1928

From now till November neither of the boys can be themselves. They are on parade. They are eating and sleeping in a show window. They are acting every minute.

Coolidge is the only one nobody ever knew when he was acting and when he wasn't. He was like a ukulele. You can't tell when somebody is playing one or just monkeying with it.

August 20, 1928

Smith, when he accepts on Wednesday night (as he probably will) I bet he will tell how he and Tammany used to lay awake at nights just to think up ways to help the farmer and skin the city slicker.

Yours in sympathy for those that fall for this.

. . . .

June 12, 1932

Now a delegate . . . is bad enough, but an alternate is just a spare tire for a delegate. An alternate is the lowest form of political life there is. He is the parachute on a plane that never leaves the ground.

June 28, 1932

Ah! They was Democrats today. They fought, they fit, they split and adjourned in a dandy wave of dissension. Thats the old Democratic spirit.

A whole day fighting over what? A President? No. A Platform? No. "Well then what did they take up eleven hundred deligates and 12 thousand spectators time for?" Why to see whether Huey Long (the Louisiana porcupine) was to sit on the floor or in the gallery. Well the "porcupine sticks right on the floor." And the other four hours was fighting over who would be chairman of a convention thats already a week old.

You can't beat the old Democrats for comedy. Time means no more to them than to a Mexican "Burro."

The Democrats are the only known race of people that give a dinner and then wont decide who will be toastmaster till they all get to the dinner and fight over it. No job is ever too small for them to split over. But you would a loved 'em today. They was real Democrats.

June 30, 1932

Did the Democrats go wet? No, they just layed right down and wallowed in it. They left all their clothes on the bank and dived in without even a bathing suit. They are wetter than an "organdie" dress at a rainy day picnic.

The plank was made from cork wood nailed together with a sponge.

I just want to know what all these old dry office holders that went wet over night are going to tell those Baptist preachers back home. They going to say, "Father, I cant tell a lie. I saw the votes going and I had to go after 'em."

June 30, 1932

You remember away back in the late part of 1927 I had a piece in the Saturday Evening Post asking Smith not to run that year; that things wasn't right; that anti-prohibition was growing but not enough. I told him that it was a Republican year and no Democrat could be elected; that anti-prohibition feeling would be strong enough in 1932 to put him over.

Well, you will pardon me for bringing that up now, but I just can't help it. Us folks that write are right so little of the time that we have to brag on these very rare occasions. . . .

PHILIP HAMBURGER

Sculling on the Schuylkill

1948

Our delegation to the 1948 Republican National Convention consisted of Mr. Stanley, who hung around Philadelphia for a day and then took a train to Hot Springs for a deserved rest. We received the following memo from him, written in his porch chair:

Having wonderful time, wish you were here. Coming along as well as can be expected, but still dizzy when I try to walk. Philly pretty much of a blur. Got pushed into lobby of Bellevue-Stratford at 10 A.M. Reached elevators at ten-fourteen. Pushed into elevator at ten-thirty. Pushed out at fourteenth floor. "May I inquire what type of razor blade you used this morning?" asked a man standing in front of the elevator. Told the man Gillette, and was pushed into down elevator, arriving back in lobby at ten-thirty-six. Nothing gained, nothing lost. Swept up by brass band headed for Stassen headquarters, at rear of lobby, walking alongside large lady trumpet player, who whispered, "McArthur just flew in from Japan!" Man even larger than lady trumpet player shoved her aside and handed me pamphlet titled "Presenting Some Facts on the Gang from Michigan." Pushed into Stassen headquarters at ten-fifty. "Right this way, Commissioner!" a little lady without a trumpet cried, and placed me in a reception line, where I shook hands for an hour with string of very nice people, mostly family types. Was called Governor thirteen times, Senator four times, and turned down the nomination twice. Terrific pressure from behind took me up stairs to second floor, where a man solemnly pinned on my lapel a bronze medal, dangling from a red, white and blue ribbon, and engraved "Newsreel Operator." "With this, doors open," the man said. A door opened and I found myself in taxi with group of Landon rooters, all very nice people. "What newsreel company you with?" someone asked. I told him Gillette. We disgorged before Independence Hall. Visited the Hall and some adjoining buildings, saw Washington's Masonic apron, some clean-cut and quiet rooms where the Senate and House of Representatives met from 1790 to 1800, several splendid glass decanters, and the Liberty Bell. Crack in bell is bigger than you'd think.

Shook off the Landon rooters and walked down Chestnut Street. Alone at last. Pondered whether I should have accepted nomination. Terrible responsibility. Ran into crowd surrounding man with pins and pennants. "William Howard Taft buttons, first-class curio, fifty cents," he said. Was pushed straight through Wanamaker's Grand Court into taxi with Taft supporters, very nice people. Pushed out at Benjamin Franklin Hotel, handed cardboard four-leaf clover attached to blue ribbon reading, "Taft Greeters," and into room with the Senator, who was holding press conference. He said he heartily endorsed the platform but hadn't read it thoroughly. "Tsina aid, Senata?" cried a Chinese newspaperman from the rear of the hall. "Wha-at?" said Taft. "Senata endorse Tsina aid, economic, military?" elaborated the Chinese newspaperman. "I'm for China aid," said the Senator. "Turkey, Greece?" shouted a swarthy gentleman. "I'm for Turkey, Greece," said the Senator. "Thank you, Senator," said another newspaperman, and the crowd rose to leave. A man went past with a walkie-talkie. "The crowd is now rising to leave," he said into the walkie-talkie. Into taxi with fellow newsreel operators, to Hotel Warwick, where found Stassen seated on large bar alongside huge Wisconsin cheese, holding press conference. Stassen heartily endorsed the platform but said he hadn't read it thoroughly. Cheese at Stassen's very good. Propelled out to street.

At door of Bellevue-Stratford, stopped by man who asked, "May I inquire what type of razor blade you used this morning?" Was escorted by four young ladies wearing Warren buttons into Dewey fashion show in Grand Ballroom. Mrs. Dewey, in bottle green, entered box overlooking stage, accompanied by Mrs. Worthington Scranton, Mrs. Randolph Wilkes-Barre, and Mrs. Herbert Harrisburg. A Mrs. Hogan introduced a Mrs. McMullan as "the ringmaster of the Philadelphia social circus."

Mrs. McMullan introduced the models. "Wrinkle-proof and washable shorts, delightful to relax in with a good book and a nice man," said Mrs. McMullan. Handed bottle of Pepsi-Cola by man wearing Vandenberg cummerbund, and got whisked into back elevator, up to sixth floor, and into room thick with smoke. Met a senator, and a senator's dog. Very nice dog. The senator was in a huddle with two men, reading a note. "Never heard of them," said the senator, handing the note to one of the men. "But Harry," said the man, "that's where your wife said to meet her for supper." The senator extended his hand to me. "Never saw you looking so well," he said. "How things shaping up?" Pushed into elevator again. "Want to read a beautiful letter?" asked a lady wearing a big purple orchid. There were tears in her eyes. The letter was from General Wainwright, addressed to the delegates. Couldn't read the letter, because of too many people. Shoved out at eighteenth floor and into another ballroom, face to face with Governor Dewey, who wore a fixed smile and looked as though he were being operated by strings. ". . . think of the platform?" someone was asking. "Looks good," Dewey said, swinging to the right to shake hands with three small boys, swinging front to write four autographs, and swinging left to read eight messages handed him by aides. "Ed Martin . . . good government . . . old friends . . . certain victory . . . breaking new ground," said the Governor, swinging slowly from side to side. Caught the eight-twenty-three out of town. Good sleep on the way down.

MORRIE RYSKIND

The Rover Boys in Los Angeles

1960

The last tremors of the Democratic earthquake have subsided, and Los Angeles is just now beginning to snap out of it. Everybody has his own version of what happened, but one thing is clear: the Kennedy Blitzkrieg at the Sports Arena definitely separated the men from the boys—and put the men out to pasture. The accent is on youth and from now on the kindergarteners are going to run the country.

And don't think it was just Democrats who were affected. Even sturdy, hard-bitten Taft-Knowland-Goldwater Republicans who have hitherto ignored the march of time are enrolling themselves as Senior Citizens, conceding that the jig is up. And I am frank to say that I hadn't realized before how jolly bowling on the green can be.

What is still being debated, as the rubble is cleared away, is whether that scrubbed, fresh-looking pack of Massachusetts Cub Scouts who visited us were really the Rover Boys or the Jesse James Gang in disguise. We had expected some youthful mischief and were fully resigned to having our house numbers turned upside down and a wooden gate or two being carted away as a souvenir. But now that it turns out that the train was derailed; that the mail and the moneybags and the delegates went thataway instead of thisaway; and that Adlai's shoes—holes and all— Symington's shirt, and Lyndon's trousers also disappeared, we can't help wondering.

It started out, heaven knows, innocently enough. Bob Kennedy, looking for all the world as though he were wearing his first long pants, got into town a little earlier than his brother in order to size up the situation, or, if you prefer, case the joint. Interviewed by ex-Governor Goodwin Knight over a local TV station the Friday night before the convention, he was boyishly confident but restrained about his brother's chances and altogether charming as he answered all questions with artless frankness. When a listener telephoned in a query about the Connally Amendment, Bob said he didn't know just what that was. That startled me, I must admit, but at that moment I would have sworn he was either telling the truth or had the best poker face I have ever seen —and I have looked into some famous ones in my time. Goody explained the amendment and noted that both Bob's brother and Dick Nixon were for repealing it. "In that case," said Bob, "I presume it should be repealed but, frankly, that's not my province. I'm just on the team and Jack's the captain."

What do you do against naïveté like that? I even forgave him—for the moment—the things he had done as counsel for the Labor Committee. After all, a kid who had never heard of the Connally Reservation could hardly be expected to know what went on in the goon squads that were used in the Kohler strike.

ACCENT ON YOUTH

Monday night, in common with a lot of old gaffers whose memories went all the way back to 1956, when Tennessee's Governor Clement brought the house down with his hillbilly jeremiad, I awaited eagerly the keynote speech of 1960. Up came Frank Church, the boy orator of Snake River, Idaho, and the nation's youngest senator. He looked like a public school valedictorian, but we had been assured that he was one of the great speakers of our time, having, at the ripe age of 16, won an American Legion oratorical contest. And, for 45 minutes or so, he bored the hell out of everybody, leaving us grateful for only one thing: that we didn't have to listen to the runner-up in the Legion's contest. As it was, only the fact that the Arena's acoustics were so bad that many of the delegates were unable to follow the address prevented a mass exodus.

The accent was still on youth Tuesday, when the platform was revealed. If one may judge by internal evidence, this remarkable document was probably composed by Frank Church's youngest child as a letter to Santa Claus. I don't want to break the kid's heart but, frankly, I don't see how Santa can deliver all the things asked for unless he is able to double his gross national product. She may have to settle for a tricycle this year.

Wednesday morning I visited the Biltmore, where many of the delegates and the newsmen were billeted. And I have never seen so many kids in my life. There were thousands of them, from six to sixteen, plastered from head to foot with hats and kerchiefs and buttons that heralded their favorite candidates. I knew some states had lowered the voting-age requirements, but I hadn't realized how far the movement had spread. The next step, obviously, is to fix it so nobody *over* 21 can vote. Or maybe that's in the platform—I don't remember *all* of it.

With the nominations that afternoon, there were a few moments when I thought my generation had a fighting chance. Sam Rayburn got the respect due him as he offered Texas' favorite son; Eleanor Roosevelt made far and away the most effective speech; and Adlai got the demonstration. But came the roll call and the Rover Boy got the votes.

And Thursday, Old Man Johnson bowed to the inevitable and settled for place money.

And now we can all turn our attention to the free and open Chicago convention—free, that is, except for the fact that Barry Goldwater, who had expected to address the delegates, has been quietly informed that the invitation, like Kishi's to Ike, has been withdrawn. This is thoroughly understandable, because a Republican convention listening to a clear-cut enunciation of Republican principles might stampede and start a riot that the government couldn't put down.

I merely want to add for the record that I am perfectly happy in my job as an Associate Editor of this magazine [*National Review*] and would not willingly trade it for any other job in the world. These, however, are perilous days that call for greatness and I owe it to my country to serve it in any capacity to which it calls me. So, if the GOP is looking for an Elder Statesman as a running mate with Dick or Barry or Nelson, somebody give me a buzz. Move over, Lyndon.

NORMAN MAILER

Some Notes from the 1960 Democratic National Convention*

. . . And panic it was I think which sat as the largest single sentiment in the breast of the collective delegates as they came to convene in Los Angeles. Delegates are not the noblest sons and daughters of the Republic; a man of taste, arrived from Mars, would take one look at a convention floor and leave forever, convinced he had seen one of the drearier squats of Hell. If one still smells the faint living echo of a carnival wine, the pepper of a bullfight, the rag, drag, and panoply of a jousting tourney, it is all swallowed and regurgitated by the senses into the fouler cud of a death gas one must rid oneself of—a cigar-smoking, stale-aired, slack-jawed, butt-littered, foul, bleak, hardworking, bureaucratic death gas of language and faces ("Yes, those *faces*," says the man from Mars: lawyers, judges, ward heelers, *mafiosos*, Southern goons and grandees, grand old ladies, trade unionists and finks), of pompous words and long pauses which lay like a leaden pain over fever, the fever that one is in, over, or is it that one is just behind history? A legitimate panic for a delegate. America is a nation of experts without roots; we are always creating tacticians who are blind to strategy and strategists who cannot take a step,

* from *The Presidential Papers*.

and when the culture has finished its work the institutions handcuff the infirmity. A delegate is a man who picks a candidate for the largest office in the land, a President who must live with problems whose borders are in ethics, metaphysics, and now ontology; the delegate is prepared for this office of selection by emptying wastebaskets, toting garbage and saying yes at the right time for twenty years in the small political machine of some small or large town; his reward, one of them anyway, is that he arrives at an invitation to the convention. An expert on local catch-as-catch-can, a small-time, often mediocre practitioner of small-town political judo, he comes to the big city with nine-tenths of his mind made up, he will follow the orders of the boss who brought him. Yet of course it is not altogether so mean as that: his opinion is listened to—the boss will consider what he has to say as one interesting factor among five hundred, and what is most important to the delegate, he has the illusion of partial freedom. He can, unless he is severely honest with himself—and if he is, why sweat out the low levels of a political machine?—he can have the illusion that he has helped to choose the candidate, he can even worry most sincerely about his choice, flirt with defection from the boss, work out his own small political gains by the road of loyalty or the way of hard bargain. But even if he is there for no more than the ride, his vote a certainty in the mind of the political boss, able to be thrown here or switched there as the boss decides, still in some peculiar sense he is reality to the boss, the delegate is the great American public, the bar he owns or the law practice, the piece of the union he represents, or the real-estate office, is a part of the political landscape which the boss uses as his own image of how the votes will go, and if the people will like the candidate. And if the boss is depressed by what he sees, if the candidate does not feel right to him, if he has a dull intimation that the candidate is not his sort (as, let us say, Harry Truman was his sort, or Symington might be his sort, or Lyndon Johnson), then vote for him the boss will if he must; he cannot be caught on the wrong side, but he does not feel the pleasure of a personal choice. Which is the center of the panic.

.   .   .   .

It is not that Los Angeles is altogether hideous, it is even by degrees pleasant, but for an Easterner there is never any salt in the wind; it is like Mexican cooking without chile, or Chinese egg rolls missing their mustard; as one travels through the endless repetitions of that city which is the capital of suburbia with its milky pinks, its washed-out oranges, its

tainted lime-yellows of pastel on one pretty little architectural monstros-
ity after another, the colors not intense enough, the styles never pure, and
never sufficiently impure to collide on the eye, one conceives the people
who live here—they have come out to express themselves, Los Angeles is
the home of self-expression, but the artists are middle-class and middling-
minded; no passions will calcify here for years in the gloom to be revealed a decade later as the tessellations of a hard and fertile work, no, it
is all open, promiscuous, borrowed, half bought, a city without iron,
eschewing wood, a kingdom of stucco, the playground for mass men—
one has the feeling it was built by television sets giving orders to men.
And in this land of the pretty-pretty, the virility is in the barbarisms, the
vulgarities, it is in the huge billboards, the screamers of the neon lighting, the shouting farm-utensil colors of the gas stations and the monster
drugstores, it is in the swing of the sports cars, hot rods, convertibles, Los
Angeles is a city to drive in, the boulevards are wide, the traffic is nervous
and fast, the radio stations play bouncing, blooping, rippling tunes, one
digs the pop in a pop tune, no one of character would make love by it
but the sound is good for swinging a car, electronic guitars and Hawaiian
harps.

So this is the town the Democrats came to, and with their unerring
instinct (after being with them a week, one thinks of this party as a
crazy, half-rich family, loaded with poor cousins, traveling always in cara-
vans with Cadillacs and Okie Fords, Lincolns and quarter-horse mules,
putting up every night in tents to hear the chamber quartet of Great
Cousin Eleanor invaded by the Texas-twanging steel-stringing geetarists
of Bubber Lyndon, carrying its own mean high-school principal, Doc
Symington, chided for its manners by good Uncle Adlai, told the route
of march by Navigator Jack, cut off every six months from the rich will
of Uncle Jim Farley, never listening to the mechanic of the caravan,
Bald Sam Rayburn, who assures them they'll all break down unless
Cousin Bubber gets the concession on the garage; it's the Snopes family
married to Henry James, with the labor unions thrown in like a Yankee
dollar, and yet it's true, in tranquility one recollects them with affection,
their instinct is good, crazy family good) and this instinct now led the
caravan to pick the Biltmore Hotel in downtown Los Angeles for their
family get-together and reunion.   . .

So here came that family, cursed before it began by the thundering
absence of Great-Uncle Truman, the delegates dispersed over a run of
thirty miles and twenty-seven hotels: the Olympian Motor Hotel, the
Ambassador, the Beverly Wilshire, the Santa Ynez Inn (where rumor

has it the delegates from Louisiana had some midnight swim), the Mayan, the Commodore, the Mayfair, the Sheraton-West, the Huntington-Sheraton, the Green, the Hayward, the Gates, the Figueroa, the Statler Hilton, the Hollywood Knickerbocker—does one have to be a collector to list such names?—beauties all, with that up-from-the-farm Los Angeles decor, plate-glass windows, patio and terrace, foam-rubber mattress, pastel paints, all of them pretty as an ad in full-page color, all but the Biltmore where everybody gathered every day—the newsmen, the TV, radio, magazine, and foreign newspapermen, the delegates, the politicos, the tourists, the campaign managers, the runners, the flunkies, the cousins and aunts, the wives, the grandfathers, the eight-year-old girls, and the twenty-eight-year-old girls in the Kennedy costumes, red and white and blue, the Symingteeners, the Johnson Ladies, the Stevenson Ladies, everybody—and for three days before the convention and four days into it, everybody collected at the Biltmore, in the lobby, in the grill, in the Biltmore Bowl, in the elevators, along the corridors, three hundred deep always outside the Kennedy suite, milling everywhere, every dark-carpeted grey-brown hall of the hotel, but it was in the Gallery of the Biltmore where one first felt the mood which pervaded all proceedings until the convention was almost over, that heavy, thick, witless depression which was to dominate every move as the delegates wandered and gawked and paraded and set for a spell, there in the Gallery of the Biltmore, that huge depressing alley with its inimitable hotel color, that faded depth of chiaroscuro which unhappily has no depth, that brown which is not a brown, that grey which has no pearl in it, that color which can be described only as hotel-color because the beiges, the tans, the walnuts, the mahoganies, the dull blood rugs, the moaning yellows, the sick greens, the greys and all those dumb browns merge into that lack of color which is an over-large hotel at convention time, with all the small-towners wearing their set, starched faces, that look they get at carnival, all fever and suspicion, and proud to be there, eddying slowly back and forth in that high block-long tunnel of a room with its arched ceiling and square recesses filling every rib of the arch with art work, escutcheons and blazons and other art, pictures I think, I cannot even remember, there was such a hill of cigar smoke the eye had to travel on its way to the ceiling, and at one end there was galvanized-pipe scaffolding and workmen repairing some part of the ceiling, one of them touching up one of the endless squares of painted plaster in the arch, and another worker, passing by, yelled up to the one who was working on the ceiling: "Hey, Michelangelo!" . . .

THE MORNING AFTER

ARTEMUS WARD

(CHARLES FARRAR BROWNE)

How Old Abe Received the News of His Nomination

1860

There are several reports afloat as to how Honest Old Abe received the news of his nomination, none of which are correct. We give the correct report.

The Official Committee arrived in Springfield at dewy eve, and went to Honest Old Abe's house. Honest Old Abe was not in. Mrs. Honest Old Abe said Honest Old Abe was out in the woods splitting rails. So the Official Committee went out into the woods, where sure enough they found Honest Old Abe splitting rails with his two boys. It was a grand, a magnificent spectacle. There stood Honest Old Abe in his shirt-sleeves, a pair of leather home-made suspenders holding up a pair of home-made pantaloons, the seat of which was neatly patched with substantial cloth of a different color.

"Mr. Lincoln, Sir, you've been nominated, Sir, for the highest office, Sir—"

"Oh, don't bother me," said Honest Old Abe; "I took a *stent* this mornin' to split three million rails afore night, and I don't want to be pestered with no stuff about no Conventions till I get my *stent* done. I've only got two hundred thousand rails to split before sundown. I kin do it if you'll let me alone."

And the great man went right on splitting rails, paying no attention to the Committee whatever. The Committee were lost in admiration for a few moments, when they recovered, and asked one of Honest Old Abe's boys whose boy he was?

"I'm my parent's boy," shouted the urchin, which burst of wit so convulsed the Committee that they came very near 'givin' eout' completely.

In a few moments Honest Old Abe finished his task, and received the news with perfect self-possession. He then asked them up to the house, where he received them cordially. He said he split three million rails every day, although he was in very poor health.

Mr. Lincoln is a jovial man, and has a keen sense of the ludicrous. During the evening he asked Mr. Evarts, of New York, "Why was Chicago like a hen crossing the street?" Mr. Evarts gave it up. "Because," said Mr. Lincoln, "Old Grimes is dead, that good old man!" This exceedingly humorous thing created the most uproarious laughter.

PHILIP HAMBURGER

Hq.

1948

We blissfully dispatched our man Stanley to Mr. Dewey's headquarters, at the Hotel Roosevelt, on the Truman-Dewey election night. He returned to the office next afternoon, unshaven and rumpled:

Reached Roosevelt at 8:03. Cops, cops, cops, cops outside, cops on the stairs, cops inside. Lobby filling up with happy, buzzing citizens. Most ladies wearing orchids. Big, purple ones. Men well barbered. Aglow. Absolutely aglow. Went to rooms for press, on mezzanine. Sign by coat racks said, "No tipping." "On the house tonight," said check girl. Vast quarters for press, no stone unturned. Historic night. Room each for newsreels, radio men, photographers, wire services, television. Another room with nothing but tables and telephones. Telephones free. Pitchers of ice water all over the place. Not many press people around—too early—so made five or six phone calls. Wonderful feeling. Spotted George Sokolsky and Robert Considine outside in corridor, aglow, and realized pundits arriving, things getting under way. Nodded to Sokolsky. "Hello, Dick," he said. "What a night!" Went to big ballroom, also on mezzanine. More bunting than Fourth of July. Orchestra playing quiet dinner music at one side of ballroom. Hundreds of chairs facing big election-returns board. Room getting crowded. Boys in green jackets lettered

"THE PHILIPS COMPANY—BEAUTIFUL SIGNS" putting paper numerals on hooks on big board. Returns coming in slowly. Ruddy-type man in dress suit watching returns in doorway, smoking biggest cigar in the world. Asked him how things shaping up. Blew thick cloud and said, "Early big-city returns for Truman, natch. Wait for the grass roots, boy. Have a cigar." Gave me second-biggest cigar in the world. Back to press rooms and made more phone calls. Press rooms getting crowded. Sokolsky center of jovial group. Spotted me and said "Hello, Paul!" Blew smoke at him and went to watch television sets. Gallup talking, impressive, calm, collected. Gallup replaced by Winchell, wearing hat. Real newspaper-man. No nonsense tonight, no amateurs. Pearson followed Winchell on screen, also wearing hat. A Lee. Pearson predicting like crazy man. (How he know so much, anyway?)

Back to ballroom. Filled now. Healthy crowd, well rested. Boy rushed to board with new figures. Dewey forging ahead in Kansas. Now two hundred ahead in Kansas. Cheers from crowd. Man who gave me cigar slapped my back. "This is it, boy!" he said. "Grass roots coming in. Have a cigar." Took third-biggest cigar in the world. Man also handed me engraved card. "Special invitation to hear returns on second floor," he said. "Use it, boy." Used it. Found dressy group of men and women watching television sets in fine suite of rooms. Quiet group. Seemed cautious. Selected rye highball from liquor tray, took it to empty place on sofa, and picked up pile of Tuesday's newspapers. Read Danton Walker column (". . . Dewey's first official act as President-elect will be to name a new Secretary of State . . ."). Read John O'Donnell column (". . . most important problem facing the Republic in the next few days is how Dewey and Truman will work out a method of handling our foreign affairs until Jan. 20 rolls around . . ."). Read column in *Journal-American* by George Rothwell Brown ("The President has been unable to overtake Gov. Dewey in the conclusive area of electoral votes, and these, under the Constitution, are what count . . ."). Brown had something there. Back to ballroom. Ballroom restive. Boy rushed over to blackboard with flash. Dewey ahead by 2,800 in Philadelphia. Cheers. Carbon statement from Brownell: ". . . so we conclude . . . that Dewey and Warren are elected." Sokolsky walked past, said, "Evening, Charles." Some of the glow gone. Gallup on television again. Looked older. Back to ballroom. Orchestra playing "When Irish Eyes Are Smiling." No eyes smiling. Newsreel men on balcony asked crowd to cheer wildly for news-of-victory pictures. Crowd cheered wildly on second try, settled back quietly. Man in dress suit still standing by door. Looked hurt. "Boy," he said, "here's a ticket for very private party in Mr. Ho-

gan's room. Closest friend of Governor. Use it." Used it. Inside, Henry
J. Taylor, pundit, sitting by radio, head in hand. Nobody speaking. William Gaxton entered, smiling. Wiped it off. Hogan very serious. "Can't
understand it," he said. Told him to wait for grass roots. He seemed
grateful. Lady in pink organdie and hair like curry powder said, "He
didn't campaign right. Too damn respectable." Taylor departed clasping
and unclasping hands. Large gentleman in tuxedo said, "It's what you
call winning the hard way." Mild laughter. Back to ballroom. People
putting on coats, consulting timetables. Boys in green jackets mostly
standing around, putting up very few figures. Sat down beside man who
looked like Truman. Thought maybe it *was* Truman. "Tom's dying by
inches," he said. "Have a cigar." Rumor Governor coming down to
speak. Sat there two hours. No Governor. Edwin F. Jaeckel, Dewey adviser, appeared on balcony with foolish grin. Lowell Thomas walked
through ballroom. Same grin. Back to press rooms. Sokolsky clamping
hat on head, putting on coat. Didn't recognize me. Definitely time to go
home.

MARYA MANNES

Sales Campaign

1952

Hail to B.B.D. & O.
It told the nation how to go;
It managed by advertisement
To sell us a new President.

EISENHOWER HITS THE SPOT,
ONE FULL GENERAL, THAT'S A LOT.

FEELING SLUGGISH, FEELING SICK?
TAKE A DOSE OF IKE AND DICK.

PHILIP MORRIS, LUCKY STRIKE,
ALKA-SELTZER, I LIKE IKE.

MURRAY KEMPTON

The Sorehead

1952

The sun was shining, just as it always does, yesterday morning; the elevator operators, the charwomen and the waiters went about their business at the Hotel Commodore with no visible signs of enchainment.

Downstairs at Eisenhower's headquarters, they moved in silence and slow time, still prisoners of the dream. The mimeograph machine ground forth the itinerary of the General's newest flight; reading it, there was a moment when you were hearing again the marching orders of the crusade, but this was only the winner going off to play golf on a ten-day pass.

The sun was shining, and it was the same 42d Street; the taxi drivers growled the old fraternal obscenities at one another. Nothing had changed; nothing ever will, I suppose. There was no surface sign that this was the end of the world. But for my money, it was the end of world; and neither sun nor the amenities is going to trap me into saying something pleasant about it.

The knuckleheads have beaten the egg-heads. You're not going to catch this baby jumping over the net and extending his hand to the winner. Would Colonel McCormick extend his hand to me?

The difference between me and the General is that I may be just and I may be fair, but I sure ain't friendly. David Dubinsky can go ahead and call up Winthrop Aldrich any time he chooses.

The Republicans were sitting in the Commodore celebrating their deliverance Tuesday night. One of the attendants came in and asked whether a Dr. Hartman was in the house. "Oh, Harry needs a doctor tonight, oh, Harry needs a doctor," some wit sang out again and again in one long croon of hate. The man sitting at my right hand said in tones of the philosopher that, after all, these people had been losing for twenty years and they deserve a chance to win.

What is this, Ebbets Field? The Republicans haven't deserved to win since Lincoln and they don't deserve to win this one. The only justification for their quadrennial assault on truth and reason was the kind of excuse people used to give for holding debutante parties during the depression; it gave employment to a lot of people. But it was one thing to put up with a campaign pretested by B.B.D. and O. and something else again to have it win.

I suppose the woman with the diamond lattice work who was pointed out to me as Mrs. Alfred Gwynne Vanderbilt has been losing for twenty years, and I've been winning. Man and boy, I've been losing since birth, and the only time I've ever won has been with the Democrats. Couldn't George Sokolsky and Fred Waring at least leave me that?

I've been a Giant fan since 1930—four miserable pennants. When a ball player breaks his ankle, it has to be Monte Irvin. When a pitcher shows up with a back ailment defying medical science, it has to be Sal Maglie. Why does it always have to be my team?

During the war, I had a brief, tenuous relationship with an outfit called the 38th Division. Its nickname was the Cyclone Division. Do you think they called it the Cyclone Division because it had swept through the enemies of freedom? Of course not. They called it the Cyclone Division because all its tents got blown down on maneuvers. That's how it is with my team every time. I can't even persuade my kids to be Republicans and escape the family curse.

There are those who say at least Adlai Stevenson was right, and we have the satisfaction of knowing we lost in a good cause. I think it would be a little better to know you'd lost in a bad cause. The notion that you deserved to win and didn't may bring some lonely gratification to the noble of spirit; for me, it makes the whole thing twice as bad.

I should have spent election night with Tallulah Bankhead croaking curses upon the electorate, with Joe Bushkin playing a little blues through the smoke behind. That would have been the way to go out —not watching some idiot girl with a dress imprinted with her affection for Ike in five different languages waving a megaphone around the Commodore. The sun yesterday may have shined on the just and the unjust. It didn't shine on me, Mac; it didn't shine on me.

When we got into office, the thing that surprised me most was to find that things were just as bad as we'd been saying they were.
—*John F. Kennedy*

KARLA KUSKIN

The Rocky Road Upward

A STIRRING STORY OF SUCCESS

IT COULD ONLY HAPPEN HERE

1961

Once upon a time
at different ends of a great
land of opportunity
there were two little fellows.

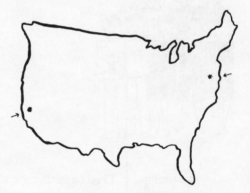

One was very rich and
handsome.

The other had
tasted poverty.

He had a beautiful mummy and a very smart daddy who made huge amounts of money in shrewd and sometimes shady ways.

THIS IS THE JACK THAT JOE BUILT

He had a plain-looking mummy and a daddy who tried but never made it.

And he had an awful lot of beautiful sisters and small, handsome brothers and he went to all the very best schools.

SO IS THIS

He had a couple of siblings one of whom got fat and borrowed money. He struggled against tremendous odds and went to second-rate schools.

 Then came the great war.

The rich little boy, who was now a rich young man, marched off to defend his nation. He returned covered with medals and glory.

The poor little boy, who was now a poor young man, marched off to defend his nation. When it was over he came home.

The rich young man
married the most
beautiful girl around.
She had an aptitude
for languages and
dressed marvelously.

The poor young man worked
long hard hours and gave
of himself unstintingly.
He married Pat.
She worked hard too.

Ouvre la fenêtre "

Où sont les neiges d'antan ?"

Dove 1600 Pennsylvania Avenue?"

The rich young man
loved filet mignon
with mushrooms, yachts
and the Riviera.

The poor young man had
simple tastes. There was
nothing he liked quite so
well as a medium
hamburger on a toasted bun
with relish.

The rich young man
and the poor young man
went to Washington, D. C.

The rich young man's
hair fell over his eyes
and he had a splendid
smile. Inside, some said,
he was cold and hard.

The poor young man's
hair receded. On advice
from friends, he smiled
infrequently. He spoke
with kindness to
shoeshine boys.

On January 20th, 1961,
the rich young man became President of the United States of America.
His beautiful wife was there to see him take the oath of office.
So were his mummy and daddy and his sisters and brothers
and masses of glorious people like statesmen and humanitarians.
Robert Frost and Tony Curtis were there.

The poor young man
was forty-seven years old,
and he went home with Pat.

Think it over,
Horatio, baby.

CLOSER TO HOME

AMBROSE BIERCE

Man and Lightning*

A Man Running for Office was overtaken by Lightning.

"You see," said the Lightning, as it crept past him inch by inch, "I can travel considerably faster than you."

"Yes," the Man Running for Office replied, "but think how much longer I keep going!"

DAVID CROCKETT

The Coon-Skin Trick

1834

While on the subject of election matters, I will just relate a little anecdote about myself, which will show the people to the East how we manage these things on the frontiers. It was when I first run for Congress; I was then in favor of the Hero (Andrew Jackson), for he had chalked out his course so sleek in his letter to the Tennessee legislature that, like Sam Patch, says I, "There can be no mistake in him," and so I went ahead. No one dreamt about the monster and the deposits at that time, and so, as I afterward found, many like myself were taken in by these

* from *Fantastic Fables*.

fair promises, which were worth about as much as a flash in the pan
when you have a fair shot at a fat bear.

But I am losing sight of my story. Well, I started off to the Cross
Roads dressed in my hunting shirt, and my rifle on my shoulder. Many
of our constituents had assembled there to get a taste of the quality of
the candidates at orating. Job Snelling, a gander-shanked Yankee, who
had been caught somewhere about Plymouth Bay, and been shipped to
the West with a cargo of codfish and rum, erected a large shantee, and
set up shop for the occasion. A large posse of the voters had assembled
before I arrived, and my opponent had already made considerable headway with his speechifying and his treating, when they spied me about a
rifle shot from camp, sauntering along as if I was not a party in business.
"There comes Crockett," cried one. "Let us hear the colonel," cried
another; and so I mounted the stump that had been cut down for the
occasion, and began to bushwhack in the most approved style.

I had not been up long before there was such an uproar in the crowd
that I could not hear my own voice, and some of my constituents let me
know that they could not listen to me on such a dry subject as the welfare of the nation until they had something to drink, and that I must
treat them. Accordingly I jumped down from the rostrum, and led the
way to the shantee, followed by my constituents, shouting, "Huzza for
Crockett!" and "Crockett forever!"

When we entered the shantee Job was busy dealing out his rum in a
style that showed he was making a good day's work of it, and I called
for a quart of the best; but the crooked critter returned no other answer
than by pointing to a board over the bar, on which he had chalked in
large letters, "*Pay to-day and trust to-morrow.*" Now that idea brought
me up all standing; it was a sort of cornering in which there was no back-
out, for ready money in the West, in those times, was the shyest thing
in all natur, and it was most particularly shy with me on that occasion.

The voters, seeing my predicament, fell off to the other side, and I was
left deserted and alone, as the Government will be, when he no longer
has any offices to bestow. I saw as plain as day that the tide of popular
opinion was against me, and that unless I got some rum speedily I
should lose my election as sure as there are snakes in Virginny; and it
must be done soon, or even burnt brandy wouldn't save me. So I walked
away from the shantee, but in another guess sort from the way I entered
it, for on this occasion I had no train after me, and not a voice shouted,
"Huzza for Crockett!" Popularity sometimes depends on a very small

matter indeed; in this particular it was worth a quart of New England rum, and no more.

Well, knowing that a crisis was at hand, I struck into the woods, with my rifle on my shoulder, my best friend in time of need; and, as good fortune would have it, I had not been out more than a quarter of an hour before I treed a fat coon, and in the pulling of a trigger he lay dead at the foot of the tree. I soon whipped his hairy jacket off his back, and again bent my steps towards the shantee, and walked up to the bar, but not alone, for this time I had half a dozen of my constituents at my heels. I threw down the coon-skin upon the counter, and called for a quart, and Job, though busy dealing out rum, forgot to point at his chalked rules and regulations; for he knew that a coon was as good a legal tender for a quart in the West as a New York shilling any day in the year.

My constituents now flocked about me, and cried, "Huzza for Crockett!" "Crockett forever!" and finding the tide had taken a turn, I told them several yarns to get them in a good humor; and having soon dispatched the value of the coon, I went out and mounted the stump without opposition, and a clear majority of the voters followed me to hear what I had to offer for the good of the nation. Before I was half through one of my constituents moved that they would hear the balance of my speech after they had washed down the first part with some more of Job Snelling's extract of cornstalk and molasses, and the question being put, it was carried unanimously. It wasn't considered necessary to tell the yeas and nays, so we adjourned to the shantee, and on the way I began to reckon that the fate of the nation pretty much depended upon my shooting another coon.

While standing at the bar, feeling sort of bashful while Job's rules and regulations stared me in the face, I cast down my eyes, and discovered one end of the coon-skin sticking between the logs that supported the bar. Job had slung it there in the hurry of business. I gave it a sort of quick jerk, and it followed my hand as natural as if I had been the rightful owner. I slapped it on the counter, and Job, little dreaming that he was barking up the wrong tree, shoved along another bottle, which my constituents quickly disposed of with great good humor, for some of them saw the trick; and then we withdrew to the rostrum to discuss the affairs of the nation.

I don't know how it was, but the voters soon became dry again, and nothing would do but we must adjourn to the shantee; and as luck would have it, the coon-skin was still sticking between the logs, as if Job had flung it there on purpose to tempt me. I was not slow in raising it to the counter, the rum followed, of course, and I wish I may be shot if I didn't, before the day was over, get ten quarts for the same identical skin, and from a fellow, too, who in those parts was considered as sharp as a steel trap and as bright as a pewter button.

This joke secured me my election, for it soon circulated like smoke among my constituents, and they allowed, with one accord, that the man who could get the whip hand of Job Snelling in fair trade, could outwit Old Nick himself, and was the real grit for them in Congress. Job was by no means popular; he boasted of always being wide awake, and that any one who could take him in was free to do so, for he came from a stock that, sleeping or waking, had always one eye open, and the other not more than half closed. The whole family were geniuses. His father was the inventor of wooden nutmegs, by which Job said he might have made a fortune, if he had only taken out a patent and kept the business in his own hands; his mother, Patience, manufactured the first white oak pumpkin seeds of the mammoth kind, and turned a pretty penny the first season; and his aunt Prudence was the first to discover that corn husks, steeped into tobacco water, would make as handsome Spanish wrappers as ever came from Havana, and that oak leaves would answer all the purpose of filling, for no one could discover the difference except the man who smoked them, and then it would be too late to make a stir about it. Job himself bragged of having made some useful discoveries, the most profitable of which was the art of converting mahogany sawdust into cayenne pepper, which he said was a profitable and safe business; for the people have been so long accustomed to having dust thrown in their eyes that there wasn't much danger of being found out.

The way I got to the blind side of the Yankee merchant was pretty generally known before election day, and the result was that my opponent might as well have whistled jigs to a milestone as attempt to beat up for votes in that district. I beat him out and out, quite back into the old year, and there was scarce enough left of him, after the canvass was over, to make a small grease spot. He disappeared without even leaving a mark behind; and such will be the fate of Adam Huntsman, if there is a fair fight and no gouging.

After the election was over, I sent Snelling the price of the rum, but took good care to keep the fact from the knowledge of my constituents. Job refused the money, and sent me word that it did him good to be taken in occasionally, as it served to brighten his ideas; but I afterwards learnt when he found out the trick that had been played upon him, he put all the rum I had ordered in his bill against my opponent, who, being elated with the speeches he had made on the affairs of the nation, could not descend to examine into the particulars of a bill of a vendor of rum in the small way.

JAMES RUSSELL LOWELL

What Mr. Robinson Thinks

1847

Gineral B. is a sensible man;
   He stays to his home an' looks arter his folks;
He draws his furrer ez straight ez he can,
    An' into nobody's tater-patch pokes;
          But John P.
          Robinson, he
  Sez he wunt vote for Gineral B.

My! ain't it terrible? Wut shall we do?
   We can't never choose him, o' course—that's flat:
Guess we shall hev to come round (don't you?),
    An' go in for thunder an' guns, an' all that;
          Fer John P.
          Robinson, he
  Sez he wunt vote for Gineral B.

Gineral C. is a dreffle smart man:
   He's been on all sides that give places or pelf;
But consistency still was a part of his plan—
   He's been true to *one* party, and that is himself;
          So John P.
          Robinson, he
  Sez he shall vote fer Gineral C.

Gineral C. goes in for the war;
   He don't vally principle mor'n an old cud;
What did God make us raytional creeturs fer,
    But glory an' gunpowder, plunder an' blood?

So John P.
Robinson, he
Sez he shall vote fer Gineral C.

We're gettin' on nicely up here to our village,
　With good old idees o' wut's right an' wut ain't;
We kind o' thought Christ went against war and pillage,
　An' that eppyletts worn't the best mark of a saint;
　　　　　But John P.
　　　　　Robinson, he
　　Sez this kind o' thing's an exploded idee.

The side of our country must ollers be took,
　An' President Pulk, you know, *he* is our country;
An' the angel that writes all our sins in a book,
　Puts the *debit* to him, an' to us the *per contry*;
　　　　　An' John P.
　　　　　Robinson, he
　　Sez this is his view o' the thing to a T.

Parson Wilbur he calls all these arguments lies;
　Sez they're nothin' on airth but jest *fee, faw, fum*;
An' that all this big talk of our destinies
　Is half on it ignorance, an' t'other half rum;
　　　　　But John P.
　　　　　Robinson, he
　　Sez it ain't no such thing; an', of course, so must we.

Parson Wilbur sez *he* never heered in his life
　Thet the Apostles rigg'd out in their swallow-tail coats,
An' marched round in front of a drum an' a fife,
　To git some on 'em office, an' some on 'em votes;
　　　　　But John P.
　　　　　Robinson, he
　　Sez they didn't know everythin' down in Judee.

Wal, it's a marcy we've gut folks to tell us
　The rights an' the wrongs o' these matters, I vow—
God sends country lawyers an' other wise fellers
　To drive the world's team wen it gits in a slough;
　　　　　For John P.
　　　　　Robinson, he
　　Sez the world'll go right, ef he hollers out Gee!

MARK TWAIN

(SAMUEL L. CLEMENS)

*Senator Dilworthy Campaigns**

1873

. . . Senator Dilworthy rose and beamed upon the assemblage for a full minute in silence. Then he smiled with an excess of sweetness upon the children and began:

"My little friends—for I hope that all these bright-faced little people are my friends and will let me be their friend—my little friends, I have traveled much, I have been in many cities and many states, everywhere in our great and noble country, and by the blessing of Providence I have been permitted to see many gatherings like this—but I am proud, I am truly proud to say that I never have looked upon so much intelligence, so much grace, such sweetness of disposition as I see in the charming young countenances I see before me at this moment. I have been asking myself, as I sat here, Where am I? Am I in some far-off monarchy, looking upon little princes and princesses? No. Am I in some populous center of my own country, where the choicest children of the land have been selected and brought together as at a fair for a prize? No. Am I in some strange foreign clime where the children are marvels that we know not of? No. Then where am I? Yes—where am I? I am in a simple, remote, unpretending settlement of my own dear state, and these are the children of the noble and virtuous men who have made me what I am! My soul is lost in wonder at the thought! And I humbly thank Him to whom we are but as worms of the dust, that He has been pleased to call me to serve such men! Earth has no higher, no grander position for me. Let kings and emperors keep their tinsel crowns, I want them not; my heart is here!

"Again I thought, Is this a theater? No. Is it a concert or a gilded opera? No. Is it some other vain, brilliant, beautiful temple of soul-stain-

* from *The Gilded Age*.

ing amusement and hilarity? No. Then what is it? What did my consciousness reply? I ask you, my little friends, What did my consciousness reply? It replied, It is the temple of the Lord! Ah, think of that, now. I could hardly keep the tears back, I was so grateful. Oh, how beautiful it is to see these ranks of sunny little faces assembled here to learn the way of life; to learn to be good; to learn to be useful; to learn to be pious; to learn to be great and glorious men and women; to learn to be props and pillars of the state and shining lights in the councils and the households of the nation; to be bearers of the banner and soldiers of the cross in the rude campaigns of life, and ransomed souls in the happy fields of Paradise hereafter.

"Children, honor your parents and be grateful to them for providing for you the precious privileges of a Sunday-school.

"Now, my dear little friends, sit up straight and pretty—there, that's it—and give me your attention and let me tell you about a poor little Sunday-school scholar I once knew. He lived in the Far West, and his parents were poor. They could not give him a costly education, but they were good and wise and they sent him to the Sunday-school. He loved the Sunday-school. I hope you love your Sunday-school—ah, I see by your faces that you do! That is right.

"Well, this poor little boy was always in his place when the bell rang, and he always knew his lesson; for his teachers wanted him to learn and he loved his teachers dearly. Always love your teachers, my children, for they love you more than you can know, now. He would not let bad boys persuade him to go to play on Sunday. There was one little bad boy who was always trying to persuade him, but he never could.

"So this poor little boy grew up to be a man, and had to go out in the world, far from home and friends, to earn his living. Temptations lay all about him, and sometimes he was about to yield, but he would think of some precious lesson he learned in his Sunday-school a long time ago, and that would save him. By and by he was elected to the legislature. Then he did everything he could for Sunday-schools. He got laws passed for them; he got Sunday-schools established wherever he could.

"And by and by the people made him governor—and he said it was all owing to the Sunday-school.

"After a while the people elected him a Representative to the Congress of the United States, and he grew very famous. Now temptations assailed him on every hand. People tried to get him to drink wine, to dance, to go to theaters; they even tried to buy his vote; but no, the memory of his Sunday-school saved him from all harm; he remembered the fate of the bad little boy who used to try to get him to play on

Sunday, and who grew up and became a drunkard and was hanged. He remembered that, and was glad he never yielded and played on Sunday.

"Well, at last, what do you think happened? Why the people gave him a towering, illustrious position, a grand, imposing position. And what do you think it was? What should you say it was, children? It was Senator of the United States! That poor little boy that loved his Sunday-school became that man. *That man stands before you!* All that he is, he owes to the Sunday-school.

"My precious children, love your parents, love your teachers, love your Sunday-school, be pious, be obedient, be honest, be diligent, and then you will succeed in life and be honored of all men. Above all things, my children, be honest. Above all things be pure-minded as the snow. Let us join in prayer."

When Senator Dilworthy departed from Cattleville, he left three dozen boys behind him arranging a campaign of life whose objective point was the United States Senate.

When he arrived at the state capital at midnight Mr. Noble came and held a three hours' conference with him, and then as he was about leaving said:

"I've worked hard, and I've got them at last. Six of them haven't got quite backbone enough to slew around and come right out for you on the first ballot tomorrow, but they're going to vote against you on the first for the sake of appearances, and then come out for you all in a body on the second—I've fixed all that! By supper-time to-morrow you'll be re-elected. You can go to bed and sleep easy on that."

After Mr. Noble was gone, the Senator said:

"Well, to bring about a complexion of things like this was worth coming West for."

ROGER PRICE

*J. G. Meets the Candidate**

1960

After a few moments, two more young men came into the room with the Candidate, George Stanley Jenkermill.

* from *J. G., The Upright Ape.*

George Stanley Jenkermill was tall and broad-shouldered with a round, innocent face and beautiful, silver-grey hair which swept back from his unlined forehead in precise and graceful waves. On entering, he began circling the room clockwise, giving each of the young men a firm handshake and a brief smile and saying, "Glad to have you on the team!"

When Muddington saw him his face seemed somehow to assume a less rancid expression, and he lumbered forward. "Jenk," he said, "you old Horse Thief!" He threw his arms around Jenkermill and thumped him on the back. "By God, you're all right, Jenk," he said.

Jenkermill smiled broadly and said, "Glad to have you on the team."

"Look at that smile," Muddington shouted. "It's worth a million votes!"

Jenkermill smiled even more broadly.

"By God, you're all wet," Muddington said, feeling his shoulders. "They shouldn't let you get wet." He turned suddenly and shouted at Bustabutton, "Get this dam' meeting on the road. Time is money! Not one of you ever had to meet a payroll or you'd know it. Lazy loafers sitting around in cocktail bars. Don't know the first thing about the oil and gas business. Don't know how to pump or wipe a windshield or anything. Don't even know enough not to let ol' Jenk stand in the rain."

Bustabutton went to the head of the long table and rapped on it with a gavel and said that the first strategy meeting of the Planning Committee for the Election of George Stanley Jenkermill was called to order. The Patriots sat in the large leather chairs at one end of the table, flanked by several young men holding cigars and lighters at the alert. The rest, including J. G. and McKooly, grouped themselves against the wall opposite Bustabutton. Bustabutton spoke directly to Muddington, who sat in the center of the Patriots holding Jenkermill's hand.

"We have every confidence in the reelection of our great and glorious candidate, Mr. Jenkermill," Bustabutton said. "Our confidence is not based upon hope, idle speculation or an emotional belief in the rightness of the high principles which Mr. Jenkermill holds. Our confidence is based upon scientific knowledge. We have applied the scientific yardstick to our efforts and science has assured us that we have put the ball over the goal line for a touch-down." Obviously pleased with this last sentence, Bustabutton paused and smiled proudly.

"Crap!" Muddington said.

"I should now like to introduce the head of our Research Department, formerly the dean of the State University Psychology School, holder of the Nobel Prize, former director of the National Clinic for Mental Health, Dr. Emil Menzig."

On cue, Dr. Menzig entered rapidly from a door behind Bustabutton. He was portly and was dressed the same as Bustabutton, except that across his vest he wore a chain from which hung numerous small keys and amulets. Under his arm he carried a number of charts and graphs, which several of the young men took from him and whipped onto an easel with the practiced efficiency of a mortar squad under fire.

"Good afternoon, Gentlemen," Dr. Menzig said deferentially.

Muddington leaned forward, breathing heavily, and waved his finger at Dr. Menzig. "You!" he shouted, "are you a foreigner?"

Dr. Menzig shook his head violently and said, "No, no, no, no," and then smiled to show that he did not consider Muddington's question at all untoward.

"Dr. Menzig is fourth generation, one hundred percent," Bustabutton said jovially. "We checked him thoroughly, you can be sure of that." Muddington muttered something and fell back in his chair.

"Good afternoon, Gentlemen," Dr. Menzig repeated. "I will discuss first the problem of non-negative identification, as it appears in the subliminal receptor centers of the average voter.

"Applying the most modern techniques to a broad sampling, we have discovered that Mr. Jenkermill possesses the prime prerequisites necessary for a successful candidate. He has no attitudes, mannerisms or physical characteristics which the voter would even notice, much less take offense at. During a later survey in depth, we found that sixty-seven out of one hundred adults, when asked if Mr. Jenkermill reminded them of their father, replied affirmatively. This is an amazing figure when you realize that, out of these sixty-seven adults, only thirty-four had ever seen or heard of Mr. Jenkermill."

Dr. Menzig nodded to the young men, who displayed a large photograph on the easel. "Now here we have some photographs prepared by Mr. Bustabutton, under my direction, for general release," Dr. Menzig continued. "This one shows the candidate smoking a cigarette in a holder. The hand holding the holder, you will notice, has a simulated tattoo mark on it. The holder and the tattoo are psychological symbols, scientifically created, to appeal to the unconscious mind of the voter. The tatoo appeals to the uneducated workingman, while the holder appeals to the so-called intellectual type."

Muddington leaned forward and cleared his throat and a young man lunged forward with a silver spittoon. He was too late.

"Next," Dr. Menzig said, "we have a photograph showing the candidate wearing an army helmet and lit so as to resemble, in only a symbolic way of course, a phallus. This phallic symbolism, coupled with the candidate, will make him seem more attractive to two of the largest and most important sections of the electorate, the housewives and the non-heterosexuals."

The young men substituted a third photograph.

"This one shows the candidate leaving a church, presumably after hearing the sermon. The beatific expression on his face is the direct result of the use of Orposil, the new tranquilizing drug, which is handled, I might add, by Bustabutton, Hokins and Valence. We feel that wide distribution of this photograph, showing the candidate, as it does, speaking with this actor costumed as a small-town non-denominational minister, should prove highly effective."

"Good stuff," Muddington growled. "Worth a million votes." The other Patriots nodded and repeated this phrase.

"The value of constant research into hidden motivations, whether in computing the drawing power of advertising or of personalities in the political arena cannot be underestimated . . ." Dr. Menzig seemed prepared to go on in this vein, but just then Muddington lurched to his feet.

"By God, you just see that he gets elected," he said. "Lousy Professor, think you're so dam' smart. You just do what you're paid to do. You hear?" he raised his voice and shook his fist at Dr. Menzig. "You hear. Lousy egghead!"

A. J. LIEBLING

*Governor Long Speaks**

1958

Hurrying through otherwise undistinguished streets, we passed between cars parked thick along the approaches to the courthouse square and heard the loud-speaker blaring long before we got there. Somebody was on the platform in front of the courthouse steps, standing too close to

* from *The Earl of Louisiana*.

the microphone and blasting. The crowd, massed immediately around the speaker's stand, thinned out toward the sidewalks.

My companion let me out and drove on to find a parking space, and I ran onto the lawn for my first look at the Imam in the flesh. As I crossed over to the forum, a boy handed me a pink throwaway, which I examined when I got within range of the light diffused from the floodlamps over the platform:

GOVERNOR LONG SPEAKS

Governor Long Opens Campaign for Re-Election

Come Out and Bring All your friends to hear the truth.
Come out and see Governor Long in person. Nothing
will be said to offend or hurt anyone.

The Governor, on the platform, was saying to somebody I could not see over in the other wing of the audience:

"If you don't shut up your claptrap, I'm going to have you forcibly removed. You just nothing but a common hoodlum and a heckler."

"Amen," an old man in front of me yelled. "Give it to him, Earl."

Whoever it was that Earl was talking to in the crowd had no microphone, so we couldn't hear him, but he must have answered in tones audible to the Governor, because the latter shouted into the mike:

"I knew your daddy, Camille Gravel, and he was a fine man. But you trying to make yourself a big man, and you nothing but a little pissant."

"Amen, Earl," the old man yelled. "Give it to him."

The fellow in the crowd, now identified for me as a lawyer from Alick who was the Democratic National Committeeman from Louisiana, must have spoken again, for the Governor thundered:

"Mr. Gravel, I got nothing against you personally. Now you keep quiet and I won't mention your name. If you don't I'll have you removed as a common damn nuisance." He paused for the answer we couldn't hear and then bellowed:

"If *you* so popular, why don't *you* run for Governor?"

It sounded like a dialogue between a man with the horrors and his hallucinations. But the National Committeeman, Earl's interlocutor, was there in the flesh. He had brought his ten children, and they were all mad at the Governor.

The night was like a heavy blanket pressed down on the lawn. Men stood in their sleeveless, collarless shirts, and sweat caked the talcum powder on the backs of the women's necks. Anti-Long newspapers the next day conceded the crowd was between three and four thousand, so there may well have been more. Plenty of Negroes, always in little groups, were scattered among the whites, an example, I suppose, of Harry Golden's "vertical integration," because in public gatherings where there are seats, the two colors are always separated into blocs.

"That's the way I like to see it," the Governor said, from the stand. "Not all our colored friends in one spot and white friends in another. I'm the best friend the poor white man, and the middle-class white man, and the rich white man—so long as he behave himself—and the poor colored man, ever had in the State of Loosiana. And if the NAACP and that little pea-headed nut Willie Rainach will just leave us alone, then *sensible* people, not cranks, can get along in a *reasonable way. That Rainach wants to fight the Civil War all over again."

There were two colored couples, middle-aged, in front of me, next to the old white man who didn't like Gravel, and now one of the colored men shouted "Amen!" The old white man gave him a reproving look, but he couldn't bawl him out for agreeing with a Long. Nobody can object to *reasonable* and *sensible*, but Long hadn't said what he thought *reasonable* and *sensible* were, and it occurred to me that he probably never would.

I had been looking at him with an amateur clinical eye since I got there, and his physical condition seemed to me to have improved several hundred percent since his stump appearance with Joe Sims on the Fourth of July. Late hours and a diet of salted watermelon, buttermilk, and Vienna sausages cut up in chicken broth had put a dozen pounds back on his bones. Walking between grandstands and paddocks had legged him up, and he pranced under the floodlights that must have raised the temperature to a hundred and ten or so. I remembered when I had seen first the referee, Rudy Goldstein, and then the great Sugar Ray Robinson himself collapse under the heat of similar lights in a ring on a less oppressive night in New York.

Uncle Earl wore a jacket, shirt and tie, a pattern of statesmanlike conventionality on a night when everybody off the platform was coatless and tieless. The tie itself was a quiet pattern of inkblots against an olive-and-pearl background, perhaps a souvenir Rorschach test from Galveston. The suit, a black job that dated from the days when he was fat and sassy, hung loosely about him as once it had upon a peg in the supermarket where the Governor liked to buy his clothes.

He left the dude role to Morrison. And in fact, before the evening was over, he said:

"I see Dellasoups has been elected one of the ten best-dressed men in America. He has fifty-dollar neckties and four-hundred-dollar suits. A four-hundred-dollar suit on old Uncle Earl would look like socks on a Rooster."

It is difficult to report a speech by Uncle Earl chronologically, listing the thoughts in order of appearance. They chased one another on and off the stage like characters in a Shakespearean battle scene, full of alarums and sorties. But Morrison, good roads and old-age pensions popped in quite often.

Of Dodd, the State Auditor, a quondam ally and now a declared rival for the Governorship, he said, "I hear Big Bad Bill Dodd has been talking about the inefficiency and waste in this administration. Ohyeah. Ohyeah. Well let me tell you, Big Bad Bill has at least six streamlined deadheads on his payroll that couldn't even find Bill's office if they had to. But they can find that *Post Office* every month to get their salary check—Ohyeah."

It was after the "*reasonable and sensible*" bit that he went into his general declaration of tolerance. "I'm not against anybody for reasons of race, creed, or any ism he might believe in except nuttism, skingameism or communism," he said.

"I'm glad to see so many of my fine Catholic friends here—they been so kind to me I sometimes say I consider myself forty percent Catholic and sixty percent Baptist" (this is a fairly accurate reflection of the composition of the electorate). "But I'm in favor of *every* religion with the possible exception of snake-chunking. Anybody that so presumes on how he stands with Providence that he will let a snake bite him, I say he deserves what he's got coming to him." The snake-chunkers, a small, fanatic cult, do not believe in voting.

"Amen, Earl," the old man said.

The expressions on the Governor's face changed with the poetry of his thought, now benign, now mischievous, now indignant. Only the moist hazel eyes remained the same, fixed on a spot above and to the rear of the audience as if expecting momentarily the arrival of a posse.

"I don't *need* this job," he said. "I don't *need* money." He stopped and winked. "I don't miss it except when I run out."

There were shouts of laughter, the effect he courted.

"Amen, Earl. You tell 'em, Earl."

His face turned serious, as if he had not expected to be so cruelly misunderstood.

"I'm serious about that," he said. "You know I'm no goody-goody. But if I have ever misappropriated one cent, by abuse of my office, and anyone can prove it, I'll resign.

"I know lots of ways to make a living. I know how to be a lawyer, and a danged good one. I know how to be a traveling salesman. I know how to pick cotton, and have many times, although I've seen the days when to get my hundred pounds I had to put a watermelon in the bag."

There were gales of tolerant laughter now, even from farmers who would shoot any of their own help they found cheating on weight.

"All I ask," he said, with the honesty throbbing in his voice like a musical saw, "is a chance once again to help the fine people of the Great State of Loosiana, and to continue to serve them as their Governor."

Even a group of great louts in T shirts, perhaps high-school football players, were silent and by now impressed; earlier in the address they had made a few feeble attempts at heckling, like yelling, "Hey, Earl, what's in the glass?" when the Governor paused for a drink of water. These boys might be from well-to-do anti-Long families, but they had the endemic Southern (and Arabic) taste for oratory, and they knew a master when they heard him.

Mr. Gravel, down near the platform, must have again attracted the Governor's attention, but now Uncle Earl, the creature of his own voice, was in a benign mood from offering his own body to the Great State of Loosiana.

"Mr. Gravel," he said, "you got ten beautiful children there, I wish you would lend five of them to me to bring up." It was one of Earl's well-publicized sorrows that he, like the Shah of Iran then, had no legitimate heir, and he handed peppermint candies or small change to all children he saw, even in years when there was no election. "He bought those candies by grosses of dozens," an ex-associate told me.

Mr. Gravel, still inaudible except to Earl, must have declined this overture, because the Governor shouted to the crowd: "He used to be a nice fellow, but now he just a goddamn hoodlum!"

"Leave him alone, Earl, we come to hear *you* talk!" the old man near me shouted back.

"I was in Minneannapolis once, talking to the Governor of Minnesota, a great expert on insanity," Uncle Earl said, "and he told me an astonishing fact—there are ten times as many crazy people in Minnesota as Louisiana. I suppose that is on account of the cold climate. They cannot go around in their shirt sleeves all year around, go huntin' and fishin' in all seasons, as we do. We got a wonderful climate," he said, and paused to wipe the sweat from his face with a handkerchief soaked in Coca-Cola, which he poured from a bottle out of a bucket of ice handed him by one of the lesser candidates on his ticket. The bugs soaring up at the edge of the lighted area and converging on the floodlights formed a haze as thick as a beaded curtain.

"On account we got so few crazy people, we can afford to let Camille Gravel run around."

"Leave him up, Earl," the old man yelled. "You got him licked."

"Some sapsuckers talk about cutting down taxes," the Governor said, apropos of nothing he had been talking about. "Where are they going to start cutting expenses? On the *spastic* school?" (When any opponent suggests a cut in welfare expenditures, Earl accuses him of wanting to take it out on the spastics. This is the equivalent of charging the fellow would sell his mother for glue.) "They want to cut down on the *spastics?* On the little children, enjoying the school lunches? Or on those fine old people, white-haired against the sunset of life—" and he bowed his own white head for a split second—"who enjoy the most generous state pensions in the United States?

"We got the finest roads, finest schools, finest hospitals in the country —yet there are rich men who complain. They are so tight you can hear 'em squeak when they walk. They wouldn't give a nickel to see a earthquake. They sit there swallowin' hundred-dollar bills like a bullfrog swallows minners—if you chunked them as many as they want they'd bust."

"Amen, Earl," the old man said. "God have mercy on the poor people."

"Of course, I know many *fine* rich people," the Governor said, perhaps thinking of his campaign contributors. "But the most of them are like a rich old feller I knew down in Plaquemines Parish, who died one night and never done nobody no good in his life, and yet, when the Devil come to get him, he took an appeal to St. Peter.

" 'I done some good things on earth,' he said. 'Once, on a cold day in about 1913, I gave a blind man a nickel.' St. Peter looked all through the records, and at last, on page four hundred and seventy-one, he found the entry. 'That ain't enough to make up for a misspent life,' he said. 'But wait,' the rich man says. 'Now I remember, in 1922 I gave five cents to a poor widow woman that had no carfare.' St. Peter's clerk checked the book again, and on page thirteen hundred and seventy-one, after pages and pages of how this old stump-wormer loan-sharked the poor, he found the record of that nickel.

" 'That ain't neither enough,' St. Peter said. But the mean old thing yelled, '*Don't* sentence me yet. In about 1931 I gave a nickel to the Red Cross.' The clerk found that entry, too. So he said to St. Peter, 'Your Honor, what are we going to do with him?' "

The crowd hung on Uncle Earl's lips the way the bugs hovered in the light.

"You know what St. Peter said?" the Governor, the only one in the courthouse square who knew the answer, asked. There was, naturally, no reply.

"He said: 'Give him back his fifteen cents and tell him to go to Hell.'"

He had the crowd with him now, and he dropped it.

"Folks," he said, "I know you didn't come here just to hear me talk. If this big mouth of mine ever shut up I'd be in a devil of a fix. I want to introduce to you some of the fine *sincere* candidates that are running with me on my ticket. My ticket and the independent candidates I have endorsed are trained, skilled, and have the wisdom and experience to make you honest, loyal and *sincere* public servants."

He turned to the triple row of men and women who sat behind him on undertaker's chairs, the men swabbing, the women dabbing, at their faces with handkerchiefs, while the Governor talked like an intrepid trainer who turns his back on his troupe of performing animals.

A reporter who had his watch on the Governor said that his talk had lasted fifty-seven minutes, and he was not even blowing.

"And first," he said, "I want to introduce to you the man I have selected to serve under me as Lieutenant Governor during my next term of office—a fine Frenchmun, a fine Catholic, the father of twenty-three children, Mr. Oscar Guidry."

The number of children was politically significant, since it indicated that Mr. Guidry was a practicing, not a *soi-disant*, Catholic. The candidate for Lieutenant Governor had to be a Frenchman and a Catholic, because Uncle Earl was neither.

Mr. Guidry, a short, stocky man who reminded me of a muscular owl, arose from his chair like a Mr. Bones called to front center by Mr. Interlocutor. He appeared embarrassed, and he whispered rapidly to Uncle Earl.

"Oscar says he has only fourteen children," the Governor announced. "But that's a good beginnin'."

Mr. Guidry whispered again, agitated, and Earl said, "But he is a member of a family of twenty-three brothers and sisters." He turned away, as if washing his hands of the whole affair, and sat down.

Mr. Guidry, throwing back his head and clasping his hands in front of him, as if about to intone the "Marseillaise," began with a rush, sounding all his aitches:

"I am *honored* to be associated with the Gret Governeur of the Gret Stet on his tiquette. Those who have conspired against him, fearing to shoot him with a pistol-ball . . ." and he was off, but Earl, seated directly behind him, was mugging and catching flies, monopolizing attention like an old vaudeville star cast in a play with a gang of Method actors.

Pulling his chair slightly out of line, he crossed his legs and turned his profile to the audience, first plucking at his sleeves, which came down about as far as his thumbnails, then, when he had disengaged his hands, picking his nose while he looked over at Alick's leading hotel, the Bentley, across the street, described by the Louisiana State Guide as "a six-story building of brick and stone, with a columned façade and a richly decorated interior." He stared at it as if it contained some absorbing riddle.

When he had finished with his nose, he began to bathe his face, his temples and the back of his neck with Coca-Cola from the cold bottle, sloshing it on like iced cologne.

"Cool yourself off, Earl," a voice piped up from the crowd, and the Governor shouted back, "I'm a red-hot poppa."

When he had wet himself down sufficiently, he drank the heel-tap and set the bottle down. Then he lit a cigarette and smoked, dramatically, with the butt held between his thumb and middle finger and the other fingers raised, in the manner of a ventriloquist. While he smoked right-handed he pulled out his handkerchief and blotted his wet face with his left.

He sat unheeding of the rumpus raised by his adherents, like a player in a jazz band who has finished his solo, or a flashy halfback who poses on the bench while the defensive team is in. The candidates ranted and bellowed, putting across a few telling although familiar points.

"In the great state of Texas, biggest and richest in the United States, there is an old-age pension of thirty-one dollars a month. Here in Loosiana we got seventy-two."

But the bored crowd stood fast, knowing that a whistle would blow and the star would throw off his blanket and come onto the field again to run rings around the forces of Mammon. Sure enough, after what seemed to me an endless session of subordinate rant, the Governor threw away the last of a chain of cigarettes and shook his head like a man waking up on a park bench and remembering where he is. He got up and walked to the microphone so fast that the man using it had barely time to say "I thank you" before the Governor took it away from him.

"You shall know the truth, and the truth shall set you free," the Governor said, "but you will never get to know the truth by reading the

Alexandria *Town Talk*. You all read in that paper that I am crazy. Ohyeah. Do I look any crazier than I ever did? I been accused of saying the fella that owns that paper is a kept man. Maybe he ain't, but I'd like to be kep' as good as he is. He married a rich woman. That's about the best way I know to save yourself about ninety-eight years' hard work."

"Amen, Earl, it's the truth," the old man in front of me cried, and the Negroes laughed at what was apparently a well-established local joke.

"Maybe some of you are here because you've never seen a man out of a nuthouse before," the Governor said tolerantly. "Maybe you want to see a man who has been stuck thirty-eight times with needles. Oh, the first man stuck me, stuck me right through the britches. He didn't get me in the fat part, either, and oh, how it hurt! Maybe I lost a little weight, but you would have, too. Occasionally I say hell or damn, but if it had happened to you all, you'd say worse than that. Christ on the Cross Himself never suffered worse than poor old Earl!

"Oh, not that I'm fit to walk in Christ's shoes!" he bellowed to preclude any confusion. "I'm not good enough, when a fellow slugs me on one cheek, to turn the other side of my scheming head. I'm going to slug him back."

"Amen, Earl. You tell him, Earl. Who you goin' to hit first, Earl?"

"Down there in that court in Texas in Galveston before that Texas judge, I felt like Christ between the two thieves. He reared back his head and he said, 'Father forgive them, for they know not what they do!' "

At this point he was interrupted by wild handclapping from a group of elderly ladies wearing print dresses, white gloves, straw hats and Spaceman eyeglasses, who had been seated quietly on the platform through the earlier proceedings. They were under the impression that it was an original line.

I next remember the Governor in his seat again, head down, exhausted, having given his all to the electorate, in a pose like Bannister after running the first four-minute mile. It occurred to me that he was like old blind Pete Herman fighting on heart alone, by a trained reflex. Pete is a friend of the Governor's.

As Earl sat there, one of the assisting speakers, a fellow with a strong voice, grabbed the microphone and declaimed the family battle ode, "Invictus."

When the man came to the part where it says:

> "Under the bludgeonings of fate
> Ma haid is bloody, but *unbowed*"

Earl flung up his head like a wild horse and got up like a fighter about to go into a dance to prove he hasn't been hurt. He called for a show of hands by everybody who was going to vote for him, and I waved both of mine.

I left him surrounded by children to whom he was passing out coins, "a quarter to the white kids and a nickel to the niggers."

My companion had rejoined me after parking the car, and we walked together through the breaking crowd.

"How could his wife have done him like she done?" a woman was asking another, and a man was saying, "Got to give da ol' dawg what's coming to him."

ROGER EDDY

Why I Won't Be Governor of Connecticut

1962

First, let it be said that I started my quest for the Governorship of Connecticut with a serious handicap. The office was not seeking me. I was seeking the office. I very much wanted that mansion, and that chauffeur-driven limousine. Also I had long been intrigued by the power that goes with the Governor's office.

Therefore, the customary press release that, "After much urging by friends I have thrown my hat into the ring," was not suitable in my case, since there had never been a time since I first entered politics when my hat was out of the ring. Nor could I announce that, "After many hours of soul-searching, and consultation with my family, I have decided that it is my duty to accept the great challenge offered me by the people of our state," because it was I who had been challenging the people. *In other words, in my case, humility was out.*

Therefore, I chose the next most popular method of announcing a candidacy. *I denied it.*

My first official denial appeared in Connecticut newspapers about a year ago. At that time there were at least twenty other candidates issuing denials, but in general the impression seemed to be that my denials were the most statesmanlike and that of all the candidates issuing denials I had the best chance of going on to get the nomination. A member of my staff had made an exhaustive study of political denials, going all the way back to the press conference that Caesar held on the day he crossed the Rubicon. Reporters from Rome asked Caesar if "crossing the Rubicon means that you are now a candidate for Emperor?"

"Gentlemen," Caesar answered, reading from a prepared statement, "I am not a candidate for Emperor now, nor is it my intention to become a candidate in the future. The rumors that I am not happy in Gaul are totally false. I find my work there both interesting and rewarding. No, Gentlemen, while our incumbent Emperor is obviously not a big enough man for the job, and while he has surrounded himself with men who are interested only in feathering their own political nests, and while it is obvious that unless someone returns sound fiscal policies to our government, our Empire is doomed—it is not up to me to say that I am the man needed to save Rome. It is up to the people. Therefore, let's set the record straight once and for all. I am crossing the Rubicon for just one reason—to get to the other side."

Caesar then departed from his written text, and said, "The rest is off the record, boys. *The die is cast.*"

However—to return to my own campaign—my first step was to hire a professional manager.

I was severely criticized by some members of my own party for hiring a Democrat. I did this for two reasons. First, party labels mean nothing to me, particularly when I am a member of a minority party. And, secondly, Republicans these days seem to be amateurs. Now professional politicians do not manage a candidate for nothing. My own manager, for instance—an "old pro" who had been mixed up in the political wars for many years—only agreed to manage me after obtaining my promise that, if elected, I would create an entirely new department in our state government, and make him the head of it. I might have gotten other men to manage me for less. But in politics, as in any other business, it's essential to obtain the best talent available, *and then to pay the price.*

Naturally I utilized a great deal of television time in my campaign. If a candidate does not "project" on television, he might just as well go back to making money. Before my first appearance I engaged a firm of political consultants to "evaluate" me. In other words, I wanted to know where I was weak, and where I was strong. Here were a few of my strong points, as far as television was concerned.

In "Humility Rating" I ranked near the top. I was above average in "Sincerity Projection." In "Ability to Mouth Platitudes" I was fair. I was also fair when it came to "Saying Nothing With Conviction." However, the part of my evaluation report which really shook me and my staff, almost destroying our will to fight, was the final sentence:

"Your nose is too big."

It was the considered judgment of these political consultants that my nose was too large for me to be elected Governor of Connecticut, or in fact Governor of any state. Before the advent of television a candidate with a nose like mine might have made it. After television—no. Obviously, something had to be done about my nose.

I had it removed. The nose I now have is not my own. It belonged to a member of my staff. We also fixed my eyes. My eyes had been a cold, watery gray. Thanks to contact lenses, they are now large, brown, and soulful. These, and other changes I had made in my appearance, when seen on a television screen, all add up to the word, "Leadership."

It is generally conceded that I now have the finest political face ever to be televised.

In all, I appeared a total of thirty times on television, each time giving the same speech. After each appearance my staff circulated a questionnaire designed to gauge my impact on women. Every word I said, every gesture I made, had been pretested to appeal to women. The questionnaire was distributed wherever women congregate, in supermarkets, beauty parlors, discount houses, and men's bars. It was brief, and to the point.

"Judging from the grasp he has of the issues, his intelligence, his qualities of leadership, and his sincerity, and now that you have seen him on television, and knowing your great interest in your state and your nation —would you like him as your lover?"

Like every American politician I came face to face with the problem of minority groups. Unfortunately, before I was able to deny it, the word was circulated that I was of Anglo-Saxon ancestry, and even worse, a Protestant. After a stormy, all-night meeting with my advisers, during which seventy-eight of them resigned, I decided to meet this issue head on.

I called a press conference. In a prepared statement I said: "While I am aware that those of Anglo-Saxon ancestry are no longer needed in politics, except at fund-raising time, and while I am aware that I am a member of a *bad* minority group, rather than a *good* minority group, it is my hope that the time will come again when a Yankee can aspire to high political office, even in Connecticut."

Most of the comments in the press were favorable, one editor even pronouncing, "He must be commended for not trying to weasel out of it."

It is painful to walk the political streets these days and hear the refrain, "Sorry, our ticket is already balanced." Did they balance the ticket when they drafted us into the Army? And when they were choosing candidates for the Tomb of the Unknown Soldier? Yet it's reported that an office in Hartford has a sign which says: "No Anglo-Saxons need apply. We already have one as Comptroller."

I had to face still another problem in my quest for the Governorship. People wanted to know what I was. Was I a Liberal, a Conservative, or a Middle-of-the-Roader?

Politicians have trouble answering this question because they usually don't know what they are. It was my policy to employ a variety of answers, depending on whom I was talking to. For instance, when I spoke before the radicals on the Yale faculty, I admitted to them that I had espoused some conservative legislation, but insisted that I had done it in a radical way. When I spoke to some of the right-wing students, I told them that while I might *act* like a Liberal, in my *heart* I was a Conservative.

The real answer may lie in the clothing a politician wears. I wore only forward-looking suits, cut conservatively, but with liberal styling. My neckties were Liberal-Conservative, or Conservative-Liberal. My shoes were always strictly Middle-of-the-Road.

My campaign is now at the end. I have traveled over eight hundred thousand miles, without once leaving the state of Connecticut. I have shaken two and one half million human hands. I have spoken to fifteen hundred women's clubs, two thousand labor unions, three thousand PTAs, and four thousand service organizations. I am close to the people. I know what they are thinking. I know what they want, and I know who they want to lead them. Therefore, I am now going to make an announcement that few candidates have ever dared make.

I'm beaten, and I'm withdrawing from the race.

3 THE
NAME OF THE GAME

PATRONAGE AND PRACTICAL POLITICS

The subjects dealt with in this section are essentially the local, microcosmic applications of political power—jobs for the faithful, "pork" for the district, municipal services or the lack of them, corruption and reform, and the day-to-day workings of a political organization. Although the issues are generally close to the grass roots (or the asphalt gutters), the White House itself is the target in one instance. We are talking here about power and its lubrication—what makes the wheels go 'round, oils the machinery, and, occasionally, greases the skids.

MARION K. SANDERS

Meet the Boys*

1956

As the party Faithful near senescence, they are often honored at testimonial dinners. These are jolly gatherings, resembling a preview of one's own wake. Tickets for such events command a fair price, so the party treasury benefits, despite the high cost of the classic prop, a lushly embossed scroll. In later years, the male recipient derives much private mirth from this souvenir, recalling with particular gusto the bombast of old John, his lifelong foe, who was forced by protocol to make the presentation speech. In females, on the other hand, similar memories evoke a dewy-eyed nostalgia.

"Women take the world as it is too seriously," says Simone de Beauvoir, who has gotten precious few laughs out of life herself.

Humor, which sometimes blunts the sharp edge of conscience, has also helped men to outdistance women in American politics. The fact that they get a great deal of fun out of it and, at times, hold up the mirror to their own absurdities is a well-guarded masculine secret, for the public deportment of office seekers and partisan leaders must be dull and pompous. Ladies of waggish tendencies do well to conceal them, for the boys like to crack their own jokes, preferably in the University Club or some other gloomy sanctum barred to feminine eavesdroppers.

Because of his rich diversity, *homo politicus Americanus* cannot be squeezed into a composite portrait. However, a few subspecies can be identified by the perceptive feminine wayfarer at headquarters, rally, clubhouse or convention.

* from *The Lady and the Vote.*

WE GOTTA TAKE CARE OF JOE

This explains the snarling character with the smudged collar who tells you the chief is out, even though you have a firm appointment. Joe cannot remember names or faces. He has never been known to write anything down and if you give him a note he will lose it. He is headquarters receptionist, not alone because of these qualifications but because he is otherwise unemployable, and the party is permanently indebted to him for carrying his dear old mother to the polls during the blizzard of '88.

Joe is a one-man WPA for ladies eager to do political work, for, at campaign time, it takes two shifts of competent volunteers to unscramble the chaos he generates, soothe the contributors he snubs, and win back the votes he loses.

Though he is a minor bit of political flotsam, you might as well make friends with Joe. Conceivably, the party may decide to run him for sheriff some day. And, besides, he has his uses. These are mostly manual. Joe is good at moving furniture or typewriters and may, if coddled, disclose the hideouts of the people you want to see.

He also knows many other things but few of them are true. To rely on him for political tips is equivalent to letting a Paris taxi driver plan your tour of the Louvre.

LOVER BOY

This is any politician when addressing a group of women. The performance is designed to convey with puissant charm the message, "The Ladies, God bless 'em—I hope they'll vote for me."

There are a half dozen popular variations on this theme. The uxorious approach was favored, for example, by William R. Stubbs, one-time Governor of Kansas, who used to bring his mate into the act during the opening paragraphs of a speech by pulling from his pocket a tattered handkerchief and remarking, as he mopped his brow, "My, my, this certainly was careless of my wife. She doesn't do this sort of thing often. Usually, she looks after me real well and I must say she makes the finest salt-rising bread anyone ever ate in their lives."

This gambit is said to have cost Governor Stubbs a lot of handkerchiefs but won him a great many votes.

In an attempt to hoe the same row, John Foster Dulles, who is often unlucky in his public utterances abroad, got into some domestic hot water a couple of years ago. During an appearance on Ed Murrow's TV show, *See It Now*, he decided (for no clear reason, since he was not running for anything) to dwell upon his own domestic felicity. It seems he had had a lot of fun, during a recent vacation, helping Mrs. Dulles do the dishes. His favorite chore, he said, was producing a fine burnish on the copper bottom of the Dulles skillet.

I was glad to have the Secretary of State set this fine example for my own husband who takes no interest whatever in our Revere copper set. Less appreciative was the sponsor of the program, the Aluminum Company of America, which is trying to lure copper addicts back to plain old aluminum pots.

Men with small waistlines or no wives go in for the gay *caballero* touch. This is achieved through unctuous references to the charm and beauty of the audience and the dazzling chic of their hats. Democratic State Senator Francis J. Mahoney of New York sometimes gets so involved in such blandishments that he forgets to talk about anything else.

Spurred, no doubt, by the current religious revival, some of the boys are dusting off a technique which flourished in the great days of temperance—the choirboy approach. Distinguished Senators have taken to falling on their knees for public prayer with their WCTU constituents. President Eisenhower habitually gives Republican ladies a fatherly pat on their moral and spiritual values.

The lover-boy routine is, of course, shrewd politics. It is particularly devastating to women who swoon when hairdressers find hidden highlights in their hair or buy dresses they can't afford when saleswomen praise their figures.

THE WORKING PRO

"Speculators about democracy seemed to believe that by some mystic process the 'will of the people' would be expressed and the rulers elected," says Professor V. O. Key of Harvard. "But a mass of people cannot act as a unit; a small inner circle has to narrow the choice for public offices and to formulate questions of public policy."

Perennial residents of this inner circle are the Working Pros, who are not always popular among those excluded. There is, for example, a discernible note of pique in John Adams' words when he wrote in his diary in 1763:

> "The caucus club meets at certain times in the garret of Tom Dawes. . . . There they smoke tobacco till you cannot see from one end of the room to the other. There they drink flip, I suppose, and there they choose a moderator who puts questions to the vote regularly; and selectmen, assessors, collectors, firewards and representatives are regularly chosen before they are chosen in the town."

Professional politicians, says Theodore H. White, are "the most maligned folk characters in our national life." I am inclined to agree. Among them I have encountered about the same ratio of reprobates as one meets in rotary clubs, bar associations or county medical societies. The Working Pros I have studied are not lone and cynical Machiavellis but compulsively gregarious men who can endure a quiet evening at home only if the phone rings unremittingly.

Although I do not go as far as the feminists who rate civilization by the status of women, a modern politician's acumen can be tested by his attitude toward women workers. The smart ones know that there are votes in those coffee hours and, when they think of it, try to make amends for past neglect. . . .

Nor can you [be a successful politician] unless you spend eighteen hours a day, or more, talking, listening, negotiating, browbeating, cajoling and compromising. This is the standard program of the Working Pro and in the process he gets very little sleep. His constitutional insomnia is a trait which readily distinguishes him from his imitators. Commonest of these is the Vegetable—the leader unaware that anyone has moved in or out of his district in the last twenty years, who assures the candidate, on election eve, that everything is under control and is not around headquarters on election night when the dismal returns roll in. Since he never wins an election and politics is his only visible means of support, one sometimes wonders how he sustains life. Frequently he survives by trading with the enemy, which tosses him an occasional patronage crumb. In return, he is expected to prevent any outcropping of eager beavers in his ranks; this he does by example as well as precept. Such an arrangement is known as a "coalition" by those who profit from it, a "deal" by those who don't. The Vegetable is a man to avoid and will thank you for staying out of his path.

In contrast, the Working Pro, if you can corner him in a relaxed mood (say around 3 A.M. when his pace has slowed), is cordial, direct and knowledgeable. He is also a man of his word who holds a promise sacred. Not until some hours after your conference will you realize that he has not, in fact, promised you anything at all.

THE WHEEL

Grand Marshal of the St. Patrick's Day Parade, darling of the NAM and Honorary Chairman of all campaign committees is the Wheel. Often he is a politician *emeritus* like Herbert Hoover or Jim Farley. The Wheel's mannerisms recall a retired Notre Dame football coach. The boys listen to him reverently but seldom heed his counsel, for those who are running with the ball prefer to call their own signals. And when a politician is on the sidelines, quaintness sets in rapidly. Exceptions are Tom Dewey and Harry Truman whose wind and speed are so far unimpaired.

Pretenders to the Wheel's throne can become quite a nuisance. Pretenders are collateral descendants of Presidents, Kentucky colonels, prizefight managers and others who feel, for tenuous reasons, that the party owes them special deference. They may also be young men with political science degrees and rich fathers or attorneys who know everything about politics except the election laws. The ceremonial brush-off is the best treatment for Pretenders.

An authentic but troublesome Wheel is the Big Contributor, especially when he gets bored with meeting deficits and takes to making policy and speeches. Having spent most of his adult life in a top-executive vacuum, as befits a full-fledged Payroll Meeter, he is a vote-loser par excellence. Once he gets the bit in his teeth he tends, like Charlie Wilson, to announce that what's good for General Motors is good for the country or to tell the voters that they remind him of kennel dogs. . . .

THE BRAIN

Notwithstanding the egghead quips, erudition has been respectable in twentieth-century U.S. politics ever since Roosevelt proved that a man can be on speaking terms with Ph.D.'s and still be elected President four times. . . .

The Brain is most admired by politicians who are given to reading books. However, mystery story and comic fans are also glad to have someone around the house to ride herd on the opinion researchers, whip up a handy constitutional precedent or locate Uzbekistan without the aid of an atlas.

Republican Thinkers are generally Yale men and constitute a small elite corps. The Democratic Party, which draws on land-grant as well as Ivy League colleges, is sometimes overstocked with First-Rate Minds. For instance, Louis Howe, Raymond Moley and Sam Rosenman gave FDR a rather hard time by each drafting an acceptance speech for him to deliver when he flew to the Chicago convention in 1932. Having had a lot of practice in the use of a pencil during his long polio convalescence, FDR found it easy to mingle tidbits from all the manuscripts in the speech he had already written for himself. Few men are equally adroit in keeping a whole stable of geniuses content and, for most politicians, a solo Brain suffices. Such monopolies can safely be granted only to Senior Brains. Junior Brains suffer from infatuation with their own notions. Over the years, this gives speeches, platforms and official statements a certain sameness. When this happens, it is sometimes possible to persuade Junior that a new idea is his own and thus assure its inclusion in future party litanies.

This can seldom be accomplished by a woman. Junior regards all females as promising undergraduate students or cub reporters with small potential beyond typing or research of dubious scholarship.

Afflicted by well-founded doubts of his own maturity, Junior craves, above all, to be One of the Boys. He is hypersensitive about his own semi-amateur status in politics. This I noted recently when I was ruminating on the incompatibility of old hands and newcomers like myself.

"We are a bunch of intruders," I said morosely, "awkwardly trying to muscle into our own political parties."

"You are doing us a great disservice," Junior retorted hotly, "with all this talk of amateurs and professionals in politics. There are no real differences between us. This is a completely artificial dichotomy and we should strive to obliterate it, not to perpetuate it."

I did not argue the point. Still, from where I sit, there is a perceptible distance between those who seek to obliterate dichotomies and those who know which end is up.

BELOVED CANDIDATE

Whatever he may be running for, this, for the duration of the campaign, is the object of your affection. For full effectiveness, the emotional transference should be complete but temporary. This is easy if you are lucky enough to draw one of the "personable" candidates lately glorified by TV. Robert Montgomery has given his disciples a knack with the girls as well as the teleprompter.

Other specimens are less beguiling. For instance, I know a man who has been regularly elected to public office for twenty years because he always campaigns in a threadbare suit. This reminder of his shiftless family and leaky roof proves that the poor fellow really needs the job and attracts quite a few votes. John Cashmore, the perpetual Borough President of Brooklyn, won his first elective office by plodding from door to door, looking neat but shabby and assuring his neighbors that he knew he had no chance but would surely appreciate their votes just to make his mother happy. He was swept in by the "sympathy" vote and has not lost an election in Brooklyn since.

Just as the sad sack has his place on the hustings, so do the dull, the mediocre and the passive. Poor, silver-tongued William Jennings Bryan was regularly trounced by the likes of McKinley who seldom moved off his front porch and said little when he did. Some sort of record for inactive campaigning was set in 1907 by Governor Austin L. Crother of Maryland who caught typhoid fever the week he was nominated and stayed in bed until Election Day, when he won handily.

On the other hand, the Meat Axe or "give-'em-hell" type of candidate is also a good man to put your money on. This genus long predates President Truman. Congressman John Phillip Hill of Baltimore used to hurl water glasses out of the window, during his antiprohibition speeches in the nineteen-twenties. . . .

Because they are perpetually wooing the public fancy, all elected officials are chronic candidates. Thanks to their six-year tenure, Senators lapse into a subacute state at mid-term. But it is always open season on Representatives who must let the people choose every two years. This choice is thought to be closely related to the number of favors done for individual constituents in the interval. It is not considered cricket to keep pestering a man for whom you don't intend to vote, but many citizens lack a sense of sportsmanship and, irrespective of their allegiance, require of their Congressman a continuous federal information, tax advisory and personal job counseling service. This provides steady employment for a large corps of swift and smooth letter writers on Capitol Hill.

The Candidate's arts can advance not only his own political cause but also international harmony. Historian Richard Hofstadter reports that Franklin D. Roosevelt could say "my old friend" in eleven languages, a skill useful in winning allies as well as votes.

The ideal Candidate has an unlimited appetite for human contacts and the intention, which he somehow projects, of performing, if elected, in the manner suggested by his campaign promises. To a gratifying degree, those so endowed win. However, political workers must be ready to take pot luck when the party offers less toothsome fare. Some years ago, at a village caucus, the chairman unveiled the least-loved man in the county as candidate for Trustee.

"Why, he's a sonofabitch," a young and startled committeeman blurted out.

"I remind you, sir," said the chairman sternly, "that this year he's *our* sonofabitch."

CONGRESSMAN ALBERT BROWN

Some Pork for Pascagoula
(*excerpts*)

1852

I have offered that Pascagoula amendment for the last time. (Laughter.) I stand here pretty much in the attitude of the man who visited General Jackson when he was President. He came on to Washington asking for the mission to England. It was refused him. He then asked for a Cabinet appointment. That was refused him. He came down to a collectorship, and when that was refused him, he said he would put up with a clerkship. But that also was denied him. As a last dying hope he inquired of the old General if he could not give him a pair of old boots; and when they were refused he swore he would not be a Jackson man any longer. (Laughter.)

I have asked sixty thousand dollars to make improvements on the Pascagoula, and I have come down by little and little until now I ask only two thousand dollars for a survey. If you do not give it to me I shall certainly vote against this bill. (Laughter.) Gentlemen do not seem to understand the value of the Pascagoula River. Let me tell them it is a river of national importance and ought to be improved by the nation. Three rules have been prescribed by distinguished men for governing cases like this. One by General Jackson, another by Mr. Calhoun, and the third by someone else—I do not know who. This third party said a work to be national ought to be in salt water. But General Jackson thought you could improve up to the last port of entry on a river, whether it was on salt or fresh water; and Mr. Calhoun laid down the rule that a river flowing through three states could properly claim the jurisdiction and protection of the national Treasury.

Now, this improvement on the Pascagoula is in salt water, for it is in the Gulf of Mexico, and besides, I understand there was a salt barge sunk there about ten years ago. (Laughter.) Then it may be called a port of entry; for the river at this point enters directly into the County of Jackson, in my state. The Pascagoula River flows through three states. It rises in a state of prosperity—it flows through a state of affluence—but it empties into a state of embarrassment. If, however, you will only give me this two thousand dollars to make the survey, I have no doubt it will empty, ultimately, into a state of extraordinary wealth, and that will make four states. I will not take less than two thousand dollars for this survey. That is the last and lowest proposition. If you do not give me that I shall vote against the bill most certainly. (Laughter.) I do believe you think I mean to do it anyhow.

CONGRESSMAN J. PROCTOR KNOTT

The Duluth Speech
(*excerpts*)

1871

The House having under consideration the joint resolution (S.R. No. 11), extending the time to construct a railroad from the St. Croix river or lake to the west end of Lake Superior and to Bayfield—

Mr. Knott said:—

Years ago, when I first heard that there was somewhere in the vast *terra incognita*, somewhere in the bleak regions of the great Northwest, a stream of water known to the nomadic inhabitants of the neighborhood as the river St. Croix, I became satisfied that the construction of a railroad from that raging torrent to some point in the civilized world was essential to the happiness and prosperity of the American people, if not absolutely indispensable to the perpetuity of republican institutions on this continent. (Great laughter.) I felt instinctively that the boundless resources of that prolific region of sand and pine shrubbery would never be fully developed without a railroad constructed and equipped at the expense of the Government, and perhaps not then. (Laughter.) I had an abiding presentiment that, some day or other, the people of this whole

country, irrespective of party affiliations, regardless of sectional prejudices, and "without distinction of race, color, or previous condition of
servitude," would rise in their majesty, and demand an outlet for the
enormous agricultural productions of those vast and fertile pine barrens,
drained in the rainy season by the surging waters of the turbid St. Croix.
(Great laughter.)

These impressions, derived simply and solely from the "eternal fitness
of things," were not only strengthened by the interesting and eloquent
debate on this bill, to which I listened with so much pleasure the other
day, but intensified, if possible, as I read over this morning the lively
colloquy which took place on that occasion, as I find it reported in last
Friday's "Globe." I will ask the indulgence of the House while I read a
few short passages, which are sufficient, in my judgment, to place the
merits of the great enterprise contemplated in the measure now under
discussion beyond all possible controversy.

The honorable gentleman from Minnesota (Mr. Wilson), who, I believe, is managing this bill, in speaking of the character of the country
through which this railroad is to pass, says this:—

"We want to have the timber brought to us as cheaply as possible.
Now, if you tie up the lands in this way, so that no title can be obtained
to them—for no settler will go on these lands, for he can not make a
living—you deprive us of the benefit of that timber."

Now, sir, I would not have it by any means inferred from this that the
gentleman from Minnesota would insinuate that the people out in his
section desire this timber merely for the purpose of fencing up their
farms, so that their stock may not wander off and die of starvation
among the bleak hills of the St. Croix. (Laughter.) I read it for no such
purpose, sir, and make no such comment on it myself. In corroboration
of this statement of the gentleman from Minnesota, I find this testimony given by the honorable gentleman from Wisconsin (Mr. Washburn). Speaking of these same lands, he says:

"Under the bill, as amended by my friend from Minnesota, nine
tenths of the land is open to actual settlers at $2.50 per acre; the remain-
ing one tenth is pine-timbered land, that is not fit for settlement, and
never will be settled upon; but the timber will be cut off. I admit that it
is the most valuable portion of the grant, for most of the grant is not
valuable. It is quite valueless; and if you put in this amendment of the
gentleman from Indiana, you may as well just kill the bill, for no man
and no company will take the grant and build the road."

I simply pause here to ask some gentleman better versed in the science of mathematics than I am to tell me, if the timbered lands are in fact the most valuable portion of that section of country, and they would be entirely valueless without the timber that is on them, what the remainder of the land is worth which has no timber on it at all. (Laughter.) . . .

And further on I find this pregnant question, the joint production of the two gentlemen from Wisconsin:—

"Mr. Paine: Does my friend from Indiana suppose that in any event settlers will occupy and cultivate these pine lands?

"Mr. Washburn, of Wisconsin: Particularly without a railroad?

Yes, sir, "particularly without a railroad." It will be asked after a while, I am afraid, if settlers will go anywhere unless the Government builds a railroad for them to go on. (Laughter.) . . .

Now, sir, who, after listening to this emphatic and unequivocal testimony of these intelligent, competent and able-bodied witnesses (laughter), who that is not as incredulous as St. Thomas himself, will doubt for a moment that the Goshen of America is to be found in the sandy valleys and upon the pine-clad hills of St. Croix? (Laughter.) Who will have the hardihood to rise in his seat on this floor and assert that, excepting the pine bushes, the entire region would not produce vegetation enough in ten years to fatten a grasshopper? (Great laughter.) Where is the patriot who is willing that his country shall incur the peril of remaining another day without the amplest railroad connection with such an inexhaustible mine of agricultural wealth? (Laughter.) Who will answer for the consequences of abandoning a great and warlike people, in possession of a country like that, to brood over the indifference and neglect of their Government? (Laughter.) How long would it be before they would take to studying the Declaration of Independence, and hatching out the damnable heresy of secession? How long before the grim demon of civil discord would rear again his horrid head in our midst, "gnash loud his iron fangs, and shake his crest of bristling bayonets"? (Laughter.)

.   .   .   .

Ah, sir, I could very well understand why my amiable friends from Pennsylvania (Mr. Myers, Mr. Kelley and Mr. O'Neill) should be so earnest in their support of this bill the other day, and if their honorable colleague, my friend, Mr. Randall, will pardon the remark, I will say I considered his criticism of their action on that occasion as not only unjust, but ungenerous. I know they were looking forward with the far-reaching ken of enlightened statesmanship to the pitiable condition in which Philadelphia will be left, unless speedily supplied with railroad connection in some way or other with this garden spot of the universe. (Laughter.) . . .

Now, sir, I repeat I have been satisfied for years that if there was any portion of the inhabited globe absolutely in a suffering condition for want of a railroad it was these teeming pine barrens of the St. Croix. (Laughter.) At what particular point on that noble stream such a road should be commenced I knew was immaterial, and so it seems to have been considered by the draughtsman of this bill. It might be up at the spring or down at the foot-log, or the watergate, or the fish-dam, or anywhere along the bank, no matter where. (Laughter.) But in what direction should it run, or where should it terminate, were always to my mind questions of the most painful perplexity. . . .

Hence, as I have said, sir, I was utterly at a loss to determine where the terminus of this great and indispensable road should be, until I accidentally overheard some gentleman the other day mention the name of "Duluth." (Great laughter.) Duluth! The word fell upon my ear with peculiar and indescribable charm, like the gentle murmur of a low fountain stealing forth in the midst of roses, or the soft, sweet accents of an angel's whisper in the· bright, joyous dream of sleeping innocence. Duluth! 'Twas the name for which my soul had panted for years, as the hart panteth for the water-brooks. (Renewed laughter.) But where was Duluth? Never, in all my limited reading, had my vision been gladdened by seeing the celestial word in print. (Laughter.) And I felt a profounder humiliation in my ignorance that its dulcet syllables had never before ravished my delighted ear. (Roars of laughter.) I was certain the draughtsman of this bill had never heard of it, or it would have been designated as one of the termini of this road. I asked my friends about it, but they knew nothing of it. I rushed to the library, and examined all the maps I could find. (Laughter.) I discovered in one of them a delicate, hairlike line, diverging from the Mississippi near a place marked Prescott, which I supposed was intended to represent the river St. Croix, but I could nowhere find Duluth.

Nevertheless, I was confident it existed somewhere, and that its discovery would constitute the crowning glory of the present century, if not of all modern times. (Laughter.) I knew it was bound to exist in the very nature of things; that the symmetry and perfection of our planetary system would be incomplete without it (renewed laughter); that the elements of material nature would long since have resolved themselves back into original chaos, if there had been such a hiatus in creation as would have resulted from leaving out Duluth. (Roars of laughter.) In fact, sir,

I was overwhelmed with the conviction that Duluth not only existed somewhere, but that, wherever it was, it was a great and glorious place. . . . Yet, sir, had it not been for this map, kindly furnished me by the Legislature of Minnesota, I might have gone down to my obscure and humble grave in an agony of despair, because I could nowhere find Duluth. (Renewed laughter.) Had such been my melancholy fate, I have no doubt that, with the last feeble pulsation of my breaking heart, with the last faint exhalation of my fleeting breath, I should have whispered, "Where is Duluth?" (Roars of laughter.)

But, thanks to the beneficence of that band of ministering angels who have their bright abodes in the far-off capital of Minnesota, just as the agony of my anxiety was about to culminate in the frenzy of despair, this blessed map was placed in my hands; and as I unfolded it a resplendent scene of ineffable glory opened before me, such as I imagine burst upon the enraptured vision of the wandering peri through the opening gates of paradise. (Renewed laughter.) There, there for the first time, my enchanted eye rested upon the ravishing word "Duluth." . . .

If gentlemen will examine it, they will find Duluth not only in the centre of the map, but represented in the centre of a series of concentric circles, one hundred miles apart, and some of them as much as four thousand miles in diameter, embracing alike in their tremendous sweep the fragrant savannas of the sunlit South and the eternal solitudes of snow that mantle the ice-bound North. (Laughter.) How these circles were produced is perhaps one of those primordial mysteries that the most skillful paleologist will never be able to explain. (Renewed laughter.) But the fact is, sir, Duluth is preeminently a central place, for I am told by gentlemen who have been so reckless of their own personal safety as to venture away into those awful regions where Duluth is supposed to be that it is so exactly in the center of the visible universe that the sky comes down at precisely the same distance all around it. (Roars of laughter.)

I find by reference to this map that Duluth is situated somewhere near the western end of Lake Superior; but as there is no dot or other mark indicating its exact location, I am unable to say whether it is actually confined to any particular spot, or whether "it is just lying around there loose." (Renewed laughter.) I really can not tell whether it is one of those ethereal creations of intellectual frostwork, more intangible than the rose-tinted clouds of a summer sunset—one of those airy exhalations of the speculator's brain, which I am told are ever flitting in the forms of towns and cities along those lines of railroad, built with Government subsidies, luring the unwary settlers as the mirage of the desert lures the famishing traveler on, and ever on, until it fades away in the darkening horizon—or whether it is a real *bona fide*, substantial city, all "staked off," with the lots marked with their owners' names, like that proud commercial metropolis recently discovered on the desirable shores of San Domingo. (Laughter.) . . .

Then, sir, there is the climate of Duluth, unquestionably the most salubrious and delightful to be found anywhere on the Lord's earth. Now, I have always been under the impression, as I presume other gentlemen have, that in the region around Lake Superior it was cold enough for at least nine months in the year to freeze the smokestack off a locomotive. (Great laughter.) But I see it represented on this map that Duluth is situated exactly half-way between the latitudes of Paris and Venice, so that gentlemen who have inhaled the exhilarating airs of the one or basked in the golden sunlight of the other may see at a glance that Duluth must be a place of untold delights (laughter), a terrestrial paradise, fanned by the balmy zephyrs of an eternal spring, clothed in the gorgeous sheen of ever-blooming flowers, and vocal with the silvery melody of nature's choicest songsters.

.   .   .   .

As to the commercial resources of Duluth, sir, they are simply illimitable and inexhaustible, as is shown by this map. I see it stated here that there is a vast scope of territory, embracing an area of over two million square miles, rich in every element of material wealth and commercial prosperity, all tributary to Duluth. Look at it, sir (pointing to the map). Here are inexhaustible mines of gold, immeasurable veins of silver, impenetrable depths of boundless forest, vast coal-measures, wide, extended plains of richest pasturage, all, all embraced in this vast territory, which must, in the very nature of things, empty the untold treasures of its commerce into the lap of Duluth. (Laughter.)

Look at it, sir! (Pointing to the map.) Do not you see from these broad, brown lines drawn around this immense territory that the enterprising inhabitants of Duluth intend some day to inclose it all in one vast corral, so that its commerce will be bound to go there, whether it would or not? (Great laughter.) And here, sir (still pointing to the map), I find within a convenient distance the Piegan Indians, which, of all the many accessories to the glory of Duluth, I consider by far the most inestimable. For, sir, I have been told that when the smallpox breaks out among the women and children of that famous tribe, as it sometimes does, they afford the finest subjects in the world for the strategical experiments of any enterprising military hero who desires to improve himself in the noble art of war (laughter); especially for any valiant lieutenant general, whose

> "Trenchant blade, Toledo trusty,
> For want of fighting has grown rusty,
> And eats into itself for lack
> Of somebody to hew and hack."

(Great laughter.)

. . . .

And here, sir, recurring to this map, I find in the immediate vicinity of the Piegans "vast herds of buffalo" and "immense fields of rich wheat lands."

(Here the hammer fell.)

(Many cries: "Go on!" "Go on!")

The Speaker: Is there objection to the gentleman from Kentucky continuing his remarks? The Chair hears none. The gentleman will proceed.

Mr. Knott: I was remarking, sir, upon these vast "wheat fields" represented on this map as in the immediate neighborhood of the buffaloes and the Piegans, and was about to say that the idea of there being these immense wheat fields in the very heart of a wilderness, hundreds and hundreds of miles beyond the utmost verge of civilization, may appear to some gentlemen as rather incongruous, as rather too great a strain on the "blankets" of veracity. But to my mind there is no difficulty in the matter whatever. . . .

Here, you will observe (pointing to the map), are the buffaloes, directly between the Piegans and Duluth; and here, right on the road to Duluth, are the Creeks. Now, sir, when the buffaloes are sufficiently fat from grazing on these immense wheat fields, you see it will be the easiest thing in the world for the Piegans to drive them on down, stay all night with their friends, the Creeks, and go into Duluth in the morning. (Great laughter.) I think I see them now, sir, a vast herd of buffaloes, with their heads down, their eyes glaring, their nostrils dilated, their tongues out, and their tails curled over their back, tearing along toward Duluth, with about a thousand Piegans on their grass-bellied ponies yelling at their heels! (Great laughter.) On they come! And as they sweep past the Creeks, they join in the chase, and away they all go, yelling, bellowing, ripping, and tearing along, amid clouds of dust, until the last buffalo is safely penned in the stockyards of Duluth! (Shouts of laughter.)

Sir, I might stand here for hours and hours, and expatiate with rapture upon the gorgeous prospects of Duluth, as depicted upon this map. But human life is too short and the time of this House far too valuable to allow me to linger longer upon the delightful theme. (Laughter.) I think every gentleman on this floor is as well satisfied as I am that Duluth is destined to become the commercial metropolis of the universe, and that this road should be built at once. . . .

MARK TWAIN

(SAMUEL L. CLEMENS)

Letter to the Knights of St. Patrick

1876

To the Chairman:

I am very sorry that I cannot be with the Knights of St. Patrick tomorrow evening. In this centennial year we ought to find a peculiar pleasure in doing honor to the memory of a man whose good name has endured through fourteen centuries. We ought to find pleasure in it for the reason that at this time we naturally have a fellow-feeling for such a man. He wrought a great work in his day. He found Ireland a prosperous republic, and looked about him to see if he might find some useful thing to turn his hand to. He observed that the president of that republic was in the habit of sheltering his great officials from deserved punishment, so he lifted up his staff and smote him, and he died. He found that the secretary of war had been so unbecomingly economical as to have laid up $12,000 a year out of a salary of $8000, and he killed him. He found that the secretary of the interior always prayed over every separate and distinct barrel of salt beef that was intended for the unconverted savage, and then kept that beef himself, so he killed him also. He found that the secretary of the navy knew more about handling suspicious claims than he did about handling a ship, and he at once made an end of him. He found that a very foul private secretary had been engineered through a sham trial, so he destroyed him. He discovered that the congress which pretended to prodigious virtue was very anxious to investigate an ambassador who had dishonored the country abroad, but was equally anxious to prevent the appointment of any spotless man to a similar post; that this congress had no God but party; no system of morals but party policy; no vision but a bat's vision, and no reason or excuse for existing anyhow. Therefore he massacred that congress to the last man.

When he had finished his great work, he said, in his figurative way, "Lo, I have destroyed all the reptiles in Ireland."

St. Patrick had no politics; his sympathies lay with the right—that was politics enough. When he came across a reptile, he forgot to inquire whether he was a democrat or a republican, but simply exalted his staff and "let him have it." Honored be his name—I wish we had him here to trim us up for the centennial. But that cannot be. His staff, which was the symbol of real, not sham reform, is idle. However, we still have with us the symbol of Truth—George Washington's little hatchet—for I know where they've buried it.

Yours truly,
MARK TWAIN.

BILL NYE

An Acceptance

Office of Daily Boomerang, Laramie City, Wy.
August 9, 1882.

My Dear General:

I have received by telegraph the news of my nomination by the President and my confirmation by the Senate, as postmaster at Laramie, and wish to extend my thanks for the same.

I have ordered an entirely new set of boxes and postoffice outfit, including new corrugated cuspidors for the lady clerks.

I look upon the appointment as a great triumph of eternal truth over error and wrong. It is one of the epochs, I may say, in the Nation's onward march toward political purity and perfection. I do not know when I have noticed any stride in the affairs of state, which so thoroughly impressed me with its wisdom.

Now that we are co-workers in the same department, I trust that you will not feel shy or backward about consulting me at any time relative to matters concerning postoffice affairs. Be perfectly frank with me, and feel free to bring anything of that kind right to me. Do not feel reluctant because I may at times appear haughty and indifferent, cold or absurd. Perhaps you do not think I know the difference between a general delivery window and a three-em quad, but that is a mistake.

My general information is far beyond my years.

With profoundest regard, and a hearty endorsement of the policy of the President and the Senate, whatever it may be,

I remain, sincerely yours,
Bill Nye, P.M.

A Resign

Postoffice, Divan,
Laramie City, W.T.,
Oct. 1, 1883.

To the President of the United States:

Sir: I beg leave at this time officially to tender my resignation as postmaster at this place, and in due form to deliver the great seal and the key to the front door of the office. The safe combination is set on the numbers 33, 66 and 99, though I do not remember at this moment which comes first, or how many times you revolve the knob, or in which direction you should turn it first to make it operate.

There is some mining stock in my private drawer in the safe, which I have not yet removed. It is a luxury, but you may have it. I have decided to keep a horse instead of this mining stock. The horse may not be so pretty, but it will cost less to keep him.

You will find the postal cards that have not been used under the distributing table, and the coal down in the cellar. If the stove draws too hard, close the damper in the pipe and shut the general delivery window.

Looking over my stormy and eventful administration as postmaster here, I find abundant cause for thanksgiving. At the time I entered upon the duties of my office the department was not yet on a paying basis. It was not even self-sustaining. Since that time, with the active cooperation of the chief executive and the heads of the department, I have been able to make our postal system a paying one, and on top of that I am now able to reduce the tariff on average-sized letters from three cents to two. I might add that this is rather too too, but I will not say anything that might seem undignified in an official resignation which is to become a matter of history.

Acting under the advice of Gen. Hatton, a year ago, I removed the feather bed with which my predecessor, Deacon Hayford, had bolstered up his administration by stuffing the window, and substituted glass. Finding nothing in the book of instructions to postmasters which made the feather bed a part of my official duties, I filed it away in an obscure place and burned it in effigy, also in the gloaming.

It was not long after I had taken my official oath before an era of unexampled prosperity opened for the American people. The price of beef rose to a remarkable altitude, and other vegetables commanded a good figure and a ready market. We then began to make active preparations for the introduction of the strawberry-roan two-cent stamps and the black-and-tan postal note. One reform has crowded upon the heels of another, until the country is to-day upon the foam-crested wave of permanent prosperity.

Mr. President, I cannot close this letter without thanking yourself and the heads of the departments at Washington for your active, cheery and prompt cooperation in these matters. You may do as you see fit, of course, about incorporating this idea into your Thanksgiving proclamation, but rest assured it would not be ill-timed or inopportune. It is not alone a credit to myself. It reflects credit upon the administration also.

I need not say that I herewith transmit my resignation with great sorrow and genuine regret. We have toiled on together month after month, asking for no reward except the innate consciousness of rectitude and the salary as fixed by law. Now we are to separate. Here the roads seem to fork, as it were, and you and I, and the cabinet, must leave each other at this point.

You will find the key under the door-mat, and you had better turn the cat out at night when you close the office. If she does not go readily, you can make it clearer to her mind by throwing the cancelling stamp at her.

If Deacon Hayford does not pay up his box-rent, you might as well put his mail in the general delivery, and when Bob Head gets drunk and insists on a letter from one of his wives every day in the week, you can salute him through the box delivery with an old Queen Anne tomahawk, which you will find near the Etruscan water-pail. This will not in any manner surprise either of these parties.

Tears are unavailing! I once more become a private citizen, clothed only with the right to read such postal cards as may be addressed to me, and to curse the inefficiency of the postoffice department. I believe the voting class to be divided into two parties; viz., those who are in the postal service, and those who are mad because they cannot receive a registered letter every fifteen minutes of each day, including Sunday.

Mr. President, as an official of this Government I now retire. My term of office would not expire until 1886. I must, therefore, beg pardon for my eccentricity in resigning. It will be best, perhaps, to keep the heart-breaking news from the ears of European powers until the dangers of a financial panic are fully past. Then hurl it broadcast with a sickening thud.

AMBROSE BIERCE

*The Humble Peasant**

An Office Seeker whom the President had ordered out of Washington was watering the homeward highway with his tears.

"Ah," he said, "how disastrous is ambition! how unsatisfying its rewards! how terrible its disappointments! Behold yonder peasant tilling his field in peace and contentment! He rises with the lark, passes the day in wholesome toil and lies down at night to pleasant dreams. In the mad struggle for place and power he has no part; the roar of the strife reaches his ear like the distant murmur of the ocean. Happy, thrice happy man!

* from *Fantastic Fables*.

I will approach him and bask in the sunshine of his humble felicity. Peasant, hail!"

Leaning upon his rake, the Peasant returned the salutation with a nod, but said nothing.

"My friend," said the Office Seeker, "you see before you the wreck of an ambitious man—ruined by the pursuit of place and power. This morning when I set out from the national capital—"

"Stranger," the Peasant interrupted, "if you're going back there soon maybe you wouldn't mind using your influence to make me Postmaster at Smith's Corners."

The traveler passed on.

The Honest Citizen*

A Political Preferment, labeled with its price, was canvassing the State to find a purchaser. One day it offered itself to a Truly Good Man who, after examining the label and finding that the price was twice as great as he was willing to pay, spurned the Political Preferment from his door. Then the People said: "Behold, this is an honest citizen!" And the Truly Good Man humbly confessed that it was true.

FINLEY PETER DUNNE

Reform Administration

1902

"Why is it," asked Mr. Hennessy, "that a rayform administhration always goes to th' bad?"

"I'll tell ye," said Mr. Dooley. "I tell ye ivrything an' I'll tell ye this.

* from *Fantastic Fables*.

In th' first place 'tis a gr-reat mistake to think that annywan ra-aly
wants to rayform. Ye niver heerd iv a man rayformin' himsilf. He'll rayform other people gladly. He likes to do it. But a healthy man'll niver
rayform while he has th' strenth. A man doesn't rayform till his will has
been impaired so he hasn't power to resist what th' pa-apers calls th'
blandishments iv th' timpter. An' that's thruer in politics thin annywhere else.

"But a rayformer don't see it. A rayformer thinks he was ilicted because he was a rayformer, whin th' thruth iv th' matther is he was ilicted
because no wan knew him. Ye can always ilict a man in this counthry on
that platform. If I was runnin' f'r office, I'd change me name, an' have
printed on me cards: 'Give him a chanst; he can't be worse.' He's ilicted
because th' people don't know him an' do know th' other la-ad; because
Mrs. Casey's oldest boy was clubbed be a polisman, because we cudden't
get wather above th' third story wan day, because th' sthreet car didn't
stop f'r us, because th' Flannigans bought a pianny, because we was near
run over be a mail wagon, because th' saloons are open Sundah night,
because they're not open all day an' because we're tired seein' th' same
face at th' window whin we go down to pay th' wather taxes. Th' rayformer don't know this. He thinks you an' me, Hinnissy, has been
watchin' his spotless career f'r twenty years, that we've read all he had to
say on th' evils iv pop'lar sufferage befure th' Society f'r the Bewildher-
mint iv th' Poor, an' that we're achin' in ivry joint to have him dhrag us
be th' hair iv th' head fr'm th' flowin' bowl an' th' short card game, make
good citizens iv us an' sind us to th' pinitinchry. So th' minyit he gets
into th' job he begins a furyous attimpt to convart us into what we've
been thryin' not to be iver since we come into th' wurruld.

"In th' coorse iv th' twenty years that he spint attimptin' to get office,
he managed to poke a few warrum laws conthrollin' th' pleasures iv th'
poor into th' stachoo book, because no wan cared about thim or because
they made business betther f'r th' polis, an' whin he's in office, he calls
up th' Cap'n iv the polis an' says he: 'If these laws ar-re bad laws th' way
to end thim is to enfoorce thim.' Somebody told him that, Hinnissy. It
isn't thrue, d'ye mind. I don't care who said it, not if 'twas Willum
Shakespere. It isn't thrue. Laws ar-re made to throuble people an' th'
more throuble they make th' longer they stay on th' stachoo book. But
th' polis don't ast anny questions: Says they: 'They'll be less money in
th' job but we need some recreation,' an' that night a big copper comes
down th' sthreet, sees me settin' out on th' front stoop with me countenance dhraped with a tin pail, fans me with his club an' runs me in. Th'

woman nex' dure is locked up f'r sthringin' a clothes line on th' roof, Hannigan's boy Tim gets tin days f'r keepin' a goat, th' polis resarves are called out to protict th' vested rights iv property against th' haynyous pushcart man, th' stations is crowded with felons charged with maintainin' a hose conthrary to th' stachoos made an' provided, an' th' tindherline is all over town. A rayformer don't think annything has been accomplished if they'se a vacant bedroom in th' pinitinchry. His motto is 'Arrest that man.'

"Whin a rayformer is ilicted he promises ye a business administhration. Some people want that but I don't. Th' American business man is too fly. He's all right, d'ye mind. I don't say annything again' him. He is what Hogan calls th' boolwarks iv pro-gress, an' we cudden't get on without him even if his scales are a little too quick on th' dhrop. But he ought to be left to dale with his akels. 'Tis a shame to give him a place where he can put th' comether on millions iv people that has had no business thrainin' beyond occasionally handin' a piece iv debased money to a car conductor on a cold day. A reg'lar pollytician can't give away an alley without blushin', but a business man who is in pollytics jus' to see that th' civil sarvice law gets thurly enfoorced, will give Lincoln Park an' th' public libr'y to th' beef thrust, charge an admission price to th' lake front an' make it a felony f'r annywan to buy stove polish outside iv his store, an' have it all put down to public improvemints with a pitcher iv him in th' corner stone.

"Fortchnitly, Hinnissy, a rayformer is seldom a business man. He thinks he is, but business men know diff'rent. They know what he is. He thinks business an' honesty is th' same thing. He does, indeed. He's got thim mixed because they dhress alike. His idee is that all he has to do to make a business administhration is to have honest men ar-round him. Wrong. I'm not sayin', mind ye, that a man can't do good work an' be honest at th' same time. But whin I'm hirin' a la-ad I find out first whether he is onto his job, an' afther a few years I begin to suspect that he is honest, too. Manny a dishonest man can lay brick sthraight an' manny a man that wudden't steal ye'er spoons will break ye'er furniture. I don't want Father Kelly to hear me, but I'd rather have a competint man who wud steal if I give him a chanst, but I won't, do me plumbin' thin a person that wud scorn to help himsilf but didn't know how to wipe a joint. Ivry man ought to be honest to start with, but to give a man an office jus' because he's honest is like ilictin' him to Congress because he's a pathrite, because he don't bate his wife or because he always wears a right boot on th' right foot. A man ought to be honest to start with an' afther that he ought to be crafty. A pollytician who's on'y honest is jus' th' same as bein' out in a winther storm without anny clothes on.

"Another thing about rayform administhrations is they always think th' on'y man that ought to hold a job is a lawyer. Th' raison is that in th' coorse iv his thrainin' a lawyer larns enough about ivrything to make a good front on anny subject to annybody who doesn't know about it. So whin th' rayform administhration comes in th' mayor says: 'Who'll we make chief iv polis in place iv th' misguided ruffyan who has held th' job f'r twinty years?' 'Th' man f'r th' place,' says th' mayor's adviser, 'is Arthur Lightout,' he says. 'He's an ixcillent lawyer, Yale, '95, an' is well up on polis matthers. Las' year he read a paper on "The fine polis foorce iv London" befure th' annyal meetin' iv th' S'ciety f'r Ladin' th' Mulligan Fam'ly to a Betther an' Harder Life. Besides,' he says, 'he's been in th' milishy an' th' foorce needs a man who'll be afraid not to shoot in case iv public disturbance.' So Arthur takes hold iv th' constabulary an' in a year th' polis can all read Emerson an' th' burglars begin puttin' up laddhers an' block an' tackles befure eight A.M. An' so it is on ivry side. A lawyer has charge iv the city horse-shoein', another wan is clanin' th' sthreets, th' author iv 'Gasamagoo on torts' is thryin' to dispose iv th' ashes be throwin' thim in th' air on a windy day, an' th' bright boy that took th' silver ware f'r th' essay on *ne exeats* an' their relation to life is plannin' a uniform that will be sarviceable an' constitchoochinal f'r th' brave men that wurruks on th' city dumps. An' wan day th' main rayformer goes out expictin' to rayceive th' thanks iv th' community an' th' public that has jus' got out iv jail f'r lettin' th' wather run too long in th' bath tub rises up an' cries: 'Back to th' Univarsity Settlemint.' Th' man with th' di'mon' in his shirt front comes home an' pushes th' honest lawyers down th' steps, an' a dishonest horse shoer shoes th' city's horses well, an' a crooked plumber does th' city's plumbin' securely, an' a rascally polisman that may not be avarse to pickin' up a bet but will always find out whin Pathrolman Scanlan slept on his beat, takes hold iv th' polis foorce, an' we raysume our nachral condition iv illagal merrimint. An' th' rayformer spinds th' rest iv his life tellin' us where we are wrong. He's good at that. On'y he don't undherstand that people wud rather be wrong an' comfortable thin right in jail."

"I don't like a rayformer," said Mr. Hennessy.

"Or anny other raypublican," said Mr. Dooley.

SENATOR GEORGE WASHINGTON PLUNKITT*

The Curse of Civil Service Reform

1905

This civil service law is the biggest fraud of the age. It is the curse of the nation. There can't be no real patriotism while it lasts. How are you goin' to interest our young men in their country if you have no offices to give them when they work for their party? Just look at things in this city today. There are ten thousand good offices, but we can't get at more than a few hundred of them. How are we goin' to provide for the thousands of men who worked for the Tammany ticket? It can't be done. These men were full of patriotism a short time ago. They expected to be servin' their city, but when we tell them that we can't place them, do you think their patriotism is goin' to last? Not much. They say: "What's the use of workin' for your country anyhow? There's nothin' in the game." And what can they do? I don't know, but I'll tell you what I do know. I know more than one young man in past years who worked for the ticket and was just overflowin' with patriotism, but when he was knocked out by the civil service humbug he got to hate his country and became an Anarchist.

This ain't no exaggeration. I have good reason for sayin' that most of the Anarchists in this city today are men who ran up against civil service examinations. Isn't it enough to make a man sour on his country when he wants to serve it and won't be allowed unless he answers a lot of fool questions about the number of cubic inches of water in the Atlantic and the quality of sand in the Sahara desert? There was once a bright young man in my district who tackled one of these examinations. The next I heard of him he had settled down in Herr Most's saloon smokin' an drinkin' beer and talkin' socialism all day. Before that time he had never

---

* Recorded by William L. Riordan in *Plunkitt of Tammany Hall.*

drank anything but whisky. I knew what was comin' when a young Irish-
man drops whisky and takes to beer and long pipes in a German saloon.
That young man is today one of the wildest Anarchists in town. And just
to think! He might be a patriot but for that cussed civil service.

Say, did you hear about that Civil Service Reform Association kickin'
because the tax commissioners want to put their fifty-five deputies on
the exempt list, and fire the outfit left to them by Low? That's civil
service for you. Just think! Fifty-five Republicans and mugwumps
holdin' $3000 and $4000 and $5000 jobs in the tax department when
1555 good Tammany men are ready and willin' to take their places! It's
an outrage! What did the people mean when they voted for Tammany?
What is representative government, anyhow? Is it all a fake that this is a
government of the people, by the people and for the people? If it isn't a
fake, then why isn't the people's voice obeyed and Tammany men put
in all the offices?

When the people elected Tammany, they knew just what they were
doin'. We didn't put up any false pretenses. We didn't go in for humbug
civil service and all that rot. We stood as we have always stood, for re-
wardin' the men that won the victory. They call that the spoils system.
All right; Tammany is for the spoils system, and when we go in we fire
every anti-Tammany man from office that can be fired under the law. It's
an elastic sort of law and you can bet it will be stretched to the limit.
Of course the Republican State Civil Service Board will stand in the way
of our local Civil Service Commission all it can; but say!—suppose we
carry the State sometime, won't we fire the upstate Board all right? Or
we'll make it work in harmony with the local board, and that means
that Tammany will get everything in sight. I know that the civil service
humbug is stuck into the constitution, too, but, as Tim Campbell said:
"What's the constitution among friends?"

Say, the people's voice is smothered by the cursed civil service law; it is
the root of all evil in our government. You hear of this thing or that
thing goin' wrong in the nation, the State or the city. Look down beneath the surface and you can trace everything wrong to civil service. I
have studied the subject and I know. The civil service humbug is under-
minin' our institutions and if a halt ain't called soon this great republic
will tumble down like a Park Avenue house when they were buildin'
the subway, and on its ruins will rise another Russian government.

This is an awful serious proposition. Free silver and the tariff and
imperialism and the Panama Canal are triflin' issues when compared to
it. We could worry along without any of these things, but civil service is

sappin' the foundation of the whole shootin' match. Let me argue it out for you. I ain't up on sillygisms, but I can give you some arguments that nobody can answer.

First, this great and glorious country was built up by political parties; second, parties can't hold together if their workers don't get the offices when they win; third, if the parties go to pieces, the government they built up must go to pieces, too; fourth, then there'll be h____ to pay.

Could anything be clearer than that? Say, honest now; can you answer that argument? Of course you won't deny that the government was built up by the great parties. That's history, and you can't go back of the returns. As to my second proposition, you can't deny that either. When parties can't get offices, they'll bust. They ain't far from the bustin' point now, with all this civil service business keepin' most of the good things from them. How are you goin' to keep up patriotism if this thing goes on? You can't do it. Let me tell you that patriotism has been dying out fast for the last twenty years. Before then when a party won, its workers got everything in sight. That was somethin' to make a man patriotic. Now, when a party wins and its men come forward and ask for their rewards, the reply is, "Nothin' doin', unless you can answer a list of questions about Egyptian mummies and how many years it will take for a bird to wear out a mass of iron as big as the earth by steppin' on it once in a century?"

I have studied politics and men for forty-five years, and I see how things are driftin'. Sad indeed is the change that has come over the young men, even in my district, where I try to keep up the fire of patriotism by gettin' a lot of jobs for my constituents, whether Tammany is in or out. The boys and men don't get excited any more when they see a United States flag or hear "The Star-Spangled Banner." They don't care no more for firecrackers on the Fourth of July. And why should they? What is there in it for them? They know that no matter how hard they work for their country in a campaign, the jobs will go to fellows who can tell about the mummies and the bird steppin' on the iron. Are you surprised then that the young men of the country are beginnin' to look coldly on the flag and don't care to put up a nickel for firecrackers?

Say, let me tell of one case. After the battle of San Juan Hill, the Americans found a dead man with a light complexion, red hair and blue eyes. They could see he wasn't a Spaniard, although he had on a Spanish uniform. Several officers looked him over, and then a private of the Seventy-first Regiment saw him and yelled, "Good Lord, that's

Flaherty." That man grew up in my district, and he was once the most patriotic American boy on the West Side. He couldn't see a flag without yellin' himself hoarse.

Now, how did he come to be lying dead with a Spanish uniform on? I found out all about it, and I'll vouch for the story. Well, in the municipal campaign of 1897, that young man, chockful of patriotism, worked day and night for the Tammany ticket. Tammany won, and the young man determined to devote his life to the service of the city. He picked out a place that would suit him, and sent in his application to the head of department. He got a reply that he must take a civil service examination to get the place. He didn't know what these examinations were, so he went, all lighthearted, to the Civil Service Board. He read the questions about the mummies, the bird on the iron, and all the other fool questions—and he left that office an enemy of the country that he had loved so well. The mummies and the bird blasted his patriotism. He went to Cuba, enlisted in the Spanish army at the breakin' out of the war, and died fightin' his country.

That is but one victim of the infamous civil service. If that young man had not run up against the civil examination, but had been allowed to serve his country as he wished, he would be in a good office today, drawin' a good salary. Ah, how many young men have had their patriotism blasted in the same way!

Now, what is goin' to happen when civil service crushes out patriotism? Only one thing can happen: the republic will go to pieces. Then a czar or a sultan will turn up, which brings me to the fourthly of my argument—that is, there will be h____ to pay. And that ain't no lie.

Tammany the Only Lastin' Democracy

1905

I've seen more than one hundred "Democracies" rise and fall in New York City in the last quarter of a century. At least a half-dozen new so-called Democratic organizations are formed every year. All of them go in to down Tammany and take its place, but they seldom last more than a year or two, while Tammany's like the everlastin' rocks, the eternal hills and the blockades on the "L" road—it goes on forever.

I recall offhand the County Democracy, which was the only real opponent Tammany has had in my time, the Irving Hall Democracy, the New York State Democracy, the German-American Democracy, the Protection Democracy, the Independent County Democracy, the Greater New York Democracy, the Jimmy O'Brien Democracy, the Delicatessen Dealers' Democracy, the Silver Democracy, and the Italian Democracy. Not one of them is livin' today, although I hear somethin' about the ghost of the Greater New York Democracy bein' seen on Broadway once or twice a year.

In the old days of the County Democracy, a new Democratic organization meant some trouble for Tammany—for a time anyhow. Nowadays a new Democracy means nothin' at all except that about a dozen bone-hunters have got together for one campaign only to try to induce Tammany to give them a job or two, or in order to get in with the reformers for the same purpose. You might think that it would cost a lot of money to get up one of these organizations and keep it goin' for even one campaign, but, Lord bless you! it costs next to nothin'. Jimmy O'Brien brought the manufacture of "Democracies" down to an exact science, and reduced the cost of production so as to bring it within the reach of all. Any man with $50 can now have a "Democracy" of his own.

I've looked into the industry, and can give rock-bottom figures. Here's the items of cost of a new "Democracy":

A dinner to twelve bone-hunters	$12.00
A speech on Jeffersonian Democracy	00.00
A proclamation of principles (typewriting)	2.00
Rent of a small room one month for headquarters	12.00
Stationery	2.00
Twelve secondhand chairs	6.00
One secondhand table	2.00
Twenty-nine cuspidors	9.00
Sign painting	5.00
Total	$50.00

Is there any reason for wonder, then, that "Democracies" spring up all over when a municipal campaign is comin' on? If you land even one small job, you get a big return on your investment. You don't have to pay for advertisin' in the papers. The New York papers tumble over one another to give columns to any new organization that comes out against Tammany. In describin' the formation of a "Democracy" on the $50 basis, accordin' to the items I give, the papers would say somethin' like this: "The organization of the Delicatessen Democracy last night threatens the existence of Tammany Hall. It is a grand move for a new and pure Democracy in this city. Well may the Tammany leaders be alarmed; panic has already broke loose in Fourteenth Street. The vast crowd that gathered at the launching of the new organization, the stirrin' speeches and the proclamation of principles mean that, at last, there is an uprisin' that will end Tammany's career of corruption. The Delicatessen Democracy will open in a few days spacious headquarters where all true Democrats may gather and prepare for the fight."

Say, ain't some of the papers awful gullible about politics? Talk about come-ons from Iowa or Texas—they ain't in it with the childlike simplicity of these papers.

It's a wonder to me that more men don't go into this kind of manufacturin' industry. It has bigger profits generally than the green-goods business and none of the risks. And you don't have to invest as much as the green-goods men. Just see what good things some of these "Democracies" got in the last few years! The New York State Democracy in 1897 landed a Supreme Court Justiceship for the man who manufactured the concern—a fourteen-year term at $17,500 a year, that is $245,000. You see, Tammany was rather scared that year and was bluffed into givin' this job to get the support of the State Democracy, which, by the way, went out of business quick and prompt the day after it got this big plum. The next year the German Democracy landed a place of the same kind. And then see how the Greater New York Democracy worked the game on the reformers in 1901! The men who managed this concern were former Tammanyites who had lost their grip; yet they made the Citizens' Union innocents believe that they were the real thing in the way of reformers, and that they had 100,000 votes back of them. They got the Borough President of Manhattan, the President of the Board of Aldermen, the Register and a lot of lesser places. It was the greatest bunco game of modern times.

And then, in 1894, when Strong was elected mayor, what a harvest it was for all the little "Democracies" that was made to order that year! Every one of them got somethin' good. In one case, all the nine men in an organization got jobs payin' from $2000 to $5000. I happen to know exactly what it cost to manufacture that organization. It was $42.04.

They left out the stationery, and had only twenty-three cuspidors. The extra four cents was for two postage stamps.

The only reason I can imagine why more men don't go into this industry is because they don't know about it. And just here it strikes me that it might not be wise to publish what I've said. Perhaps if it gets to be known what a snap this manufacture of "Democracies" is, all the green-goods men, the bunco-steerers, and the young Napoleons of finance will go into it and the public will be humbugged more than it has been. But, after all, what difference would it make? There's always a certain number of suckers and a certain number of men lookin' for a chance to take them in, and the suckers are sure to be took one way or another. It's the everlastin' law of demand and supply.

A. J. LIEBLING

The Alderman*

1952

A superb specimen of a Chicago alderman is Paddy Bauler, who represents the Forty-third Ward. Bauler's De Luxe Gardens, at North Avenue and Sedgwick, is as sedate a groggery as you will come upon in the city of Chicago. It occupies the former premises of the Immigrant State Bank, which went under in the crash, and the original lavatory solemnity of the interior's marble decor has never been altered. The high ceilings, the grilles barring the way to the vaults, and all the other accessories designed to nurture unfounded confidence remain to warn of the uncertainty of appearances, and the patrons conduct themselves as discreetly as men about to solicit a loan. It is here that the Alderman, who is also a member of the Cook County Democratic Committee, holds court, like Saint Louis of France under his tree of judgment, from nine to eleven each evening, when he is not travelling in Europe. Paddy travels often, and always in style; he says that trips to places like Rome

* from *Chicago: The Second City.*

and Palestine help him to understand the different kinds of people in his ward. The saloon's license is in his brother's name. Paddy has apparently done well at making his aldermanic salary of five thousand dollars a year stretch.

The Alderman is a mountain—or, rather, since his contours are soft, a gravel dump—of a man, with a wide pink face wearing an expression of mock truculence. Twenty years ago, when he was courting the attention of Mayor Tony Cermak, he used to roll about the floor in wrestling matches with himself to make His Honor laugh; he weighed two hundred and seventy-five pounds then, and he has put on several ounces since. He is essentially decorous, however; a few nights before Christmas of 1933 he shot a policeman who wanted him to serve a drink after hours. Paddy had locked up and was depositing the receipts from a Forty-third Ward Democratic Christmas Fund benefit show in the bank vault when the policeman came to the door raucously demanding admittance. Paddy went out to quiet him. "Johnny, why have I got this coming to me for?" the Alderman roared plaintively. "I never done anything to you." Then he shot the policeman, and nobody has used bad language or tried to get a drink after hours in the De Luxe Gardens since. Only a few years ago, a man named Kane, who was opposing Paddy in the Democratic primary in the ward, complained because the store he was using for his headquarters was bombed one night. Kane claimed to be a close friend of Mayor Kennelly's. The Alderman said things were coming to a pretty pass when a fellow would bomb his own headquarters for publicity. "I wouldn't have minded it so much," he told reporters, "if the guy hadn't run up there and stuck Kennelly's picture in the broken window before the cops came." Paddy's posters in a recent election campaign said, with elegant restraint, "Elect Mathias J. Bauler. He will appreciate your vote." Paddy doesn't have to make himself known to the voters in the Forty-third. Once, he says, he told a campaign audience that he had been the first child ever christened in St. Teresa's Church, is his ward. The pastor looked up the baptismal record and, sure enough, Paddy had been.

Paddy's father was born in Germany, and his mother in Illinois, of German descent. Like many other men of non-Irish descent who spend their lives in politics, he has acquired a Celtic manner that sometimes imposes on him, just as some non-Frenchmen who work their way up in the restaurant business begin to think of themselves as French. Paddy's ward, it happens, is so ethnologically scrambled that there is no great political profit in being any particular kind of European, but among politicians the rule is: When in doubt, be Irish. "I've almost forgotten my name is Mathias," Paddy says.

There is no entertainment—not even a dice girl—in the De Luxe Gardens. North Avenue, which begins near Lake Michigan and runs straight west through the dimness until it hits the city line, lies only a little over a mile and a half north of the Loop, but it is the axis of an autonomous dreariness. The eastern end of the avenue, which is in Paddy's ward, has a small night life, with a German-language movie house, one or two German restaurants with zither players, and some Hungarian saloons, through which wander, in the course of the evening, a few fiddlers, who say that they are gypsies but that they have forgotten the Old Country music, because they are never asked for it. The favorite request numbers of Chicago Hungarians are "Tennessee Waltz" and "When Irish Eyes Are Smiling." Also, there are numerous bars that use low prices as their chief sales argument. These places seem purposely bare and flimsy, as if to assure the customers that nothing is being wasted on overhead. The liquor-license fee is low in Chicago, and the sheer number of saloons, even in backwash neighborhoods, is amazing. Curbstones are high, often consisting of two steps instead of one, and drunks sometimes take astonishing falls. These are seldom fatal. "You're like all us Polacks," I once heard a North Avenue bartender say to a patron who had had all he could drink. "One ain't enough and a thousand ain't enough." Then the patron went out and crashed on his head. "You can't kill a Polack," the bartender said.

The Forty-third Ward is one of the most diversified in the city, containing in its lakeward corner half of the Gold Coast, including the two Ambassador Hotels, the Cardinal's Residence, and Colonel Robert R. McCormick's town house. Toward the ward's southwest frontier there is a Negro slum (not the great one but an isolated growth), in its center is the residue of the original German colony, and within its boundaries are also blocs of Nisei, Finns, Hungarians, Italians, Irish, Syrians, Armenians, Swedes, and Poles, and a couple of neighborhoods of flats and one-family residences inhabited by solid settlers of the middle class from Iowa and Nebraska. Parts of the ward look like a city, parts like a pleasant suburb, and large tracts like the less favored sections of a blighted mill town. The principle of Paddy's rule is simple. "Everybody gets something," he says.

During one of my longer stays in Chicago I lived in the Forty-third, and I ran across a friend of mine—and a constituent of Paddy's—who volunteered to take me over to the De Luxe Gardens to meet the gentleman. The friend, a fellow named Martin, was brought up in the ward, where his father, a carpenter and novelist born in Finland, owned a house. Martin started out to be a novelist, too, but somehow landed in the advertising business, which keeps him prosperous and embarrassed. He is a victim of his present environment, in which literature no longer flourishes; if he had been born ten years earlier in Chicago, I am convinced, he would have been a novelist, proud and famishing. We found Paddy sitting at a table with one of his executive assistants, a younger man, who also owns a saloon and is training to be an officeholder. "I am always here at nine o'clock, in case anybody has a brother that has been arrested or a relative he wants to get into Cook County Hospital or anything like that," the Alderman said. "I am A-1 with the Hospital," he went on, and explained that without support, a candidate for admission has to wait his turn. "You got to keep in touch," he said. "Things like that the precinct captain should be on the lookout for, if they are in his precinct, but you can't always depend on them."

Paddy told me that there were forty thousand votes in his ward, and that in his capacity as Democratic Committeeman he had seventy-six precinct captains, each with a city, state, or county job. "We have some very nice jobs to give out, from two hundred and seventy up to three hundred and fifty dollars a month," he said. "And all the fellow has to do is keep track of the votes in his precinct and get out the Democratic voters when it counts. If he says there will be one hundred votes for us and eighty for the other fellow, I would rather have it come out that way than one hundred and fifty to twenty, because if it comes out the second way, it shows the precinct captain don't know his business, or he is faking. I got to know within one percent. That's how I know if I got good precinct captains. Then I got to tell the county chairman how the vote will be in the ward. That's how he knows if he's got a good committeeman. Naturally, if I got a bum precinct captain, I got to get rid of him and give that city job to a hustler, because if I got enough bum captains, it will throw my figures out. Then I am a bum, too."

"And have you always been able to tell what the vote in the ward will be?" I asked.

"I never been off the public payroll in forty years," the Alderman replied, with modest indirection. "The second big thing a precinct captain has to do is get out the vote. The way he does that is by knowing everybody in his precinct and being nice to them. Everybody needs a favor sometimes, but some people are too dumb to ask for it. So I say to my captains, 'If you notice a hole in the sidewalk in front of a fellow's house, call on him a week before election and ask him if he would like it fixed. It could never do any harm to find out.' When you got a good precinct captain, you got a jewel. Like last year. It was an off year and hard to get people interested, but we needed some votes to elect local candidates. I asked a young fellow named Barney McGuirl how many votes he thought he'd get out in his precinct and he said about ninety-five. 'Well,' I said, 'Barney, I know you got five beautiful little children and a bailiff's salary does not go as far as it should,' I said, 'although I hope to get you something a little better soon. But if you get me a hundred and fifty votes just this time, I will present them angels with ten dollars apiece.' He got me a hundred and ninety-seven.

"We got nice people in this ward," Paddy went on. "Nice Germans, nice Poles, nice Irish, nice Jews, nice colored people, and so on, and recently we been getting a lot of Japanese, which are moving north across Division Street, and they are a very nice high-class class of Japanese. I try to see that nobody gets shut out on the jobs. The Forty-third Ward, I always say when I make a speech, is like the United Nations."

The Gold Coast, although it confers social éclat on the ward, is not Paddy's favorite corner. "The type people you got over there don't need a job as bailiff, so you got to rely on amateurs for your organization work," he said. Moreover, he holds that the inhabitants of the Gold Coast, many of whom are Republicans, expect more than their share of service. "They complain about dirty streets and bad lighting and fads like that, and about they never got enough cops, and when you come right down to it, they got only one vote apiece, like everybody else," he told me. "But it's a fine ward. We had the Massacree in this ward. Did you know that?"

"The what?" I asked.

The effect of my failure to comprehend was unfortunate. "*The St. Valentine's Massacree*, of course!" Paddy shouted. Then, regaining control of himself, he added, "Right over in a garage in the 2100 block on Clark. I knew some of the fellows." The Alderman's manner, if not his tone, was that of Dr. Douglas Southall Freeman saying, "There stood Pickett's men. . . ."

An honest politician is one who when he is bought will stay bought.—*Simon Cameron*

The "report" below is keyed to the gift of a vicuña coat by manufacturer Bernard Goldfine to Presidential assistant Sherman Adams, Adams' subsequent resignation, and Democratic and Republican attitudes towards Adams.

WHITTAKER CHAMBERS

Letter from Afar

1958

Our African correspondent writes:

They ate the Rev. Sherman Adams last night. Of course, for months, it has been a dead certainty that they would; and one or two of us at the Club even laid small wagers (an inflated £ or two) on the date, which was the only point in question. It would certainly have come sooner, but for the rains, which, this year, have been interminable, and, in the past weeks, torrential. Last night there was a letup. Before you could say "Barbecue," they had the big iron ritual pot out of the Temple of the Crocodile (where they also keep their ghastly fetish), and the Rev. Mr. Adams out of the Black House (as they call the Paramount Chief's throne-room), and the old missionary—or what was left of him—into the pot. Don't ask me how they got a fire roaring under it when there seems nothing left to burn in our jungle world but rain-soaked mildew. In such matters, I have noticed before, savages seem every bit as resourceful as we are.

There followed the usual chanting of magical spells, imprecations, exorcisms by their witch doctors, and howling of responses by their hand-clapping public, foaming to hysteria as the tom-toms stepped up their beat. After that, on signal, came the traditional rush for the pot, and snatching and gobbling of choicer gobbets from the stew, resulting in the usual recriminations, and all ending after repletion (or spiritual exhaustion) in some almost American tribal dances. That is, if accounts of your rock and roll that reach us here in Africa are true.

Of course, I am simply a businessman, so, for me, it was a little on the boring side: one has seen so many cannibal feasts. Besides, something *was* missing. Civilization *does* take its toll; but the restraint, or damp-ener, or whatever it was, was not, I think, due so much to the weeks of rain, as to the presence of the UN observer, who got up-river just in time to witness the fun. Awful little busybody called Hammerhead, or some such name, who sits, or so they tell me, for the Falkland Islands in the General Assembly. He ate nothing (a grave breach of manners on these occasions). What is worse, all through the ceremony, he had his note-book and camera out. And while we may be savages, and sometimes in-cline to make a virtue of it, we don't like this kind of thing getting about recklessly, and coloring what the Falkland Islanders think of us.

They say that, if it had been anything but a gold nose-ring that the Rev. Adams accepted from Bwana Goldfa, they would never have got him into the pot. (F.y.i., Bwana Goldfa is a Syrian trader here, a great figure in the fiercely competitive loincloth market. For more on Syrian traders, read Graham Greene.) Now, the Rev. Adams, as the Old Chief's missionary counselor, had made himself the obsessive opponent of gold nose-rings. It was precisely against gold nose-rings that he preached some of his most moving sermons. Moreover, he had an em-barrassing habit of snatching and examining other people's noses on the mere suspicion of tattletale ring-marks on them. So when the Opposition came on a nose-ring among the Rev. Adams' personal possessions ("From Bwana with love"), the effect was not so much joy or sorrow, as a great surprise. The Rev. Adams took sanctuary in the Temple of the Crocodile, and, clinging to the fetish for months, mutely defied the witch doctors to pry him loose. The Old Chief pled that he could not even keep the Black House swept without the Rev. Mr. Adams to hand him the broom. The witch doctors simply kept pointing to the nose-ring. As theater, it was masterly; and the crowning touch came the day after the feast.

On the way to the cauldron, the missionary had uttered a few ex-culpatory words. Promptly, the No. 1 Witch Doctor (or, as *you* would say, Chairman of the Opposition's National Committee) rose to rebut. He remarked that the kind of feast that they had just celebrated, how-ever gratifying to ingestion, must never be taken in a spirit of shallow hedonism. "The best of barbecues," he said in a memorable period, "is a bothersome business. And, of course, there is a scruple, a vestige from the dark past, that no public servant of either party likes to form the main course on such occasions. Yet how feeble such sentiments appear beside the overriding consideration that it was only by eating the Rev. Adams that the ends of higher morality could be served or served up!" Hence no blame whatever attached to the Opposition. They had merely fanned the flames. The real sin lay in the fact that the Paramount Chief and his warriors had not eaten the Rev. Adams themselves. As he was speaking, I could not help thinking that, with the addition of a top hat, in the States the No. 1 Witch Doctor might have been taken for an undertaker's assistant, enacting a charade that stood for: pious fraud. There are times when I rather despair of Africa.

Yet to despair of Africa is to despair of the future. They are asking here: "Where else, once the rest of the world has vaporized itself with its bombs and missiles, is civilization to survive if not in the jungle?" That is, if our jungles survive civilization. So I take heart by glancing out at the modernistic structure of the national bank (they call it The Fund for the Republic), soaring five floors above the Old Chief's hutment with its old-fashioned, serpentine fence of leg-bones. Here, at least, is Progress. But I must close. For a native runner has just panted in to report that, with the rain's end, the Krushchas and Mau-tsetse, fierce tribes to the east, are raiding for heads and slaves as far as the coast. Another job for Hammerhead, I suppose.

GUY DANIELS

A Biologist Looks at the Civil Service

1959

This curious growth, labelled a noxious weed
By every politician,
Is actually part plant, part pedigreed
Academician.

And though at times they scarcely seem alive,
These very much neglected
And misused florae and/or faunae thrive
Where least expected.

In fact, it has been claimed they'll live forever.
But most experts incline
Towards the French view: they sometimes die, but never
Never resign.

ENVOI

For best results, spray with Security,
Promise higher positions,
And keep in humid, crowded places, free
Of inquisitions.

JULES FEIFFER

Corruption

THE EVOLUTIONARY PROCESS IN GOVERNMENT CONTINUES. WE HAVE PASSED FROM FEUDALISM TO CAPITALISM. OUR CURRENT STAGE, AS WE ALL KNOW, IS **CORRUPTION**.

CORRUPTION AS A FORM OF GOVERNMENT IS, ITSELF, WITHIN VARYING STAGES OF DEVELOPMENT. IN THE SOVIET UNION, WHERE YOU HAVE THE "**STATE**" OR "**TRICKLE DOWN**" THEORY OF CORRUPTION, IT OPERATES WITH THE **MOST** EFFICIENCY.

IN OUR **OWN** COUNTRY WE ARE IN THE TRANSITIONAL, MORE DYNAMIC PHASE -**FREE FORM** CORRUPTION. IT IS AN UNPREDICTABLE PHASE BECAUSE IT CONTINUES, SELF CONSCIOUSLY, TO DENY ITS EXISTENCE IN FEAR THAT, WERE ITS **TRUE** NATURE MADE KNOWN, IT WOULD BE OVERTHROWN.

THEREFORE, IN LINE WITH THE CURRENT PRACTICES OF ENLIGHTENED LEADERSHIP, IT PUBLICLY **DEPLORES** WHAT IT PRIVATELY OWES ITS EXISTENCE TO.

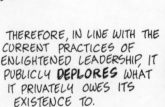

AS PART OF THIS PHILOSOPHY IT OFFERS A REGULAR PROGRAM OF PLANNED EXPOSURES TO SATISFY THE PUBLIC'S APPETITE- A BUILDING INSPECTOR ONE MONTH, A CITY OFFICIAL ANOTHER MONTH- **ANYTHING** WHICH WILL MISDIRECT THE GAZE OF AN ANTI-CORRUPT CITIZENRY.

THUS THE PUBLIC IS ENCOURAGED TO THINK OF CORRUPTION AS AN UNWELCOME STRANGER IN ITS HOUSE RATHER THAN AS THE HOST.

IN THE MEANTIME, TO SOFTEN THE PUBLIC'S ANTI CORRUPTION NEO-IDEALISM, THERE WILL BE A GROWING LIST OF **PEER GROUP** EXPOSURES- PROMINENT PRIVATE CITIZENS, IMPORTANT BUSINESS LEADERS, LEADING INTELLECTUALS -

WITH SO MUCH CORRUPTION MADE SO APALLINGLY EVIDENT, PUBLIC RESPONSE WILL DEADEN AND WITHDRAW. ACCEPTANCE WILL SET IN. CORRUPTION'S TAKE OVER WILL BE **COMPLETE**.

IN EVERY SCHOOL IN THE LAND WILL BE ENGRAVED OUR **NEW** MORAL BANNER ———

"WHAT CAN YOU EXPECT? I'D DO IT MYSELF."

LEO ROSTEN

An Open Letter to the Mayor of New York

1963

Dear Mr. Mayor:

There's a fellow I want to report—so's you can arrest him or deport him or what. He's a real troublemaker who goes around saying awful things about you. I think he's a Communist, or even a Republican.

Last night, whilst shooting the breeze, How do you like living in little old NY? he asks.

I like NY fine, I said.

He looks at me like I'm some kind of Astronut. I mean NY the capital of Noise, Dirt, Muggings and Holes in every street, he says. (Right there I should of realize this guy is carrying around some grudge to grind.) How long, he asks, does it take you to commute to and fro your place of work?

I do not commute, I say, as I work only 30 blocks from here, in the Umpire State Bilding, which takes me 45 minutes to 1 hour.

If that ain't commuting I'd like to know what is, he says. How do you like our Mayor?

OK, I said. His heart's in the right place.

If his heart wasn't in the right place it couldn't pump enough blood to his head to keep him awake, he said, which there's no proof he is.

Ha, ha, ha, I argued.

Want a bargain in a gasmask? he said.

What do I want a gasmask for? I ask.

So's you can survive from the fumes, he says. Don't you know the pop. of NY is *being gassed to death* from the xhaust pipes of Trucks, Buses and Cars?

I told him I didn't notice, as I am from the soft-coal belt of Pa.—and back home people are kind of proud of the fact we have the lowest oxygen rate in the entire USA.

O my God, he groned. Do you realize that even air conditioners only last 4–5 years in NY, on account of the gas and acid fumes eat away the metal parts?

Well, I'm not an air conditioner, I said.

I hate to think what they will find when they open up *your* lungs, he said, assuming there are any lungs left to describe. Why can't the Mayor make every Truck, Bus and Car clean its filters and fix its carboretors?

You can't see your own xhaust fumes if you are driving, I said, as you drive in front whereas the xhaust pipes are in *back*.

That is why I am organizing a Comittee, he said, so when a citizen sees a Bus, Truck or Car trying to kill people by poisoning the air, he slaps 1 of these stickers on the vehicle. (He shows me a sticker and you know what it says? So help me, Mayor, it says—

> STOP POISONING YOUR FELLOW AMERICANS!
> Your xhaust is black filth!
> You are choking our lungs!
> You are shriveling our leafs!

That won't do no good, I said. They will just scrape them stickers off.

In that case, we go into action! (Now he wips out a long Rubber Hose.) You attach 1 end to the xhaust pipe and stick the other end in the window, right next to the Driver's puss. If he loves fumes, let him breathe them!

What if the window ain't open? I said.

Brake it, he said simply.

I said, Braking car windows is a crime.

He said, Poisoning 8,000,000 NYorkers is a worse crime. Why, I went up to Conn. last week to visit a refugee from NY, and the fresh air there made me so sick they had to blow carbon monoxy in my face to revive me.

By now he looks ready to split a gut, so I decide to quiet him up. Why don't you write all these beefs, I ask, to Mayor Wagner in person?

He laughed so hard you could scramble eggs on his stomack. Write the *Mayor?* he strangles. I have already wrote that Boy Scout a dozen letters, and I get back a dozen replies from some stoodge, saying the Mayor has turned my complaints over to "the proper dept." Well, they are so damn proper they don't even answer—because we ain't been formally introduced. What do you do with your Old Rubbers?

I give them to the Salvation Army, I said.

What? he cries. You are suppose to take them to one of the bildings where they burn old rubber and hot-water bags in the incinerators. Why, old rubber is one of our finest products for making Smog and Smoke. I can see you are low in civic spirit, he says. I bet you ain't even been in Central Park resently.

Why should I go in Central Park? I said.

So's you can be mugged like everyone else, he said, and push up our crime statistiks.

You don't have to go in Central Park to get mugged, I said. We have had 2 muggings, 3 break-ins and a stabbing right on this block.

That shows what a great Mayor we have, he said.

Ain't there even 1 good thing you can say about him? I challendged.

He closed his both eyes and took so long thinking I wondered is he coming down with the African Sleeping Sickness, which strikes without warning. Finally he said, I admit Wagner is doing more than any man alive to solve the Number 1 Problem of the World today—Do you know what the Number 1 Problem is?

Overweight, I said.

God, he groned. Try again.

Cavities, I said.

Lay down and rest, he says, you sure need it. The Number 1 Problem of the World is—OVERPOPULATION. And no one is doing more to reduce it than Bewildred Bob. As for NY, it's a race between moving out and getting ulcers.

What are you dragging ulcers in for? I said.

Take a ride in a NY taxi and see, he said. We have cabs no other city would allow in a amusement park for midgets. First, the doors barely open, so you have to turn sideways to try and get in. Then you bang your head against the top, which is made low for this purpose. You have to corkscrew in, thus spraining a mussel or your sacrediliac, and if it's raining or snow, you are in for a dandy surprise—because these taxis have a hump in the floor in back, and on each side of that hump is a 4 in. well, like two dishpans. Each citizen brings in snow and rain, which drips down and fills up the dishpans, and since NY cabbies feel it against their relidgion to ever clean out their cabs, which are moving garbage disposals, a very interesting collection of bilge floats in those dishpans. . . .

. . . You can't sweep it out, on account of the dishpans being lower than the doors. You can't vacuum it out, it being mostly water. The only defense is this—(and now he hawls out a Carpenters Drill!) Make holes in the floor.

Water will certainly run right out of a hole, I decided.

Your mother would be proud of you at this moment, he said. And how about the Bus and Subway torture?

How's the Mayor suppose to even know what goes on in Buses or Subways? I said. He rides in a offishul limozine, with a driver to take him to and fro.

Then let's pass a law, he said, making the Mayor and all the politicians *ride in public transportation* for 1 week each year. Just 1 *week* of them dumbells waiting for Buses, getting hijacked into Subways, getting nauzeated from the stink of hotdogs and piazzas frying underground—just 1 week and Brother, you'd get some action!—Take Buses. Rush hour, they pass you in wolf packs, they're so full—while right across the street, going in the opp. direction, a fleet of empty Buses is racing like hell to the Bronx, 10 miles away, *so's they can turn around!* Why can't every 2nd or 3rd empty turn around *right there*, instead of racing all the way up to the Bronx?

That would foul up their skedules, I said.

They are suppose to serve people, not skedules, he hollers. What about the holes in the streets?

With all this new bilding, they have to tear up the ground, I said.

They could put a limit on the number of holes, he said, like Mayor La Gardia used to. But not this Mayor, xcuse the xpression. He has raised the Art of making holes to new hights. He has xperts who do nothing but dig holes inside the holes already there. He has inspectors who, if there's a stretch of 3 blocks without a hole, the mistake is corrected before morning.

With so many holes, I am amazed you do not have to crawl to and fro, I said (but he don't even see I have throwed him a spitball).

I carry a board, he said. (You won't believe this, Mr. Mayor, but this kook is now showing me a Ironing Board!) This is part of the NYorker's Survival Kit, to get you across Bewildred Bob's trenches, foxholes, soors and open graves. He is changing NY from a Summer Festival to a All-Year Obstacle Race.

If you don't dig holes you don't get bildings, I defended.

Do you know what type monsterosities they now call bildings? he said.

Sure, I said. There's a new one right outside these windows.

That's why it's so nice and dark in your apt. all day, he said.

I'm not there much during the day, I said.

From the look of things you're not all there most of the time, he said. I will give you a refresher course on Wagner's Bilding Code, or How to Drive Americans Crazy in their Own Home. First, they make the ceilings so low you get an xtra floor every 4 floors—and that overloads all the elevators right there. Second, they make all the walls so thin no one will ever get lonesome. Everyone hears his neighbors gargling, taking a bath, or worse. In 1 new bilding, a tenant went to Florida leaving his TV on and it took the endgineers 2 days to figure out from which apt. the *Sunrise Semester* was coming to educate everyone at 6:30 A.M. . . .

Let's get back to the traffick, I said coldly, which if you don't like you can always walk.

Walk? In NY? He laughed so hard you think he's watching Red Skeleton. You don't walk if you want to keep your love of animals. The Pidgeons decorate your head and the dog-do lubricates your shoes. "Curb Your Dog" it says, but dogs don't read. . . . What type earplugs do you use?

My ears do not hurt, I said.

You mean you sleep in NY without plugging your ears up? he xclaims. Even through this Croak of Doom horn the Fire Dept. shrewdly added to the heebie-jeebie sirens?

Which would you rather have, I said, people being woke up or the whole NY burning down?

Don't press me, he said. I'd burn ¾ of the new bildings with pleasure, starting with that Pan Am warehouse in the sky which will bring 25,000 more cattle to the worst crowded place they could find.

Mayor Wagner probably didn't even *know* the Pan Am bilding is going up there, I said.

That's true, he said.

I'm glad you give him 1 benefit of a dout, I said. . . .

Well, Mr. Mayor, what's the use? This screwball went on like that must of been 2 hours. By the time I manadge to get away, my mind is so xhausted from his Gasmask and Stickers and Rubber Hose and Ironing Board and Drill for draining out Taxis couldn't sleep a wink all night. That's when I heard the Croak of Doom horns. They were going like crazy.

Yours truly,
J. R. Jukes

4 WHAT DO THEY MEAN?

POLITICS AS A FOREIGN LANGUAGE

The abuse of language and meaning lies close to the heart of whatever is funny, or outrageous, in politics. Cant phrases, ambiguous clichés, soothing euphemisms, and meaningless slogans take root more readily and flourish more abundantly here than in any other garden, or weedpatch, of our civilization. Politics, more than academe or Madison Avenue, is the refuge of the vogue word; for all their other useful applications, how long would "dialogue," "consensus," "viable," "spectrum," or "pragmatic" survive in common parlance were it not for their capacity to transform the patter of a political dopester into the pretentious meditations of a pundit?

One reason for this, of course, is that in our tradition political situations seem to call for rhetorical hyperbole, which in turn encourages redundancy, ambiguity, tautology, and the non-sequitur. Another is that American politics requires continual commitments—but no contracts. The purpose of legal jargon is to define an obligation; the purpose of political prose, more often than not, is ot obscure it. A third is the more general truism: We—the people, the voters—have been so conditioned by an advertising culture to exaggeration and deception as the norms of public statement that we are suspicious of the modest claim and the simple truth.

This section starts off with some of Ambrose Bierce's durable definitions. Bierce was not the nihilist or arch cynic he appeared to be, according to Carey McWilliams, but a severe moralist: "He turned the values of the day inside out, and found, as men will find if they try the same experiment today, that the inside-out version is a fairly reliable guide to social reality."

SOME GENERAL INSTRUCTION AND GLOSSARIES

It is remarkable how very debased the language has become in a short period in America.

—*Frederick Marryat*

AMBROSE BIERCE

from *The Devil's Dictionary*

1911

ADMINISTRATION, *n.*: An ingenious abstraction in politics, designed to receive the kicks and cuffs due to the premier or president. A man of straw, proof against bad-egging and dead-catting.

ALDERMAN, *n.*: An ingenious criminal who covers his secret thieving with a pretence of open marauding.

ALLIANCE, *n.*: In international politics, the union of two thieves who have their hands so deeply inserted in each other's pocket that they cannot separately plunder a third.

AMNESTY, *n.*: The state's magnanimity to those offenders whom it would be too expensive to punish.

BOUNDARY, *n.*: In political geography, an imaginary line between two nations, separating the imaginary rights of one from the imaginary rights of the other.

CONSERVATIVE, *n.*: A statesman who is enamored of existing evils, as distinguished from the Liberal, who wishes to replace them with others.

DICTATOR, *n.*: The chief of a nation that prefers the pestilence of despotism to the plague of anarchy.

DIPLOMACY, *n.*: The patriotic art of lying for one's country.

FREEDOM, *n.*: Exemption from the stress of authority in a beggarly half-dozen of restraint's infinite multitude of methods. A political condition that every nation supposes itself to enjoy in virtual monopoly. Liberty. The distinction between freedom and liberty is not accurately known; naturalists have never been able to find a living specimen of either.

HARANGUE, *n.:* A speech by an opponent, who is known as an harangue—outang.

INSURRECTION, *n.:* An unsuccessful revolution. Disaffection's failure to substitute misrule for bad government.

LABOR, *n.:* One of the processes by which A acquires property for B.

MACHINATION, *n.:* The method employed by one's opponents in baffling one's open and honorable efforts to do the right thing.

MUGWUMP, *n.:* In politics, one afflicted with self-respect and addicted to the vice of independence. A term of contempt.

NOMINEE, *n.:* A modest gentleman shrinking from the distinction of private life and diligently seeking the honorable obscurity of public office.

PATRIOTISM, *n.:* Combustible rubbish ready to the torch of anyone ambitious to illuminate his name. In Dr. Johnson's famous dictionary patriotism is defined as "the last resort of a scoundrel." With all due respect to an enlightened but inferior lexicographer, I beg to submit that it is the first.

PLEBISCITE, *n.:* A popular vote to ascertain the will of the sovereign.

POLITICS, *n.:* A strife of interests masquerading as a contest of principles. The conduct of public affairs for private advantage.

PRESIDENCY, *n.:* The greased pig in the field game of American politics.

RADICALISM, *n.:* The conservatism of tomorrow injected into the affairs of today.

RECOUNT, *n.:* In American politics, another throw of the dice, accorded to the player against whom they are loaded.

REFERENDUM, *n.:* A law for submission of proposed legislation to a popular vote to learn the nonsensus of public opinion.

REVOLUTION, *n.:* In politics, an abrupt change in the form of misgovernment. Specifically, in American history, the substitution of the rule of an Administration for that of a Ministry, whereby the welfare and happiness of the people were advanced a full half-inch.

SENATE, *n.:* A body of elderly gentlemen charged with high duties and misdemeanors.

SUFFRAGE, *n.:* Expression of opinion by means of a ballot. The right of suffrage (which is held to be both a privilege and a duty) means, as commonly interpreted, the right to vote for the man of another man's choice, and is highly prized.

TARIFF, *n.:* A scale of taxes on imports, designed to protect the domestic producer against the greed of his consumer.

TRUST, *n.:* In American politics, a large corporation composed in greater part of thrifty working men, widows of small means, orphans in the care of guardians and the courts, with many similar malefactors and public enemies.

ULTIMATUM, *n.:* In diplomacy, a last demand before resorting to concessions.

UN-AMERICAN, *adj.:* Wicked, intolerable, heathenish.

VOTE, *n.:* The instrument and symbol of a freeman's power to make a fool of himself and a wreck of his country.

WESTBROOK PEGLER

Little Words of Big Men

1936

An examination of the pat remarks of famous men reveals how very little wit it takes to create a reputation as a phrasemaker or humorous philosopher if the author happens to be a man in public life.

I am thinking at the moment of Mr. Charles G. Dawes's expression, Hell-an'-Maria, which made him Vice-President of the United States, and of Mr. Al Smith's scornful reference to the baloney dollar. Only a very dull comedian or sports writer would be satisfied with Hell-an'-

Maria as original material, but so little is ever expected of men so highly placed that when Mr. Dawes began to say it, that was news.

You may challenge the notion that his use of this remark made him Vice-President, but it did, all right, with the assistance of his character pipe, his comedy collar and political circumstances. That was back in the he-man era, and Mr. Dawes's expression made him famous and popular where his record had failed to distinguish him in the public imagination. Later on, when the Republicans moved into Cleveland to nominate Mr. Coolidge and startled statesmen were fleeing the vice-presidency in wild alarm, Mr. Dawes was the obvious one. When Mr. Frank Lowden finally refused and almost threatened to sue the party, Mr. Dawes expressed a willingness, and he was it.

Certainly the word baloney had lost its humorous quality, if it ever had any, long before Mr. Smith got around to it. His reference to alphabet soup in connection with the new government agencies set up under the Roosevelt administration was belated too, for it occurred more than once in Mr. Bugs Baer's syndicated nonsense in the papers as far back as 1920. Yet when Mr. Smith said baloney and alphabet soup he was making language.

The human, folksy, philosophical quality of Mr. Smith's salutation, "Hello, you old potato," on the night of his famous reconciliation with Mr. Roosevelt in Madison Square Garden defied inspection. When you examined it, there was nothing there. Still, it was accepted as being characteristic and somehow very good until Fred Storm, of the United Press, admitted some time afterward that nobody had been able to hear just what Mr. Smith did say and that he had taken the liberty of putting the words in Mr. Smith's mouth.

The best-quoted phrase of all attributed to Mr. Smith, somehow, lacked staying qualities. That was the expression with which he finally and completely did away with young Theodore Roosevelt the time Mr. Roosevelt was running against him for Governor of New York. Perhaps running is an exaggeration. Toddling would be more like it.

Mr. Smith listened tolerantly to Mr. Roosevelt's campaign and at the climax said simply, "The young feller ain't there."

It was Mr. Joe Tumulty, then secretary to Woodrow Wilson, who first described as boll weevils the new Southern Congressmen and deserving Democrats from below the line, but out of consideration for his position he was not charged with it at the time. There were some amazing specimens of wild life in Washington just then, and some of the sockless types newly elected to the lower house charged into town under the impression that the government furnished barracks or dormitories for the statesmen. Finding no such accommodations, certain of them carried bedding into their offices and moved in.

Boll weevil was a term destined to live long and prosper. It is useful again nowadays, with many political parasites established in office and the soft magnolia drawl of the Southern appointee murmuring in every corridor of the government.

The same tactful forbearance that shielded Mr. Tumulty then now protects the man who recently referred to a clerical demagogue as the "mad monk."

Senator Huey Long was not at his best when he was deliberately coining phrases, but in unguarded moments he sometimes spoke a language true to his country. He was sounding his A when, in a speech on patronage, he spoke of God and hell and cesspools of vice, but he was talkin' Southe'n when, in the same address, he said the blame would come home as straight as the swallow to the gourd.

I never thought there was half the quality to Theodore Roosevelt's "Speak softly and carry a big stick," that would have been seen in the remark if it had been uttered by a salesman. In fact, it is the stuffiness of statesmen on the average which exaggerates the wit and originality of the few unusual utterances which they do get rid of now and again.

There is a much brighter wit to the language of the sports business, particularly the racing, fighting and baseball branches, but originality is routine there, and few men have become associated with a particular phrase. One of them was Willie Keeler, who said, "Hit 'em where they ain't."

And in all the sports business there never was a phrasemaker comparable to the late Phocian Howard, the horse journalist who ran a little gamblers' trade journal called the New York *Press*, which he always mentioned as the Fireside Companion. Mr. Howard bundled up the whole thought behind the professional gamblers' business in the phrase "Suckers can't wait."

ROBERT BENDINER

How to Listen to Campaign Oratory If You Have To

1960

To help voters make their choices this year, enough words will be spoken to fill three thousand books, each the size of *Gone with the Wind* and each rating that title. Fortunately, most of this outpouring will not get into print. But you will probably catch two or three volumes' worth, and maybe you will want a guide throught the verbiage.

The first rule for penetrating the underbrush of words is to keep always in mind that a candidate is not out to explain anything to you. It is not your mind he is after; it is your glands. He is out to show you, above all, that he is *your* kind of man—only more so. For this reason, a good campaign talk always starts out with the speaker finding a link to his listeners —no matter how hard he has to stretch for it. Here is the same candidate addressing three different audiences:

TO A VETERANS' CONVENTION—"I am proud to be here, among my former comrades in arms. I was not 'big brass,' but I think I know the thoughts and feelings of a humble soldier . . ." (He was, in fact, at Camp Yaphank in World War I, when the Armistice happily cut off his military career.)

AT A COUNTY FAIR AND PLOUGHING CONTEST—"My Grandfather Richards, on my mother's side, had a small farm, like most of you folks here, and many's the day I spent getting to know the backbreaking work that makes the farmer this country's forgotten man . . ." (He spent three summer vacations there as a growing, eating boy.)

IN A TRADE-UNION HALL—"I am delighted to be here, because this is where I belong. I am proud to have in my pocket right now a membership card in one of the great trade-unions of this country . . ." (An honorary card bestowed on him by a bricklayers' union when, as an alderman, he laid the cornerstone for a new local.)

Where the audience is a mixed group, the speaker finds a quick kinship in geography. He will always have a soft spot for Devil's Gulch, Ariz., because his mother was born 18 miles from there. Or for East Overshoe, Ill., because his Uncle Henry ran a poolroom there in 1912. At worst, he can always call a town his "second home" on the ground that he once stayed overnight at the local hotel and had his laundry done.

Once past the amenities, our man is ready to plunge into serious matters, equipped as he is with a life belt of ready-made phrases to keep him afloat. The kind he chooses depends on whether his party is in or out of office. If he belongs to the "out" party, government expenditures are *criminal waste and extravagance*. And all members of the executive branch of government automatically become *bureaucrats*.

If our man belongs to the "in" party, government expenditures are *the best return on his dollar the American taxpayer has ever had*. As for executive personnel, they are *dedicated public servants*, who daily sacrifice themselves for you and me when they could be making millions in some other job.

There are, of course, turns of phrase that are common to both the "ins" and the "outs." In this category are the diminutives—*little man, common man, small businessman, small farmer* and the like. In an election year, we seem to have an enormous population of midgets. The candidate's immediate audience, however, is never made up of these wee folk; it is made up of *the great people of this great state*. That's you. The little people are your relatives and neighbors. They don't happen to be there, but on their behalf, you will no doubt appreciate this unselfish champion of the underdog.

Having mastered these semantic twists, the student of campaign oratory is ready to move on to those tags that politicians hang on each other in the hope that voters will treat the wearer like a medieval leper. In this category are the various Red labels, ranging from *pro-Communist* to *fellow traveler* to the newest variants, *soft on communism* or *soft on Russia*. Every candidate has to run against two opponents—the other party's candidate and Nikita Khrushchev. It might be assumed at this stage in history that every American politician is against communism, just as he is against barracuda in the bath. But unless his views are the exact opposite of the Russian leader's on everything from astrophysics to the can-can, he may be put down as *playing into Khrushchev's hands*. In common with certain head-hunting natives of Borneo, both John F. Kennedy and

Richard M. Nixon relish a good meal, but it would probably be wrong to assume on that evidence that either of them is soft on cannibalism. Unless this particular trick is held in check, anyone who lights a match may be put down as soft on arson.

In a milder category are the hundreds of clichés, rubber stamps and warmed-over metaphors, mixed and unmixed, that make the padding of campaign oratory. Most of them are so washed out by waves of repetition that they call up no pictures at all and are intended only to get the speaker from one sentence to the next with the least resistance. He thinks it sounds good to work in references to *our Founding Fathers, Old Glory, hearths and homes, our children and our children's children.* These are not really words at all. They are red-white-and-blue cement.

Now that you have been warned, how are you to get through the next few weeks? Here are a few rules that may help:

1) Spend a preliminary month in a Trappist monastery, so that the sound of even a politician's voice, no matter what he says, will have a certain welcome freshness.

2) Decide in advance on three or four questions that a candidate ought to deal with in this year of 1960. If he dodges or skirts all four of them the first time you hear him, ignore him the next time and go back to Bat Masterson.

3) If he answers even one of these questions to your satisfaction, give him a second try. If he answers two or three, vote for him. And if he successfully answers all four, go out and work for him.

4) Try listening to a candidate in the company of someone who generally opposes your views. If the two of you can't get up a good row about the talk afterwards, the chances are that the speaker didn't say anything.

5) No matter how frighteningly the campaigners warn you that the salvation of the world depends on their winning, remember that on November 9, half of them will be wiring congratulations to the other half on their great victory and promising to co-operate fully in the predicted disaster.

THEY SAY	*THEY MEAN*
My opponent is making a political football out of this grave and complicated issue.	*He has a good thing going for him there. If my party was on the paying end of that issue, I'd sure know what to do with it.*

THEY SAY	THEY MEAN
Let us return to spiritual values.	*Let's put my party in again and see what happens.*
Clean up the mess in Washington (or Boston or Albany).	*Clean up their mess in Washington (or Boston or Albany). It will take a few years before we have a mess of our own.*
We will conduct a vigorous, fighting campaign.	*We will smear them.*
They are trying to smear us.	*They are conducting a vigorous fighting campaign.*
It is time to close ranks.	*It is time to close ranks behind us. (If the opposition wins, it is time for honest criticism.)*
I am not here to make a speech.	*I mean to talk for another 40 minutes. Don't anyone leave.*
I am not suggesting that my opponent is personally dishonest.	*He is a willing dupe.*
This is the speech *they* wrote for me, but I'm going to throw it away and speak from the heart.	*They slipped me tomorrow's speech, which would lay an egg with this audience.*
I cannot go into the details now, but I think I may say without fear of contradiction that our policies have proved to be sound.	*All sound.*
We will take the American people into our confidence.	*We will let them in on all the opposition's scandals we can uncover.*
They are playing into the hands of our country's enemies.	*They are criticizing us again.*
You may hear talk that they have reformed, my friends, but the leopard doesn't change its spots.	*We haven't been able to get anything new on them lately.*

THEY SAY	*THEY MEAN*
We have had enough of their defeatist talk.	*Let's forget the facts for awhile. Things are tough all over.*
They have made a tragic blunder, for which we must all pay the price.	*They have had a nasty break, and it looks as though we can cash in on it.*

RUSSELL BAKER

The Vast Wasteland
of Hard-Nosed Multi-Gigaton Words

1961

After an emergency meeting to expel all members of the Kennedy Administration from its ranks, the National Society for the Preservation of the English Language to Say What You Mean has just issued one of its rare "condemned" lists.

Under society rules, any member who catches himself using a "condemned" word or phrase must do penance by parsing the collected news conference transcripts of former President Eisenhower.

Mostly, the society states, the new list consists of "clichés, jargon, misleading slogans, deceptive euphemisms and meaningless polysyllabics created or popularized by Kennedy administrators, journalists, sociologists, bureaucrats, advertising agents and such, whose survival often depends upon a talent for abusing the language."

The new "condemned" list appears below, with the society's guess about how each item might be defined in pure English.

TASK FORCE, *n.*: any group appointed by the President to devise a program for Congress to ignore.

AUTOMATION, *n.*: an industrial trend leading inexorably to the day when Presidents will urge machines to ask not what their country will do for them, but what they can do for their country.

BATTLE FOR MEN'S MINDS (*cliché*): an effort to sell the starving on credit-card living.

RESPONSIBLE, *adj.*: used to describe a speech, decision, action, etc., conforming to your personal prejudices about what is good for the country.

IRRESPONSIBLE, *adj.*: describing any course of conduct likely to cost you votes in the next election.

THE HARVARD GROUP, *n.*: assorted professors with entree to the "rat pack."

TO BE PERFECTLY CANDID: a meaningless phrase interjected to avoid awkward silences while mentally concocting an uninformative reply to a delicate question. (Popularized by Secretary of State Rusk.)

SURVIVABILITY, *n.*: (Pentagonese): the prerequisite to enjoyment of post-World-War-III society.

FALLOUT SHELTER, *n.*: a hole where the family with survivability can thank their lucky stars until the looters arrive.

MULTI-GIGATON BOMB, *n.*: Doomsday in the big economy package.

ESCALATION, *n.* (Pentagonese): two sides are fighting sportingly with rifles; one side is about to lose, so stops being sporting and hits the other side with a multigigaton bomb; the contest is thus subjected to "escalation."

RACE FOR SPACE (*cliché*): a euphonious justification for spending billions to export snappy new earth ideas like "escalation" to other words.

CHALLENGES OF THE SIXTIES (*cliché*): (1) producing an eyeball stabilizer to destroy the evidence of a three-martini lunch; (2) convincing Congress that the twentieth century is already out of hand; (3) persuading James Bond to come to work for the C.I.A.; (4) stamping out television; (5) liberating Dad from the charcoal grill.

FRUITFUL, *adj.*: any diplomatic gathering that does not produce war.

INCREASED READINESS, *n.*: a uniformed solution to the unemployment problem.

WE WILL MAKE A JUDGMENT (Kennedyism): roughly, "Sorensen thinks we ought to keep quiet on this one until the next Gallup poll is in."

I AM HOPEFUL (Kennedyism): "Well, there's always the chance somebody will pull off a miracle."

EXTREMISTS, *n.*: public nuisances whose insistence upon their legal rights may jeopardize your special privileges.

VAST WASTELAND, *n.*: the American home with all its television sets simultaneously out of order.

GENEVA CONFERENCE, *n.*: a sweet way of life which allows diplomats to live, love, marry, rear families, grow old and die in pleasant surroundings while preserving insoluble international problems on ice.

THE NEW CONSERVATISM, *n.*: a political philosophy born under the conjunction of Arizona, Yale and Adam Smith; it holds that the United States must get tougher with the Communists and expand its influence around the world while cutting the budget, dismantling the Federal Government and bringing the boys home, thus turning a tide of events that has been running against the country since the last Federalist Administration.

PRAGMATIST, *n.*: an important politician whom you approve of despite his readiness to kick you if you get in his way.

ON THE ORDER OF MAGNITUDE (gobbledygook): a bureaucrat's phrase for estimating costs which may later prove to be $1 billion to $5 billion higher. (Example: Inquiring Senator: What will be the cost of this highway the State Department proposes to build from Rabat to Madagascar Junction? Bureaucrat: On the order of magnitude of $2 billion. Inquiring Senator Three Years Later: How do you explain the fact that the trans-African highway has already tripled your original estimate without even reaching Buganda? Bureaucrat: Senator, the best I could give you then was an estimate of the order of magnitude.)

BACKDOOR SPENDING: epithet used by Republicans to describe Democratic use of financing techniques invented by Herbert Hoover.

A POSITION OF RESPONSIBILITY SECOND TO NONE (*euphemism*): an inconsequential sinecure for sensitive ex-Governors.

HARD-NOSED, *adj.*: used to describe someone who is convinced the Russians are just bluffing, wants the United States to get tough, thrills ladies at Georgetown dinner parties by proposing that the United States foment rebellion in Poland, and is ready to fight to the last drop of your blood.

GEORGETOWN DINNER PARTY, *n.*: any meal from Wheaton, Md., to Bailey's Crossroads, Va., at which a Washington pundit finds a Kennedy Administration functionary willing to spill the beans provided he isn't quoted.

STEPPED-UP (Pentagonese): what the President orders done to programs, producing, planning, etc., when under pressure to do something fast without any idea of what to do. (Curiously, things are never "stepped down" in Washington, but are, instead, "phased out." Things to be "phased out" did not get under way by being "phased in," but by the cumbersome process of being "initiated," "definitized," "implemented" and "stepped up.")

NEW FRONTIER, *n.*: the great crusade with less golf.

CASKIE STINNETT

Only in America

CHAIRMAN (*banging gavel*): The Civil Service Review Board is now in session. What is the charge against this defendant?

INVESTIGATOR (*seats government worker on witness stand*): He refuses to use the approved forms of expression.

CHAIRMAN (*peering over glasses*): Perhaps he's just ignorant.

INVESTIGATOR (*laughs hollowly*): There's no one in government so ignorant he doesn't know better than to say "pass along" when he means "channelize." Furthermore, on one occasion he wrote "general situation" instead of "overall picture."

CHAIRMAN (*shocked*): This is serious. Do you have any documents? (*coughs apologetically*) I mean documentary support?

INVESTIGATOR: There is an abundance of supporting data, which will be submitted in quintuplicate. That reminds me the defendant has been heard—in the cafeteria and other public places—substituting the word "information" for "data."

CHAIRMAN (*sternly*): Is this true?

DEFENDANT (*hanging head*): I didn't mean to use the—

INVESTIGATOR (*sharply*): Utilize.

DEFENDANT: Utilize the wrong term. I was worried about—

INVESTIGATOR: Concerned with—

DEFENDANT: I was concerned with the safety of the information and—

INVESTIGATOR: He means security of the data.

DEFENDANT: That's right. I didn't want certain letters to—

INVESTIGATOR: Certain correspondence.

DEFENDANT: Certain correspondence to be seen by other employees—

INVESTIGATOR (*wearily*): Other *personnel*, please.

DEFENDANT: Other personnel before I could put it in the files. So I—

INVESTIGATOR (*translating*): He means integrate it with the files. Mr. Chairman, this man is so obviously unfit to serve the government that continuation of this hearing is merely a regularization and formalization (*Savors terms*). Regularization and formalization.

CHAIRMAN: Have you anything to say before I—

INVESTIGATOR: Excuse me, Mr. Chairman, but you must mean "prior to." After all, "before" hasn't been used since prior to the Coolidge Administration.

CHAIRMAN: (*flushing*): Of course. The defendant has me making errors. I find him guilty and the punishment is termination by—by— (*He looks hopefully at Investigator*).

INVESTIGATOR (*quickly*): Involuntary separation for cause, fully supported by documentation and concurrence of principal supervisory personnel.

CHAIRMAN (*nods appreciatively*): Thank you.

Gavel Falls

THE NEW YORK TIMES

No Clear Reply at Foggy Bottom; Official
Prose a Thing to Behold

1963

State Department prose, like a garden, "is a lovesome thing, God wot," and the noon briefing for reporters today produced a rare bloom.

It all began when Joseph W. Reap, acting press officer, was asked to comment on a dispatch in *The New York Times* today that said South Vietnam had agreed to finance the $17,000,000 cost of the strategic-hamlet program.

Mr. Reap is a straightforward fellow who would prefer his communications to be "Yea, yea and nay, nay." But this is not permitted, and somewhat diffidently Mr. Reap pulled from his pocket a statement prepared by the Bureau of Far Eastern Affairs, whose style is the envy of all other bureaus in the department.

Mr. Reap prefaced his reading by saying that "this is all I have" and "I hope this will be helpful." What followed, which is a fair sample of what happens every day at the noon briefing, is here set down:

MR. REAP—We are talking and negotiating every day with the Vietnamese Government on the best means of defending that country against the Communist attack. We are naturally—

QUESTION—Just a minute, please. Against Communist attack?

ANSWER—Against the Communist attack. We are naturally going to try to bring American assistance to bear in the most effective ways possible, and this requires a continuous process of discussion, agreement and implementation in Saigon.

Q.—Process of discussion, what?

A.—Agreement, and implementation. This whole process involves fiscal and economic considerations as well as the purely military. The Communist threat is not all confined to the military.

Q.—Is not confined to the what?

A.—To the military, and our two Governments have tried to design and put into effect an effective response which is economic—(laughter).

Q.—Financial.

A.—and social.

Q.—Which is economic what?

A.—Which is economic and social as well as military.

Q.—Financial and social?

Q.—You have to learn this by rote, economic, social.

Q.—When is the exam going to be?

Q.—Are you free to disclose the basis of the hope that you express, this statement would be helpful? (laughter)

Q.—Don't stop him; maybe he has more.

Q.—I suggest we give this man a medal, who ever wrote this.

A.—I will stand on the statement.

Q.—Mr. Chairman, I suggest the absence of a quorum (laughter).

Q.—I have really missed this place.

Q.—We have missed you.

Q.—What we are trying to determine is whether this process, which has been so philosophically described here, applies to the particular problem mentioned, that is, the financing of the strategic-hamlet program.

A.—What this paper is trying to say is those things are a matter of continuing discussion (laughter). There has been no agreement signed, sealed and delivered, as such.

Q.—You mean the discussion goes on and on and it never comes to a conclusion?

A.—I gather that these are bits and pieces of agreements to do this thing, and then to do another thing.

Q.—Seventeen million dollars. That is a pretty big bit, Joe.

A.—I ask you to please recall my preamble to this statement.

Q.—You said you thought it would be helpful (laughter).

A.—I expressed that as a hope.

Q.—We recognize that this is not your statement.

A.—Thank you.

Q.—But we also recognize that somebody upstairs should really have a medal for this one. We hope that you will see that they get it.

Q.—This is on the record, isn't it, Joe? It isn't background? (laughter).

A.—Since you insist, I will put it on the record.

KARL E. MEYER

That Image in the White House*

1961

You have shown me a strange image, and they are strange prisoners.

Like ourselves, I replied; and they see only their own shadows, or the shadows of one another, which the fire throws on the opposite wall of the cave.

* from *The New America*.

True, he said; how could they see anything but the shadows if they were never allowed to move their heads? . . .

To them, I said, the truth would be nothing but the shadows of the image.

—PLATO, *The Republic*

It must have begun in a flossy executive suite on Madison Avenue. The year was 1952, the subject was the latest account—a product named Eisenhower—and the momentous words might have been these:

"He's not penetrating, J. B. There's no smack, no punch, no consumer impact. What we've got to do is to crystallize a new—a new *image*."

And there it was. We've been stuck with the word ever since, and no political discussion seems authoritative without a respectful allusion to the candidate's image. It goes beyond politics. By now, everyone has discovered that everything has an image—from people and parties down to the lowly prune (depth interviews showed that the prune's image "was ridden with meanings, all unfortunate," according to Vance Packard).

The term has become so widely accepted that it seemed wholly in order during the 1960 campaign for an Associated Press profile of Richard M. Nixon to be subheaded "Man and Image"—with the undeniable implication that there was a difference between the two. Inevitably, Rabbi Max Nussbaum of Los Angeles opened the third session of the Democratic Convention by beseeching divine assistance for an "America with a new image." At the Republican Convention, images flew like hailstones —most memorably, perhaps, when the Governor of West Virginia retroactively endowed Lincoln with the "image of freedom."

During the campaign, the combatants hurled loaded images at each other. This came to a crescendo at the end of October, when President Eisenhower accused Candidate Kennedy of having "cruelly distorted the image of America." On the same day, the Washington *Post* quoted Mr. Kennedy's rejoinder: "Our prestige is not so high. No longer do we give the image of being on the rise. No longer do we give an image of vitality." . . .

II

At the risk of grievously damaging my own personalized image, I have consulted the dictionary to see what all the talk is about. The *Pocket Oxford Dictionary* scarcely affords comforting reading. An image by definition is a polite kind of fraud, a trick with mirrors, as well as a symbol or conception. The meaning of image (root: *imitari*, to imitate) is:

Imitation of object's external form, *e.g.,* statue esp. as object of worship; form, semblance; counterpart; type; simile; metaphor; optical counterpart produced by rays of light reflected from mirror, etc.

Now the primary meaning clearly conveys the impression of humbug, and the final meaning suggests compellingly that an image is a deceptive optical illusion. Surely it is appropriate that the word image came into currency after the 1952 Presidential campaign introduced, in a big way, two miracle ingredients into politics: (1) advertising agencies, and (2) television.

The coincidence is revealing. An image, like an advertisement, is not the substance of an object but its ephemeral shadow; it is the beguiling package, not the reality within. Most important, in all its meanings an image connotes something contrived. Whether in the fine arts or the black arts, an image is a conceit, a concoction, a cabalistic device. Hence, in the familiar usages, images are "projected," "created," "updated," and even (see above) "standardized." The shaping of an image, then, is a technique of manipulation, not of reasoned persuasion.

Above all, the image is associated with visual presentation. In the years when radio was the chief tool of mass communications, there was little talk about images and a good deal of solemn discourse about the intangible quality known as "radio personality." The change came swiftly. In 1948, Thomas E. Dewey defeated Harold Stassen in the pivotal Oregon Presidential primary after a radio debate. In 1950, Governor Dewey market-tested television by centering his campaign for re-election on a carefully staged question-and-answer TV show. It worked. In 1952, General Eisenhower was the first candidate to be retailed nationally over television, chiefly through spot announcements. (Voice: "Mr. Eisenhower, can you bring taxes down?" Eisenhower: "Yes. We will work to cut billions in Washington spending and bring your taxes down.") . . .

But to connoisseurs, the campaign of 1956 was a letdown. . . .

"I can't recall a national advertising campaign which was so poorly conceived, so badly written, so clumsily managed and produced, so misdirected and so dishonest as the political campaign of 1956," concluded John G. Schneider, author of *The Golden Kazoo* and an adman himself. "Maybe if we get some smart, amoral, know-how boys into the act, we'll get a better show in 1960."

Mr. Schneider had his wish. We went from the mellow, kindly gramps from old Abilene to a college quiz show. Both candidates in 1960 sought exposure on TV in every possible way—filmed biographies, spot announcements, rallies, and debates—but Mr. Nixon was the more enterprising of the two. He wound up his campaign with "Dial Dick Nixon," a one-man telethon which reached new heights, or touched new depths, depending on your view. Mr. Nixon answered questions from viewers, chatted with his family and with movie stars, and heard fervent appeals for his election from Jinx Falkenberg and Ginger Rogers (who spoke for the *rentier* class in recalling that she too lived on a fixed income).

But Mr. Nixon, with a sure showman's instinct, sensed that too much floss and furs could blemish his image. "Let's cut the junk," he snapped at one point. "Let's just have questions for the next hour."

III

A good deal of the preoccupation with the image is of course pretense and fad, springing from an innocent desire to appear *au courant*. But there is more to it than that. It can be plausibly argued that the advent of the image is a symptom of potential corruption of our political system.

In essence, the assumption behind the talk about imagery is that appearance is far more important than substance. It is not whether the candidate *is* folksy, vigorous, experienced, and pious, but whether he *appears* to have those qualities. This is hardly an original doctrine; Machiavelli phrased it in its classic form four centuries ago. . . .

What *is* startling is that this dissembling quality should now be treated as a matter of course—and that psychiatrists, theologians, and political writers should engage in solemn public autopsies on the candidate's phantom self. This is not only startling; it is alarming. . . .

IV

In pragmatic political terms, too, the cult of the image has a disturbing implication. It is that a candidate's potential for the White House is measured not only by his true qualities but also by the astral personality he manages to project through a vacuum tube. The most convincing demonstration of the shortcomings of this approach can be made by taking an image inventory of Presidents past.

Let us begin in the approved IBM manner by turning the image into a statistical formula. Let us divide the image into seven components—manner, health, background, appearance, experience, viewpoint, and religion. In order for a candidate to compile a perfect score, he must: (1) appear to have an acceptably homey manner; (2) seem in robust health; (3) suggest a background of modest means; (4) look like a heroic marble bust; (5) possess an apparent record of extensive experience; (6) seem moderate in all his views; and (7) appear to be a model of Protestant piety.

It is a revelation to measure our Chief Executives by this standardized image yardstick. George Washington, for example, would score a meager four, because of his hopeless dentures, his insufficient informality, and his wealthy plantation background. John Adams would do little better, by virtue of his dubious Unitarian affiliation, his crotchety personality, and his Harvard taint.

Jefferson's image rating is a dismaying three. His eccentric religious views, his immoderate espousal of liberty and revolution, his affluence, and his withdrawn, intellectual manner would hardly provide an image adequate to the election of a county coroner. Andrew Jackson might do a little better (4.5), but his abrupt manner, his gaunt and gnarled appearance, and his splenetic partisanship would give an account executive cause to reconsider.

Of all our Presidents, Lincoln has the most dismal image; it is obvious why Stephen Douglas trounced Lincoln in the race for the Senate (I would give Douglas a 6-plus)-Odd-ball views on religion, an almost total lack of experience, rumors of illegitimacy, scarecrow appearance, melancholy disposition, an unfortunate ribald streak, *and warts*—all this adds up to what the PR boys would call a big nothing. One can hear the authentic voice of Madison Avenue: "J.B., there'd be a civil war if the Republicans put up that village crank."

Cleveland, of course, is automatically out of the running because he publicly admitted to fathering a bastard child, and Teddy Roosevelt is too bumptious, too toothy, too dogmatic, and too wealthy. Mark Hanna, who knew a good image when he saw one, spoke for the ages when he gasped, "Now look, that damned cowboy is President of the United States!" Wilson would get the same low rating (3.2) for the opposite reasons: too aloof, too highbrow, too frail-looking, too sanctimonious.

As for Franklin Roosevelt (4.9), the negative factors are physical infirmity, excessive wealth, and a Harvard degree. Harry Truman is impossible: a failure in business, immoderate language, flashy sport shirts—how he ever beat the superbly imaged Thomas E. Dewey (6.95) is matter for wonder.

On the other hand, if we peer backward, certain Presidents emerge with impeccable images:

James Buchanan: A muscular six-footer with an impressive record of experience (Secretary of State, Minister to Great Britain, Congressman), magnificent bearing, a stout Presbyterian.

Ulysses S. Grant: Humble origins, a salty virility, sound experience, a good Methodist, and—as a bonus—name well-known.

Rutherford B. Hayes: Stately appearance, with a reassuring patriarchal beard, moderate views, ample experience (Governor of Ohio), eight children, regular Methodist church-goer.

William McKinley: Stunning profile, impression of enormous vitality, sound and sane views, well-seasoned (Governor and Congressman), a pillar of Methodism.

Warren G. Harding: Handsomest President of this century, a staunch Baptist but with winning bonhomie, broad experience (Lt. Governor, Senator), sturdily moderate.

The clinching point is that all of these Chief Executives look far more impressive on a postage stamp than a Lincoln or Jefferson. It is strange that the Post Office Department relegates Harding and Buchanan to such exotic denominations as fifteen cents and two dollars.

Coming to the present, there can be little debate as to which of the two candidates in 1960 had the more salable image. Mr. Nixon's persona is marred only by a trace of Quakerism. Self-made, brimming with experience, prodigiously moderate, and as folksy as a Sears, Roebuck catalogue, Mr. Nixon deserves a respectable 6.54 rating. Then let us examine John Fitzgerald Kennedy: Controversial religious affiliation, callow appearance, a trace of arrogance in manner, the Harvard blot, millionaire background, an author. "He'll never do, J.B.," says a voice on the thirty-sixth floor, "with that corny New Frontier routine and that lover-boy look."

One wonders whether it is not time to halt this degrading game by burying the mischievously occult word. An appropriate epitaph might be the Commandment which, as you recall, warns the children of Israel: "Thou shalt not make unto thee any graven image. . . ."

JOSEPH KASELOW

*P.R. Brains in Birmingham; Task: Lift Image**

May, 1963
A group of Birmingham public relations men is going to fight the city's public image of police dogs and fire hoses with press releases and paperback books. The group is setting up a Birmingham public relations office to counteract what it calls the "holier-than-thou" reporting in the Northern press.

The development, probably the most formidable undertaking in history for the public relations business, is reported in today's PR Reporter, which is published in Meriden, N.H. Fred A. Wondress, a Birmingham public relations consultant, told the newsletter: "Excellent writers here who know and love Birmingham feel it is a hopeless task to get their viewpoints published in national magazines. A few eager newsmen, photographers and TV men, ambitious for better jobs in New York and good freelance pay, continue to distort Birmingham's public image."

The p.r. man said real progress was being made in improving the city's image "before Martin Luther King moved in and caused the current unrest." In addition to the p.r. office being set up, the group will call on the top p.r. brains in the community to help with the world image problem, according to the newsletter.

Said Mr. Wondress: "After all, with all this interest in Birmingham, it should be easier to tell the world what's good about us because it's been hearing so much bad."

In other words, there's no way to go but up.

The PR Newsletter also spoke with a Negro p.r. man in Birmingham who told them he hadn't noticed any special p.r. activity there and that the "situation hasn't caused any change in our regular p.r. activities except to make it pretty difficult getting in and out of the building."

Probably slipped on the wet pavement.

* from the *New York Herald Tribune*.

SOME SPECIAL EXERCISES, AD HOMINEM

H. L. MENCKEN

Gamalielese

1921

On the question of the logical content of Dr. Harding's harangue of last Friday I do not presume to have views. The matter has been debated at great length by the editorial writers of the Republic, all of them experts in logic; moreover, I confess to being prejudiced. When a man arises publicly to argue that the United States entered the late war because of a "concern for preserved civilization," I can only snicker in a superior way and wonder why he isn't holding down the chair of history in some American university. When he says that the United States has "never sought territorial aggrandizement through force," the snicker arises to the virulence of a chuckle, and I turn to the first volume of General Grant's memoirs. And when, gaining momentum, he gravely informs the boobery that "ours is a constitutional freedom where the popular will is supreme, and minorities are sacredly protected," then I abandon myself to a mirth that transcends, perhaps, the seemly, and send picture postcards of A. Mitchell Palmer and the Atlanta Penitentiary to all of my enemies who happen to be Socialists.

But when it comes to the style of a great man's discourse, I can speak with a great deal less prejudice, and maybe with somewhat more competence, for I have earned most of my livelihood for twenty years past by translating the bad English of a multitude of authors into measurably better English. Thus qualified professionally, I rise to pay my small tribute to Dr. Harding. Setting aside a college professor or two and half a dozen dipsomaniacal newspaper reporters, he takes the first place in my Valhalla of literati. That is to say, he writes the worst English that I have ever encountered. It reminds me of a string of wet sponges; it reminds me of tattered washing on the line; it reminds me of stale bean soup, of college yells, of dogs barking idiotically through endless nights. It is so bad that a sort of grandeur creeps into it. It drags itself out of the dark abysm (I was about to write abscess!) of pish, and crawls insanely up the topmost pinnacle of posh. It is rumble and bumble. It is flap and doodle. It is balder and dash.

But I grow lyrical. More scientifically, what is the matter with it? Why does it seem so flabby, so banal, so confused and childish, so stupidly at war with sense? If you first read the inaugural address and then heard it intoned, as I did (at least in part), then you will perhaps arrive at an answer. That answer is very simple. When Dr. Harding prepares a speech he does not think it out in terms of an educated reader locked up in jail, but in terms of a great horde of stoneheads gathered around a stand. That is to say, the thing is always a stump speech; it is conceived as a stump speech and written as a stump speech. More, it is a stump speech addressed primarily to the sort of audience that the speaker has been used to all his life, to wit, an audience of small town yokels, of low political serfs, or morons scarcely able to understand a word of more than two syllables, and wholly unable to pursue a logical idea for more than two centimeters.

Such imbeciles do not want ideas—that is, new ideas, ideas that are unfamiliar, ideas that challenge their attention. What they want is simply a gaudy series of platitudes, of threadbare phrases terrifically repeated, of sonorous nonsense driven home with gestures. As I say, they can't understand many words of more than two syllables, but that is not saying that they do not esteem such words. On the contrary, they like them and demand them. The roll of incomprehensible polysyllables enchants them. They like phrases which thunder like salvos of artillery. Let that thunder sound, and they take all the rest on trust. If a sentence begins furiously and then peters out into fatuity, they are still satisfied. If a phrase has a punch in it, they do not ask that it also have a meaning. If a word slides off the tongue like a ship going down the ways, they are content and applaud it and wait for the next.

Brought up amid such hinds, trained by long practice to engage and delight them, Dr. Harding carries over his stump manner into everything he writes. He is, perhaps, too old to learn a better way. He is, more likely, too discreet to experiment. The stump speech, put into cold type, maketh the judicious to grieve. But roared from an actual stump, with arms flying and eyes flashing and the old flag overhead, it is certainly and brilliantly effective. Read the inaugural address, and it will gag you. But hear it recited through a sound magnifier, with grand gestures to ram home its periods, and you will begin to understand it.

Let us turn to a specific example. I exhume a sentence from the latter half of the eminent orator's discourse:

> I would like government to do all it can to mitigate, then, in understanding, in mutuality of interest, in concern for the common good, our tasks will be solved.

I assume that you have read it. I also assume that you set it down as idiotic—a series of words without sense. You are quite right; it is. But now imagine it intoned as it was designed to be intoned. Imagine the slow tempo of a public speech. Imagine the stately unrolling of the first clause, the delicate pause upon the word "then"—and then the loud discharge of the phrase "in understanding," "in mutuality of interest," "in concern for the common good," each with its attendant glare and roll of the eyes, each with its sublime heave, each with its gesture of a blacksmith bringing down his sledge upon an egg—imagine all this, and then ask yourself where you have got. You have got, in brief, to a point where you don't know what it is all about. You hear and applaud the phrases, but their connection has already escaped you. And so, when in violation of all sequence and logic, the final phrase, "our tasks will be solved," assaults you, you do not notice its disharmony—all you notice is that, if this or that, already forgotten, is done, "our tasks will be solved." Whereupon glad of the assurance and thrilled by the vast gestures that drive it home, you give a cheer.

That is, if you are the sort of man who goes to political meetings, which is to say, if you are the sort of man that Dr. Harding is used to talking to, which is to say, if you are a jackass.

The whole inaugural address reeked with just such nonsense. The thing started off with an error in English in its very first sentence—the confusion of pronouns in the *one-he* combination, so beloved of bad newspaper reporters. It bristled with words misused: *Civic* for *civil*, *luring* for *alluring*, *womanhood* for *women*, *referendum* for *reference*, even *task* for *problem*. "The *task* is to be *solved*"—what could be worse? Yet I find it twice. "The expressed views of world opinion"—what irritating tautology! "The expressed conscience of progress"—what on earth does it mean? "This is not selfishness, it is sanctity"—what intelligible idea do you get out of that? "I know that Congress and the administration will favor every wise government policy to aid the resumption and encourage continued progress"—the resumption of what? "Service is the supreme *commitment* of life."—*ach, du heiliger!*

But is such bosh out of place in a stump speech? Obviously not. It is precisely and thoroughly in place in a stump speech. A tight fabric of ideas would weary and exasperate the audience; what it wants is simply a loud burble of words, a procession of phrases that roar, a series of whoops. This is what it got in the inaugural address of the Hon. Warren Gamaliel Harding. And this is what it will get for four long years—unless God sends a miracle and the corruptible puts on incorruption. . . . Almost I long for the sweeter song, the rubber-stamps of more familiar design, the gentler and more seemly bosh of the late Woodrow.

Mrs. Eleanor Roosevelt, a frequent target of Pegler's columns, was herself the author of the widely-syndicated "My Day."

WESTBROOK PEGLER

His Day

1940

Yesterday morning I took a train to New York City and sat beside a gentleman who was reading the 1937 Report of the International Recording Secretary of the World Home Economics and Children's Aptitude and Recreation Foundation of which my very good friend, Dr. Mary McTwaddle, formerly of Vassar, is the American delegate. This aroused my interest and I ventured to remark that I had once had the pleasure of entertaining a group of young people who were deeply concerned with the neglected problem of the Unmarried Father. It turned out that the gentleman himself was an unmarried father so we had a very interesting chat until he got off at Metuchen.

In the afternoon a group of young people came in for tea and we had a discussion of the effect of early environment on the efficiency of war workers. I am afraid environment is more important than many of us think and I have asked the Department of Agriculture to make a survey. Of course some people have more environment than others but then, I am afraid, very often the reverse is true and that is something that one cannot dismiss lightly these days.

Later in the day we took a train up the river where a group of young people were waiting to have a discussion of the psychology of youth in the postwar world. It is very stimulating to observe the eager interest of such young people, some of them not more than 35, in the serious problems of the world. They seem to me to face problems much more candidly than some of us seem to think they do and it is very encouraging to see this, for I believe they will have a great influence for good in the future.

I left them after a time and went over to the Big House and had a discussion with my very good friend, Dr. Fusty, formerly of Smith College. He had written an article for the World Mothers' Planning Council of which he is the Honorary International Research Adviser, Emeritus, and one paragraph in particular seemed to me so profound that I obtained his permission to quote it for my readers. It says:

"Students will not fail to value the institutions and privileges of the tradition they inherit if they resist the temptation not to keep vividly aware that their duty to society is perennial, in the larger, rather than the narrower, sense of the word."

This seemed particularly thought-provoking to me. I shall think about it one day soon.

Returning to the Little House I mounted my bicycle and rode 12 miles up and down the path to save gasoline. I have figured that if I ride 10 or 12 miles up and down the path every day that will be at least 60 miles a week and I shall save about four gallons a week.

Another group of young people had arrived at the Little House and we plunged at once into a very interesting discussion of the duty of the citizen not only toward his country but toward himself and his fellow man in relation to the past and the critical days ahead. One gentleman had rather strong ideas on the subject of nail biting and while, of course, I realize that there are two sides of the question, I am afraid capital punishment for nail biters is rather severe. I prefer what seems to me the more democratic way and proposed to approach it as a world problem, as nail biting is not a matter of race or creed. After a very spirited discussion we formed an organization which we are calling the Provisional World Extension Congress Against Nail Biting or

P.W.E.C.A.N.B. Six of the young people pledged themselves to establish local committees immediately in their home cities. After all, the eradication of this deplorable vice is in the hands of the future mothers of the world.

After dinner several old retainers came over to the Big House and together with Dr. Fusty and the young people we had a very enjoyable game of squat-tag on the lawn. This was followed by a brisk round of spin the plate and after bobbing for apples we retired at 9:45.

In bed I read Ludwig Donnervetter's *All Is Everything*. It is very beautiful and brings out powerfully the struggle of the young people to organize their world through student collaboration and discussion. I sometimes think we seem to miss many opportunities for better understanding because peoples are set apart by differences in language.

DWIGHT MACDONALD

A Note on Wallese

1947

Wallaceland is the mental habitat of Henry Wallace plus a few hundred thousand regular readers of *The New Republic, The Nation,* and *PM.* It is a region of perpetual fogs, caused by the warm winds of the liberal Gulf Stream coming in contact with the Soviet glacier. Its natives speak "Wallese," a debased provincial dialect.

Wallese is as rigidly formalized as Mandarin Chinese. The Good people are described by ritualistic adjectives: "forward looking," "freedom loving," "clear thinking," and, of course, "democratic" and "progressive." The Bad people are always "reactionaries" or "red-baiters"; there are surprisingly few of them, considering the power they wield, and they are perversely wicked, since their *real* interests would best be served by the Progressive and Realistic policies favored by the Good people. Wallese is always employed to Unite rather than to Divide (hence the fog), and to Further Positive, Constructive Aims rather than Merely to

Engage in Irresponsible and Destructive Criticism. As George F. Babbitt of Zenith City, who had his own brand of Wallese in the twenties, used to say: "It's Easy Enough to Criticize!" There are other conventions in Wallese. Issues are always Clarified, Events invariably Exert Pressure, Problems are Faced (good) or Not Faced (bad), and the World is either On the March (good) or At the Crossroads (neutral) or Facing a Crisis (bad). No article may be composed in Wallese unless it includes at least one of the following terms: "grass roots," "integration," "horizon," "general welfare." The frequent use of the "should and will" or "can and must" construction is also obligatory, as in the (imaginary) sentence: "The American people can and must free the forward march of technology from the dead hand of monopoly." The adjective "new" is much used, as: "new horizons," "new frontiers," and "the new democracy" (which means the old democracy minus all democratic elements). Like "adventure," another important word in Wallese, it suggests something Different (and God knows we're sick of what we've got now), Positive, Exciting; something, in short, to which the old critical categories, which have proved so lethal in the hands of Irresponsible and Destructive critics, cannot be applied. Thus many of us are by now somewhat leery of both democracy and *The New Republic*, but how about the new democracy and the new *New Republic?* Perhaps the greatest sentence ever composed in Wallese is the following, from the hand of the master himself: "New frontiers beckon with meaningful adventure."

Wallese is not, of course, Henry Wallace's personal idiom. There is nothing personal about his writing—indeed, alienation from his own individual interests, values and enjoyment is the most striking thing about Wallace's whole "style" as a political figure. Unlike Churchill or Roosevelt, for example, who clearly got a big kick out of exercising power and hurling around the thunderbolts of political rhetoric, Wallace is lumpish, depressed, weighed down by a sense of duty (or of guilt?). His political personality curiously resembles Herbert Hoover's. "The words that spring from his mind," writes an admirer, "sometimes stumbling, sometimes leaping, are those of a man troubled, deeply troubled by the far-reaching sickness of these strange times. He takes little pride in his writing. . . . 'Strangely enough, I don't like to write,' he says." As literary criticism, nothing could be wider of the mark: Wallace's words don't spring, they don't leap, and they don't even stumble; they just ooze. But it is true that his writing is that of a sick and troubled man, a man not at peace with himself, alienated from his own individuality, a man who doesn't enjoy writing because he senses obscurely that it has nothing to do with his own pleasure and convictions.

Wallese is a collective product, a style that has developed in liberal journalism more or less instinctively as a drapery for the harsh political realities of our time. The justification for calling it "Wallese" is that Henry Wallace has parlayed it into a career. . . .

JOHN UPDIKE

Mr. Ex-Resident

1961

(Assuming, unlikely though it seems at first blush, that Harry S Truman, author of "Mr. Citizen," also wrote Adam's memoirs.)

A large number of people have expressed curiosity as to how Eve and I like residing out of Eden. The answer is very simple. We like it fine.

I began as a farm boy, so the thorns and thistles of the "outer world" are not news to me. We thoroughly enjoyed our years in Eden, but now that they are over we find many things to enjoy elsewhere. Pleasant as it was, Eden always had the disadvantage for me personally of being a little too lush and orderly. As the saying goes, I like some grit to my mash.

So many contradictory accounts of what happened have been published that I think the time has come to set the record straight. Now that my grandson Enoch has builded a city of the same name, I know there is a firm watertight place where the records can be kept. I think it is very important, whether or not it causes embarrassment in Heaven, for the First Man to set down in his own words his side of the story so that the generations succeeding him in this world can understand their present condition and why things are the way they are.

When the matter first came up of eating of the tree of knowledge of good and evil, I consulted with Eve and with the serpent and their consensus seemed to be that it could do no harm and might do a lot of good. It is easy to identify mistakes in hindsight, but at the time this was the best available information I could get, and it was my responsibility to act upon it. And I did.

The following day, God came to me and asked, "Hast thou eaten of the tree, whereof I commanded thee that thou shouldest not eat?"

I thought this was a curious question, since if He were omniscient as supposed He must have already known that I certainly had. But I have never had any trouble keeping the reins on my temper. With the utmost patience and courtesy I explained the situation.

When I was done, He simply told me, "In the sweat of thy face shalt thou eat bread, till thou return unto the ground." I felt lucky at that, since what He said to Eve and the serpent was far worse.

We wasted no time getting out, once the circumstances had become definite. I expected no fanfare, so it was one of the deeply moving experiences of my life to see all the cherubim waving goodbye with their flaming swords. I had not in any way asked them to do this. It was a truly spontaneous demonstration.

Two things need to be cleared up, for the reason that there has been a lot of improper and inaccurate speculation written concerning them.

The first is this. At no time, then or since, have Eve and I exchanged recriminations. She was produced from my rib and I have never for a moment wanted my rib back. In my opinion, she did a wonderful job raising Cain and Abel in an environment that was necessarily unsettled and far from ideal. If the boys did not turn out exactly the way we had hoped, this is no excuse for the disproportionate publicity that has surrounded their quarrel. It is course a tribute to the office of First Man that everything that happens within his family circle attracts widespread comment.

Secondly, a lot of well-meaning—I will give them the benefit of the doubt—souls have expected us to resent how the serpent has insinuated himself into the good graces of subsequent administrations and is in fact enjoying a good deal of present prosperity. This shows they have no knowledge of the nature of the cosmos. It is the essence of the system that the serpent, having served his term with us, should seek "greener pastures." While I cannot feel that his advice was always in the best interests of my family, he was by his own lights successful and must be admired for it. History has been created by just this type of personality.

I have been called, among many other things, an optimist.

I do not think of myself as an optimist or a pessimist but as a normal human individual blessed with 100% excellent physical health since the day of my creation. At the time, a certain number of angels whom I do not wish to name doubted my ability to serve as First Man. I showed them that they were wrong. It is my sincere belief that any healthy man, placed in that position, could have done the job.

Though there is a lot wrong with the state of the world as we know it, I think entirely too much is made of the Fall. Eden just could not have accommodated all the men and women who now enjoy the blessings, qualified though they are in some instances, of earthly life. I lived in Eden many years and I flatter myself that I know more about its dimensions than most of the theological journals I make it my habit to read. These are written by good men, but their morbid preoccupation with Original Sin rubs me the wrong way, though I don't mind in the least whatever they say about me. I have no regrets. And I recommend that you have none either.

This famous parody was widely circulated in a variety of anonymous versions within a few weeks of its first informal appearance. The one below is the original, furnished by the author, as first published under copyright in the Virginia City, Nevada, Territorial Enterprise.

OLIVER JENSEN

The Gettysburg Address in Eisenhowerese

1957

I haven't checked these figures but eighty-seven years ago, I think it was, a number of individuals organized a governmental setup here in this country, I believe it covered certain eastern areas, with this idea they were following up based on a sort of national-independence arrangement and the program that every individual is just as good as every other individual. Well, now, of course, we are dealing with this big difference of opinion, civil disturbance you might say, although I don't like to appear to take sides or name any individuals, and the point is naturally to check up, by actual experience in the field, to see whether any govern-mental setup with a basis like the one I was mentioning has any validity, whether that dedication, you might say, by those early individuals will pay off in lasting values.

Well, here we are, you might put it that way, all together at the scene where one of these disturbances between different sides got going. We want to pay our tribute to those loved ones, those departed individuals who made the supreme sacrifice here on the basis of their opinions about how this setup ought to be handled. It is absolutely in order and one hundred percent okay to do this.

But if you look at the overall picture of this, we can't pay any tribute —we can't sanctify this area—we can't hallow according to whatever individuals' creeds or faiths or sort of religious outlooks are involved— like I said about this very particular area. It was those individuals them-selves, including the enlisted men, very brave individuals, who have given this religious character to the area. The way I see it, the rest of the world will not remember any statements issued here but it will never forget how these men put their shoulders to the wheel and carried this idea down the fairway.

Our job, the living individuals' job here, is to pick up the burden and sink the putt they made these big efforts here for. It is our job to get on with the assignment—and from these deceased fine individuals to take extra inspiration, you could call it, for the same theories about the setup for which they did such a lot. We have to make up our minds right here and now, as I see it, that they didn't put out all that blood, perspiration and—well—that they didn't just make a dry run here, and that all of us here, under God, that is, the God of our choice, shall beef up this idea about freedom and liberty and those kind of arrangements, and that government of all individuals, by all individuals, and for the individuals, shall not pass out of the world-picture.

What made this burlesque of an Eisenhower press briefing into an international incident was the reaction of the President's press secretary, James Hagerty. Denouncing Buchwald's "transcript" as "unadulterated rot," Hagerty demanded (and got) equal space from the New York Herald Tribune *for his denial.*

ART BUCHWALD

P.S. from NATO

1957

The NATO conference now going on in Paris is being covered by 1,700 top-flight, highly paid journalists from every corner of the globe. Every detail of the conference is being given careful and thorough coverage. The star of the show is President Eisenhower, and every facet of the President's stay in Paris is being reported to the public in detail. In order to keep the press up on the President's activities, briefings are held at the Hotel Crillon in the morning, at noon and in the early evening, and there is even a special one held late at night for reporters who can't sleep.

We happened to attend one of these late-night briefings with several correspondents of early-morning newspapers. To give you an idea of what takes place at one of these briefings, we took down a transcript.

The man behind the microphone arrived at 12:30 A.M.

"I'm sorry I'm late, gentlemen, but I thought the show at the Lido would end at 11:30. I have a few things to report. The President went to bed at 11:06 tonight."

Q.: Jim, have Premier Gaillard and Prime Minister Macmillan also retired?

A.: To my knowledge they have.

Q.: Then are we to assume that they will not meet with the President until morning?

A.: Yes, you could assume that.

Q.: Then does that mean he's going to meet with Adenauer during the night?

A.: I didn't say that. As far as I know he'll sleep until morning.

Q.: Jim, whose idea was it for the President to go to sleep?

A.: It was the President's idea. He was tired and decided to go to sleep.

Q.: Did Sherman Adams, or Dr. Snyder, or the President's son suggest he go to sleep?

A.: As far as I know, the President suggested the idea himself.

Q.: Jim, did the President speak to anyone before retiring?

A.: He spoke to the Secretary of State.

Q.: What did he say to the Secretary of State, Jim?

A.: He said: "Good night, Foster."

Q.: And what did the Secretary say to the President?

A.: He said: "Good night, Mr. President."

Q.: The Secretary didn't say: "Pleasant dreams"?

A.: Not to my knowledge. I have nothing on that.

Q.: Jim, do you have any idea what the President is dreaming of this very moment?

A.: No, the President has never revealed to me any of his dreams.

Q.: Are we to assume from that that the President doesn't dream?

A.: I'm not saying he does or he doesn't. I just said I don't know.

Q.: Jim, how will the President be waked up tomorrow morning? Will it be by alarm clock, or will someone come knock on the door?

A.: That hasn't been decided yet. But as soon as it has, I'll let you fellows know.

Q.: Do you have any idea who the President will see first tomorrow morning?

A.: I imagine he'll see the Secretary of State.

Q.: What will he say to him?

A.: The President plans to say: "Good morning, Foster."

Q.: What will the Secretary reply?

A.: "Good morning, Mr. President."

Q.: That's all?

A.: That's all I can tell you at this moment.

Q.: Jim, when the President went to bed last night, how did he feel?

A.: He was feeling chipper and in good spirits.

Q.: How many blankets were on the bed?

A.: I'm not sure. Maybe two or three. But certainly no more than he uses in Washington.

Q.: Could we say three?

A.: I better check that. I know three blankets were made available but it's possible he didn't use all of them.

Q.: One could have been kicked off during the night?

A.: Yes, that could be possible, but it's unlikely.

Q.: Was there a glass of water by the bed?

A.: There was a glass of water and a pitcher.

Q.: Jim, could we have another briefing before morning?

A.: I don't see what would be accomplished by that.

Q.: It might tend to clarify the situation.

A.: I think the best thing would be to have the briefing after the President gets up.

Q.: What about breakfast, Jim?

A.: I think we better have another briefing about breakfast, after it's over.

Q.: Thank you, Jim.

A.: Okay, see you later.

Here is another piece with references that may need explanation. The important ones are a) *the failure of world heavyweight boxing champion Ingemar Johansson to defend his title successfully against Floyd Patterson, and* b) *the cancellation of President Eisenhower's trip to Japan shortly before, under pressure of hostile Japanese student demonstrations, but presented as a kind of diplomatic victory.*

JAMES RESTON

To Ingemar Johansson with Love

1960

Dear Ingemar:

You asked me what you should say in your forthcoming TV report to the Swedish people about the recent regrettable incident with Mr. Floyd Patterson at the Polo Grounds in New York.

I have three suggestions. The best thing is to say nothing. The next best thing is to deny that you ever went to America. But if you have to make a report, I suggest that you follow the victory-through-defeat system used by President Eisenhower in his report on Japan, speaking—if you are now able to speak—as follows:

My friends:

I have just returned to Sweden from America, where almost everybody treated me very kindly. It has been a trip so marked by events that I shall try this evening to give you a simple background of fact against which these recent events can be viewed in perspective.

First, Swedish relations with the United States have been strengthened. I wish that every one of you could have accompanied Birgit and me to New York and thus witnessed for yourselves the outpouring of friendship and respect for Sweden and the Swedish way of life.

Second, the happiness created among the Colored people of America as a result of my appearance there this time was not only heartwarming but surpassed by far their reaction to my last visit.

Finally, as the Marquis of Queensberry once said, it matters not in this life whether you win or lose, but how you play the game, especially when economic rewards are so agreeable.

Now, let's look at the background of this trip and the others I have taken in the interests of world understanding. For some years the world has been inclined to think only of the beauty of Swedish women.

Meanwhile, the heroism and warrior tradition of Swedish men had long been overlooked, not only by atheistic international communism, but even among the peoples of our sister democracies.

Accordingly, I have traveled tirelessly around the world, seeking lucrative personal contacts in my own people-to-people program, and belting old retreads regardless of race, creed or color.

With the passage of time I began to receive urgent invitations to attend a heavyweight summit meeting in America. Many months ago I concluded that I should accept these invitations whenever the price was right. In this decision Birgit enthusiastically concurred.

Incidentally, I have never believed that victory and money were the only things in life, although, as the Americans say in their picturesque way, these things are not to be sneezed at. What matters is the international goodwill that results from bilateral reciprocal aggression before multitudes of well-heeled savages in the overdeveloped and under-educated areas of the globe.

Now as to the incident at the Polo Grounds, I have been assured that the people there were, in overwhelming majority, anxious to welcome me as a representative of a nation with which they wished to cooperate and have friendly relations.

It is true that the outrageous conduct of a violent and disorderly minority prevented me from achieving all of my objectives, and that Mr. Patterson displayed toward me, especially in the fifth round, a certain animus and even hostility, which temporarily interrupted my mission.

Nevertheless, if you could have heard the cheering that filled that great arena, when I finally regained consciousness, I think you would agree with me that a great many peace-loving Americans were actually overjoyed at my survival.

I shall never forget the look of relief on the face of Mr. Patterson at the end. He kept saying in a faraway voice: "Wake up, Ingemar. Wake up!" It is in such moments a man realizes there is no defeat.

Now, a final personal word:

Sweden has nothing to regret. In the long history of human conflict no man has ever lost and regained the heavyweight championship of the world until now.

As I said to Birgit, this is our consolation: We have made it possible for Mr. Patterson to lose and regain a crown, and all I can hope is that he will do the same for me.

Thank you and—good night!

KARL E. MEYER

JFK's Pressmanship

1962

Mr. Stephen Potter, if the idea has not already occurred to him, ought to begin work instantly on another volume in his useful series of manuals on how to win an argument without actually trying. There is need for a scholarly and specialized work to be entitled *Presidential Pressmanship*,

A Guide for the Executive Gamesman in the White House. Each American President has his own style in dealing with prying reporters at the weekly news conferences, and the work ought properly to begin with a thoughtful historical survey.

Franklin Roosevelt, for example, employed the methods of a smiling charmer and was an adroit fencer who could occasionally untip his blade. Mr. Truman specialized in the brisk, lecturing tone. And President Eisenhower, of course, was known for his exotic syntactical flights that bemused and bewitched. There is the Classic Eisenhower Balk-Line Thrust, which goes like this:

Q.: Mr. President, what is your position on the Gregorian calendar?

A.: Well now, I will say this. These things—the sort of things to which I assume that your question may refer—these sort of things, as I say, are not subject to the kind of answer, let me put it this way, that makes black only black and white only white, but you have to re- member this—check me if my memory is wrong, Jim—in this kind of governmental setup we have here, these types of problems, you might say calendrical questions, are best approached in a middle- of-the-road manner, as I believe I have said many times. Besides, I never deal in personalities. Who was that fellow Gregor?

In his short time in office, President Kennedy has revolutionized Press- manship. He has given to his responses the cultivated cadences of Harvard mixed in with some peculiar Kennedy nasal quirks ("Cuba" is "Cuber," and "idea" is "ideer"). His essential approach is flat, his idiom curiously bureaucratic, his tone chillingly sober. As a result, his occa- sional embellishments of wit sparkle with special brightness because the setting is so drab; it is like encountering a pun in a telephone directory.

After a few faltering moments last year, Mr. Kennedy has established himself as a master of Pressmanship. With the bland assurance of a seasoned practitioner, the President can deflect a question and leave the beguiling impression that a response has been given when in fact nothing has been said at all. He frequently relies on what can be called the No-Comment Bank-Shot. Consider these variants:

Q.: Can you tell us, sir, what your Administration plans to do to imple- ment Physical Fitness Week?

(Variant #1)

A.: These are, I know, difficult questions and there are no simple answers. We intend to hear all views on the subject and to reach a judgment that will protect the vital interests of this country.

(Variant #2)

A.: I am hopeful that proper consideration will be given to this matter, and that the interests of all concerned can be met in a responsible way that takes account of the basic rights of those who wish to be fit.

(Variant #3)

A.: It should be a source of satisfaction to all of us that the appropriate agencies of this Government are deeply concerned with the problem you have mentioned. There is every intention of meeting our commitments fully in lessening any tensions that may arise from the implementation of this program.

Of late, specialists in Pressmanship have noticed that the President, perhaps out of an increased self-confidence based on practice, has relied heavily on the Massive Deterrence Response, frequently modified by a Statistical Twist. The essential strategy is to engulf the questioner in a torrent of facts, thereby paralyzing the auditory senses. For example:

Q.: Mr. President, what are your plans for dealing with the surplus stockpile of ostrich feathers accumulated under our barter program?

A.: If my recollection is correct, a seven-man task force was appointed under Executive Order 3255 to report back on inter-departmental usages of this commodity. That task force, I believe, has held three meetings, one on August 27, 1961, another on December 4, 1961, and a final one on March 13 of this year. Under legislation enacted by the 14th Congress on October 2, 1863, passed, as I recall, by a 67 to 14 vote, there is a limit of 2.4 million tons set on surplus stocks. There is a difficult problem in balancing various interests, but when the task force has completed its assignment, I fully intend to see that the results are made available. Mr. Salinger has passed me a note indicating that the date will be announced some time in the future.

These specimens of JFK's Pressmanship are familiar to millions who watch in expectant admiration for the most spectacular of the devices used by the President. This technique, which might be called the Rhetorical Ricochet or Dialectical Drop-Shot, is employed only at strategic moments and is intended to silence the questioner with an aggressive counterattack. If there is a trace of ill-temper in the President's reply, he seeks to offset the effect by promptly recognizing one of the lady reporters who can be counted on to ask a silly question. Here is the Rhetorical Ricochet:

Q.: Sir, what is the policy of your Administration concerning the excessive use of adverbs in your state papers? As you yourself remarked—

A.: What's that?

Q.: As you yourself remarked, more action verbs are desirable to get America moving again, and—

A.: Excuse me, you haven't stated my position correctly. I refer you to a speech delivered in Eugene, Oregon, that explicitly states: "We intend to yield neither to the tyranny of words nor to the words of tyranny. The extremes of using too many words to say too little and of using too few words to say too much are equally abhorrent to this Government."

That is our duty as I see it. I intend to see that we meet that obligation. Over there, Mrs. Craig?

Q.: Mr. President, sir, is it true that Caroline is taking courses in Esperanto?

A.: No. (Laughter.)

Thank you, Mr. President.

ROGER ANGELL

The Great Starch Debate

(*Mr. Nixon Encounters Still Another Crisis*)

1962

My experience has taught me that the first step in facing a crisis is the ability to recognize that the crisis does in fact exist. This requires a cool head and considerable personal background in crisis-recognition. Looking back on it now, I am certain that no one in our group but I sensed that a full-scale crisis was in the making on that warm evening, early in my campaign for the governorship of my native state, when we returned to our hotel and I discovered that my shirts had not come back from the laundry. We had enjoyed a busy and deeply satisfying day of campaigning in the upper San Fernando Valley. I had made a number of hard-hitting points in thirteen separate speeches, and from the emotional point of view I had had the always enriching experience of shaking hands with hundreds of folks who seemed decidedly pleased with the principles I had laid before them. It had been another mountaintop experience, and after it was over there was a distinct temptation for my campaign staff and me to relax momentarily and indulge ourselves in the luxury of retrospection and self-congratulation. My discovery, at this juncture, that my shirts had not come up from the laundry was at first only an irritation. I had exhausted my small personal stock of clean white shirts in the previous few days on the road, and the hotel laundry had made a firm commitment to me of delivery by 5 P.M. I had made it entirely clear to them that I required a clean shirt for that evening, when I was scheduled to address a Republican Peach-Pickers' Rally and then to participate in a brass-tacks public debate on the issue of water fluoridation in parochial schools. When a thorough search of my suite turned up no package of clean shirts, I knew I had to take decisive action. I got busy on the telephone, speaking in person first to the front desk, then to the laundry room. Were my shirts ready? If not, would they be ready within the next hour?

Answer: negative. No one appeared to know where my shirts were. I hung up.

My estimate of the situation sharpened. As I sat by the bedroom telephone, engaged in inner debate, Earl Mazo, Bill Key, Alvin Moscow, Don Hughes, Jim Bassett, and several other members of my team came in. They sensed that something was "up." I quickly spelled out the facts for them and asked them for their evaluations. I told them I wanted advice, not sugar-coating.

The gist of their group opinion was at first glance both sensible and attractive. They urged me to take the easy way, to ride with the punch. They pointed out that a search for the shirts and a full disclosure of the reasons for their disappearance could be time-consuming and, in the long run, frustrating. They outlined the potential political dynamite that could be touched off if some member of our press entourage got wind of any "scene" that might ensue if I determined to follow through personally and find my shirts in the hotel. Several opinions pinpointed the fact that I could still in all probability go out and buy a new shirt before the beginning of the evening schedule. At least two of my companions kindly offered to lend me one of their own clean shirts—a warm expression of personal loyalty that I still cherish. As far as content went, their advice was excellent.

Nevertheless, I asked them to leave me alone for a few minutes while I made a deeper evaluation. I explained to them that a leader must do more than count the noses of his advisers. Left alone, I realized that I would be fully pardoned if I came to the conclusion that the situation I faced lay in one of life's gray areas, where the easier decision was called for. But there were principles involved, and I knew that any man who shirked the inner struggle at a time like this was guilty of irresponsibility. I saw at once that this was a crisis of an entirely new kind. This was not simply a case of Nixon being inconvenienced by the carelessness of one hotel or one laundry. If I were to permit myself to be bluffed out at this stage, it would mean that a citizen was acquiescing to the inefficiencies that woolly-thinking apologists often declare to be an innate part of the American system. It would be a case of Nixon putting his tail between his legs and surrendering to bureaucracy. I could not in conscience take such a course and then go before the people as their candidate. My philosophy has always been to do what is right. My instinct in this case was to act, to find the shirts.

Once I saw the course I had to take, any tension I might have felt disappeared. Courage—that is, the absence of fear—comes from conviction. I had long since learned that the decision-making process—that is, thinking—is the most trying part of any crisis. Now that my mind was made up, I felt cool and ready for battle. But merely to be doubly sure, I put long-distance calls through to Herb Brownell, Tom Dewey, Allen Dulles, and Charlie Halleck. All of them concurred, in broad terms, with the wisdom of my decision, and Charlie added that I had again made him proud to be an American. Tom Dewey was most specific. "This is a matter you must decide for yourself, Dick," he stated.

I summoned my staff back into the room. Quickly, I laid the program before them. We would act, I said, because we were on the right side. But we would act responsibly, after thorough preparation and with proper respect for the workings of the hotel's administrative apparatus. I asked them to prepare the necessary background material I would require, including data on laundry operations in general in the Free World, average delivery time of shirts by non-private launderers, wages and working conditions enjoyed by union and non-union ironers and folders, and so forth. I asked them to have this material before me in fifteen minutes, which would allow me perhaps another fifteen minutes for a crash briefing and intensive homework before we swung into action. They hurried off eagerly, and then for the first time I allowed myself to relax for a moment and reflect on what curious but perennially stimulating encounters history continued to place before the man who had once, back in a plain boy's bedroom in Yorba Linda, allowed his modest daydreams to encompass only the possibility of one day making the high-school junior-varsity debating team. Now, as far as background was concerned, the stage was set for that encounter that the American press, with more enthusiasm than accuracy, was later to call the Great Starch Debate.

Accompanied by two of my aides, I stepped into the elevator, turned, and faced the front of the car. "Laundry room, please," I said in a firm voice. The operator stole a puzzled glance at me, but I looked straight ahead. As we went down, I took stock of my physical condition. I was a trifle edgy, my palms were damp, and there was an empty feeling in the pit of my stomach. I suppose some might say that I was "nervous," but by drawing on personal experience I was able to recognize and even welcome these signs for what they were—the symptoms of a normal man in descent in a fast elevator.

We alighted in the sub-basement and I strode directly through the doors of the laundry room. I was at once enveloped in clouds of steam, but my painstaking briefing had prepared me for this eventuality, and I did not hesitate. In spite of the steam and the hiss and roar of washers and pressing machines, I was able to single out my man, the laundry manager, at once. He was behind a counter, wearing a white undershirt and white trousers. I introduced myself, and we shook hands. While our aides grouped themselves around us in the manner prescribed by protocol and roughed out between them the substance of the conversations to come, I took stock of my man. He exuded an unmistakable impression of weariness and ennui. Here, I knew, was a powerful adversary —a hard-core laundry manager, steeled to complaints, magnificently trained in evasion.

I got off to a particularly good start by pointing out to him that his failure to deliver my shirts constituted a breach of contract. In effect, I told him, he had failed to live up to his end of one of those countless small but vital agreements that permit men of good will to function together in our increasingly complex world.

He feigned bewilderment. The delivery of shirts was not in his province, he stated—only their processing.

Instinctively, I knew I had to press my attack. I asked him if he ever had any difficulty sleeping at night if he knew that even one of his customers felt less than complete satisfaction with the laundry service that day. I roughed out for him a broad panoramic view of the operations of our vast mercantile system and its concomitant and essential service subdivision.

He seemed reluctant to debate the points I had raised. He pounded the counter and, with some vivid and distinctly non-diplomatic peasant adages, stated that I was adding to, rather than clarifying, our differences.

My intensive preparations allowed me to absorb and counter his attack without being thrown off balance. I knew that from the standpoint of temper control this would be the worst possible time for me to blow my stack. I decided to shift tactics. An "end run" was called for. I pointed out that while over fifty-one million American males owned white shirts, the average per-capita ownership (including steelworkers) was still only 2.3 shirts each, a figure that did not allow for any slipups in the laundry-processing industry. *Time* magazine later characterized this as "a beefed-up riposte that scored heavily in the drama."

Now it was his turn to change the pace. Forcing a laugh, he asked me if I was not being guilty of obscurantism.

"That's not my way," I retorted. "I shall never be guilty of obscurantism."

He poked a pudgy finger at me. "We are capable of dialectics, too, you know," he said menacingly.

Now we were going at it hammer and tongs. I was vaguely aware that a considerable crowd of laundresses, waiters, bellboys, and house detectives had surrounded us. None of them had ever heard anything like this before behind the doors of their laundry room, and I knew that even if I failed now in my primary mission, my journey would not prove to have been entirely in vain.

At this moment, one of the manager's assistants pressed a note into his hand. We both paused, panting in the steam, while he read its contents. He hesitated. "It seems," he said at last, "that your laundry has been found. It is in this room. Our position has been entirely justified. Your shirts are washed and ironed, but they have been detained here for reprocessing, because by inadvertence the starch was omitted. You will have them tomorrow, starched."

The day was won. Without knowing it, he had played directly into my hands, but years of experience in dealing with success now warned me that this was the time for magnanimity, not crowing. Smiling, I quoted to him Abraham Lincoln's remark, made in reference to one of his generals, that he preferred "starch in the man rather than in his shirt." It was my way of telling him that I never have my own shirts ironed with starch.

The manager shrugged. He turned, received the package of shirts from an assistant, and handed them to me. We shook hands warmly. Although the one-hundred-percent-successful outcome of our meeting had been largely unexpected, I was not unprepared even for this eventuality. Still holding his hand, I clapped him on the shoulder and said, "Isn't it fine that two men, each trained to a peak of creative usefulness by our great system of economic and personal incentives, can meet as we have and exchange views openly and without fear, thus adding to man's centuries-long struggle for understanding and freedom?"

He nodded wordlessly, and we parted. I turned and walked toward my elevator, ignoring the confused babble of voices behind me engaged in excited interrogation, recapitulation, and speculation. I pressed the elevator button. As I stood there, it occurred to me that many American men in their middle years might be suddenly depressed to find themselves, immediately after a personal success, standing in a hotel sub-basement with a package of laundry in their arms. I knew, however, that the most dangerous part of any crisis is its aftermath, the time of letdown. This is when the human system, wearied by tension and hyperbole, is all too apt to become exhausted and to indulge itself in destructive reflection. This knowledge enabled me to put the thought aside. I watched the needle on the indicator above the elevator door. The car was moving downward, but soon, I knew, it would rise again, taking me with it.

JAMES A. WECHSLER

Dry Spell

1963

(*Transcript of an unrehearsed, unrecorded, unconducted interview with Senate Republican leader Dirksen on the day's burning issue.*)

Q.: Senator, I am sure you are aware that there is growing concern in much of the country over the lack of rainfall in recent weeks. Have you been studying the problem?

DIRKSEN: Indeed I have. If I may say so, I have been thirsting for every available piece of information on this very grave situation.

Q.: Have you reached any conclusions?

DIRKSEN: Well, first let me say, gentlemen, that I hope this crisis will be approached in a full spirit of bipartisanship. Past mistakes are, one must say, water over the dam—

Q.: You mean you feel the long absence of rain is a matter for which the Administration must bear—

DIRKSEN: Now, I said nothing of the kind. It is, obviously, a matter of record that this prolonged dryness has occurred during Mr. Kennedy's reign, or perhaps I should say tenure, and if there has been negligence in high places, it should be exposed. But certainly I make no such charge at this time. I have always said, in this and similar circumstances, that politics must stop at the water's edge.

Q.: When you say "negligence in high places," sir, are you asserting that the Administration might be deliberately withholding rain until we get closer to the 1964 election?

DIRKSEN: I did not state any such thing. I remind you gentlemen that you brought this matter up. But since you did I merely call attention to the fact that, as a nation, we have again been caught high and dry, in a manner of speaking.

Q.: Then you would say this is a federal matter—that you don't hold Governor Rockefeller responsible for the absence of rain in New York?

DIRKSEN: Well, I have never minimized the role and responsibilities of the states. But this is not a local phenomenon we have been experiencing. It has blighted many states. There is a federal agency concerned primarily and indeed exclusively with the analysis and prognostication of weather. Without, I repeat, making any charges, in this very, uh, fluid situation, it is legitimate to ask why the federal administration apparently did nothing to prepare us for this ordeal—why Mr. Kennedy and his associates have spent so much time discussing the so-called perils of nuclear tests in the atmosphere and diverted our attention from the immediate issue, which is the absence of moisture in the atmosphere. Such questions are being asked in the grass roots.

Q.: Are you contending, Senator, that the Administration should have been actively engaged in producing rain during this interval?

DIRKSEN: That is a question beyond my scientific competence. I would only remark that the government which had the foresight to anticipate this situation might have taken some steps—

Q.: In short, you think its intelligence was faulty.

DIRKSEN: This would not be the first time. Now, gentlemen, I do not want to squeeze this subject dry; I do not doubt that the Administration's desire for rain is as strong as that of the opposition party. I merely say that it is too often taken in by the sunny appearance of things, without realizing that there is always a day of reckoning.

Q.: There are reports that the latest hurricane may move in and create flooding. Is the Congress giving any thought to more comprehensive flood-control measures?

DIRKSEN: I have heard such alarmist reports but they have often proved to be wrong in the past; I do not think we should be stampeded into any hasty federal moves until there is a genuine emergency. And I suspect—this is only a suspicion, mind you—that we are being saturated with such reports by Administration spokesmen in an attempt to divert attention from the immediate crisis, which is the shortage of rain.

Q.: There was also a radio report this afternoon, Senator, that it has begun raining in Pittsburgh.

DIRKSEN: Again, I do not want to comment until such information is confirmed. Naturally, if it is true, that would be a reason for bipartisan rejoicing and I pray that these dark clouds contain the proverbial silver lining.

Q.: A final question, Senator. Have you given any serious thought to experimental programs designed to convert salt water into drinking water?

DIRKSEN: I believe such experiments may be warranted at a future time, but I must warn against any panic that would lead us into reckless or costly federal action, with resultant regimentation of our drinking habits. We must choose to sink or swim as free Americans or, if I may coin a phrase, our way of life will go down the drain.

Q.: Thank you Senator, for giving us, as usual, a clear-cut, undiluted statement of your views.

PRESS AND PUNDITRY

WESTBROOK PEGLER

Myriad-Minded Us

1938

Of all the fantastic fog-shapes that have risen off the swamp of confusion since the First World War, the most futile and, at the same time, the most pretentious, is the deep-thinking, hair-trigger columnist or commentator who knows all the answers just offhand and can settle great affairs with absolute finality three days or even six days a week.

Being one of these myself, I have been trying to figure out how we came to be. Some, I know, have been pontificating for twenty years and have come to regard themselves as intellectual landmarks and American institutions as permanent as Baseball.

But I am one of the green crop, come after the panic, and my confidence in the vast public importance of my opinions, to say nothing of their sanity, has not become a fixed habit.

It takes gall to sit down to a typewriter at a certain hour every afternoon to confront a long mile of white paper and presume to tell the people what it is all about to the extent of from 500 to 1000 words.

Tell them what what is all about, says you? Oh, just anything and everything.

What is it that you would like to be told all about by your favorite myriad-minded commentator? Economics, pig prevention, the Constitution, the law, politics, war, history, labor, the C.I.O. and the A.F. of L., housing, international relations, birth control, the infield fly rule, Fascism, Nazism and Communism, inflation, agriculture or phrenology? Name me something we can't tell you all about with absolute, irrefutable authority and no two, perhaps, in agreement on any single point.

We include experts on the budget who can't balance an expense account; economic experts who can't find the 5:15 on a suburban time-table much less read a balance sheet, labor experts who never did a lick of work in their lives, pundits on the mechanical age who can't put a fresh ribbon on their own typewriters and resounding authorities on the problem of the farmer who never even grew a geranium in a pot.

We are, in short, the berries of the Fourth Estate, so passionate and self-important these last few years that some of our number, not content with telling the world what and why so on paper, must even rear back at public meetings and snort and sweat in the faces of our fellow citizens in outbursts of courthouse forensics intended to make them think, or any-way think they do.

Not only that, but these oral remarks are sometimes deemed to be of such priceless originality and wisdom as to justify reprinting in full next day, lest some immortal truth be gone with the wind when the cleaners air out the joint.

What causes us? Well, as nearly as I can figure it out, this trade began as a sort of journalistic vaudeville intended to entertain the customers and exert a little circulation pull of a slightly higher tone than that of the comics. Actually, even now at our grimmest, we aren't one, two, six with a real good comic strip in which some evil man is plotting to put out a little girl's eyes or throw a little boy into a blast furnace, a reassur-ing fact, if you are considering the good sense of the nation, as the syndi-cate managers, in their nasty way, are always reminding us.

In the days of the wham-sock strips our trade was just olives, requiring a cultivated taste, and as the comics veered off into tragedy and we drifted into isms and causes, the salesmen on the road found, as they continue to find today, that it was much easier to peddle serious funnies than funny seriousness. The comic artists still ride in the big cars and spend their winters shooting in the eighties down South, while we drive the light models and interview ourselves day after solemn day on the state of the nation and the wrongs of a woeful world.

You might think that once in a great while we would run out of intelligence, and I often marvel at my own inexhaustible fund of knowl-edge, but it just keeps on bubbling up. Nowadays, numbers of our set even get into rather acrimonious clothesline spats figuring, like the old-time fight promoters, that a grudge fight is good for the gate. And the one sure way to drive a small competitor nuts, as Mr. Lippmann has demonstrated in several instances where efforts were made to smoke him out, is to ignore him as though he didn't exist.

Maybe I shouldn't be writing like this, revealing secrets of the trade and all, but I just got to thinking it over and, honest to God, it is getting plumb ridiculous.

This early pundit, a Whig wag, was also one of the most prudent. Most of his "forecast" had already taken place.

PHILIP FRENEAU

The Prophecy

1782

When a certain great king, whose initial is G,
Shall force stamps upon paper, and folks to drink tea;
When these folks burn his tea and stampt paper, like stubble,
You may guess that this king is then coming to trouble.
But when a petition he treads under his feet,
And sends over the ocean an army and fleet;
When that army, half-starved, and frantic with rage,
Shall be cooped up with a leader whose name rhymes to cage;
When that leader goes home dejected and sad,
You may then be assured the king's prospects are bad.
But when B and C with their armies are taken,
This king will do well if he saves his own bacon.
In the year seventeen hundred and eighty and two,
A stroke he shall get that will make him look blue;
In the years eighty-three, eighty-four, eighty-five,
You hardly shall know that the king is alive;
In the year eighty-six the affair will be over,
And he shall eat turnips that grow in Hanover.
The face of the Lion shall then become pale,
He shall yield fifteen teeth, and be sheared of his tail.
O king, my dear king, you shall be very sore;
The Stars and the Lily shall run you on shore,
And your Lion shall growl—but never bite more!

EMERY KELEN

*Press Gallery**

1960

"Platypus," Max said, "you've met a lot of politicians now, and you've seen how they look after your interests by jaw-jaw instead of war-war. They are your guardians. There remains the eternal question: *Who guards the guardians?*

"The answer is: The press does.

"Press and politicians are a perfect team. The politician knows that what the press didn't mention didn't happen. The press knows that what the politicians mention is not *all* that happened. There is a jolly vacuum of truth left over in which they can all play blindman's buff.

"Intercourse between journalist and politician takes place by *communiqué*, by *press conference*, by *interview* and by *leak*.

"A *communiqué* is a carefully worded document containing all the information healthy for you, Platypus, to know, and for the politician to have you know. The journalist's job is to read between the lines.

"The *press conference* is a politician's way of being informative without actually saying anything. Should he accidentally say something, he has at his side a *press officer* who immediately explains it away by 'clarifying' it.

"The *interview* is an intimate conversation between journalist and politician wherein the journalist seeks to take advantage of the garrulity of the politician, and the politician of the credulity of the journalist.

"The *leak* is a sneaky way of handing out information, deniable at any time.

"The *press officer* is responsible for the *press conference*, and *communiqués*. The *journalist* is responsible for *interviews*. Nobody is responsible for *leaks*.

"The *politician* is not responsible for anything."

* from *Platypus at Large.*

This parody of a prominent political columnist was part of a complete parody issue of the New York Post, *prepared by the staff and contributors of* Monocle *magazine during the New York newspaper strike of 1962–63.*

DAN WAKEFIELD

("MAX LEARNED")

Wags and the West

1962

As I read the final chapter spun out by the mass media of the gruesome story of the death of little Wags, the spotted and lovable pet of little Jane Schwartz of the Bronx, I was struck, as I often am, by how small our modern world has become and how rich in complexity and paradox. The lessons in this microcosmic human drama cry out to be reflected on, calling to mind as they do the current East-West struggle and, of course, the fate of America as a civilization. Nor can we for a moment hope to brush aside the even darker, deeper-flowing stream of Freudian motivation infusing, if not pervading the entire sordid—and yet, in a curious way, heartwarming—little tale.

I spoke above of "paradox"—as I often do—which calls to mind my recent trip to India, which is indeed a Land of Paradox—the mountains and the valleys, the people and the animals, the past and the present, the day and the night, all of which lend a subtle irony to that large and often misunderstood nation. In India, where religious ideas are quite different from our Judeo-Christian heritage, the cow is a sacred animal. Here in America, with its strong Puritan tradition and its eco-politico-sexio revolutions which have gone so far to emancipate us from the shackles of the past, no animal is "sacred."

Yet the dog—"man's best friend"—has always been regarded with warmth and affection, sometimes bordering on a kind of primitivistic love-cult phenomenon. It was perhaps such an underlying current which pulsed through the warm relationship between little Jane and her little dog; and when Wags fell the victim of a deranged and troubled ax murderer, our hearts were wrung by the grief which came to little "Dardy" so early in her previously innocent life.

There are, of course, those among us who cry out that Clem Roosevelt, the itinerant trash collector who brought this foul deed to its untimely fruition, be drawn and quartered. My own feelings are mixed. On the one hand, as I look down even now at my own little dog (his name is Justice Holmes, though my youngest daughter, Eve, insists on calling him Bow-Wow), I feel a burning indignation which cries out for punishment to anyone who would inflict harm on his playful little life.

Yet we cannot overlook the fact that Clem Roosevelt was deformed, not only physically, but mentally—and, what is even more important, emotionally. We have learned now that his tyrannical mother was rarely at home but spent most of her time as a volunteer worker for the ASPCA which explains fully the working out of poor Clem's Oedipal syndrome in this senseless slaying.

The fact that little Wags happened to be a mongrel does not in any sense lessen our grief at his passing; we mourn him with all the feeling we would mourn a poodle of the finest pedigree. Our Judeo-Christian tradition, leavened with the wisdom of Freud, Schweitzer, John Dewey, Justice Holmes, Jefferson, Thoreau, Vance Packard, Jane Addams, Liz Taylor, David Reisman, Shoeless Joe Jackson, Arthur M. Schlesinger, Jr., and Charles "The Bird" Parker, has created a kind of socio-cultural *zeitgeist* culminating in a sense of fair play, which, though often distorted into cults such as "Togetherness" foisted upon us by the subliminal techniques of the Hidden Persuaders of Madison Ave., nevertheless has raised us above the basest instincts of the herd and thus acts as a kind of checks-and-balances system against the pitfalls of herd-mindedness. Sometimes, as in the McCarthy Era, we fall prey to the baser motives which make the mob the master of human events, but even though we still live in an Age of Anxiety, as I have sometimes put it, beneath the very shadow of the H-Bomb and Juvenile Delinquency, the pendulum swings back again to what is best and most life-giving in our heritage: as, for instance, Debbie-Eddie-Liz, The Peace Corps, and Huckleberry Finn, to cite but a few examples.

No one can say what good may eventually come from the darkest deeds such as the senseless thrill-murder of Wags; we may find even in this evil drama a glimmer of hope, if we remain future-minded, rather than allowing the shackles of the past to mute the still voice within us all which cries out for a better tomorrow. Perhaps our national mourning for the mongrel may instill in our national conscience a new sense of relatedness to the Underdeveloped Nations, where cows, and sometimes, I understand, oxen, are thought of as sacred. An understanding of the mutual superstitious heritage of all mankind, linking men and nations, may be one of the positive results that flow from the tears of little Jane over her dog; and, indeed, little Wags—and the ill-starred Roosevelt himself—may serve as a bridge between East and West.

These are only a few of the implications of the drama upon which I will have more reflections tomorrow, and tomorrow, and tomorrow, in the words of Justice Holmes. Next week I go to receive an honorary degree at Sioux U., the first Indian Reservation University in the country to boast a department of sociology, and I shall no doubt find still more lessons there to be drawn from this story of love and death, hope and heartbreak, passion and pity, for this, indeed, like life itself, is an Unfinished Column.

This constitutes the "funny" part of a long, not entirely hostile discussion of Murray Kempton, then a columnist; the greater part of it consists of quotations, and a large part of that of quotations within quotations. I hope both readers and typesetters can keep their bearings.

WILLIAM F. BUCKLEY, JR.

Two excerpts from *A Fortnight with Murray Kempton*

1962

WEDNESDAY

One of the most satisfying things about K is his impartial iconoclasm. There are a few—a very few—graven images he won't profane—some because he truly admires them (A. Stevenson, E. Fitzgerald); some because they are too overwhelmingly ridiculous (E. Roosevelt); and he tires of overkill, except perhaps when dealing with institutionalized enemies (J. Eastland). I remember his writing when Roy Cohn was finally and ignominiously forced out of McCarthy's Committee, *"So help me God, I feel sorry for Roy Cohn."*—which I am sure he did, as well he might have, having for months galloped miles ahead of the posse (never did so many supererogate upon so little!). It is as distasteful to use a machine gun to deliver the coup de grâce as it is to have to wait for the fourth coda to terminate a Tschaikowsky symphony. In 1960 he didn't want to go to Chicago. *"If I do,"* he told me, *"I'll knock Nixon— it's like junk. But I like Nixon!"* He does feel sorry for the mangled corpse; but it is also for artistic reasons he feels the need to back away. Today he goes after Robert Wagner again. K, of course, immediately saw through the phoniness of the anti-DeSapio frenzy of last summer and fall (ironically, his employer was much responsible for stirring the thing up). K passed the day of the Execution with DeSapio, following him around everywhere, closely observing his manners,. and reacting prodigally to his remarkable personal gentility (*"I sometimes think that if Carmine DeSapio were running against Lucifer he would consider it ungentlemanly to mention that little trouble in heaven."*). When it was finally clear that he had been overthrown by the ideological janissaries and the playboy reformers, there were still the conventional and highly poignant rituals to go through. And then DeSapio walked out alone, after midnight, into the streets. *"His visitor"* (K's wonderfully unobstrusive way of designating himself, in all his interviews) *"left him and walked into the streets and noticed that there were no slums any more, and no landlords, and the Age of Pericles had begun because we were rid of Carmine DeSapio. One had to walk carefully to avoid being stabbed by the lilies bursting in the pavements. I wish the reformers luck—with less Christian sincerity than Carmine DeSapio does. I will be a long time forgiving them this one."*

Enter Wagner. *"The Mayor of New York,"* he writes today, opening his column, *"has hired a $40,000-a-year team to improve his press relations. His image in the press already seems to any detached observer somewhat better than it should be."* (He likes a good first sentence or two, as Pegler does. All K's sentences are good, of course—it is even suggested, by a critic on whom they happen to cloy, that they are too good. "If you try to slay your audience with every sentence," the critic once wrote me, "you run the great danger that you might succeed.") And then he goes after Wagner on highly demagogic grounds (when K is putting forth demagogy, he almost surely doesn't realize that is what he is doing: he is still enough the old socialist to react conventionally to the old demonology . . .). *"If I were a union electrician at this hour, I should suggest that someone be found to preach to me besides a mayor who took a 26 percent salary increase two weeks ago."* As ever, the little-manliness. It is utterly irrelevant to the question whether an electrician should get full pay for a twenty hour week (that is what the electricians in the instant case were demanding), whether the Mayor of New York, commonly understood as occupying the nation's third most important electoral office, should get a salary increase from $30,000 to $40,000. And it makes no difference at all that the Mayor getting the increase is, so far as being Mayor goes, a notorious incompetent. He is certainly not an incompetent at getting to *be* Mayor. Modern Democracy holds that no man who wins landslide political victories is an incompetent, and on such matters Modern Democracy is sovereign. But the crack about the salary turns out to be just an aside, and K ends up back on the subject of the press agent. *"[Wagner] is the full flower of Mencken's law that no man ever went broke underestimating the intelligence of the American voter. I resent having to pay taxes for press agents to protect a man whose magnificent effrontery already makes him invulnerable."* There aren't six men in the country who could have composed that last sentence.

. . . .

TUESDAY

Incomparable. Absolutely nowhere else, save possibly in *National Review,* can you find such a thing. It is practically all quotations, and the very best evidence that selective quotations are all that is really needed to finger the nation's ironic pulse. *"Comes now Public Document 75452,"* K announces starchily, *"from the Subcommittee of the Subcommittee of the Senate Committee on Commerce, the sober record of the fall of 1960 when America was deciding whether to move again:*

Vice President Nixon: Could I ask you one favor, Jack?

Jack Paar: Yes sir; you can ask any favor you'd like.

Vice President Nixon: Could we have your autograph for our girls?

"The notes on the particular meeting at the summit (Paar: I can't tell you how much this means to our show. It gives us 'class.') *are the opening exhibit in a Senate report labeled. 'The Joint Appearances of Senator John F. Kennedy and Vice-President Richard M. Nixon and*

other 1960 Campaign Presentations.' That was September 11, 1960, and Nixon had packed [for the White House]. The Kennedys rallied two weeks later.

Charles Collingwood: Hello, Caroline.

Caroline: Hello.

Mrs. Kennedy: Can you say hello?

Caroline: Hello.

Mrs. Kennedy: Here, do you want to sit up in bed with me?

Mr. Collingwood: Oh, isn't she a darling?

Mrs. Kennedy: Now, look at the three bears.

Collingwood: What is the dolly's name?

Mrs. Kennedy: All right, what is the dolly's name?

Caroline: I didn't name her yet.

(It reminds me of Vincent Sheean, King of *Gemütlichkeit*, exuberantly opening the first recorded interview by a Western newspaperman with Stalin, and trying to put Stalin at ease. "Comrade Stalin, *all* the world *over* you are associated with your *pipe*, and here I sit down with you and I see *no pipe!* Where *is* your *pipe?*" "I left it at home," said Stalin.)

K continues after having quoted much more of the same kind of thing: *"This painful, vulgar record evokes [the campaign] again, but the mystery of [Nixon's] collapse taunts us yet. Still it was a terribly close election and who can say what small mistake cost him it?*
"There is one clue:

Bill Henry of NBC: I am so fascinated with that little kitten. Does the kitten have a name?

Julie Nixon: Yes, its name is Bitsy Blue Eyes.

"Maybe Caroline saved the package when she held off naming the doll."

M. J. ARLEN

Who Wants to Know?

Senator Mildred H. Paulding Answers the Mail

1962

Q.: My husband who is active in business circles says it is all the talk these days how the Democratic Administration is planning to move the Federal Capitol back to Philadelphia. What is your opinion of this proposal?

A.: In my many years in Washington, I have heard numerous rumors about moving the Federal Capitol back to Philadelphia, but, to the best of my knowledge, nothing has ever come of them. Philadelphia, however, has always been one of my favorite cities, and I recall we often spent happy minutes, and even hours, there as children.

Q.: What is your own personal definition of an isosceles triangle?

A.: I have always felt that an isosceles triangle is a triangle in which the angles at the base are equal, and in which the two longest sides (AB and AC) are also equal.

Q.: What is your private opinion of the Algeciras Incident?

A.: I am sorry not to have answered this letter sooner. It is always difficult for someone not actually "on the scene" to speak accurately about this kind of situation, but I should say that although there is a good deal to be said for one side, there is at least as much, or possibly more, or even less, to be said for the other. Nonetheless, Algeciras remains one of my favorite cities and contains many interesting sights, including streets, sidewalks, and buildings.

NORMAN MAILER

*Newspapers and Politics**

1963

The newspapers are rich in self-examination these last two mornings. Like beatniks or poets they are studying themselves, their digestion, their elimination, their neuroses, their arts. They are examining the secrets of their own formula for making history. They are trying to decide whether Adlai Stevenson is in serious disfavor with President Kennedy or is not. As in a laboratory experiment, they have a specimen to examine, tests to make.

* from *The Presidential Papers*.

The specimen is an article in *The Saturday Evening Post* by Stewart Alsop and Charles Bartlett. The article finds Stevenson guilty of express-ing a *soft* policy toward Cuba during several *secret* conferences, those talks of the Executive Committee in which Kennedy discussed what to do about Soviet missiles in Cuba. Since Charles Bartlett is known to the newspaper business as a *leak* for the President, one basic theme proposes itself immediately: the President, or somebody very close to the Presi-dent, gave Bartlett the idea that an attack upon Stevenson was not im-permissible. It is an administrative way of seizing Stevenson by the throat and slamming him against a wall.

What? Soft on Cuba you son of a bitch?

Newspapers and politics are married. One cannot have a theme with-out its development. So a contrary and second hypothesis emerges from the first; it goes: Bartlett is not merely a leak for the President, but indeed has a set of spigots for a dozen different members of the administration. The President knew nothing in advance of Alsop and Bartlett's article, goes the second interpretation. On the contrary it is a plot by the Right Wing of the administration to eat up the Left Wing. Since this second conception is Liberal, it concludes that the President will not destroy Adlai Stevenson but rescue him.

Then there is a full theory in the center. It is created out of the other two theories. It supposes that Kennedy gave the secret of the conver-sations to Bartlett in order to rescue Adlai Stevenson later. By this sup-position, John F. Kennedy must be much like Madame de Staël. It was remarked of this heroine that she liked to throw her friends into the pool in order to have the pleasure of fishing them out again.

I do not think the President throws his assistants into the pool for such a ladylike reason. Doubtless, he acts more like the pure moon man and good scientist he is. He knows that polls are not enough to test the pulse of the public. One needs a small explosion here, a bit of blast there. Hot ore to examine. Hot ants. One way to test the ferment of the extreme Right is to tie Adlai Stevenson to their anthill, put a splash of gasoline at his feet, and strike a match. Will he be burned? will he be bitten to death by ants? will he recover? . . .

I make a prediction. I think Stevenson will still be Ambassador to the U.N. Once the President proved he was ready for an atomic war, the

National Ticket was finally created. John F. Kennedy for President, Barry Goldwater for Vice-President. Adlai Stevenson and William F. Buckley, Jr. to stand on the platform beside them.

The only people who will vote against the National Ticket will be a few hundred unreconstructed Birchites, a few followers of George Lincoln Rockwell, fifty very old socialists loyal to Daniel De Leon, five or six junkies, eighty-two beatniks brave enough to keep wearing beards, a covey of vegetarians, a flying squad of pacifists, the three remaining bona-fide Communists of America, and the ten thousand members of the FBI who have infiltrated the Communist Party and will be afraid to vote for fear that one of the three bona-fide live Communists might see them and expose them to the wrath of the Party.

After the National Ticket is elected, we could have the Jack and Barry show. Edward Murrow might see his way clear to give us a tour of the Vice-President's electronic shack in Arizona.

. . . .

It used to be, not very many years ago, that politicians could use the Washington Press Corps as a series of Certified Leaks. They could play the body politic like the strings of a harp. A piece of news was rarely what it presented itself to be—it was rather a lie which, put next to other lies, gave the intimation of a clue. At its best, a news story was the key to a cryptogram.

One offers a mythical example. *The New York Times* on a given day some ten or twelve years ago has a story with by-line on page three. It is trivial and it is dull. But it is on page three. So its importance is underlined. The story states that an "undisclosed reliable source" has said today that sentiment among the West Germans to end the Nuremberg Trials is increasing. One knows the "source" is the Secretary of State because the reporter is his Certified Leak. Now of course this story has no sociological bottom. The Secretary of State did not conduct a private poll of West Germans. Nor is he interested to serve the public with the latest information available to him. On the contrary he has no information: he is simply announcing to various experts in America, Europe, and West Germany that America is getting ready to end its de-Nazification program. Since the Secretary of State does not speak in his own name but through his Certified Leak, the experts are also advised to ad-vise their particular institutions that the announcement of this new policy is several weeks to several months away. Objections by the separate institutions may be considered. Democratic process.

Those were the good old days of the Truman or Eisenhower Administration. With a code-breaking machine at hand, it was a high navigational pleasure to read a paper. Supplied with a handbook of Certified Leaks, one could explore the news tributaries of the world. A genius could have put out a great newspaper without ever leaving his room. He just had to be a plumber with a plumber's snake.

But the Serpent entered Paradise. The Certified Leaks began to make news independently. Sometimes they were even known to betray their officials. The strings of the Goat's harp began to move in new ways. An official would try to play the harp, and a string would call, it would say, "Come here, index finger, touch me. If you don't, I'll start to vibrate without you." The Twist had entered History.

Who knows? Playing touch football, Kennedy gives the ball to Bartlett on an end around. "Don't give Adlai the ax," whispers the quarterback. "Oh, Jeez, dad," says Charley B. after his touchdown is called back, "I thought you said, *give* Adlai the ax." In such a game, which playmaker can know if his tongue is thickening or son is hip to Dad?

5 CULTURE AND CENSORSHIP

POLITICS IN ART AND MANNERS

Here's a small sampler of the side effects of the impingement of politics on arts and mores; it should come as no great surprise to observe that some form of censorship is usually at issue. Sculpture, pornography, poetry, music, drama; prohibition, ornithology, and women's rights. A little something for everybody, folks, and don't forget to vote—

CONGRESS

Abraham Lincoln's Statue

1866

MR. WADE: I move to take up the joint resolution authorizing a contract with Vinnie Ream for a statue of Abraham Lincoln.

MR. SUMNER: I hope that will not be taken up.

SEVERAL SENATORS: Oh, let us vote.

MR. SUMNER: Senators say, "Oh, let us vote." The question is about giving away ten thousand dollars.

MR. CONNESS: Taking it up is not giving money away, I hope.

MR. SUMNER: The question is, I say, about giving away ten thousand dollars; that is the proposition involved in this joint resolution.

MR. CONNESS: For a statue?

MR. SUMNER: The Senator says "for a statue"—an impossible statue, I say; one which cannot be made.

MR. McDOUGALL: I am somewhat surprised to hear the Senator from Massachusetts, who professes to be not merely an amateur but a connoisseur in art and an admirer of beautiful things and a person understanding them well, object to a proposition of this kind. We are all informed that the person who makes this proposition to us is an artist; she has evinced her skill. . . .

MR. SUMNER: I am unwilling to utter a word that would bear hard upon any one, least of all upon a youthful artist where sex imposes reserve, if not on her part, at least on mine; but when a proposition like this is brought forward I am bound to meet it frankly. You might as well place her on the staff of General Grant, or put General Grant aside and place her on horseback in his stead. . . .

MR. NESMITH: Sir, the Senator might have raised the same objection to Mr. Lincoln, that he was not qualified for the Presidency because his reading had not been as extensive as that of the Senator, or because he had lived among rude and uncultivated society. I claim for this young lady, sprung from a poor family, struggling with misfortune and adversity, that she has developed such natural genius that her talents in this direction should be fostered and cultivated in preference to our giving this work to any foreigner. The Senator from Massachusetts has pandered so long to European aristocracy that he cannot speak of anything that originates in America with common respect.

If this young lady and the works which she has produced had been brought to his notice by some near-sighted, frog-eating Frenchman, with a pair of green spectacles on his nose, the Senator would have said that she was deserving of commendation. If she could have spoken three or four different languages that nobody else could have understood, or, perhaps, that neither she nor the Senator could understand, he would vote her fifty thousand dollars. (Laughter.) He is a great patron of art, but not a patron of domestic art. He is a patron of foreign art; he is a patron of those who copy and ape European aristocracy, and he does not propose to patronize or encourage the genius which grows up in our own great country, particularly in the wilds of the West. . . .

I challenge the Senator from Massachusetts to produce one of the foreign artists, of whom he boasts so much, who can produce the equal of that bust. I deprecate his panegyrics upon foreign artists in derogation of those raised in our own country, and particularly those of the great West.

MR. SUMNER: Where have I said anything in praise of a foreign artist in depreciation of the artists of our own country? I have alluded with praise to the artists of our own country.

MR. NESMITH: I heard nothing of that. I heard the Senator speak with particular reference to that door which was cast in Munich.

MR. SUMNER: Which is by a western artist, Mr. Rogers, reared in the West. I give him praise for what he has done.

MR. NESMITH: I appeal to Senators on this floor, to those who have natural taste, to those who have an eye for beauty, as I admit the Senator from Massachusetts has not, to support this young lady in her efforts to produce what will be a magnificent statue of Mr. Lincoln.

MR. McDOUGALL: This young lady is undoubtedly a lady of marked genius; and she has proved, so far as the bust is concerned, that she has produced the best likeness of Lincoln of any person that has attempted it. I have the right to say so, because I was perhaps better acquainted with Mr. Lincoln in his lifetime than any gentleman on this floor; he was a companion of mine many years ago, with whom I was long familiar. I have not been satisfied with any attempt to reproduce his features till I saw the bust produced by this lady. She has achieved a success, showing that she has true genius; and if she is young, the better for her. In five years more she will be as great a genius as she ever will be, no matter how long she may live. "Whom the gods love die young." . . .

MR. HOWARD: Now, sir, I am willing to vote the sum of ten thousand dollars for the purpose of securing a good statue of Abraham Lincoln; but I am not willing to vote that sum or any other sum to this person and take the risk of an entire failure in the end. If this country in its history has ever produced a statesman, and a great man deserving to be memorialized in its annals, not only upon the pages of history but in the works of art, it is Abraham Lincoln. . . . I would as soon think of a lady writing the *Iliad* of Homer; I should as soon think of placing at the head of an army a woman for the conduct of a great campaign.

MR. COWAN: They have done both.

MR. HOWARD: It has not been their general history.

MR. McDOUGALL: They have done it.

MR. HOWARD: No, sir. I would as soon expect from the pen of a woman the *Paradise Lost* or any other great work of genius which has honored our race.

MR. McDOUGALL: Did you ever read the fragments of Sappho?

MR. HOWARD: I have read the fragments of Sappho.

MR. McDOUGALL: What do you say about that?

MR. HOWARD: That certainly does not prove that Sappho was capable of writing Homer's *Iliad*.

MR. McDOUGALL: She exceeds Homer in many respects.

MR. HOWARD: In many respects—in erotic expressions she certainly exceeds Homer. Whether the proposed work in the present case would have a similar merit I cannot say.

But, sir, without trifling on the subject, and without meaning to say a word in disparagement of this young lady, whom I suppose to be a young lady of genius, I insist that we are taking a great risk in entrusting the execution of this work to her.

MR. SUMNER: A statue is one of the highest forms of art. There have been very few artists competent to make a statue. There is as yet but one instance that I can recall of a woman successful in such an undertaking. But the eminent person to whom I refer had shown a peculiar genius early in life, had enjoyed peculiar opportunities of culture, and had vindicated her title as artist before she attempted this difficult task. . . .

MR. COWAN: I shall vote for this resolution, Mr. President, because I understand that this little child of genius has struggled up amid poverty and difficulty to this great result through the medium of her statuary. I must confess I do not know much about statuary myself. Modern statuary, I think, would be about as well made by the tailor and the shoemaker, all except the head, as by anybody else. (Laughter.) Ancient nude statuary required an exact knowledge of anatomy and of the human form in the natural state. How it is proposed to have this statue of Mr. Lincoln I am not advised. Whether it is to be draped with a Roman toga, or with a white jacket and black coat and blue pantaloons, I do not know. (Laughter.)

MR. WADE: Perhaps with a cannon ball in his hand.

DONALD OGDEN STEWART

The Whisky Rebellion

(*In the Bedtime Story Manner of Thornton W. Burgess*)

1921

"Just the *day* for a Whisky Rebellion," said Aunt Polly and off she ran, lipperty-lipperty-lip, to get a few shooting rifles.

"Oh goody goody," cried little Emily. "Now we can all shoot at those horrid Revenue Officers," for the collectors of internal revenue were far from popular with these kindly Pennsylvania folk and Aunt Polly Pinkwood had often promised the children that if they were good some day they would be allowed to take a shot at a Revenue Officer.

Soon she returned, bearing in her arms a number of bright shiny new guns. The children crowded around in glee and soon all were supplied with weapons except little Frank who of course was too young to use a gun and was given a two-gallon jug of nice, old whisky to carry. Jed hitched up old Taylor, the faithful farm horse, and as quick as you could say Jack Robinson the little ones had piled into the old carryall. Round Mr. Sun was just peeping over the Purple Hills when the merry little party started on its way, singing and laughing at the prospect of the day's sport.

"I bet I kill five Revenue Officers," said little Edgar.

"Ha Ha Ha—you boaster, you," laughed Aunt Polly. "You will be lucky if you kill two, for I fear they will be hard to find today."

"Oh do you think so, Aunt Polly?" said little Elinor and she began to cry, for Elinor dearly loved to shoot.

"Hush dear," said Miss Pinkwood with a kindly pat, for she loved her little charges and it hurt her to see them unhappy. "I was only joking. And now children I will tell you a story."

"Oh goody goody," cried they all. "Tell us a true story."

"All right," said Aunt Polly. "I shall tell you a true story," and she began.

"Once there was a brave handsome man—"

"Mr. Welsbach," cried the children with one voice, for it was well known in the neighborhood that Aunt Polly had long been sweet on Julius Welsbach, the popular superintendent of the Sabbath School and the best whisky maker for miles around.

"Hush children," said Aunt Polly blushing in vexation. "Of course not. And if you interrupt me I shall not tell my story at all." But she was not really angry.

"And one day this brave handsome man was out making whisky and he had just sampled some when he looked up and what do you suppose he saw?"

"Snakes," cried little Elmer, whose father had often had delirium tremens, greatly to the delight of his children.

"No, Elmer," said Miss Pinkwood, "not snakes."

"Pink lizards," cried little Esther, Elmer's sister.

"No," said Aunt Polly, with a hearty laugh, "he saw a—stranger. And what do you suppose the stranger had?"

"A snoot full," chorused the Schultz twins. "He was pie-eyed."

"No," replied Miss Pinkwood laughing merrily. "It was before noon. Guess again children. What did the stranger have?"

"Blind staggers," suggested little Faith whose mother had recently been adjudged insane.

"Come children," replied Aunt Polly. "You are not very wide awake this morning. The stranger had a gun. And when the brave handsome man offered the stranger a drink, what do you suppose the stranger said?"

"I know," cried little Prudence eagerly. "He said, 'Why yes, I don't care if I do.' That's what they all say."

"No, Prudence," replied Miss Pinkwood. "The stranger refused a drink."

"Oh come now, Aunt Polly," chorused the boys and girls. "You said you were going to tell us a true story." And their little faces fell.

"Children," said Miss Polly, "the stranger refused the drink because he was a Revenue Officer. And he pointed his gun at the brave handsome man and said he would have to go to jail because he had not paid the tax on his whisky. And the brave handsome man would have had to have gone to jail, too; but fortunately his brother came up just at the right time and—"

"Shot the Revenuer dead," cried the children in glee.

"Yes children," said Miss Polly. "He shot the Revenue Officer dead."

"Oh goody goody," cried all. "Now tell us another story. Tell us about the time your father killed a Revenue Officer with an ax."

"Oh you don't want to hear that again, do you children?" said Aunt Polly.

"Oh yes—yes—please," they cried, and Aunt Polly was just going to begin when Jed the driver stopped his horses and said:

"This hilltop is as good a place to shoot from as I know of, Miss Pinkwood. You can see both roads, and nobody can see you."

"Thank you, Jed," said Aunt Polly giving him a kindly smile, and without more ado the children clambered out of the carryall and filled their guns with powder and bullets.

"I get first shot," proudly announced Robert, the oldest boy, and somewhat of a bully.

"Robert!" said Aunt Polly severely, and she looked almost ready to cry, for Aunt Polly had tried hard to teach the boys to be true knights of chivalry and it hurt her to have Robert wish to shoot a Revenue Officer before the girls had had a chance. Robert had not meant to hurt Aunt Polly's feelings but had only been thoughtless, and soon all was sunshine again as little Ellen the youngest made ready to fire the first shot.

The children waited patiently and soon they were rewarded by the sight of a Revenue Officer riding on horseback in the distant valley, as pretty a target as one could wish.

"Now do be careful, dear," whispered Miss Pinkwood, "for if you miss, he may take alarm and be off." But little Ellen did not miss. "Bang" went her gun and the little Merry Breezes echoed back and forth, "She got him. She got him," and old Mother West Wind smiled down at the happy sport. Sure enough, when old Mr. Smoke had cleared away there was a nice dead Revenue Officer lying in the road. "Well done, Ellen," said Miss Pinkwood, patting her little charge affectionately which caused the happy girl to coo with childish delight.

Mary had next shot and soon all were popping away in great glee. All the merry wood folk gathered near to watch the children at their sport. There was Johnny Chuck and Reddy Fox and Jimmy Skunk and Bobby Coon and oh everybody.

Soon round Mr. Sun was high in the Blue Sky and the children began to tire somewhat of their sport. "I'm as hungry as a bear," said little Dick. "I'm as hungry as two bears," said Emily. "Ha Ha Ha," laughed Miss Pinkwood, "I know what will fix that," and soon she had spread out a delicious repast.

"Now children," said Miss Pinkwood when all had washed their faces and hands, "while you were busy washing I prepared a surprise for you," and from a large jug, before their delighted gaze, she poured out—what do you think?" "Bronxes," cried little Harriet. "Oh goody goody." And sure enough Aunt Polly had prepared a jug of delicious Bronx cocktails which all pronounced excellent.

And after that there were sandwiches and olives and pie and good three-year-old whisky, too.

"That's awfully smooth rye, Aunt Polly," said little Prudence smacking her two red lips. "I think I'll have another shot."

"No dear," said Miss Pinkwood, pleased by the compliment, but firm withal. "Not now. Perhaps on the way home, if there is any left," for Aunt Polly knew that too much alcohol in the middle of the day is bad for growing children, and she had seen many a promising child spoiled by over-indulgent parents.

After lunch those children who could stand helped Aunt Polly to clear away the dishes and then all went sound asleep, as is the custom in Pennsylvania.

When they awoke round Mr. Sun was just sinking behind the Purple Hills and so, after taking a few more scattered shots at Revenue Officers, they piled once more into the carryall and drove back to town. And as they passed Mrs. Oliphant's house (Aunt Polly's sister) Aunt Flo Oliphant came out on the porch and waved her handkerchief at the merry party.

"Let's give her a cheer," said Fred.

"Agreed," cried they all, and so twelve little throats united in three lusty "huzzahs" which made Auntie Flo very happy you may be sure.

And as they drove up before the Pinkwoods' modest home twelve tired but happy children with one accord voted the Whisky Rebellion capital fun and Aunt Polly a brick.

The South is dry and will vote dry. That is everybody that is sober enough to stagger to the polls will.—*Will Rogers*

RING LARDNER

On Prohibition

1923

When it was suggested that I write something about prohibition, I snapped at the idea as a starving dog goes after a deck of cards. Here was a subject that had escaped the attention of other members of the writing graft, and you don't have to be so skillful in the handling of a given theme if the theme itself is sufficiently novel.

I thought I could tear off two or three thousand words almost as fast as I could type. I forgot that even a mental contact with the Demon or anything pertaining to same always filled me with an almost overwhelming desire to abstain from work for a period of thirty-four days. So the composition of this article has been a tough job and not a siesta, and I ask my friends to bear that in mind while they are thinking what a tough job it is to read it.

I do not believe I am betraying a confidence when I say that there are, in this country, several organizations whose aim is to effect the modification or repeal of the Eighteenth Amendment.

Nearly every citizen who isn't living under an assumed name has received invitations to join one or more of these tongs. If I have been asked once, I have been asked twice. But I have consistently declined to go into them because I figure it is silly to interfere in any way with the efforts of the Drys to knock their own pet legislation for a nose dive. If they fail, it will be time for outsiders to step in.

But they won't fail. They are experienced Gummers and we should be grateful that they are not enlisted on the side of some more salutary statute such as the one which restricts husband-killers to four kinds of dessert during the week of penal servitude.

The Drys of our land are to a large extent identical with the people who have fought the good fight for purity and decency in books and plays. If their war on rum is conducted only half as shrewdly as the struggle against literary and dramatic dirt, we boy scouts need have no fear. You can hardly name one legitimate show of the past season that could possibly give offense to any 125-year-old paralytic who was unable to attend it, and parents are safe in leaving a volume of Milne or Guest on the living-room table, while the children are away at kindergarten.

With a modicum of the same energy and skill applied to the anti-alcohol campaign, the Pros will soon have it fixed so a person can't buy a drink from a horse. It were folly for an amateur to offer advice to these needle-witted strategists, but it does seem to me that if the idea is to stop tippling by homicide, bigger results could be obtained, and at less expense, through the withdrawal of artillery and snipers from the border and the free and untrammeled admittance of all the stuff the consumer wants.

The price of what is screamingly called liquor would shortly drop to a point where even actors could afford it and the consequent fatalities would outnumber those resulting from the present system by at least a hundred to one.

Moreover, this sort of war of attrition would be carried on at little or no cost to the government; the customers would have to pay for their own demise unless they died before they settled, in which case the laugh would be on the bootlegger where it belongs.

But even if the current scheme is adhered to, I believe it should be carried out with more thoroughness and zeal.

In the first place it should be under the auspices of the War Department instead of the Secretary of the Treasury. Revolvers, shotguns, small-bore rifles and pea-shooters ought to be supplanted by long-range cannon, and bullets that can kill only one man or child at a time, replaced by high explosives, shrapnel and all the latest delicacies in the way of gas.

Electrically charged wire should guard the Canadian border from ocean to ocean and the Mexican border from the Pacific to the Gulf. Scout planes and observation balloons should locate Canada's distilleries and direct our shell fire, and the fields of hay from which the liquor is made could be destroyed by poisoned confetti.

The entire eastern half of the Dominion to the north of us might be inundated by a company of volunteers under Capt. Gertude Ederle, who would stand at the bottom of Niagara Falls and splash the water back as fast as it came over. Our aces could drop souvenir post cards from George Creel assuring the Canadians that we have no quarrel with them as a nation, that all we want is peace without whisky, and that this is merely a war to make the United States safe for the soda fountains. An armistice would be granted, we'd tell them, as soon as they pledged themselves to eliminate entirely the alcoholic content of the stuff they have been selling to our importers. This would mean a reduction of nearly two percent.

Some of the war-time regulations should be in effect once more. No meat on Mondays; no heat on Tuesdays; no sweet on Wednesdays; no wheat on Thursdays; no treat on Fridays, and no eat on Saturdays. Censorship of all mail passing between us and Canada and Mexico; four-minute speeches; adoption of Belgian orphans; purling; saving fingernail parings to fill in the shell holes on the Texas and the Minnesota thoroughfares.

I do think, though, that this war should be made much more bearable and entertaining to the stay-at-homes by the adoption of a liberal policy in regard to press dispatches. I never did understand what good was accomplished by the exclusion of the names of people and places from the dull, daily stories from France in 1917 and 1918.

The theory seemed to be that if the *Grand Rapids Herald* printed the news that Hendrik Van Hooten of Holland, Michigan, was in hospital at Chalons-sur-Marne with anthrax, a German spy employed by the Grand Rapids Furniture Company would call up the Kaiser who would thus suspect that a division containing Michigan regiments was, or had been, somewhere near Chalons. Wilhelm would then confer with Ludendorff on what style of defense to use against Michigan's passing game with Van Hooten on the sidelines.

Let's cut down on caution this time; the danger of disclosing military secrets would be more than offset by the certainty of improving the country's morale with a few human-interest stories such as:

El Paso, Tex., Aug. 2—Corporal Charley Judson of Company B, Fourth Regiment of the Eighth (Hawkeye) Division, American Prohibitionary Force, was being congratulated by his buddies tonight for shooting the left ear off a two-year-old child who was crossing the bridge from Juarez with a peculiar waddling gait. Corporal Judson said he had witnesses to prove that the fellow had been seen drinking out of a bottle; he fired at his ear instead of his heart because he just wanted to frighten him. The bottle was found to contain a little over an ounce of a liquid identified as milk. "Yeh?" said the Corporal, who has a certain dry humor. "Well, milk don't make people walk funny."

Sault St. Marie, Mich., Aug. 2—Miss Muriel Chapin of this place was scattered all over the Northern Peninsula today by a machine-gun squad in charge of Capt. Felix Lord of Houghton. The captain picked up one of the girl's lips and showed it to his colonel, H. R. King of Calumet. The lip was a pale red. "That's what fooled me," said Captain Lord. "It's just some kind of rouge, but I thought it was grenadine."

Niagara Falls, N.Y., Aug. 2—A depth bomb dropped by Lieut. Ed. Frawley of Herkimer demolished a barrel that was seen shooting the Falls late today. Frawley suspected that the barrel was full of liquor, but it developed that the contents had been John E. Gardner and wife and two children, a Buffalo family out for an outing. "This was self-defense if there ever was one!" declared Lieut. Frawley. "I acted only after assuring myself that the barrel was shooting the Falls."

Plattsburg, N.Y., Aug. 2—A bearded man on a bicycle was stopped here today by Clarence Dutton, an M.P. of the A.P.F. Dutton demanded the man's name and the man said he was Eli Kolp, a farmer residing three miles south of Plattsburg.

"Then why are you wearing a beard?" asked Dutton.

"I look funny without one," replied the bicyclist.

"You look funny with one," retorted Dutton. "You look suspicious to me. How do I know what you've got in those tires?"

"I've got nothing but some air. I'll open them and let it out."

"I'll let some into you," said Dutton, shooting him full of holes.

The bicyclist was later identified as Eli Kolp, a farmer residing three miles south of Plattsburg.

HERBERT ASBURY

The Noble Experiment of Izzy and Moe

(excerpts)

1946

In a $14-a-month flat on Ridge Street, in New York's lower East Side, lived a bulbous little man named Isadore Einstein, whom everyone called Izzy. He had been a salesman, both inside and on the road, but was now a minor clerk at Station K of the New York Post Office. It required very shrewed management to feed, house, and clothe his family—his wife and four children and his father—on the meager salary of a postal employee. He was looking for something better, and decided that he had found it when he read in his newspaper about the government's plans to pay enforcement agents up to $2,500 a year.

But James Shevlin, Chief Enforcement Agent for the Southern District of New York, was not enthusiastic about Izzy. "I must say, Mr.

Einstein," he said, "you don't look much like a detective." And that was the truth. Probably no one ever looked less like a detective than Izzy Einstein. He was forty years old, almost bald, five feet and five inches tall, and weighed 225 pounds. Most of this poundage was around his middle, so that when he walked, his noble paunch, gently wobbling, moved majestically ahead like the breast of an overfed pouter pigeon.

But Izzy was accomplished. Besides English and Yiddish, he spoke German, Polish, and Hungarian fluently, and could make headway, though haltingly, in French, Italian, and Russian. He had even picked up a few words and phrases of Chinese. Moreover, Izzy had a knack of getting along with people and inspiring confidence. No one, looking at his round, jolly face and twinkling black eyes, could believe that he was a government snooper. Down on the lower East Side in New York he was the neighborhood cutup; whenever he dropped into the corner cigar stores and the coffee houses his witticisms and high spirits never failed to draw an appreciative crowd.

"I guess Mr. Shevlin never saw a type like me," Izzy said afterward. "Maybe I fascinated him or something. Anyhow, I sold him on the idea that this prohibition business needed a new type of people that couldn't be spotted so easy."

Whatever the reason, Izzy got the job.

"But I must warn you," said Shevlin, "that hunting down liquor sellers isn't exactly a safe line of work. Some law violator might get mad and try to crack a bottle over your head."

"Bottles," said Izzy, "I can dodge."

Izzy's first assignment was to cleanup a place in Brooklyn which the enforcement authorities shrewdly suspected housed a speakeasy, since drunken men had been seen staggering from the building, and the air for half a block around was redolent with the fumes of beer and whisky. Several agents had snooped and slunk around the house; one had watched all one afternoon from a roof across the street, and another had hidden for hours in an adjoining doorway, obtaining an accurate count of the number of men who entered and left. But none had been able to get inside. Izzy knew nothing of sleuthing procedures; he simply walked up to the joint and knocked on the door. A peephole was opened, and a hoarse voice demanded to know who was there.

"Izzy Einstein," said Izzy. "I want a drink."

"Oh, yeah? Who sent you here, bud? What's your business?"

"My boss sent me," Izzy explained. "I'm a prohibition agent. I just got appointed."

The door swung open and the doorman slapped Izzy jovially on the back.

"Ho! ho!" he cried. "Come right in, bud. That's the best gag I've heard yet."

Izzy stepped into a room where half a dozen men were drinking at a small makeshift bar.

"Hey, boss!" the doorman yelled. "Here's a prohibition agent wants a drink! You got a badge, too, bud?"

"Sure I have," said Izzy, and produced it.

"Well, I'll be damned," said the man behind the bar. "Looks just like the real thing."

He poured a slug of whisky, and Izzy downed it. That was a mistake, for when the time came to make the pinch Izzy had no evidence. He tried to grab the bottle but the bartender ran out the back door with it.

"I learned right there," said Izzy, "that a slug of hooch in an agent's belly might feel good, but it ain't evidence." . . .

Izzy used his original device of giving his real name, with some variation, more than twenty times during the next five years. It was successful even after he became so well known, and so greatly feared, that his picture hung behind the bar in many speakeasies, that all might see and be warned. Occasionally Izzy would prance into a gin-mill with his badge pinned to his lapel, in plain sight, and shout jovially, "How about a drink for a hardworking prohibition agent?" Seeing the round little man trying so hard to be funny, everyone in the place would rush forward to hand him something alcoholic, and Izzy would arrest them and close the joint.

. . . .

After Izzy had been an enforcement agent for a few weeks, he began to miss his old friend Moe Smith, with whom he had spent many pleasant evenings in the East Side coffee houses. Like Izzy, Moe was a natural comedian, and, also like Izzy, he was corpulent. . . .

Moe could probably have got on the enforcement staff by his own efforts, for his background and experience were at least as good as those of nine-tenths of the agents who were hired, but he obtained the post a little quicker through Izzy's recommendation. As soon as he was sworn in as an agent, he and Izzy teamed up together, and most of the time thereafter worked as a pair. Their first assignment took them to Rockaway Beach, near New York, where they confiscated a still and arrested the operator. This man apparently took a great liking to Izzy, for after he got out of jail he made several trips to New York especially to urge Izzy to go on a fishing trip with him.

"I'll take you three miles out to sea," he said. "You'll have quite a time."

But Izzy firmly declined the invitation. "Sure he'll take me out to sea," he said, "but will he bring me back? He could leave me with the fishes."

In those early days of the noble experiment everything that happened in connection with prohibition was news, and some of New York's best reporters covered enforcement headquarters. Casting about for a way to enliven their stories and provide exercise for their imaginations, they seized upon the exploits of Izzy and Moe. The two fat and indefatigable agents supplied human-interest material by the yard; moreover, they were extraordinarily co-operative. They frequently scheduled their raids to suit the convenience of the reporters and the newspaper photographers, and soon learned that there was more room in the papers on Monday morning than on any other day of the week. . . .

For more than five years the whole country laughed at the antics of Izzy and Moe, with the exception of the ardent drys, who thought the boys were wonderful, and the bootleggers and speakeasy proprietors, who thought they were crazy and feared them mightily. And their fear was justified, for in their comparatively brief career Izzy and Moe confiscated 5,000,000 bottles of booze, worth $15,000,000, besides thousands of gallons in kegs and barrels and hundreds of stills and breweries. They smashed an enormous quantity of saloon fixtures and equipment, and made 4,392 arrests, of which more than 95 percent resulted in convictions. No other two agents even approached this record. . . .

During the summer of 1925 the almost continual stories about Izzy and Moe in the newspapers got on the nerves of high prohibition enforcement officials in Washington, few of whom ever got mentioned in the papers at all. National headquarters announced that any agent whose name appeared in print in connection with his work would be suspended, and perhaps otherwise punished, on the ground that publicity brought discredit to the service. At the same time a high official called Izzy to Washington and spoke to him rather severely. "You get your name in the newspaper all the time, and in the headlines, too," he complained, "whereas mine is hardly ever mentioned. I must ask you to remember that you are merely a subordinate, not the whole show." For a while Izzy really tried to keep away from the reporters and out of the papers, but both he and Moe had become public personages, and it was impossible to keep the newspapermen from writing about them. When they refused to tell what they had done, the reporters invented stories about them, so a stream of angry denials and protests continued to come from Washington.

Finally, on November 13, 1925, it was announced that Izzy and Moe had turned in their gold badges and were no longer prohibition agents. Izzy's story was that he had been told he was to be transferred to Chicago. He had lived in New York since he was fifteen years old, and had no intention of ever living anywhere else, so he refused to go, and "thereby fired myself." Government officials, however, said that Izzy and Moe had been dismissed "for the good of the service." Off the record they added, "The service must be dignified. Izzy and Moe belong on the vaudeville stage." Most of the newspapers took the position that the whole problem of enforcement belonged on the vaudeville stage. . . .

OGDEN NASH

Invocation

1930

("Smoot Plans Tariff Ban on Improper Books"—NEWS ITEM)

> Senator Smoot (Republican, Ut.)
> Is planning a ban on smut.
> Oh root-ti-toot for Smoot of Ut.
> And his reverent occiput.
> Smite, Smoot, smite for Ut.,
> Grit your molars and do your dut.,
> Gird up your l——ns,
> Smite h——p and th——gh,
> We'll all be Utah
> By and by.
>
> Smite, Smoot, for the Watch and Ward,
> For Hiram Johnson and Henry Ford,
> For Bishop Cannon and John D., Junior,
> For Governor Pinchot of Pennsylvunia,
> For John S. Sumner and Elder Hays
> And possibly Edward L. Bernays,

For Orville Poland and Ella Boole,
For Mother Machree and the Shelton pool.
When smut's to be smitten
Smoot will smite
For G——d, for country,
And Fahrenheit.

Senator Smoot is an institute
Not to be bribed with pelf;
He guards our homes from erotic tomes
By reading them all himself.
Smite, Smoot, smite for Ut.,
They're smuggling smut from Balt. to Butte!
Strongest and sternest
Of your s——x
Scatter the scoundrels
From Can. to Mex.!

Smite, Smoot, for Smedley Butler,
For any good man by the name of Cutler,
Smite for the W.C.T.U.,
For Rockne's team and for Leader's crew,
For Florence Coolidge and Admiral Byrd,
For Billy Sunday and John D., Third,
For Grantland Rice and for Albie Booth,
For the Woman's Auxiliary of Duluth,
Smite, Smoot,
Be rugged and rough,
Smut if smitten
Is front-page stuff.

RUSSELL MALONEY

Short-Wave Propaganda Program

Suitable for Jamming by an Axis Power

1942

(*Theme music fades in and under.*)
ANNOUNCER: Listen, Hitler! Listen, Hirohito! Listen, Mussolini!
Night has fallen over the continent of North America, but the people

are not sleeping! The factories are running—

(*Roar of blast furnace in background.*)

The trains are running—

(*Train whistle.*)

The *Herald Tribune* has just gone to press with an editorial urging support of certain provisions of the new tax program—

(*Rumble of newspaper presses.*)

And the poets of America are hard at work, dozens and hundreds and thousands of poets, stripped to the waist in the fierce white light of their study lamps, writing poems. *War* poems, Hitler! *Morale* poems, Hirohito! Radio continuities like this one, Mussolini—radio continuities, cinema sound tracks, picture captions, they are all poems. Nouns, pronouns, verbs, adverbs, adjectives, prepositions, conjunctions—

(*The Announcer's voice is drowned out by the rising sound of a multitude of typewriters. Starting at thirty words a minute, they go faster and faster, reaching a crescendo which is abruptly cut off.*)

It was not always like this. Before we tapped the vast natural resources of our city directories, our maps, our gazetteers, our telephone books, our *Directory of Directors, Hotel Red Book, Who's Who, Railroad Guide, Lloyd's Register of Yachts, Horses in Training, Social Register, Spalding's Baseball Guide*—before we discovered the new kind of poetry, the kind of poetry any strong young American could write, it took a long time to write a poem. There was a man named Poe—

VOICE OF EDGAR ALLAN POE (*an irritated mumble*): Helen, thy beauty is to *me*, like those Nicæan barks of *yore* . . . ee, ore . . . see, be, me, he, she, we, thee, glee, tree, flee, store, more, gore, snore, whore, floor, bore, lore, poor, roar, sore, tore . . . Oh, God!

ANNOUNCER: In England there was a man named Wordsworth, who lived with his sister and wrote poems the old-fashioned way—

VOICE OF DOROTHY WORDSWORTH, READING FROM HER JOURNAL: William tired himself today, seeking an epithet for the cuckoo.

ANNOUNCER: But our poets today are not Poes, Adolf! They are not Wordsworths, Hirohito! Think about this, Mussolini—our poets can send over to England thousands of epithets for the cuckoo. The sleeping giant of American poetry production is awakening—

VOICE OF DORTHY WORDSWORTH: An epithet for the cuckoo—

VOICE OF A POETRY COÖRDINATOR: O.K., leave it blank in your copy. We'll get somebody to do it, pencil it in before we go on the air. We'll have it ready for you at the Garden by eight sharp. Or is it for that luncheon at the Waldorf?

ANNOUNCER (*in tones of thoughtful reminiscence*): Who was it, I wonder, who discovered that poetry didn't have to rhyme, or scan, or even mean anything in particular? Whoever made that discovery, and whenever it was made, that was an evil day for the enemies of the United States. We can all write poems now, Adolf. Think what that means—WE CAN ALL WRITE POEMS NOW, EVERY GODDAMN ONE OF US! The plump, wealthy dialogue writer from Hollywood—

VOICE OF HOLLYWOOD DIALOGUE WRITER (*back*): A poem? Sure. When do you want it, tomorrow?

ANNOUNCER: The tall, dyspeptic agency man from Chicago—

VOICE OF CHICAGO AGENCY MAN (*back*): A poem? O.K., how long of a poem?

ANNOUNCER: The lady novelist from the South—

VOICE OF THE LADY NOVELIST (*back*): A poem? Why, yes, if y'all can read mah handwritin'.

ANNOUNCER: I don't know how it is in your country, Adolf. Maybe your people do things differently, Benito, and very likely you, Hirohito, won't understand this. Over here, you see, we have more poems than we can use. We're poem-poor. ANY LIST OF ANYTHING IS A POEM OVER HERE, IF CLEARLY ENUNCIATED THROUGH A MICROPHONE. Any kind of a list. Today's menu at the Astor—

VOICE OF THE HEADWAITER AT THE ASTOR: Cold jellied consommé madrilène, crême vichyssoise, petite marmite, cold cuts, baked Alaska salmon, omelette fines herbes—

ANNOUNCER: All we have to do is add a couple of lines pointing out that this is what we're fighting for, and we have another poem, Adolf. A poem every hour, just like Willow Run . . . Do you know the stations on the Highland branch of the Boston & Albany, Adolf? Another poem—

TRAIN ANNOUNCER: Longwood, Brookline, Brookline Hills, Beaconsfield, Reservoir, Chestnut Hill, Newton Centre, Newton Highlands, Eliot, Waban, and Woodland.

VOICE OF A POET: (*back; slowly, accompanied by tapping of a typewriter*): "Eliot, Waban, and Woodland. Land of the free." O.K., take this one away, Joe.

ANNOUNCER: Poems—

1ST VOICE: Coming up!

ANNOUNCER: More poems!

2ND VOICE: Right!

ANNOUNCER: And more and more and MORE!

3RD VOICE: O.K.!

ANNOUNCER: Poems, *poems*, POEMS, *Directory of Directors, Hotel Red Book, Who's Who, Railroad Guide, Lloyd's Register of Yachts, Horses in Training* . . .

(*Again his voice is drowned out by the rising clatter of typewriters.*)

(*Theme music up and out.*)

MARYA MANNES

Postmaster Versus Poet

1958

Concerning attempts to bar *Lysistrata* from the mails: "Mr. Summerfield's charges . . . assert that certain passages in *Lysistrata* are 'well calculated to deprave the morals of persons . . . and almost equally certain to arouse libidinous thoughts in the minds of the average normal reader.' "—*New York Herald Tribune*

> Is your libido, normal mite,
> Roused by the birds and bees?
> If so, Mr. Summerfield is right
> To ban Aristophanes.
>
> For pleasure and wit in amorous play
> Are depraving and profane,
> But never the bloody kill-a-day
> On the pages of Spillane.
>
> Censor the healthy urge of man
> Especially if it's fun,
> But never stop an American
> From making love with a gun.

JULES FEIFFER

Bureau of Images

HELLO? MR. MILES TOOMUCH, THE JAZZ MUSICIAN? THIS IS THE **STATE DEPT.- BUREAU OF IMAGES** - VICTOR VENEER SPEAKING. I'M CALLING, SIR, IN REGARD TO THE ATTORNEY GENERAL'S PLAN FOR IMPROVING OUR IMAGE ABROAD BY SENDING OVER OUR INTELLECTUAL AND ARTISTIC **ELITE** - OH, YES, YOU ARE, MR. TOOMUCH! - WELL, **WE** SAY SO!

ANYHOW, WE DOWN HERE AT **IMAGE** JUST WANTED TO CHECK YOU OUT ON SOME DIFFICULT QUESTIONS YOU MIGHT BE ASKED ON YOUR TRIP - YOU KNOW - BY RIOTING STUDENTS OR SOMETHING.
FOR INSTANCE WHAT WOULD YOU SAY ABOUT OUR RESUMPTION OF ATMOS- PHERIC TESTING ?

OH, YOU'D SAY **THAT** WOULD YOU ? AND HOW WOULD YOU HANDLE DIVISIVE QUESTIONS ON RACE RELATIONS? - I SEE -. AND ABOUT OUR BERLIN, NATO AND ASIAN POLICIES? - - MMM - **HMMMM** -

WELL, MR. TOOMUCH, INSTEAD OF ALL **THAT** COULDN'T YOU JUST **PLAY** SOMETHING ON YOUR HORN?

I MEAN ISN'T **MUSIC** TRULY THE BEST COMMUNICATOR?

HEAVENS, **NO** ONE IS TRYING TO SUPPRESS YOU, MR. TOOMUCH, BUT IT **IS** SORT OF **YOUR** IMAGE OF OUR IMAGE AGAINST **OUR** IMAGE OF OUR IMAGE, ISN'T IT? AND SHOULDN'T IMPORTANT DECISIONS ON IMAGE BE LEFT IN THE HANDS OF THE PUBLIC RELATIONS EXPERTS WHO MAY HAVE ACCESS TO CLASSIFIED PUBLICITY THAT YOU DON'T KNOW ABOUT?

WELL, LOOK, MR. TOOMUCH, BEFORE WE REISSUE YOU YOUR PASSPORT WHY DON'T I SEND YOU OUR SAMPLE IMAGE SALES KIT, INCLUDING PAMPHLETS, FILM STRIPS AND VISUAL AIDS - ALL UNDER THE GENERAL TITLE OF **"OPERATION : GOOD GUY."** WE'D LIKE YOU TO HAVE THE RIGHT SLANT BEFORE YOU WENT ABROAD, SIR.

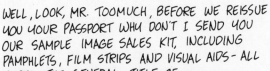

AFTER ALL **IMAGE** IS **EVERYBODY'S** JOB.

SENATOR J. W. FULBRIGHT

Seagull Wisdom

1963

Mr. President, I recently came across an article in *National Wildlife* magazine on the mores and mating habits of seagulls. My initial reaction to the article was that I had learned somewhat more about seagulls than I really cared to know, but on further reflection I realized that I was manifesting the rather stuffy and superior attitude which we humans all too often direct at our inarticulate fellow creatures.

The seagull in fact is a marvelous bird. Unlike many other species, it is entirely free of socialistic tendencies. It is in fact a capitalist bird, a rugged individualist with a highly developed regard for the sanctity of private property. Every family of seagulls has its own nesting land, about seven feet square, and the family estate is absolutely inviolable. To invade one of these private preserves is the gravest of offenses, punishable by swift and stern retaliation.

In addition to his sound economic doctrine, the seagull is guided by rigorous standards of morality in his private life. Courting is conducted with dignity and ceremony and, once wed, the seagull is monogamous and devoted to family. Divorce is unknown and scandals of the sort which rock great empires in the world of men are considered by seagulls to be in unacceptably bad taste.

More impressive still is the high regard which seagull society holds for the principle of seniority. Every gullery has its venerated senior citizens, newcomers working their way up, and a few members whom everybody is allowed to pick on. Under the seniority system the young chick is required to keep his neck tucked in because a high head and a stretched neck is a status symbol among gulls. Nothing is more infuriating to an adult than the sight of a juvenile with his neck stuck out. This is the ultimate in presumption, and the bumptious youngster who holds his head high is likely to be struck dead by an adult who sees him. Where, Mr. President, outside a gullery and the United States Senate, is the principle of seniority more faithfully observed?

The most ingenious and civilized of seagull folkways are the rules of chivalrous combat. A head held high is the most heinous of offenses, but so long as a gull holds his neck in, he is immune from attack, even if he invades the private property of another bird. The tucked in head is a permanently available form of diplomatic immunity, sacred and inviolable. There is no real equivalent to it in human society except for certain rather limited forms of political asylum for heretics and dissenters. Surely with our superior mental endowment we humans ought to be able to devise a form of protection for our free thinkers and dissenters as safe and as convenient as the pulled-in neck.

When seagulls do actually fight, they seldom go beyond ceremonial expressions of hostility. When two enemies face each other, they are likely to stand puffing out their wings until one or the other commits the ultimate provocation of leaning over and pulling grass. So terrifying is this act that most fights usually end at this point. Only the gravest of conflicts actually reaches the point of whacking and biting.

It takes little imagination to conceive of the benefits which would accrue to humanity if we were able to apply such civilized techniques to our own rivalries. Pulling grass hardly seems an appropriate expression of hostility for so elevated a creature as man, but certainly we should be able to devise more suitable forms of ceremonial combat. Consider, for example, the battle of Agincourt. It would have been almost as exciting and a great deal safer if the English had tipped their arrows with suction cups instead of sharp metal points.

Or consider the hydrogen bomb. Wouldn't it be a fine thing if we could agree with the Russians to replace all our nuclear bombs with smoke bombs—huge smoke bombs which could set off immense unradioactive mushroom clouds and even make a tremendous noise but to do so without a lethal explosion. Surely it is not beyond the genius of modern science to invent such a weapon, one which would permit us the fun and excitement of nuclear war without getting killed.

But all this, I suppose, is idle nonsense, suitable enough for the mindless seagull but hardly worthy of the most exalted of God's creatures.

ART BUCHWALD

I Have a Lady in the Balcony

1963

One of the things that came out of the March on Washington was a protest by women reporters that they were discriminated against by their male counterparts at Washington's National Press Club.

Miss Elsie Carper, president of the Women's National Press Club, protested to A. Philip Randolph, chairman of the March on Washington, who was scheduled to be guest speaker at the men's National Press Club, last Monday that women would have to sit in the balcony during his talk.

She asked that Mr. Randolph change the site of his speech so that the men and women reporters would be allowed to sit together.

The embarrassed Mr. Randolph turned down Miss Carper's request, though he did come out for equality for women and said he was against discrimination of any kind. He went ahead and gave the talk to an all-male audience with a few women sitting in the balcony.

The question of discriminating against women has always been a ticklish one in the nation's capital. Although the majority of members of the National Press Club consider that some of their best friends are women, the feeling is that women aren't ready to take their places as men's equals, and no amount of legislation will change the attitude towards the female reporter by male members of the Press Club.

One correspondent spoke for several members at the bar when he said, "Our women were very happy to sit in the balcony until outside agitators from the North came down here and started causing trouble. Women prefer to be together. That's why they have women's colleges and women's magazines. We've always treated our women good, but they wouldn't know what to do with equal rights if we gave it to them."

Another newspaper man agreed. "You said it. You start mixing the sexes and you know what you'll wind up with? Babies! I've seen it happen during the war."

"I don't mind women asking for equal pay and wanting their children to go to school with our children," said a third reporter. "But what I'm worried about is that if we let them eat with us, pretty soon they'll want to dance with us, and neck with us, and before you know it all the barriers will be down, they'll be wanting to play poker with us."

"We don't ask to go to their beauty parlors," a columnist said. "Why should they ask to come to our club?"

Everyone at the bar nodded his head.

A young reporter said, "I was in Chicago recently at the Playboy Club and you know what was going on there because women are permitted to sit downstairs? The women were kissing the men, right in public. I saw it with my own eyes."

"I hope you walked out," the others said.

"You bet your life I did," the reporter replied. "I told them we don't do things like this in Washington, and they accused me of being a bigot."

"Damn Yankees," someone muttered.

"I said," the reporter continued, "that our women know their place and if a woman in Washington attempted to kiss a man in public she'd be tarred and feathered and rode out of town on a rail."

"Good for you," the others said.

A public relations man said, "I heard that the agitation at the Press Club for women to sit with men is Communist-inspired."

"It's got to be," a fellow drinker said. "They would never have thought of it themselves."

"I sure would like to know who is behind it."

"The Communists have the most to gain," a Hearst man said. "You desegregate the sexes and you have chaos—marriages, divorces, fights, riots, and crime, everything the Communists are working for."

"Our mistake was letting them sit in the balcony in the first place," a TV commentator said. "We opened the door an inch and now that they've got their foot in they want to squeeze in the rest of their anatomy."

"You can say all you want about women," a man from a wire service said. "You can talk about equal rights, equal job opportunities, equal schooling, and equal public accommodations, but it still boils down to one question: Would you want your brother to marry one?"

Everyone at the bar, including the bartender, shouted, "No."

SENATOR KENNETH KEATING

*Mine Enemy—The Folk Singer**

1963

MR. KEATING: Mr. President, it will come as a shock to many Senators, but according to a resolution of a certain Los Angeles civic organization the Communists have developed a new secret weapon to ensnare and capture youthful minds in America—folk music . . .

The resolution adopted by this organization, called the Fire and Police Research Association of Los Angeles, Inc., describes folk music as—and I quote from the resolution—"an unidentified tool of Communists psychological or cybernetic warfare." . . .

Mr. President, this amazing document maintains that "the dialectics of the Communist movement have successfully used, and are now using all modes and media of communication with young people, including the subtleties and the verbal subterfuges of applied dialectics in both poems and songs" and that "it is becoming more and more evident that certain of the 'Hootenannies' * * * in this country and in Europe have been used to brainwash and subvert"—and now, listen to this—"in a seemingly innocuous but actually covert and deceptive manner, vast segments of young people's groups." It closes with a fervent plea for a congressional investigation of this "unidentified tool of Communist psychological and cybernetic warfare" which is being used "to ensnare and capture youthful minds in the United States as it has so successfully and effectively captivated them abroad."

I had always had the impression that if anything was thoroughly American in spirit, it was American folk music. To be sure, I was perfectly aware of certain un-American influences in it, like Elizabethan balladry, English Protestant hymns and spirituals, and, with respect to

* from the *Congressional Record.*

jazz and in some cases the Negro spiritual, native African rhythms. But in my naïveté I had never considered these un-American influences to be of a sinister nature and simply passed them off as part and parcel of the melting-pot tradition which has contributed so much in the way of variety and interest to the American cultural heritage.

In the light of this resolution, however, I have given this subject renewed attention. Have we ever considered, for example, that the music of our national anthem, the Star-Spangled Banner, is based upon an English folk melody—a drinking song, no less—"To Anacreon in Heaven"?

Of course, I realize that folk music tradition is grounded in movements of political, economic, and social unrest and I did not expect to find in music which originated among sharecroppers, miners, union organizers, factory workers, cowboys, hill folk, wanderers, and oppressed Negroes—a pattern of tribute and praise to such symbols of orthodoxy as the gold standard, the oil depletion allowance, and the standing rules of the U.S. Senate. . . .

No one could possibly imagine the members of the board of directors of General Motors sitting around a conference table composing ditties in honor of defense contracts, while it is not surprising that coal miners should have come up with a protest song, "Sixteen Tons," crying "Saint Peter, don't call me, 'cause I can't go; I owe my soul to the company store." . . .

The first significant discovery I made was that from this Nation's very beginnings folk music had indeed been used, "in a seemingly innocuous but actually covert and deceptive manner, to incite violations of the laws of the United States." Why, even "Yankee Doodle" has fallen victim to misuse in this fashion, as it did during President Jefferson's embargo of 1808 imposed to prevent our embroilment in the Napoleonic wars. Just listen to this plea to run the embargo:

> Attention pay ye bonny lads
> And listen to my Fargo
> About a nation deuced thing
> Which people call Embargo
>
> Yankee doodle, keep it up
> Yankee doodle, dandy
> We'll soak our hide in home-made rum
> If we can't get French brandy

I've got a vessel at the wharf
　Well loaded with a cargo
And want a few more hands to help
　And clear the cursed Embargo

Yankee doodle, keep it up
　Yankee doodle, dandy
We'll soak our hide in home-made rum
　If we can't get French brandy

. . . Apparently, some of our folk music takes a pretty cavalier attitude toward the enforcement of our Internal Revenue laws and could easily brainwash our young people into total disrespect for all law and order. The song, "Darlin' Cory," is a prime example of this:

Wake up, wake up, darlin' Cory
　What makes you sleep so sound?
The revenue officers a-comin'
　Gonna tear your still house down

Or, for another example, the now very popular, "Copper Kettle," which contains the lines:

My daddy he made whisky
My granddaddy did, too
We ain't paid no whisky tax
Since 1792.

If enough people went around singing this at hootenannies, Americans might soon get the idea that they don't have to pay their taxes. After all, the family in the song got away without paying them for 171 years. And if the Government loses its ability to collect taxes to pay for our defense effort, we would be wide open for a Communist takeover, would we not?

This sinister folk music plot for disarmament takes more direct form than merely inciting Americans not to pay their taxes. Consider, for example, this pacifist Negro spiritual:

Gonna lay down my sword and shield
Down by the river-side
Down by the river-side
Down by the river-side

Gonna lay down my sword and shield
Down by the river-side
And study war no more.

. . . If we do not realize that this "seemingly innocuous" Negro spiritual is "actually covert and deceptive," we have obviously been duped.

Now the Communists have also been known to sow the seeds of dissension in capitalist countries by turning people against their own political leaders. There's an Ozark folk song—and perhaps one of the Senators from Arkansas can enlighten me as to its origin—that goes like this:

Yes, the candidate's a dodger, yes, a well-known dodger
Yes, the candidate's a dodger, and I'm a dodger, too
He'll meet you and greet you and ask you for your vote
But look out, boys, he's dodging for a note.

. . . These examples must give pause to every patriotic American who may have taken folk music for granted in the past. But there is one concern I still have about a congressional investigation of folk music such as proposed by the Fire and Research Association of Los Angeles. What I fear is that [it] would stimulate the writing of new folk music making fun of congressional investigations. This shows how devious the Communists really are. . . .

Once a congressional investigation of folk music is held, the Communists set about composing new folk music impugning the integrity of congressional investigations, like this folk song of a few years ago:

Who's gonna investigate the man who investigates me?
I don't doubt my loyalty
But how about what his may be?
Who'll check the record of the man who checks the record of me?
Seems to me there's gonna be an awfully long line.

One more problem puzzles me
Pardon my strange whim
But who's gonna investigate the man who investigates the
    man who investigates him? . . .

It all boils down to a gigantic plot, one that has been brought to our attention before, most notably, by the assistant minority leader, the senior Senator from California [Mr. Kuchel], based on letters he has received from constituents whose keen alertness to matters involving our national security is fully equal to that of the Fire and Police Association of Los Angeles, Inc. And so, now, to the list of subversive individuals, institutions, and ideas, which presently includes the United Nations, the income tax, the Chief Justice of the United States, the Girl Scouts of America, fluoridation of the water supply, the last four Presidents of the United States, beatniks, Harvard University, civil rights demonstrations, expenditures for mental health, the Arms Control and Disarmament Agency, coffee houses, every Secretary of State since William Jennings Bryan, professors of anthropology, back-door spending, metro government, Jews, *Time* magazine, the Council on Foreign Relations, firearms registration, the Protestant clergy, the two United States Senators from New York plus between 77 and 83 of their colleagues and proposals for Federal aid to mass transportation—to this list of Communist-inspired persons and ideas we must now add, merciful heavens, American folk music. And who knows what lies ahead?

6 BREAD AND BUTTER

WAYS AND MEANS AND THE GENERAL WELFARE

This is the place for a comment on Will Rogers, since he is the closest to a bread-and-butter (meat-and-potatoes, grits-and-gravy) political humorist we have had. Nowadays he is most often thought of as a kind of good-natured crackerbarrel philosopher, given to sententious witticisms, "beloved" by one and all. But this was only a part of Rogers' repertoire, as some of the quotations in this book will indicate; for all his cowboy clowning, he was a genuine satirist, and occasionally his insights were searing.

This may also be the place for a different kind of comment on two political antagonists of a generation ago, since both are represented here. Westbrook Pegler, says Murray Kempton, in a review of Oliver Pilat's recent biography, "found it sacrilegious that Heywood Broun would cast off in 40 minutes something so extraordinary as a newspaper column." Broun, on the other hand, "thought it unreasonable for . . . Pegler to sit for eight hours with the blood running into his shoes for nothing more consequential." Broun is not as well represented in this volume as Pegler, because his most trenchant political writings were rarely funny, his funny pieces seldom political. (Other writers one might expect to find in a book of this kind are, regrettably, missing entirely from it, for the same reason.)

WILL ROGERS

Chamber of Commerce

1923

Well, they had another big Convention here this week—the Chambers
of Commerce from all over the U.S. Being big sound business men,
they wanted some good conservative business man to address them, and
also wanted some frivolous or light talker that would sound amusing but
mean nothing.

So Herb. Hoover drew this last frothy or carefree assignment. He had
those BABBITS just rolling off their seats telling them about the
prosperous conditions of this Country.

Then he knocked 'em Coo Coo with a gag for the Government not
to go into business. He said the standard of living had advanced so far
in this country that we could lay off two million men from work and
the rest of the people would live just as good as they did 10 years ago.

He didn't say what would become of the 2 Millions he laid off. But
you take a busy man like that, he can't stop to worry about trifles like a
couple of million men.

Well, the next night after Mr. Hoover spoke, why, they were ready
for some real conservative business talk. So I went over and instructed
them.

You know what the Chamber of Commerce is, don't you? You
remember the Old Ladies' sewing circle in towns years ago that knew
everybody's business and were into everything. Well, this is the Male
end of that same organization. They fix everything from the local
Marble Championship to the next War. The minute a fellow gets into
the Chamber of Commerce he quits mowing his own lawn.

Sick Hogs

1924

You wire the State or the Federal Government that your Cow or Hog is sick and they will send out experts from Washington and appropriate money to eradicate the Cause. You wire them that your Baby has the Diphtheria or Scarlet Fever and see what they do. All you will do is hire your own Doctor if you are able, and there will be a Flag put up on your front Gate. Where Children that don't know can still go in and perhaps be exposed to certain Death, the Government won't have Guards at every Entrance to keep you back from that Exposed House.

If your Hog has the Cholera the whole State knows it and everybody is assisting in Stamping it out. You can have 5 Children down with the Infantile Paralysis, more deadly 10 times over than any Foot and Mouth disease, and see how many Doctors they send out from Washington to help you.

There is more Money spent on Hogs' sickness by State and Federal Governments than there is on Children, when one child's life is worth all the Hogs and Cows that ever had a Disease. If you want the Government to help you, don't tell them it is any Human Sickness. Tell them it is Boll Weevil or Chich Bugs, and they will come a running, because they have big appropriations and men paid for that.

How many Children die every day from some contagious disease, that would be Living if we exercised the same vigilance over a Child that we do over a Cow?

I fully believe that every sane Precaution that is being exercised is necessary, but while we are all thinking of it, why can't we get the Government to at least do for a Child's protection, what they do for a Cow or a Hog?

When more and more people are thrown out of work, unemployment results.—*Calvin Coolidge*

VARIOUS VOICES

*The Great Depression**

Herbert Hoover, accepting Republican nomination, August, 1928—"Unemployment in the sense of distress is widely disappearing. . . . We in America today are nearer to the final triumph over poverty than ever before in the history of any land. The poor-house is vanishing from among us. We have not yet reached the goal, but given a chance to go forward with the policies of the last eight years, and we shall soon with the help of God be in sight of the day when poverty will be banished from this nation. There is no guarantee against poverty equal to a job for every man. That is the primary purpose of the economic policies we advocate."

November, 1929—"Any lack of confidence in the economic future or the basic strength of business in the United States is foolish."

Robert P. Lamont, Secretary of Commerce
March, 1930—"Business will be normal in two months."
May, 1930—"Normal conditions should be restored in two or three months."
September, 1930—"Our information indicates that the decline in business has substantially if not wholly ceased."
March, 1931—"There has been evidence of a slight but unmistakable improvement in the employment situation."

Charles M. Schwab, of the Bethlehem Steel Corporation
October, 1930—"Looking to the future I see in the further acceleration of science continuous jobs for our workers. Science will cure unemployment."
February, 1931—"I am not predicting anything."

* Some of the quotations collected by Edward Angly in *Oh, Yeah?*, Viking Press, 1931.

Simeon D. Fess, Chairman, Republican National Committee
  October, 1930—"Persons high in Republican circles are beginning to believe that there is some concerted effort on foot to utilize the stock market as a method of discrediting the administration. Every time an Administration official gives out an optimistic statement about business conditions, the market immediately drops."

Arthur Brisbane, syndicated columnist
  November, 1929—"It ought to be a good year."
  November, 1929—"All the really important millionaires are planning to continue prosperity."
  January, 1931—"Sometimes when things go wrong, it is a comfort to be reminded that nothing matters very much. If the earth fell toward the sun, it would melt like a flake of snow falling on a red-hot stove."
  October, 1931—"You can get all the money you want, up to a hundred million or more, if you have the right collateral and enough of it."

By 1935, the New Deal administration of Franklin D. Roosevelt was in full swing, and so was the opposition. The Democratic campaign song of 1932 had been "Happy Days Are Here Again," (Die Zeiten, etc.)

JOHN T. FLYNN

Von Pleesemall of Schlumpberg

1935

Once upon a time there lived in the little village of Schlumpberg the good burgomaster von Pleesemall. He was a pleasant fellow if ever there was one. He was in truth the very model of an agreeable man. That is, he loved to have around him only men who agreed with him, while he, on his part, set an excellent example of this virtue by agreeing with all who came to him with advice.

The village of Schlumpberg was a place where the good burghers had enjoyed the greatest abundance, so much indeed that they supposed they had actually solved the ancient riddle of poverty. But then, one day, in the midst of their vainglory, it was observed that honest Hans was out of work. The burghers promptly met this challenge by eager contributions to aid Hans. But when Fritz and Honus and several others turned up without work, it was seen that a major disaster was upon them.

The people were greatly exercised. They threw out the reigning burgomaster and chose the good von Pleesemall in his place. This agreeable man had endeared himself to all with his ready smile and a merry tune he played upon his oboe. He loved to sit at his window and toot merrily away his favorite tune, *"Die Zeiten sind wieder glücklich."* And so when the good man was elevated to his high post of burgomaster, the joyous burghers gathered around the little guild hall and sang merrily *"Die Zeiten sind wieder glücklich."*

Von Pleesemall had many clever stratagems for ending the tribulations of Schlumpberg. But the one that brought the greatest results was his plan to move all the leaves in Schlumpberg from where they were to some other place. The oak leaves were collected and put under the linden trees and the linden leaves were put under the locust trees. It was called the Emergency Rearrangement Plan and it kept Hans and Honus and Fritz busy.

But smartest of all was the way in which von Pleesemall got the money for this. One of his counsellors said:

"Your worship, you should lay a heavy tax on old Guldenrocks, the rich banker and merchant. He has gotten more than his share of our abundance. Take it from him to pay Hans and Fritz and Honus."

"No, no, my good friend," replied the burgomaster, with a sly glance. "That would displease Guldlenrocks. He would be very angry and cease to love me. And I wish all men to be pleased with me. I will be more clever. Remember, my friend, the cure for all ills is cleverness. I will not take Guldenrocks' money. I will borrow it from him."

So von Pleesemall went over to Guldenrocks' counting room, which was right next to his store. He asked him to lend him 5,000 guilders on the credit of the village to pay the wages of Hans and Honus and Fritz and others. Guldenrocks was greatly relieved to see von Pleesemall come as a borrower rather than a tax collector and he granted the loan forthwith.

"And how much did you have in the bank this morning, Herr Guldenrocks?" asked the burgomaster.

"One hundred thousand guilders."

"And so now you will have only 95,000 guilders."

"No, your worship. I had 100,000 guilders before I lent you 5,000 guilders. But since making the loan I have 105,000 guilders."

"And how is that?" asked the puzzled burgomaster.

"I had 100,000 guilders. Now give me the town's bankbook. See! I write in 'On Deposit for Schlumpberg, 5,000 guilders.' You have 5,000 guilders on deposit here. So my deposits are 5,000 more than they were."

"Marvelous!" cried the happy von Pleesemall. "What could be finer? I do not tax you. I borrow from you, pay Hans and Fritz and Honus for their useful work and you have more money in your bank than you started with and we pay you interest. Hans is happy, Fritz is happy, you are happy, everyone is pleased with me. Everyone is happy!"

Von Pleesemall drew the money from the bank, paid it out to Fritz and Hans and the others each week. Fritz and Hans promptly took it to old Guldenrocks' store and spent it there and Guldenrocks put it back in the bank.

Von Pleesemall thought this such a sublime performance that he announced Schlumpberg was "on its way" and he tooted away more lustily upon the oboe *"Die Zeiten sind wieder glücklich."*

For four years von Pleesemall repeated this. Then one day he found that Schlumpberg owed old Guldenrocks 20,000 guilders and that each year he had to pay him 1,000 guilders interest. When he realized this, he tried to forget it by playing on his oboe. He blew sweetly into the little reed but the notes came out sourly from the other end. It is a plaintive instrument at best and hardly suited to the mood of *"Die Zeiten sind."*

By this time old Guldenrocks was growling about all the money due him. Hans and Fritz and Honus had grown lazy and listless and the good burghers were muttering.

Then one of von Pleesemall's counsellors said:

"Your worship, there is one thing left for you to do to please the burghers. You must soak old Guldenrocks. That fellow Koenigsmelt is stirring up the people telling them he will 'share-the-wealth.' You must strike first. Make a great speech saying you will tax old Guldenrocks— that you will take from him and give to Hans and Fritz and Honus."

And so von Pleesemall did this. He found that Guldenrocks was paying to the village in taxes 1,000 guilders a year. "Let them be doubled," cried von Pleesemall. And this was done.

When the tax collectors returned they found the burgomaster tooting gleefully on his oboe.

"Very well, my men," he cried. "Has the wealth been shared?"

"Truly, your worship."

"You took the extra 1,000 guilders from old Guldenrocks?"

"Yes, your worship."

"And what did you do with it?"

"We took it to his bank and paid it back to him in interest."

Von Pleesemall looked a little crestfallen.

"We have borrowed 20,000 guilders from him," he said, "and given them to Hans and Fritz and Honus. But they spent all these guilders in Guldenrocks' store. And so he has them all back and we owe them besides. Now I tax him 1,000 guilders to 'share-the-wealth' and we pay them to him as interest. He still has them. What of Hans and Fritz and Honus? Did you give them some of this?"

"Nothing, your worship. They are still quite impecunious. If you want to give them aught, you must borrow from Guldenrocks."

Von Pleesemall blew fitfully into his oboe—"*Die Zeiten sind wieder glücklich.*" But the merry motif ended in a sob.

"And the leaves are all worn out," said one of his counsellors. "What will you do?"

"Here, take away this oboe. Hand me my violin. I shall play "*Die Zeiten sind*" on this. This is a merrier organ. I can play louder and faster."

And so they left von Pleesemall fiddling away.

HEYWOOD BROUN

Hints to the Epicure

1938

It is well enough for Mr. Roosevelt to eschew "grilled millionaire" as a breakfast dish, but it is disappointing to learn that he prefers scrambled eggs. Hardboiled ones are better. The reference, naturally, is to eggs rather than millionaires. A gourmet of my acquaintance says that a one-minute millionaire is not so bad, but that any boiling beyond that point is as useless as bleaching the lily. Still, one need not be an ogre or an epicure to find a millionaire quite tasty upon occasion.

For instance, did President Roosevelt ever try roasting one over a national hookup for fifteen minutes? But if you like game the best culinary approach to a millionaire is to fricassee him. Of course, you must first catch your millionaire, and it is best to get him young.

Experienced hunters go down to the blinds long before daybreak carrying an elephant gun and a set of decoys which are arranged alphabetically in a receptacle known to sportsmen as a sucker list. These decoys are cleverly carved and painted to look like innocent investors. A bright green seems to be the favorite color, and the design should resemble either a young sheep, a widow or an orphan.

After they have been placed at convenient points in some open meadow the hunter goes into hiding and bides his time. In an earlier generation the guide would try to summon millionaires by imitating a margin call. This was done under the theory that the big birds would always flock together to save the market, but scientific experiments made in the hard winter of 1929 proved that this was merely an old woodsman's legend without validity. The easiest way to spot a millionaire is to remember that he is the precise opposite of a poet or a pheasant. He flies high, and it would do you no good to dust him.

In order to bring a millionaire to earth it is necessary to score a direct hit in the pocketbook. Retrievers of any sort can be left in the kennels, because there never will be any doubt as to whether or not the millionaire has been hit. As he flutters down he emits loud squawks of protest which are very piteous. Humane hunters make it a practice to put the quarry out of its misery by clubbing the wounded bird over the head with an income tax, but even this requires almost surgical skill, because the blows must be delivered in the higher brackets.

However, even at this point the job is scarcely begun. You've got your millionaire, but before he can even be considered as potentially edible you've got to skin him. This may take days or even weeks. Some hunters can never learn the trick at all. But once the tough hide has been removed the lucky sportsman can bring the millionaire back to the cook in triumph. At that, it is likely that the chef will give the hunter a dirty look, for the fricasseeing still presents an elaborate problem.

One time-tried formula is to soak the millionaire overnight or longer in brine in proportion of sixteen to one. Then he should be baked to eliminate the water and the paper profits. After that you may add salt in generous quantities, pepper, Scotch whisky, port, one-half pint sloe gin, truffles, mushrooms and a pousse-café. Then turn the heat on and allow the whole thing to simmer over a slow fire while a group of cooks, known as an investigating committee, stirs the whole mess continuously.

If anything is left of the millionaire at the end of that time go to the nearest telephone and order a hamburger steak from your neighborhood butcher.

Maybe Mr. Roosevelt is right, after all. At least he has chosen the safer method. Any journeyman can run up a dish of scrambled eggs, but only an expert can do a millionaire.

WESTBROOK PEGLER

Those Were the Days

1938

Next time Mr. Roosevelt or Honest Hal Ickes, the House Dick of the New Deal, or Wallace or Jackson or any of those honorary proletarians who swing towels in that corner of the ring sounds off in disrespect of the Old Deal I would appreciate it if somebody would refresh my memory on just what was wrong with it. Because, checking over my recollections, that seems to have been a pretty fair sort of era, especially by comparison with this New Deal period, and if there was anything to be sore about I want to do my duty.

Wasn't that the time when they were sticking up tall buildings in all the big towns and building swell new suburbs and kicking out new cars by the millions, including some which retailed for about $6,000 and, what's more, selling them? Wasn't everybody working who could or would work? Weren't fight tickets selling at $55 a copy at the box office and $100 up at the gyps, and weren't ordinary, forgotten men able to fish up the price of $25 seats a couple of times a year? Check the files and see.

Remember how it was almost impossible to get a kid to run copy or get a can of coffee for you because they were all over in the corner reading the tape? Not the baseball tape, either. No, pals! They were reading that stock tape and forming little syndicates and buying stuff on margin and making money at it, too.

And Iowa farmers were selling out and hauling away for Southern California and Florida to take it easy, and ditch labor got $6 a day around here, anyway, and skilled men—some of whom weren't so very skilled, at that—got ten, twelve, twenty.

What do you want to bet that Jim Farley's business has made half as much under this New Deal that he goes around making neck sounds, but not heart sounds, about in duty speeches for the Boss and the Party, as it made under the rotten Republicans?

And taxes! Friend, who ever mentioned taxes in those days?

And if it is a question of wage levels are you telling me that wages are higher under the New Deal after—how long is it—six years than under the Old?

I do remember being pretty sore about prohibition, but, to be fair, it wasn't so bad after bootlegging got organized, and, moreover, we fostered a fine domestic skill in those days which is rapidly vanishing from our civilization now, I refer to the home manufacture of gin, beer and wine. Remember, you got a can of alky and some distilled water and some gin drops and a little bottle of glycerine, and it was as much a part of ma's domestic duties to sling a batch of gin together once a week as to bake a mess of bread back in the nineteen hundreds. All gone now under repeal, and the poor doctors have lost a very reliable source of practice, in addition to which, with much less money, the people have to pay much more for their square face, most of it for taxes, licenses and color-press pictures of pretty models in glove-tight swimming suits in the ads.

Yes, I know, the banker and speculators and hustlers shoved us a lot of wall-paper stocks and bonds, and everybody was knocked in the creek when the wagon threw a wheel. But you wait and see what happens to Morgenthau's Mavoureens one of these days and then tell me whether, and if so why, it's any more fun to be rooked by a political party and a lot of wabble-wits stuck away in offices in Washington than by a banker. Henry Morgenthau, for gossakes! Why, old Andy Mellon could have stolen his fillings right out of his face with boxing gloves on without Henry's even knowing it. Henry isn't the one who is shoving the queer. He just runs the building. You know, okays orders for so many mops and so many gross of paper clips and so many tons of spare parts for adding machines to keep track of that deficit. And the tape is a year behind, at that.

I just don't know, neighbor. For a long time when I would hear them say Old Deal in that curl-of-the-lip way, I went along too, feeling that, yes, it certainly was terrible, but let me ask you this: How were you doing back in those terrible days, and if this New Deal is going to be so swell when are those boys going to get through that long windup and let us see what they have got on the ball?

CONGRESSMAN FRANK THOMPSON, JR.

A *Modest Proposal for the Return to Conservatism Through Decentralization*

1962

Certain of my conservative colleagues in the Congress have recently proposed selective decentralization as the road back to "the good old days." These well-meaning individuals would destroy an occasional bloom on the weed of socialism as a token of opposition. We must reject this as an inadequate, half-way measure, which is worse than nothing at all, since this lulls the American public into believing that creeping federal controls are being effectively challenged.

Any amateur gardener knows weeds are not destroyed by plucking blooms, but by tearing them up by the roots. We must search out the beginnings of socialistic tendencies in this nation of ours and destroy them at their source. To do otherwise would be to attack the symptoms and leave the disease go unchecked.

Too often, people will accept a little bit of socialism as being all right. They must be reminded that being "a little bit socialistic" is like being a "little bit honest." Either you are or you aren't. There is no middle road. With this in mind, let us now examine the following topics to discover—in order to destroy—the tap roots of creeping socialism.

One of the earliest services performed by the Federal Government was, of course, the carrying of the mail. There is no reason why this service could not be more effectively handled by free enterprise or why, for instance, people could not deliver their own letters. Must we ask Uncle Sam to do everything for us? If things continue the way they are going, we will be sending our stamps to Washington to be licked!

Consider the basic freedoms which we have lost in this strictly socialistic postal venture. Can you design your own stamps? No! Can you decide what you will pay to mail a letter? No! These rights have been usurped by the Federal Government, which tells you what stamps you will use and sets the price. As a result, the cost of mailing letters has continued to rise. Free enterprise, on the other hand, through competition, would relentlessly drive prices down—as it has done in all fields of private industry month by month in recent years.

Let's look at the Weather Bureau. Why should Uncle Sam tell us what kind of weather we have? Is socialized weather any different than socialized medicine? No! Besides, it leads to mediocrity. In the old days, weather predictions were accurately made by a member of the family who had corns, lumbago, or a broken bone. In the more enlightened homes there was a *Farmers' Almanac*, gotten free with the purchase of fifty pounds of feed at the general store. What has happened to our self-reliance? Why must we call the Federal Weather Bureau to find out if it is safe to plan a picnic? Federally-controlled weather also infringes on states rights. In the South, "separate but equal" weather is the custom.

It is well known that there is an insidious plot for socialized medicine. This plot must be exposed. It is the most brazen attempt to convince our legislators of the benefits of socialized medicine. I refer, of course to the fact that free medical care is provided for the President. Exposed to this free medical care, the President may become convinced that this is the proper approach and would force it down the throats of the American public in the form of medical care legislation.

Let us examine next, the Federal Highway Program. If toll roads were good enough for our forefathers, they should be good enough for us. How can a bureau in Washington know anything about local needs? Individuals on the spot know what is needed and will provide it, if this power is returned to their hands. Millions in taxes could be saved by this move. Why should federal bureaucrats destroy our beautiful and historic parks and buildings? This right should belong to the state highway commissioners, who would proceed to destroy them without socialized federal interference. . . .

The National Parks have become pockets of socialism. They should be turned over to private ownership forthwith. Federal jurisdiction over these parks which belong to all the people has proved to be costly and outmoded. The Grand Canyon, for example, has not been redecorated in years and Old Faithful continues to operate on its outdated schedule. The parks should be returned to the states, which, in turn, could sell them to private enterprise for the construction of shopping plazas.

Private enterprise would, no doubt, provide grass, play areas, swings and see-saws and the other things which the Federal Government does not provide. In addition, the rateables would fatten the municipal and state tax coffers.

The Federal Bureau of Standards has inflicted almost innumerable socialistic doctrines on business. Any businessman will tell you that a definition in the field of weights and measures depends entirely upon whether you are buying or selling. The Federal Government must stop interfering with private enterprise. The government produces nothing so how can it understand the problems of buying and selling?

The position of the states' militia must be strengthened by decentralization of the Armed Forces. Should New Jersey be concerned if Khrushchev offends Long Beach, California? Should Arizona invade Cuba because Senator Smathers is piqued over Castro? On the other hand, if the Manhattan Militia invade Moscow, shouldn't it be their right, or if Senator Smathers wishes to do away with Fidel, shouldn't he be allowed to take this personal freedom? If my neighbor has a head cold, should I take the remedy? Certainly not. This basic freedom must be maintained in other matters also.

Why should Montana's tax dollars, for example, go to pay for a Navy, when that state doesn't even have a shoreline? Do they benefit from federal expenditures on aircraft carriers or naval installations? No! Montanans can't even see the ocean on a clear day. Why should they be expected to pay for something they don't see or need? . . .

These are but a few topics with which we must come to grips if we are to revitalize our moral fibre and maintain a strong America free from creeping socialism. . . .

AL CAPP

I Can Give You Anything But Love, Baby,

or the Conscience of a Conservative

1962
"*It seems to me the error of the welfare staters might be expressed in these terms. The impersonal, benevolent state offers money without*

love, assistance without concern, direction without personal involvement. And to my mind, money and assistance and direction are not enough. How do you stand, sir?"

From a Barry Goldwater column in the *Boston Globe*.

SCENE: *The home of* MR. *and* MRS. FRANKLIN P. FLEASPOT. *It is a cold-water flat in the most unlivable tenement of a crumbling slum in the nation's most depressed area.*

MR. FLEASPOT *is on the floor trying to scrape some nourishing solids off food stains left from better days.* MRS. FLEASPOT *is reading the Duchess of Windsor's article in* McCall's *magazine on the proper decoration of a dinner table for twelve. Several little Fleaspots are scattered about, not crying or fighting. They haven't the strength.*

MR. GOODPANTS, JR., of the Welfare Department enters.

GOODPANTS: Your case has just come to the attention of the Dire Emergency Section of the Welfare Department. Here is a check for groceries. Our housing section has found you a decent home, and our children's nutrition experts are on their way here to—

FLEASPOT (*interrupting—not taking the check*): Why are you doing all this for us, Buster?

GOODPANTS: Because it's our duty—

FLEASPOT (*turning triumphantly to his wife*): See!!! That's what's behind it all, honey!!! COLD, IMPERSONAL, HEARTLESS DUTY!!!

GOODPANTS: I wouldn't put it quite THAT way, sir. Our purpose is to provide the destitute with everything they need. Food, shelter, medical aid—possibly a job—

FLEASPOT (*coldly*): So that's all you think we need, eh, buddy?

GOODPANTS: You want—more?

FLEASPOT: You bet your sweet life I do!!!—LOVE!!! Before I accept any of this (*he waves the check away*) I've got one simple question to ask you. Do you love me?

GOODPANTS: Well—I wouldn't put it quite that way, sir.

FLEASPOT: Does anyone in the whole Welfare Department love me? Just give me ONE name!!!

GOODPANTS: I—I don't think I can, sir, but—

FLEASPOT (*opening the door and pointing out*): Then get out!!! I don't want the Welfare Department's money—without the Welfare Department's love!!! I don't want the Welfare Department's assistance without the Welfare Department's deep, heartfelt concern!!! And as for your giving me direction—like getting a job for me, and proper nutrition for my kids—it is a meaningless mockery without your warm, personal involvement!

(MR. GOODPANTS *leaves and the* FLEASPOTS *continue to starve and freeze to death as the destitute used to in the good old days.*)

ARTHUR HOPPE

Abundance Is a Four-Letter Word

1962

One of the things I love most about America is her abundance. Every time I hear: "Oh, beautiful for spacious skies/For amber waves of grain," I tend to get a bit misty-eyed. So, I'll bet, do our Presidents. It's the most horrendous domestic headache they've got.

But Mr. Kennedy's going to lick it. He's come up with a "drastic new Farm Program." Which happens annually. He calls his the "ABCD Farm Program." He says this stands for "Abundance, Balance, Conservation, and Development." It usually does.

You see, we've got an Abundance of good things to eat. Which is terrible. So, to achieve a Balance, we must all pitch in and grow less. That's where development comes in. This year, as usual, Mr. Kennedy has developed a whole mess more new Quotas, Acreage Allotments, Soil Banks, and Price Supports. They always work exceptionally well. In Washington.

There seems to be some confusion about our Farm Program in the minds of the lay public. It is high time, I feel, for a detailed, authoritative explanation. I'd be glad to.

Take Farmer Jones, whom we always take. Farmer Jones has one hundred acres, having owned them since I was in the fourth grade. Last year, Farmer Jones grew one hundred bushels. Which are delicious when fried in butter.

This year, the Washington experts decided that no one could possibly eat more than fifty bushels. This is called a Quota. The experts then divided one hundred acres by two, which is called Simple Division, and told Farmer Jones to plant bushels on only fifty acres. This is called

Acreage Allotment. Washington then said it would pay him for the fifty bushels he pitched in and didn't grow on his other fifty acres. This is called Soil Bank. Which is what the farmers laugh all the way on their way to.

Now we get to Conservation. What Farm Programs aim at Conserving is the Farm Vote. This is done by Serving the American Farmer Better.

You see, once we've got Farmer Jones to grow less through all these quotas and what not, we then send around federal agricultural experts to teach him how to grow more. Farmer Jones, understandably, if unpatriotically, loves to grow things. So he listens to the advice of these experts, soaks his remaining fifty acres in the latest federal fertilizers and—presto!—this year he grows seventy-five bushels. Which is twenty-five more than anybody wants.

Washington, of course, buys up these extra twenty-five bushels it helped Farmer Jones grow. This is called Price Supports. Then Washington squirrels them away in the nation's attic at a cost of more than $1 million a day. This is called Nonsense.

It would be cheaper, naturally, to give our surplus bushels away. It would also be more Christian, seeing that two-thirds of the human race goes to bed hungry each night. But we can't give away more than a dribble or we'll bust the world bushel market. And we can't have that. It would make the bushel-market proprietors mad.

Under the circumstances, I think Mr. Kennedy's ABCD Farm Program is more or less admirable. As far as it goes. But it can't compare with my EFGH Farm Program, which I thought up myself. Mine stands for Every Farmer Gets Helped.

What we do under my Farm Program is pay farmers not to grow any more farmers. If they do, we buy up the surplus farmers and store them away. We may even have to plow some under.

For it seems there is nothing more surplus in a hungry world these days than a man who loves to see good things grow.

Obviously, my EFGH Farm Program will face tough sledding in Congress. Congressmen who are elected by the Farm Vote have very little interest in decreasing it. Which, naturally, is the heart of the Farm Problem.

Should my program fail, the least we can do is change the words of "America, the Beautiful." I mean all this stuff about "amber waves of grain" and "fruited plains." Why keep reminding ourselves of our handicaps?

J. B. LEE, JR.

Letter from a West Texas Constituent

March 20, 1963

The Honorable Ed Foreman
House of Representatives
Congressional District #16
Washington 25, D.C.

Dear Sir:

My friend over in Terebone Parish received a $1,000 check from the government this year for not raising hogs. So I am going into the not-raising hogs business next year.

What I want to know is, in your opinion, what is the best kind of farm not to raise hogs on and the best kind of hogs not to raise? I would prefer not to raise Razorbacks, but if that is not a good breed not to raise, I will just as gladly not raise any Berkshires or Durocs.

The hardest work in this business is going to be in keeping an inventory of how many hogs I haven't raised.

My friend is very joyful about the future of his business. He has been raising hogs for more than 20 years and the best he ever made was $400, until this year, when he got $1,000 for not raising hogs.

If I can get $1,000 for not raising 50 hogs, then will I get $2,000 for not raising 100 hogs? I plan to operate on a small scale at first, holding myself down to 4,000 hogs which means I will have $80,000 coming from the government.

Now, another thing: these hogs I will not raise will not eat 100,000 bushels of corn. I understand that you also pay farmers for not raising corn. So will you pay me anything for not raising 100,000 bushels of corn not to feed the hogs I am not raising?

I want to get started as soon as possible as this seems to be a good time of the year for not raising hogs.

One thing more, can I raise 10 or 12 hogs on the side while I am in the not-raising-hog-business just enough to get a few sides of bacon to eat?

Very truly yours,

J. B. Lee, Jr.
Potential Hog Raiser

JBL:gb

RICHARD R. LINGEMAN

The Fleeced Land

1959

I. THE SALEMAN'S TALE

April is the accrualest month, seizing
Taxes from the clenched hand, twisting
Memory and fueling avaricious desire.
In winter, with the chorine named Torchie
I sipped orange juice at Miami Beach, and
The sun surprised us coming over the Fontainebleau.
There among the rich one feels free
And expense account largesse blesses the spree.
But the blank white heat of summer sun
Cracked the scaly skin of the land
And money's fertile green shriveled to
The barrenness of sand.
(Come under the shade of the red rock,
The rock of capital gains on stock.
A tiny spring gurgles there,
The spring of deductions rare.)

Madame La Zonga, clairvoyante, C.P.A. and
Mystic from Murmansk
Gazed at the cards
And saw the Treasury agents
And suggested death by water.

II. WHAT THE MINOTAUR SAW

Unreal City.
Into bureaucracy's labyrinth flows
A swarm of sharp-eyed drones.
(Who would have thought that Civil Service had undone so many?)
Hypocrite lecteur—mon semblable—mon frère!

It is the twilit hour, the violet hour
(Just after the 3 P.M. coffee break).
Gladys Girth, GS 7 and Treasury clerk,
Scans with tired, empty eyes
The tax form before her,
Sees the violation,
And allows a half-formed thought to appear:
"Well, *he's* had it." .
Then combs her hair and puts the record in the filing cabinet.
(So rudely enforced. Jug. Jug. Jug.)

I, Tiresias, with green eyeshade and shiny-seated pants,
Seer through the tax forms of man and woman to the reality of their souls
Know well that
Marriage flows not from the passion that burns
But from the sexless calculus of joint returns.

III. THE CRIES OF THE INFANTS

The chair he sat in creaked and groaned
As his body twisted in the agony of recall
While a single naked light
Encircled in its glare
A pile of bills curled and sere
And glanced off to glint on his steel-rimmed glasses
With lenses mistily opaque from streaming sweat.
(Those were eyes that are red-veined pearls.)
The dry bones of a year's spending
Will rattle in the rat's alley of Form 1040.

"My nerves are bad tonight. Yes bad.
What shall I do now? What shall I ever do?"
You shall play a game of solitaire
Pressing empty pockets and waiting for
The knock of the process server at the door.

So I sez to him sez I, ya can't deduct them medical expenses.
And her expecting a baby and all.

(It's her thirteenth, poor soul, and what with all those pills she takes
The exemptions hardly make up for it.)
HURRY UP PLEASE ITS TIME
An' so he sez ta me, if I deduct just a bit more for
    charitable contributions—
HURRY UP PLEASE ITS TIME
And declare my aunt as a dependent and—
HURRY UP PLEASE ITS TIME
HURRY UP PLEASE ITS TIME

IV. THE THUNDER SPEAKS

Then spoke the thunder
DA
Datta: Give—
Let not your souls grow obese
From a superfluity of riches.
Dayadhvam: Sympathize—
Unlock the strong box
And let hoarded treasure flow.
Damyata: Control—
Follow without a whimper
The torturous trails of the statutory way.

From whatever source derived
Of what comes in we must be deprived.
For money held curdles and spoils
And money spent the soul's purity soils.
Far better that the Government take
And of itself a more powerful Leviathan make.
Shantih, shantih, shantih.

NOTES ON THE FLEECED LAND

I. The imagery in this passage was suggested by the case related by an anonymous court reporter under the title *United States v. Travelinman* which, research discloses, was appealed to the Supreme Court. As a moving chronicle of the hopes and despairs of our bleak age the Supreme Court reports, as well as the reports of the U.S. Tax Court, cannot be surpassed. The richness of the mythological and folk tale material found therein has inspired me throughout this work.

II. The labyrinth imagery occurs again and again in what I consider to be one of the monumental works of American literature of the twentieth century: the Internal Revenue Code of 1954. As with all great folk sagas, this work was the product of a group of anonymous wandering story-tellers and ballad singers who were wont to assemble yearly in Washington, D.C., and join their voices in a cacophony of sound that would continue for months upon end.

III. The source material of this passage is self-explanatory. Cf. Dante, *The Divine Comedy*, Hades cantos.

IV. See the *Bhagavad Gita*. See also Buddha's admonitions to his followers on the ephemerality of worldly things, the sanctity of poverty, and the joys of giving. The close rhyming of the final passage evokes the feeling of harmony with the universe that comes to the Buddhist who obeys the Sacred Laws and follows the True Way to Enlightenment. "Shantih" may be translated as "the peace which passeth understanding." The use of a formal ending to an Upanishad as the culmination of this part of the poem is not an accident.

> One-third of the people in the United States promote, while the other two-thirds Provide.—*Will Rogers*

RUSSELL BAKER

Tax Day

1963

Philosophy to make April 15 more bearable for everybody:

First, for Mortimer Caplin, the friendly Commissioner of Internal Revenue, who wants people to like his agency:

"To tax and to please, no more than to love and to be wise, is not given to men" (Burke).*

* Many of the quotations cited have been compiled by W. H. Auden and Louis Kronenberger in the *Viking Book of Aphorisms*, published by the Viking Press, Inc.

Or, "State business is a cruel trade; good-nature is a bungler in it" (Lord Halifax).

And, "I sit on a man's back, choking him and making him carry me, and yet assure myself and others that I am very sorry for him and wish to lighten his load by all possible means—except by getting off his back" (Tolstoy).

For President Kennedy, while reading the editorials on his budget policy: "For those who govern, the first thing required is indifference to newspapers" (Thiers).

And, while reflecting that Congress probably won't do enough about taxes to get the country moving again before the 1964 campaign: "It is a certain sign of a wise government and proceeding that it can hold men's hearts by hopes when it cannot by satisfaction" (Bacon).

For his brother Robert, pondering the coming year's expenses in Mississippi: "The reluctant obedience of distant provinces generally costs more than it is worth" (Macaulay).

For politicians everywhere who campaigned in November with promises to cut taxes and then had to raise them in January: "The honest liar is the man who tells the truth about his old lies! Who says on Wednesday, 'I told a magnificent lie on Monday'" (Chesterton).

For the Administration's Congressional leaders when they despair of the Senate Finance Committee's attitude toward tax reforms: "The dismay and fury of the men who depend for their living on the dwindling horse traffic in a town is natural, and excites sympathy and pity. But these are unfortunately not the men whom it would be useful to elect on a traffic board for the consideration of the future lines on which an electrical system should be laid down and linked up" (Walter Sickert).

And for Congressmen wondering if it is worth stirring the mightiest lobby of them all by urging reduction of oil-and-gas's 27½ percent depletion allowance: "The art of taxation consists in so plucking the goose as to get the most feathers with the least hissing" (Colbert).

For the oil men, if any there be, who have had to pay taxes this weekend even after claiming their 27½ percent: "Every luxury must be paid for, and everything is a luxury, starting with being in the world" (Cesare Pavese).

For tax agents all over the country who cannot understand their low esteem in the community: "The wretched have no compassion" (Dr. Johnson). Or, "He that fears you present will hate you absent" (Thomas Fuller).

And, finally, some thoughts for the anonymous. For the low-income people promised a tax cut this year: "When the ass was invited to the wedding feast he said, 'They need more wood and water' " (Bosnian proverb).

For everybody betting that he can cheat Caplin's computers: "Harsh is the law, but it is certain" (Giovanni Vico).

And for those protesting that I. R. S. is out to trick them: "The fox condemns the trap, not himself" (Blake).

Words to be muttered in incoherent rage by the improvident waiting for April 15 midnight mail collection:

> "A dog starved at his master's gate
> Predicts the ruin of the state" (Blake).

And when the mail is gone: "God will provide—ah, if only He would till He does so!" (Yiddish proverb).

And remember, "Melancholy, indeed, should be diverted by every means but drinking" (Dr. Johnson).

And, "As he knew not what to say, he swore" (Byron).

EDWARD K. NELLOR

Office Memo on Expense Accounts

March 12, 1963

The last meeting heard the following remarks by Ralph Dawkes on the government's ruling that a businessman has to substantiate in writing all entertainment expenses over $25.

"The trouble with those boys in Washington," Ralph said, "is they've got no idea of all the hell some businessmen have to go through to get business. You can tell that from the example they give of how a businessman ought to report his entertainment. The example they sent out reads this way:

> 'Lunch with Jones, Green, Brown and Smith, trustees of P. Q. Real Estate Investment Board. Discussed architectural plans submitted for proposed Claremont Village apartment building. No other persons entertained.'

"Now that's fine and dandy, if you're entertaining trustees, but if you're entertaining the clowns I have to do business with you've got to go into all the sordid details or you don't get your deduct. To demonstrate that point, I am going to read from a carbon copy of an expense account I have just turned in, following the new Washington rules. It says:

'Dinner with Buckman, Dietzel and O'Brien of Ajax Machinery. Discuss re-tooling. Buckman says why don't we have another round, a double this time. More discussing and drinking and Dietzel says, why don't we go to some place where it's a little livelier.

'Go to Orangutang Club. More discussion and drinks. Buckman says Ajax needs heavier casings. O'Brien says, speaking of casing, he's been casing two broads at corner table and why don't I ask them over.

'Get broads over . . . Big Red and Roxy. More drinks, discussion. Dietzel starts figuring re-tooling costs on table cloth. No ink, uses ketchup. Waiter objects. Dietzel tells waiter what he can do with table cloth. Manager, eight diners object. O'Brien says he and Dietzel will clean out joint if manager, diners not careful. Tip waiter ten bucks not to call police, leave for Big Red's apartment.

'Reach Big Red's apartment, discuss contract date with Dietzel. Big Red tells Buckman to come in off fire escape. Buckman says, him Tarzan, her Jane. Big guy upstairs says Jane better get Tarzan the hell off fire escape or him calling police. O'Brien sick in kitchen sink, tie caught in garbage grinder. Big Red turns on hot water, tries scalding O'Brien. Jerk O'Brien loose, get Buckman off fire escape. Give Big Red 15 bucks for miscellaneous damage, leave for hotel.

'Don't reach hotel. Stop by Club Hotsy for six nightcaps. Listen to Buckman on following items in following order: Heavy machinery, politics, religion, sex, Mrs. Buckman, sick joke about Eskimo, heavy machinery, sex, Mrs. Buckman's mother, sick joke about Eskimo, religion, Buckman's hernia, sex, sick joke about Eskimo, religion, how Buckman is going to diddle O'Brien and Dietzel out of Ajax vice-presidency. O'Brien and Dietzel having foot race in parking lot. Winner get bartender's wife. Pull bartender off Dietzel. O'Brien sleep in shrubbery.

'Arrive hotel 4 A.M. O'Brien refreshed by sleep, crawls through lobby baying like dog. Buckman, playing little Eva, knocks over potted plant, bust of Conrad Hilton. Dietzel takes over elevator. 4:30 A.M., catch Dietzel, get them to room. Buckman starts calling old army buddy in San Francisco. Leave. Cost for evening, $117.23. Return to hotel 11 A.M., wake Buckman et al. Buckman asks what happened. Tell him, get rush order to re-tool Ajax Machinery.'

"Now that's exactly what happened and I got the bills, 3 waiters, a manager, 8 diners, 2 broads, a bartender's wife, an elevator operator, a house dick and a cold check from Dietzel to prove it. And if Washington thinks I didn't have to entertain them that way to get that order, they don't know Buckman, Dietzel and O'Brien."

All the "lobbies" are gathered in Washington to see that the tax is put on somebody else's business, but not on theirs.—*Will Rogers*

JOHN CROSBY

The Pangs of Utopia

1963
LONDON

I was reading a letter from home to my cockney friend, Alfie, who is perennially fascinated by the golden American way of life in the golden United States. "It's going to be a slim Christmas," the lady wrote. "I'm still paying off for my broken leg."

"Payin' off," said Alfie, "Y'mean the guvmint don't pye fer 'er broken leg?"

"We're a free country," I told him proudly. "We pay for our own broken legs."

"Coo," said Alfie. "We're 'obbled with socialism over 'ere. The guv'mint robs us of the pleasure of pyin' our medical bills. It must be wonderful to be free of all that guv'mint interference. How long will it tyke the poor woman to pye for 'er broken leg?"

"About 18 months, I think," I said. "Of course, she's broke—but free. That's the spirit of 1776."

"Certainly hain't the spirit of 1963," said Alfie cheerfully. "I hunnerstan' you Americans 'ave one of the 'ighest tax rates in the 'ole world. Wot do you get fer yer 'igh taxes?"

"Oh," I told him, "we get many of the good things of life. The moon probe."

"What's 'at?"

"We're preparing to land a man on the moon in 1970—or some such thing. It'll cost between $40 and $50 billion. I don't think any one really knows."

"Blimey," said Alfie. "If 'e breaks 'is leg landin' on the moon, will 'e 'ave to pye for it?"

"No," I explained. "The government will pay for his broken leg because he's on government service. It's only the taxpayers who pay for their own broken legs."

Alfie looked quizzical. "Wut uvver good things of life do you get fer them 'igh taxes?"

"Well—" I thought a bit. "The American taxpayer gets a lot of things. The Venus probe, for example, we found out that the other side of Venus is just as hot as this side."

"That must be a grite comfort to the lady wif the broken leg," said Alfie. "She c'n warm 'er broken leg on the uvver side of Venus."

"We have private medical insurance plans. That's the democratic way," I said.

"Why didn't it pay this poor woman's bills then?"

I explained that she probably couldn't afford private medical insurance after paying her taxes. And anyhow, private medical plans only paid part of the bills. "My daughter had an eye operation that cost about $700. Blue Cross paid about $150 of it. My daughter also had a tonsils and adenoids operation that cost $200. The Blue Cross paid $39."

"Oi don't think Oi could afford ter live in so free a country," said Alfie. "Oi'd much rather 'ave the guv'mint enslave me an' pye me bills."

"But we're free!" I cried. "Free! Free!"

"Free to pye the bills," said Alfie cheerfully. "Tell me, guv'nor, are there any other countries as gloriously free to pye its medical expenses as America?"

"Well, of course, there's Afghanistan, there's the Congo and Outer Mongolia. They're free too."

Alfie sniffed. "We calls 'em backward."

7 WHO'S UN-AMERICAN?

LOYALTY, LEFT AND RIGHT

The topics here are loyalty, oath-taking, security, Communism, in-vestigations, and xenophobia. This time, unsurprisingly, the 1950s are well-represented, even though their leading character in this context, the late Senator Joseph McCarthy, might not appreciate the top billing. I once heard him describe something, on a television program, as "the most unheard-of thing I ever heard of"; the phrase is brought to mind repeatedly by some of these pieces.

Two other periods are important in this section. The writings of the American Revolution were rich in political satire, much of it about "loyalty," much of it in verse; they achieved a general level of literary quality unmatched in the genre for many generations. The 1930s marked, among other things, the high-water mark of the American communist movement and its offshoots; the breadth of leftist influence at that time, recalled wistfully in "Remembrance of Past Things," provides a background to "Redder Than the Rose" and, at a different level, to "The Mugity Wumpus," that has been long absent from the political scene.

JAMES THURBER

The Very Proper Gander

Not so very long ago there was a very fine gander. He was strong and smooth and beautiful and he spent most of his time singing to his wife and children. One day somebody who saw him strutting up and down in his yard and singing remarked, "There is a very proper gander." An old hen overheard this and told her husband about it that night in the roost. "They said something about propaganda," she said. "I have always suspected that," said the rooster, and he went around the barnyard next day telling everybody that the very fine gander was a dangerous bird, more than likely a hawk in gander's clothing. A small brown hen remembered a time when at a great distance she had seen the gander talking with some hawks in the forest. "They were up to no good," she said. A duck remembered that the gander had once told him he did not believe in anything. "He said to hell with the flag, too," said the duck. A guinea hen recalled that she had once seen somebody who looked very much like the gander throw something that looked a great deal like a bomb. Finally everybody snatched up sticks and stones and descended on the gander's house. He was strutting in his front yard, singing to his children and his wife. "There he is!" everybody cried. "Hawk-lover! Unbeliever! Flag-hater! Bomb-thrower!" So they set upon him and drove him out of the country.

Moral: Anybody who you or your wife thinks is going to overthrow the government by violence must be driven out of the country.

These two excerpts of Revolutionary War satire were written from the Loyalist point of view. The title of the first refers to the notorious, perhaps apocryphal, sixteenth-century British clergyman whose "principles" reflected every change in power; the surprisingly modern ring of the "soliloquy" might give us pause.

ANONYMOUS

The American Vicar of Bray

When Royal George rul'd o'er this land,
And loyalty no harm meant,
For Church and King I made a stand
And so I got preferment. . . .

After repeal of the Stamp Act, however—

I quickly joined the common cry,
That we should all be slaves, Sir;
The House of Commons was a sty;
The King and Lords were knaves, Sir. . . .

*Independence was declared; the outlook
was unpromising, so he—*

Declar'd it was Rebellion base
To take up arms—I curs'd it.
For faith it seem'd a settled case
That we should soon be worsted. . . .

*As the fortunes of war swung back and
forth, the Vicar swung with them, until
finally—*

Since Fate has made us great and free,
And Providence can't falter;
So Cong. till death my King shall be,
Unless the times shall alter.

The Pausing Loyalist

To sign, or not to sign!—That is the question:
Whether 'twere better for an honest man
To sign—and so be safe; or to resolve,
Betide what will, against "associations,"
And by retreating, shun them. To fly—I reck
Not where—and, by that flight, t'escape
Feathers and tar, and thousand other ills
That Loyalty is heir to: 'tis a consummation
Devoutly to be wished. To fly—to want—
To want?—perchance to starve! Ay, there's the rub!
For in that chance of want, what ills may come
To patriot rage when I have left my all,
Must give us pause! . . .

ROBERT FORSYTHE
(KYLE CRICHTON)

Redder Than the Rose

1935

When I reached that portion of Isidor Schneider's interview with Gertrude Stein in which she referred to herself as more Communist than the Communists, I put my hand to my head and uttered a cry which bystanders have since told me sounded like "peep" and slid fainting into the wastebasket. From this you might assume either that I was fatally stricken by the brilliance of Miss Stein or merely irritated by her presumption, but you would be entirely wrong. It was purely a physical matter. Twice previously on the same day I had heard the same words from other lips and I very much suspected that I was being made the object of a plot.

Mr. Edmund Wilson once indicated his desire to take Communism away from the Communists, but that may have been youthful zeal and it is hardly likely that he entertains such hopes at the moment. If he feels, however, that he is more Left than the Left, he is entirely in style. Just where this new rallying cry for ex-Democrats, ex-Humanists and ex-Communists arose is not clear but it is in full swing and a revolution happening within the week would be a terrible thing with such wild people around to lead it.

Naturally it is not merely a matter of force; it is a problem of dialectics and philosophy; the philosophy is so marvelous that the historians of the future will bow in wonder before such logic and discernment. I know an interesting fellow who is a writer, a playwright, a philosophical anarchist, and a supporter of Herbert Hoover. I have never had the courage to question him about his Hoover affiliation, but he could probably sustain it on the ground that only by fostering tyranny can we have freedom. His long stay in Hollywood at a fat figure has been explained as his way of bankrupting the industry and thus bringing about its downfall. He is now said to be at work on a play which proves that Tom Mooney framed the State of California.

I have another friend who is eighteen miles east of Lenin and going rapidly further Left. He is a broker and a Trotskyite and I am no longer able to face his scorn. The last time I saw him he was coming out of the Waldorf-Astoria and although I tried to hurry by, he caught me and said some very harsh things about the timidity of the Communist Party in this country. He might still have had me there, backed against a window containing the treasures of the late Czar, if his chauffeur had not interrupted to say that the car was waiting. When I say that my friend is a Trotskyite, I must explain that he is also a Technocrat and in addition has been reading Malaparte. His theory is that Trotsky and four good engineers could put New York City at the mercy of the revolutionists by turning off the lights and overpowering Fiorello while he was scurrying about in his nightshirt hunting a candle. My friend explained this to me as the theory of permanent revolution; all you do when you want a new revolution is turn off the lights.

Unless something is done I am afraid we are going to face indignation from people who are expecting a great deal from us. Intellectually it seems that we are not as daring as we had thought. I know of a lady who has been successively a suffragette, a Catholic and a socialist. For some time she has been requesting the services of the more agile and younger male comrades in educating her in the intricacies of Communism but they have evidently failed at the job. The last report of her was as chairman of an Utopian meeting, which I am informed is much more Communist than Communism as well as much more Rosicrucian than Rosa Bonheur.

It is, however, around the tea table that the true essence of radicalism is attained. I must report a wave of indignation in such circles at the delay in the revolution. One lady only recently was remarking that her brother, a major in the army, was an excellent man to approach on the matter of revolt. She indicated that she would speak to him. But beyond that she was not pleased with the conduct of the Party. She said that although she had just been won over to Communism, she felt that she was far more advanced than many of the party members and was at a loss to account for the lag. She said she had been speaking to the servants on her estate and whereas they had all been ardent Republicans when she spoke to them in the past, they were now all ardent Communists, answering her questions if they were Communists with the reply that they were Communists indeed. She felt that if her people were of that opinion, the servants on other estates must have like views and she couldn't understand what was holding things up.

On the cultural front I have recently had contact with a Hearst reporter who rather frightens me with his enthusiasm. He has not joined the Communist Party but tells me he is far more Communist than the Communists. In covering a strike about a month ago, he wrote of the hoodlums who crawled up from the gutters like insects coming out from under a rock after a rain. I ventured to suggest that although the strikers were workers, they might not like to be called insects and besides it played into the hands of the owners, but he answered me in a manner which quite overcame my fears. If you talk about these people scornfully enough, said my friend, they will eventually become angry and revolt. In the meantime you fool Mr. Hearst by seeming to be on his side. He said that when the time came—and he had ideas on how slow the Party was about bringing it to pass—we would know what side he was on. He would stay with Hearst stirring up the workers by telling lies about them until the victory was won; after that he would bring us the technical newspaper skill a proletarian paper needed.

There is a possibility that many individuals who are more Communistic than the Communists will go completely berserk and end as Theosophists or Seventh Day Adventists but there is little that can be done about it. I had thought of offering myself as a sacrifice to the bloodthirsty by appearing at the New Masses Ball and allowing hand grenades to be hurled at me as I stood on the platform near the bass viol, but that was before I read Isidor Schneider on Gertrude Stein and before I met Mr. Cartwright. Mr. Cartwright said almost immediately that he was more Communist than the Communists and that he had great admiration for Adolph Hitler. Upon seeing my surprise, Mr. Cartwright said rather sternly that he was most certainly a Communist but an anti-Jewish Communist. It seems to me that this is carrying specialization and sectarianism so far that my death in Webster Hall would have little effect. I am afraid that even the passing of a noble fellow such as myself will not win over the groups which, when they feel the need of a name, will undoubtedly be known as the anti-proletarian Communists. Only prayer, I am afraid, will be of avail with such fine folk.

S. J. PERELMAN

Thunder Over Alma Mater

The Rover Boys and the Young Radicals
1935

"It's up to us to crush this Red menace, fellows!"

The speaker was none other than our old friend Tom Rover, and as he looked into the intent faces of his classmates, his eyes flashed fire. For once the Rover Boys, fun-loving Dick and serious-minded Tom, were united in a common purpose. Not in years had the hoary walls and storied elms of old Effluvia College been threatened with such a crisis. But let us hear it from Tom Rover's own lips as he awakened his fellow students to the danger facing them:

"I found out just in the nick of time," vouchsafed Tom in manly tones, producing several newspaper clippings. "These sneaking Reds have been plotting a revolution right here in old Effluvia! Certain weak-minded members of the faculty, goaded on by insidious alien doctrines and abetted by unscrupulous students, are preparing to seize power, set up a soviet in the Administration Building, and nationalize the girls of

Sweetbread Hall!" The collegians exchanged startled glances, but Tom's charges were irrefutable, for everything he said was supported by the clippings from the Hearst papers he held in his hand.

"This is an unexpected turn of affairs," frowned Dick gravely. "Who is responsible for this disloyalty to our ideals and institutions?" Tom's sense of sportsmanhip would have prevented him from replying, but at this juncture the culprit revealed himself unwittingly. Muttering a coarse oath, skulking Dan Baxter, followed by several of his toadies, slunk from the hall. Seizing the opportunity, Tom followed up his advantage.

"As you know, men," he continued, "one worm in an apple is often enough to spoil a whole barrel." His epigram was not lost on his hearers, as several appreciative chuckles testified. "This hulking bully whom you all know as Dan Baxter is really Dan Baxtrovitch, a notorious single-taxer, anarchist, and firebrand who has been sent here by Moscow to foment discord in the ranks of American youth." At his mention of Moscow, his audience recognized the name of a poorly-ventilated city in Russia which the unsuccessful revolutionaries were using as a base. Fortunately its downfall was imminent, as the gentle but firm armies of several nations were on their way to deliver its cowed inhabitants from a reign of terror.

"These ruffians will stick at nothing," declared Tom, compressing his lips. "Hourly they are widening the rift between capital and labor and swaying the freshmen. They use specious arguments such as our twelve million unemployed, when everybody knows that there are more than enough jobs to go around if the lazy scum would only work. But their real designs are even more loathesome. They are scheming to divide up our allowances evenly, convert our football team into shock troops, and force us to subsist on beet soup!" A great roar of protest welled up from his listeners as they realized how the subversive forces had been boring from within.

"Is there still time to outwit these destructive elements?" demanded Tom's schoolfellows in determined accents.

"If we hurry," returned Tom, alive to his responsibility. "Come closer, fellows."

With a will his friends gathered in a resolute little knot around him and in hurried whispers prepared a plan of battle to combat the impending menace to old Effluvia.

The college librarian blinked in surprise as the door of the reading-room swung open and a group of earnest students entered. In a trice he was courteously trussed up like a fowl by several juniors while the rest of the unit searched the shelves for incendiary literature and carried it outside to the waiting bonfire. Soon the works of a number of inflammatory and un-American writers of the crazy so-called modern school such as Sherwood Anderson, John Dos Passos, and Carl Sandburg were swelling the blaze amid the vociferous applause of the student body. Alert and clear-eyed volunteers joined enthusiastically in the hunt and gave vent to righteous wrath as volumes of "dry-as-dust" economics and sociology by firebrands like Veblen and Babbitt advocating the overthrow of democracy crackled into ashes.

Meanwhile another band of stalwart athletes led by Dick Rover had cornered several of the younger professors in the English department, who had openly been inciting underclassmen to revolt by sponsoring collective bargaining. The pitiable wretches were given an opportunity to recant by their gentlemanly captors but countered with stubborn refusals. Only when a copy of The Nation was found secreted under a pillow did the vigilantes' patience come to an end, and after some innocent horseplay involving castor-oil and a rubber hose, the cowardly "intelligentsia" admitted their mistake. Some of the more exuberant youngsters were for riding the offenders out of town on a rail, but under the restraining hand of Dick Rover, the chop-fallen radicals were allowed to take the oath of allegiance and remove their coats of tar and feathers.

Fifteen miles out of town Tom Rover, bending low over the wheel of his speedy rocket car, glanced hurriedly at his wristwatch and raced forward through the darkness. Would he be in time? One of Dan Baxtrovitch's minions had confessed that beautiful Eunice Haverstraw, head of the Sweetbread soccer team, had been abducted to a low roadhouse by his leader. Tom uttered a silent prayer and pressed the throttle to the floor.

Baxtrovitch, his coarse features suffused with vodka, had pinned Eunice in his non-Aryan embrace and was attempting to rain kisses on her averted face. Plucky albeit she was, Eunice's cries echoed in vain in the sound-proofed room. She was almost losing consciousness when the door crashed inward under Tom Rover's powerful shoulders. Crossing the floor at a bound, he drove several telling blows into Baxtrovitch's kidneys. Flaccid from years of easy living, and an immoderate consumption of Cotelettes Pojarski, *koulebiaka*, sturgeon, black olives, and *kvass*, Baxtrovitch realized he was through preying on young American womanhood and sank to the floor, shamming a dead faint. But close on Tom's heels a party of his fellow clansmen entered briskly, wearing conical soldier hats improvised from copies of the American Weekly and Time. The radical leader, who had hoped to escape by simulating unconsciousness, was securely bound and removed to face charges of syndicalism in California that had been pending for some time.

"Oh, Tom!" breathed Eunice, as she nestled in the protection of his brawny young arms, "I—I was afraid you might be too late!"

"Not Tom," came an unexpected voice. Turning, the pair descried the lineaments of elderly Job Haverstraw, head of the Haverstraw Woolen Mills, field officer of the Key Men of America, and Eunice's father. "I knew he'd be on the spot. Thank you, son," he added, his eyes suspiciously moist. Then a twinkle invaded them. "And after you're married, I'll need you as general manager of my plant. Some of the workmen have been grumbling about our fourteen-hour day, and I know you can set them an example of Americanism and fair play."

And there, face to face with success and their new destiny, let us leave them until the next episode, "THE ROVER BOYS AND THEIR YOUNG FINKS."

MIKE QUIN

(PAUL WILLIAM RYAN)

The Mugity Wumpus

1941

Arriving back in America after an absence of 15 years or more, Dr. Emory Hornsnagle was surprised by a strange creature approaching him along the road. At first he took it to be a weird animal or land bird of the emu or cassowary variety. It waddled clumsily on four legs and had a large, plumlike tail protruding from the rear.

As it drew nearer, he perceived it to be a man crawling on his hands and knees. His hair had been shaved off and his head was painted blue. His body was encircled by red stripes. What looked like a tail was a long stick decorated with streamers of colored paper and bearing a placard: I LOVE CAPITALISM.

As the man crawled, he muttered over and over: "I am not a Communist. I am not a Communist. I am not a Communist."

"Then what are you?" asked Dr. Hornsnagle.

The creature took one look at Hornsnagle, then turned around and began to crawl away as rapidly as its hands and knees could carry it.

Hornsnagle quickly lassoed it by one leg and tied it to a tree. "Now there is no reason for you to be frightened," he said. "I am not going to hurt you. As a scientist I would like to know what you are."

"Let me go," begged the creature. "If I am seen talking to you I will get in trouble."

"Why should you get in trouble for talking to me?" asked Hornsnagle.

"Because you are a Communist," whined the creature.

"Nonsense," said Hornsnagle. "What makes you think that?"

"Because," said the creature, "there is nothing about you to indicate you are not. If you were not a Communist you would certainly do something to indicate you were not. As for myself, you can see at a glance I am no Communist."

"Just what is a Communist?" asked Hornsnagle.

"I don't know," replied the creature, "but you certainly could not accuse me of being one."

"But crawling on your hands and knees," said Hornsnagle, "and that, er—tail—isn't it all somewhat inconvenient?"

The creature broke into tears, and Dr. Hornsnagle kindly loaned it his handkerchief.

"I used to walk erect," it said, "and speak my mind freely. It all started when they brought that resolution into the union."

"What resolution?" asked Hornsnagle.

"The resolution against communism," said the creature. "It was discovered that many of our members had Communistic books and literature in their homes."

"So what did you do?" asked Hornsnagle.

"We expelled them," said the creature, "and the rest of us burned our libraries to make absolutely sure."

"Did that convince them?" asked Hornsnagle.

"No. They said our officials were Communistic. So we expelled them too and elected new ones who were highly praised in the newspapers as reasonable and patriotic."

"What happened then?" asked Hornsnagle.

"Then we stopped holding meetings," said the creature. "There was nothing to meet about anyhow. It was impossible to make any demand or conduct any business without being called Communistic. Later we disbanded the union altogether."

"Didn't that convince them?" asked Hornsnagle.

The creature shook its head sadly. "No indeed. Employers made a rule to employ only the most non-Communistic workers who would work for the lowest wages. Everybody began to outdo each other in being non-Communistic. Some of them began to crawl, and pretty soon no one could get a job at all if he didn't crawl. Then one thing followed another. The tail piece was thought up by William Green."

"Why don't you stand up and tell them to go to hell?" asked Dr. Hornsnagle.

"That would be impossible," said the creature.

"And why so?" asked Hornsnagle.

"Because," said the creature, "that would be Communistic."

ANONYMOUS

The Parrots of Penance

1952

I

I am the very model of a member of the faculty
Because I'm simply overcome with sentiments of
    loyalty.
I daily think of reasons why I'm glad to be American,
And thank the Lord I've always been a registered
    Republican.
The thoughts I think are only thoughts approved by my
    community.
I pledge allegiance to the flag at every opportunity.
I haven't had a thing to do with Communist
    conspirators,
And neither have my relatives, descendants or
    progenitors.

I try to keep away from propositions controversial;
I've no opinions social, economic, or commercial.
And so you see that I must be, with sentiments of
    loyalty,
The very perfect model of a member of the faculty.

CHORUS:

And so you see that he must be, with sentiments of
    loyalty,
The very perfect model of a member of the faculty.

II

I'm qualified to educate in matters of heredity,
Unsullied by the taint of any doctrinaire rigidity.
I teach the Darwin theory with evaluation critical,
Uninfluenced by dogmatists, religious or political.
I understand the economic forces that have made us
    great,
The system of free enterprise I do not underestimate.
I'm well-equipped objectively to point out flaws in
    Marxist thought,
Because I've never read his work and rest assured that
    I will not.
I freely follow truth in ways which I am sure will
    satisfy
The Boards of Regents, William Hearst, and Hoover of
    the FBI.
And so you see that I must be, with sentiments of
    loyalty,
The very perfect model of a member of the faculty.

During the latter part of the so-called McCarthy period (the early 1950s) a recording of "The Investigator" had an enormous circulation, largely clandestine and largely in bootlegged pressings. Even today, the Library of Congress keeps its copies of the book version in a special collection (along with pornography) not readily accessible to readers. In the excerpt that follows, The Investigator, who has been killed in an airplane crash, has been brought by the Immigration Inspector to the Gatekeeper "Up Here." It does not take the Investigator long to make the Gatekeeper a witness before a special committee (headed by Titus Oates), or to subject him to a typical cross-examination.

REUBEN SHIP

*St. Peter Takes the Stand**

1954

"Sir, you have heard the testimony of the previous witness?" the Investigator asked the Gatekeeper.

"Yes."

"Was his testimony true?"

"Well, I want to be fair to Investigator Martin . . ."

"I think up till now we have all been so."

"I would say that his testimony is true insofar as the actual words I used. However, the intent . . ."

"I think the committee can draw its own conclusions as to the intent."

"That may be, sir. But the point is . . ."

"The point is that you actually used those words."

"Well, yes, I must say I did. However . . ."

"Very well then. If, as you admit, your department is grossly inefficient . . ."

"But I do not admit . . ." the Gatekeeper said angrily.

". . . is it not possible that certain subversive individuals," the Investigator continued, ignoring the Gatekeeper, "have managed to infiltrate Up Here by taking advantage of this laxness and gaining permanent entry?"

* from *The Investigator*.

"That is absolutely impossible. I deny it!"

"You deny they have gained entry by taking advantage of your laxness? How then did these subversives gain entry?"

"Well they got in . . ." The Gatekeeper checked himself abruptly. "I deny that any subversive elements gained entry at all. I never said they did. The charge is absurd. No one has ever gained entry here undeservedly. The committee will bear witness to that fact."

"My charge is not directed against present members of the committee. This criminal infiltration occurred before they became members of this committee. In any event you have the final responsibility for granting permanent visas."

"Well, yes . . ."

"And if certain undesirable elements have infiltrated here you admit the responsibility would be yours and yours alone?"

"Yes, it would. But I again deny that such a thing is possible. Every applicant must undergo the usual routine investigation."

"Routine!" The Investigator's voice became an angry whine. "Don't you think the applications of heretics, dissenters, rebels—many of them with prison records—should have been given more than routine consideration?"

"Sir, I . . ."

"Don't you think you should have exercised the most careful vigilance in cases of this kind?"

"Sir . . ."

"That you should have subjected such individuals to the most intensive scrutiny?"

"All our investigations follow the standard pattern. That is what I meant by routine."

"In other words, you admit that cases of individuals most likely to be subversive Up Here were investigated with no more thoroughness than you would use in the case, say, of an applicant whose record was without a blemish."

"I did not consider it necessary."

"What was your motive in coddling known subversives?"

"There was no evidence that any of them were subversive."

"But you have admitted their investigation was cursory. Do you deny the possibility that a more complete investigation would have brought forth facts which would have possibly exposed their affiliations with a foreign power? Do you deny that possibility?"

"How can I answer—" the Gatekeeper said helplessly.

"Do you deny that possibility?"

"I cannot answer such a question. No one can."

"Then you do not deny such a possibility."

"Obviously I cannot deny it. I neither deny it nor affirm it."

"Can you deny it?" the Investigator insisted.

"No matter how many times you ask me that question my answer must be that . . ."

"Mr. Chairman, the witness is not being responsive. I ask that the chair direct him to answer the question."

"I must protest, Mr. Chairman," the Gatekeeper appealed to Oates. "The nature of the question . . ."

"In the opinion of the chair the question is a proper one. Witness is directed to answer."

"Can you deny such a possibility?" the Investigator began again.

"I neither deny nor admit it," the Gatekeeper said wearily.

"But you do not deny it?"

"No, I do not deny it," the Gatekeeper said in a faint voice.

"Mr. Chairman, members of the committee. In view of the admission of gross inefficiency by the Gatekeeper—in view of the fact that he cannot deny there is a possibility that subversive persons likely to be agents of a foreign power, by taking advantage of the Gatekeeper's laxness, if indeed it is mere laxness and not a deliberate and treasonable coddling of such persons . . . have succeeded in infiltrating Up Here for the purpose of undermining our way of life . . . in view of these facts this committee has no alternative but to reopen for complete and thorough investigation a number of cases, specifically I have in mind such known subversives as . . ."

"I protest!" the Gatekeeper shouted. "This is a deliberate attempt to discredit the Immigration Service. I insist that we proceed with the regular business of the committee immediately."

"May I remind the Gatekeeper that he has temporarily relinquished the chair?" the Investigator said mildly.

"Mr. Chairman I appeal to you. How much longer are the members of this committee going to tolerate these disruptive tactics?"

Oates pounded his gavel. "The chair agrees that this committee has no alternative but to reopen a number of cases in order to determine the truth of the allegations which have been made. It therefore rules . . ."

"I will not be a party to any such undertaking! I will resign first!" the Gatekeeper protested.

"If the Gatekeeper feels that this is the only honourable course open to him . . ." Oates smiled.

"That is exactly how I feel. I am resigning . . . do you hear? I resign . . . I resign!"

RICHARD ROVERE

I've Got a Paper Here

1954

I never see a picture of McCarthy flourishing a document without thinking of a meeting I had with him in May, 1949, about a year before he went to Wheeling, West Virginia, and held aloft the piece of paper that made him famous. (He said it was a list of Communists in the State Department. It turned out to be a letter from James F. Byrnes to Adolph Sabath, and had no list of Communists or of anything else in it.) I was in Washington, and I dropped in at a Senate hearing at which testimony was being taken on the alleged mistreatment by Americans of some German S.S. men, members of an outfit called the Blowtorch Battalion, who had been accused of massacring a hundred and fifty United States troops and a hundred Belgian civilians at a crossroads named Malmédy, in December, 1944. I had been in the hearing room only a few minutes when McCarthy became involved in an altercation with Senator Raymond E. Baldwin, of Connecticut, a fellow-Republican who has since become a judge of the Supreme Court of Errors, in Hartford.

It was an angry exchange. McCarthy took the view that the Americans had in fact been guilty of brutal conduct. In this first brush with the Army, he claimed that it was coddling not Communists but sadists and crooked lawyers. He said that he had documentary proof of this but that Baldwin, intent for some unexplained reason on protecting the accused men, wouldn't pay any attention to it. Baldwin insisted he wasn't trying to protect anyone. After a while, McCarthy rose from his seat, stuffed a lot of papers into his briefcase, and left the room, saying he would no longer be a party to a shameful farce, a "deliberate and clever attempt to whitewash the American military."

Curious about the dispute and at that time ignorant of its background, I followed McCarthy into the corridor and asked him if he would be kind enough to tell me what he was in such a stew about. He said he would be glad to, and suggested that I go with him to his office. "It's time the American people knew about this," he said. "These documents will speak for themselves." He hefted up the bulging briefcase to give me some idea of the sheer bulk of them. "When you've looked at a few of my documents, you'll agree with me that this is one of the most outrageous things the country has ever known." I said that if this was the case, I'd certainly feel privileged to be allowed to inspect them. "You'll see them, all right," he said. "I'm not holding anything back. I'm through with this investigation, and I'm taking my case to the public."

He struck me as being a bit overwrought, but on the whole he seemed an earnest and plausible young senator. Though he used extravagant language, his tone was restrained, his manner almost gentle. As we walked along through the wide, echoing corridors of the Senate Office Building, he kept talking of the magnitude of his revelations, and although I had wanted—for a starter, at least—just a brief résumé of his side of the story, he succeeded in whetting my appetite for the contents of the briefcase.

We reached his office at last and sat down at his desk. He emptied the briefcase and piled the papers up in front of him. "Let's see, now," he said as he thumbed his way down toward the middle of the pile. "I know just the thing I want you to see first. I've got one thing here that's a real eye-opener. Oh, yes, here we are now." He pulled out several pages of photostat paper and handed them to me. "I think the facts will mean more to you than anything I could say. Once you've looked this over, you'll see that Baldwin has been playing a pretty sinister role in trying to whitewash the administration."

I read rapidly through what he gave me. Then I read it a second time, more carefully. When I'd finished the second reading, I was certain that the Senator had selected the wrong document. I no longer recall just what was in it, but it was a letter from one Army officer or government official to another, and although it had, as I recall, some bearing on the Malmédy affair, it didn't seem to me to prove anything about anything. I told McCarthy that as far as I could see, it was a pretty routine piece of correspondence.

"You're certainly right about that," he said. "Don't get me wrong, now. I didn't mean you'd find the *whole* story there. Standing alone, it doesn't mean much—I know that just as well as you do. But it's a link in a chain. It's one piece in a jigsaw puzzle. When you've seen some of the other documents, you'll know what I mean."

This was reassuring. In fact, I felt a bit ashamed of myself for expecting to master a complex situation in a few minutes. I began to read the next document McCarthy handed me. "Now, when you put these two together," he said, "you get a picture." The second document was mainly a listing of names. None of them meant anything to me. I tried to think what connection they might have with the letter I'd just read or with Senator Baldwin. I tried to "put them together," as McCarthy had advised, and "get a picture." No picture came. I confessed this to the Senator.

"Exactly," he said. "That's exactly my point. Those names mean nothing to you. They didn't mean anything to me, either, when I began to look into this conspiracy. But they're going to mean something to you before long, I can guarantee you that. I wanted you to have a look at them, because when you've seen some of the other things I've got here, you'll see how this jigsaw puzzle fits together. Now just bear those names in mind."

I tried to bear the names in mind and found it was impossible. Nothing unsticks faster than names you can't associate with real people. But although it was, I thought, curious that the Senator hadn't shown me the documents explaining the significance of the names before showing me the names themselves, I continued to be impressed by his manner. And the papers themselves were impressive—not by virtue of their contents but by virtue of their existence. Photostats and carbon copies and well-kept newspaper clippings have, I think, an authority of their own for most people; we assume that no one would go to the bother of assembling them if they didn't prove something.

As McCarthy sat at his desk sorting out the papers, putting some in a stack to his right and some in a stack to his left and consigning others to a filing cabinet behind him, he seemed knowledgeable and efficient. "I'm just trying to put this picture together for you," he kept saying. Two or three times in the course of our interview, which must have lasted about an hour and a half, he called in a secretary and asked her to fetch him some document that wasn't among those he had taken to the hearing. I wondered as I watched him what had become of the promise to provide a blinding illumination with a single document, but for quite a while I assumed it was my fault, not his, that I wasn't grasping the details very well.

McCarthy kept handing papers across the desk to me. "Here are a few more links in the chain," he would say as he handed me more correspondence, more lists, and a good many pictures of the Germans who had accused the Americans of brutality, of the accused Americans, of Malmédy farmhouses, and of Army barracks in Occupied Germany. None of them seemed to advance his argument by very much— by anything at all, in fact—but then he was no longer claiming very much for them.

"You don't get to the bottom of these things in a few minutes," he said. "Especially when so many powerful people are trying to hide the truth. Believe me, it wasn't easy for me to put this story together."

At one point he handed me a rather thick document. "I don't want you to leave without seeing this," he said. "Here we have the facts in the Army's own records. This is a transcript of the first hearing on this affair. This is what Baldwin and the administration are trying to cover up. Remember, now, this is from the records the Army itself kept."

I read here and there in the record the Army itself kept, and told McCarthy that, perhaps because of my ignorance, I was unable to see any holes in the Army's case.

"Of course you don't," he said. "Naturally, they're going to make out the best case they can for themselves. You wouldn't expect them to spill the beans in their own records, would you? The whole thing is a pack of lies."

I was beginning to get a bit impatient, though I tried not to show it. I said that as I understood the situation, he, McCarthy, was persuaded that the Malmédy massacre was a fiction of our own military authorities, that Germans had been tortured into confessing acts that had never been committed, and that a Republican senator, a man with a considerable reputation for probity, was trying to protect the torturers. I was about to go on to say that thus far nothing he had shown me established the truth of all this. But McCarthy interrupted me.

"That's right," he said, in a manner that suggested appreciation of my insight and my gift of summation. "You're beginning to get the picture now. I think the next thing I'll do is show you some of the affidavits we've gathered on this case."

He handed over a stack of affidavits. They were the sworn statements of the S.S. men held as war criminals, and they alleged the most hideous mistreatment by the Americans. It was because these statements were being published in newspapers throughout Germany and, the government had been advised, were being believed by large numbers of Germans that the Senate Armed Services Committee had decided to conduct its own hearings, assigning the job to a subcommittee led by Senator Baldwin and including, besides Baldwin, Senator Kefauver, of Tennessee, and Senator Lester Hunt, of Wyoming. Although McCarthy had given the impression of resigning from this group, the fact, as I later learned, was that he couldn't resign, because he hadn't been a member to begin with. He had merely exercised the senatorial privilege of sitting with the committee during the hearings, at which, from most newspaper accounts, he had done most of the talking. He was able to do this, incidentally, only after he had won a long fight to get from Senator Baldwin the right, which isn't normally regarded as part of the privilege, to cross-examine all the witnesses. Senator Baldwin later said it was McCarthy's bullyragging of him in the Malmédy affair that finally led him to give up politics.

After scanning some of the affidavits, I said that while it was entirely conceivable that a Nazi under sentence of death or imprisonment could be telling the truth about his own past behavior, it was at least equally conceivable that he would falsify. I wondered, I said, what McCarthy had in the way of evidence that it was not the convicted Nazis but the Americans who were lying.

"You've put your finger on it," he said. "Those are precisely the facts that Baldwin and the administration don't want me to bring out. That's why I walked out of that hearing. They're concealing all the evidence. I've shown you some of the pieces in this jigsaw puzzle, and believe me, when I take this story before the American people, the truth will be forced to come out."

I asked McCarthy if he had anything else he wanted to show me. "Well, I've got the affidavits of the Army people here," he said. "But I guess you can imagine what's in them. Lies from start to finish. Naturally, they're trying to protect themselves. I've got them here if you want to see what's in them."

I said I thought I'd skip them. I thanked the Senator for his courtesy and left.

The following pastiche appeared as an unsigned editorial in The New Republic. *McLeod had led the State Department's own security investigations with the kind of zealousness associated with Senator McCarthy, and had become a political hot potato.*

DONALD MALCOLM

Dooley Redivivus

1957

"Did ye see in th' papers," said Mr. Hennessy, "how they're sindin' Scott McLeod to be ambassadure to Ireland?"

" 'Tis funny ye should mention that," replied Mr. Dooley, "just when I'm standin' here thryin' to recall whether 'twas a poet or a secur-rity officer who made the famous remark: 'I care not who makes the laws iv a nation, if I can sarve on the investigatin' committees.' But ye mustn't think they're sindin' McLeod to Dublin out iv malice, Hinnissy. Very like, it just came up in a casual conversation, d'ye know. The Prisident happens to notice one day that his Sicrety iv State is back in town, an' he takes him to wan side an' says, 'While ye're here Foster,' he says, 'ye might just tell me how the wurrld is gettin' along.'

'Oh times is lookin' up,' says the Sicrety iv State, 'Our relations with England haven't been annywhere near so plisint since the Rayvelutionary War,' he says, 'an' that's nothin' to our relations with France an' Israel,' he says. 'To the oppressed peoples in the satellites,' he says, 'I just sint kind regards an' the hope iv a speedy and complete liberation,' he says, 'but not so speedy as to worry the Rooshians about losin' their empire,' he says. 'I told them,' he says, 'if they needed anny help, just say the wurrud,' he says, 'an' we will give them every assistance, short iv helpin' them,' he says. 'In short,' he says, 'by exertin' a stiddy moral pressure,' he says, 'we're bound to win some sort iv moral victory.'

'Well, you take care iv it, Foster,' says the Prisident. 'Dwight D. Eisenhower is not the man to stand in ye'er way.'

'Speakin' iv people in me way,' says the Sicrety iv State, 'I do belave I've found the place for Scott McLeod.'

'Is that a fact?' says the Prisident. 'And where is that, now?'

'Well,' says the Sicrety, 'I thought to meself, what sort of appintment wud prove that we are on such terms with McLeod as wud plaze the Old Guard, but not on anny such terms as wud make anny modhren Raypublican think we was on anny such terms as we ought not to be. Then I remembered we had a job open in Dublin, an' I says to meself, well Foster, me lad, 'tis not as good as sindin' him to th' moon, but still, 'tis better than a poke in th' ey with a sharp stick.'

'It is that,' says the President, 'but d'ye think the Irish will like it?'

'I dunnaw,' says the Sicrety, 'They're a hard lot to plaze. They didn't like the Black and Tans ayther, till they got used to them.'

'Well,' says the President, 'you always had a livvil head, Foster, an' if ye think it's a good idea, it suits me right up to the handle. Where do I sign?'

"And that, Hinnissy, is how 'twas done."

"But d'ye not think," asked Mr. Hennessy, "that th' Congress might tell the Sicrety to sind up another boy?"

"I do not," said Mr. Dooley. " 'Tis a foolish man, Hinnissy, who stands behind his own plate-glass window and makes faces at th' fellow with a brick in his pocket. Th' Congress don't dare turn down McLeod and the Sicrety knows it."

"And why is that, now?" asked Mr. Hennessy.

"Sure, an' how else wud they get him out iv the counthry?" answered Mr. Dooley.

CHARLES LEVY

*Statute of Liberty**

1959

Give me your tired unless they are aliens who are polygamists or who practice polygamy or advocate the practice of polygamy,

* The italicized portion of "Statute of Liberty" is from the poem by Emma Lazarus inscribed at the base of the Statue of Liberty; the balance is from the McCarran-Walter Immigration and Nationality Act of 1952.

Your poor unless they are aliens who are paupers, professional beggars, or vagrants,

Your huddled masses yearning to breath free unless they are aliens who are afflicted with tuberculosis in any form,

The wretched refuse of your teeming shore unless they are aliens who the consular officer or the Attorney General knows, or has reason to believe, seek to enter the United States solely, principally, or incidentally to engage in activities which would be prejudicial to the public interest,

Send these unless the President finds that the entry of any aliens or of any class of aliens into the United States would be detrimental to the interests of the United States,

The homeless unless the employment of such aliens will adversely affect the wages and working conditions of the workers in the United States similarly employed,

Tempest-tost to me unless they are aliens who have been convicted of two or more offenses,

I lift my lamp beside the golden door unless they are aliens who write or publish, or cause to be written or published, or who knowingly circulate, distribute, print, or display, or knowingly cause to be circulated, distributed, printed, published, or displayed, or who knowingly have in their possession for the purpose of circulation, publication, distribution, or display, any written or printed matter, advocating or teaching opposition to all organized government.

CHARLES J. PRENTISS

Remembrance of Past Things

1959

Oh, why has the radical
Taken a Sabbatical?
No longer is heard
A revolutionary word.

We're left with the liberal,
Pompous and glibberal;
Filled with quotations
From *Reporters* and *Nations*.
But no more fanatics
Give classes in attics
Or speeches in playgrounds.
The first day of May sounds
Of Unions parading
Are distant and fading.
The Jefferson School,
Once a cultural jewel,
Now is even more bare
Than the late Union Square.
Oh, long-haired Messiahs,
Oh, red Jeremiahs
Our culture is poorer
Without all your furor.

ART BUCHWALD

The Peril of Informing

1962

According to a story in *The Nation*, an ex-FBI agent named Jack Levine let some top secrets out of the bag. Mr. Levine said that one fifth or 1,700 of the 8,500 members of the registered Communists in the United States were FBI informers. Mr. Levine said these 1,700 were dues-paying members, who gave the party its financial support. He also predicted that as Communist membership continues to decline and the percentage of informants increases, the day will soon come when FBI informants, who are rising rapidly to the top, will capture complete control of the party.

This is something that I'm sure Mr. J. Edgar Hoover never planned on, and if what Mr. Levine says is true, he will have to revise his whole book on Communist infiltration in the United States.

It isn't too farfetched to assume that in a couple of years the entire Communist Party will be made up of FBI informants. The reason for this is that the Communists are very bad about paying their dues and the FBI informants are the only ones who have the money (provided, of course, by the FBI) to keep up their memberships.

Because they haven't paid their dues, the real Communists will be forced to leave the party, and the only ones left will be the FBI informants. Now one informant doesn't know who another informant is, so all the informants will assume the other informants are Communists. Yet in order to make his job pay off, the informant will have to justify his job and will, therefore, have to invent things to warrant his staying on the FBI payroll. The informants will be in severe competition with each other and, as time goes on, their reports will become more dramatic as each one has to outdo the other.

As these reports pour into the FBI, each one more harrowing than the last, the Justice Department will have to take some action. What they'll probably do is hire more informants to keep tabs on the party.

The new informants will increase the Communist Party membership by 10,000, then 20,000, then 30,000 members, and pretty soon the party, which had been dying out, will get a new lease on life.

The trouble is that as the membership increases, the FBI will have to increase its vigilance and hire new informants to infiltrate the party. These new members, all dues-paying members, will, in order to keep it a secret that they are informants, have to prove they are Communists, and will have to get involved in subversive activities so they won't arouse suspicion.

Once these subversive activities are exposed, there will be a public outcry, and the FBI will have to send in more informants to show it is in control of the situation. Requests will be made for more funds from Congress and hearings will be held, at which time several of the informants, with paper bags over their faces, will testify to the danger of the increasing membership of the Communist Party.

Congress will authorize the money, urging the FBI to keep them informed of the dangers involved. In order to keep them informed, new informants will have to be recruited. In no time at all a million registered party members will be on the rolls, all paid for by the Department of Justice.

With so many informants the competition among them will get

fierce. Informants will be forced to hand in longer and more complete reports. Evaluation teams will have to be set up all over the country. Each report will require new informants to check out the facts. In no time at all the Communists could become the leading political party in the country, and to show their strength would have to put up a candidate for the Presidency of the United States. And the name of the candidate? J. Edgar Hoover, of course. Who else?

RUSSELL BAKER

Security Test

1963

People who grind their teeth while sleeping may be on the road to treason. So may sleepwalkers, hair fingerers, and people who perspire easily.

The warning is implicit in the latest psychological test designed to trap security risks in the State Department. The department's security office began giving the test in October, and though its use has recently been suspended—the official explanation is that it was unduly "personal" —the questionnaire's validity as a device for detecting latent traitors remains unchallenged. Would anyone care to submit?

QUESTION: Has any member of your family ever brought "embarrassment or unpleasantness on the rest of you?" Remember, answers may be checked for perjury. What about that scene your wife threw in the principal's office after the first-quarter report card? Should you mention the evening cousin Walter got sozzled at the Smiths' and had to be put to bed? What about the night in 1931 when Uncle Jim was caught in a Hoboken police net with bootleg whisky in the glove compartment?

QUESTION: Are there any "major sources of conflict in your family life?" Here most people will write "money" and pass on, but the roots of treason lie deep. There is a man here, for example, who likes to chin himself on the hemlock in his front yard. His wife is bitterly opposed. She says the neighbors will think he is mad. Nevertheless, he goes on chinning on the hemlock, building up marital tensions that may some day lead him into the enemy camp.

QUESTION: Are you "jumpy, restless, jittery, can't seem to keep still?" This, obviously, is a trick question to catch people who are trying to outwit the test. People who answer "no" can expect to have F.B.I. dossiers opened on them immediately. Nowadays everybody is jumpy, restless, jittery and can't seem to keep still. It is a respectable condition known as *"overkill tremens."* The best answer is, "all the time."

QUESTION: Do you feel "mixed up, upset, confused, can't think straight?" Another trick question. Most people, asked if they feel "mixed up, upset, confused," will answer, "doesn't everybody?" This is a perfectly loyal reply, but the last part of the question—"can't think straight?"—is double-edged.

If the last thirty years of Congressional oratory have taught us anything, it is that a primary trait of Communists is an inability to think straight. Therefore, straight thought about this question would proceed like this: If I admit that I can't think straight, I will probably be investigated as a Communist. That would be terrible. All I want is to get through this test without being ruined. If I make it, I will get far away from Washington. Maybe I can become a gardener. Work in the sunlight.

The proper answer, then, is to lie. Write that you always think straight. The psychologists will know it is a lie, but they will approve the answer because it shows straight thinking.

QUESTION: Do you grind your teeth in your sleep? The sensible answer, of course, is: "my teeth won't tell me." Psychologists, however, do not appreciate straight-thinking answers that make them feel ridiculous. It is wiser to write something illegible suggesting vaguely that you never sleep. Your questionnaire will probably be pulled from the group's and lost while moving through channels toward the Great Psychologist, thus permitting you to leave town without a trace.

QUESTION: Do "things appear strange, peculiar, unnatural, unreal?" Be careful with this one. The examiner will be watching to see if you laugh. He will be a small metallic examiner glowing with interior tube lights, utterly humorless but totally secure. He will be looking for the totally secure man.

Write, "while many would say that we live in a strange, peculiar, unnatural, unreal world, I feel perfectly normal whenever I can garden in the sunlight." Hand in the completed test. Walk deliberately out the door. Start running. Run very fast.

MARVIN KITMAN

Confessions of an Ex-Anti-Communist

1963

Like most members of my generation, I became an anti-communist in college. I was immature and didn't know what I was doing by falling under the spell of the anti-communists at my alma mater, City College of New York. Most outsiders knew that 20 percent of the student body and faculty at CCNY were communists. But what they didn't know was that 80 percent were anti-communist. The college was riddled with anti-communists.

During my undergraduate years 1947–53 in this hot-bed of anti-communism, being an anti-communist was "in." All my close friends were anti-communists. The best fraternities on campus were all under-cover anti-communist cells. I was weak and I didn't feel that I wanted to save the world as a member of an out-group.

It made so much sense to be an anti-communist in those days. There was an economic boom on, and I was told I never had it so good because of the anti-communists. On my way to school every morning, I could see those long lines of employed men, walking to the subways and busses.

The anti-communists in the bull-sessions in the City College cafeteria warned me that I would never get a job in the communications industry unless I was a known anti-communist. Personnel departments at newspapers, magazines, TV networks, ad agencies, and Hollywood studios were all under the control of anti-communists, and they were only hiring their own people. I wanted to be a writer so much, I didn't care what I believed as long as I got a job.

On my way home from school every afternoon, I read the *Journal-American*, and somebody always seemed to be turning anti-communist: people like Harvey Matusow, Louis Budenz and Herbert Philbrick. I felt that I was joining the wave of the future.

Gradually I drifted into the Party.

I should have realized that I was being manipulated by the inner circle of the Republican Party. At the time, they were trying to inject new blood into the Party, hoping to win an election for a change. The Eastern industrialists and bankers who controlled the Party nominating apparatus sought to seduce young minds of all ages by drafting a national hero to head the ticket. I fell for the Eisenhower pitch.

The Party had other card-carrying members whose names I saw on letterheads and respected: Irving Berlin, Irene Dunne, and Jackie Robinson. Before I knew what was happening, I found myself attending meetings of anti-communist front organizations hoping to meet people like them. The only people I met seemed to be girls.

To make myself more attractive as a man, I started reading obscure anti-communist journals, like the *Herald Tribune*. I'm ashamed to admit it now, but I was influenced by the Republican press.

The Republican Party was definitely hard on communism. I really believed the Russians were our enemies in those first cold war years. Keep in mind that during the cold war, the Russians were on the other side.

I was such an innocent dupe that I even thought the Republicans were the party of the common stockholder—the little guys, widows, and orphans, none of whom owned more than half of AT&T and GM. I didn't question the party's claim, either, that they pioneered in the fight for Negro civil rights. No party would be willing to lose the South for a hundred years unless it was sincere.

Still I didn't actually join the Party. A friend sent me a gift membership. When a well-meaning relative introduced me to the *Wall Street Journal* with a gift subscription, I was finished. I wound up on every anti-communist mailing list in the nation.

I realize now that not getting out of the Party was an error in judgment. In my defense, I can only say that I was never an active member of the Party. Not wanting to be out of step with our candidates, I didn't even take the Party's platform seriously.

Neither did I play an important role in the anti-communist conspiracy outside the Party. To the best of my recollection, I never once preached or taught the violent overthrow of any communist government. I thought John Foster Dulles was out of his mind when he advocated unleashing Chiang Kai-shek. I was, in retrospect, just another dedicated, hack anti-communist who merely did what everybody else was doing the past 15 years.

Why am I the first anti-communist in America to confess in full detail his role in the anti-communist movement? If the thaw in Russian-American relations continues, one day soon I expect to be called before the House Un-American Activities Committee and asked the question I've dreaded ever since I decided to quit the movement several weeks ago: "Are you now, or have you ever been, an anti-communist?"

HUAC, of course, has no right to inquire into my political beliefs; a man's politics is his own private business. That's why I'll probably lose my job if I refuse to testify on the grounds that I might incriminate myself.

By confessing now, I will be able to say before the Committee truthfully that I have nothing to hide. I want to testify to end, once and for all, the innuendos clouding my past.

There is, however, something I won't do. I won't give the Committee the names of all the people I knew as anti-communists during the past fifteen years—unless they're needed to get my job back.

The only thing I'm worried about now is that the House Un-American Activities Committee will be abolished before I have the chance to clear my name.

8 BLACK AND WHITE

THE INSTITUTION IS STILL PECULIAR

Once upon a time the great indigenous American issue was chattel slavery; today it is civil rights. Once the specific lines of battle were drawn at the Dred Scott decision, the Missouri Compromise, or the Fourteenth Amendment; today they may converge on public accommodations, de facto integration of schools, or equalization of employment opportunities.

The basic issue has been long settled, in principle if not in practice; today's battles are rearguard delaying actions. This does not mean they are less important or less bitterly fought. The subtlety, incisiveness, and impatience demonstrated by present-day writers in their treatment of "the question" contrasts dramatically with the crudeness (and condescension) of their nineteenth-century forerunners.

The haughty American nation . . . makes the Negro clean its boots, and then proves the . . . inferiority of the Negro by the fact that he is a bootblack.—*George Bernard Shaw*

8 BLACK AND WHITE

THE INSTITUTIONS IS STILL PROBLEM

Nasby, Locke's protagonist, was presented as a morally typical "Copper-head" (pro-slavery Northern Democrat). References: the election was for ratification of the Fourteenth Amendment; "Vallandygum" (Vallandigham) was the Copperhead leader; Wade was the Radical Republican in line for the Presidency had Andrew Johnson been removed from office.

PETROLEUM V. NASBY

(DAVID ROSS LOCKE)

Mr. Nasby Assists in the Ohio Election

POST OFFIS, CONFEDRIT X ROADS
(Wich is in the Stait uv Kentucky), 1867.

Feelin that the time hed arrived which wuz to decide whether 7,000 degradid niggers wuz to grind 500,000 proud Caucashens into the dust, I felt that ef I shood fail in my dooty now, I shood be forever disgraced. Accordingly, I put in on elekshun day at a Dimocratic town in Ohio— the battlefield—the identikle place into wich I made a speech doorin the campane.

I arrived ther on the mornin uv the elekshun, and found that comperhensive arrangements hed bin made for defeatin this most nefarus and dangerous proposishen. Paradin the streets ez early ez 7 A.M. wuz a wagon containin 25 virgins, runnin from 27 to 31, the most uv em ruther wiry in texture, and over their heads wuz banners, with the followin techin inscriptions: "Fathers, save us from Nigger Ekality!" "White Husbans or nun!" It wood hev bin better, I thot, hed they bin somewhat younger. Ther wuz suthin preposterous in the ijea uv females uv that age callin upon fathers to save em from anythin, when in the course of nacher their fathers must hev bin a lyin in the silent tomb for several consecutive years, onless, indeed, they marrid young. Ef still livin (I judged from the aged appearance uv the damsels), their parents must be too far advanced in yeers to take an activ part in biznis. In anuther wagon wuz a collekshun uv men wich hed bin hired from the railrode, twelve miles distant, whose banners read, "Shel ignerent Niggers vote beside intelligint Wite men?" and the follerin verse:—

> "Shel niggers black this land possess,
>   And rool us whites up here?
> O, no, my friends; we ruther guess
>   We'll never stand that ere."

It okkurd to me that it wood hev done better hed their spellin bin more akkerit; but upon inquiry I found that it didn't make no difference. That wuz the pervailin way of spellin things in that vicinity. Hangin over the polls wuz a broad peece uv white muslin, onto wich was painted, in large letters, "Caucashuns, Respeck yer Noses—the nigger stinks!" Then I knowed it wuz safe. That odor hez never yet bin resisted by the Democrasy, and it hez its inflooence over Republikins.

I never saw sich enthoosiasm, or more cheerin indicasuns uv the pride uv race. Ez evidence uv the deep feeling that pervaded that community, I state that nine paupers in the poorhouse demanded to be taken to the polls, that they might enter their protest agin bringin the nigger up to a ekality with em, wich wuz nine gain with no offsets, ez ther wuzn't an Ablishnist in the institooshun. Two men, in the county jale for petty larceny, wuz, at their own rekest, taken out of doorance vile by the Sheriff uv the county, that they mite, by the ballot, protest agin bein degraded by bein compelled, when their time wuz out, to acknowledge the nigger ez their ekal. One enthoosiastic Dimekrat, who cost us $5, hed to be carried to the polls. He had commenced early at one uv the groseries, and hed succumbd afore votin. We found him sleepin peacefully in a barn. We lifted the patriotic man, and in percession marched to the polls. We stood him on his feet, two men supportin him—one on either side. I put a straight ticket into his fingers, and takin his wrist with one hand, held his fingers together with tother, and guided his hand to the box. Ez it neared the winder, he started ez ef a electric shock hed struck him, and, straightenin up, asked, "Is it the sthrate ticket? Is Constooshnel Amindmint No! onto it?"

Ashoorin him that it wuz all rite, he suffered me to hold his hand out to the Judge uv Eleckshun, who took the ballot and deposited it in the box. "Thank Hivin!" sed he, "the nagur is not yet my ayquil!" and doublin up at the thigh and kneejoints, he sank, limber-like, and gently, onto the ground. Ez he hed discharged the dooty uv an Amerikin freeman, we rolled him out to one side uv the house, wher the drippin uv the rain from the roof wood do suthin toward soberin him off, and left him alone in his glory.

The Amendment got but a very few votes in that locality. The Republikins jined us in repudiatin it, mostly upon ethnologikle grounds. One asserted that he hed bin in favor uv emancipashen in time uv war, becoz the Afrikin cood thereby be indoost to fite agin their Southern masters, and it wood hev the effeck uv makin the drafts come lighter in his township. He wuz a humanitarian likewise. He opposed crooelty toward em. He wept when he heerd uv the massacre at Fort Piller, becoz in the army the nigger wuz ez much a man ez anybody, and sich wholesale slaughters tendid to make calls for "500,000 more" more frekent. But when it come to givin uv em the privilege uv votin beside him, it coodent be thot uv. He cood never consent that a race whose heels wuz longer than hizzen shood rool Ameriky. "My God!" sed this ardent Republikin, "ef you give em the ballot, wat kin prevent em from bein Congrismen, Senators, Vice-Presidents, and even Presidents? I shudder when I think uv it"; and he hurried in his vote.

I didn't quite see the force uv his objecshen, for it never okkurred to me that bein sent to Congris wuz the nateral consekence uv votin. I hev voted for thirty years, at many elections four or five times, but I hev never bin to Congris. Wher is the constitooency wich wood elect me? But it wuzn't my biznis to controvert his posishen. It made no diffrence to me wat his reason wuz for votin ez I desired him to vote.

The nigger-lovers beat up one man to vote for the Amendment, wich, I saw by his dissatisfied look, hed bin overperswadid. "Sir!" sed I, "do yoo consider a Afrikin suffishently intelligent to be trustid with so potent a weapon ez the ballot?"

Bustin away from them wich hed him in charge, he exclaimed, "No, I don't! I can't vote for it. They ain't intelligent enuff. Sir, scratch off the 'Yes' from my ballot, and put onto it 'No!'"

"Here is a pensil," sed I.

"Do it yerself," sed he; "I can't write."

And I did it. Sich is the effeck uv a word in season. Words fitly spoken is apples uv gold, set in picters uv silver.

One man woodent listen to me, but votid the Amendment. He hed bin a soljer, and for eleven months pertook uv the hospitality uv the Confedrits at Andersonville. Escapin, he wuz helped to the Fedrel lines by a nigger, who wuz flogged almost to death, in his site, for not betrayin wher he wuz hid. I mite ez well hev talked to a lamp-post. Ez he shoved in his ballot, he remarkt suthin about he'd ruther see a nigger vote than a d____d rebel, any time. From the direckshun uv his eye-site, I persoom he referred to me.

I left for home ez soon ez the votes wuz counted, and the result wuz made known, only waitin till the poll-books wuz made out, and the judges uv eleckshun hed got ther names written by the clerks, and hed made their marks to em. On my way home I wuz gratified to see how the nateral antipathy to the nigger hed revived. At Cincinati, the nite uv the eleckshn, they wuz bangin uv em about, the patriotic Democrisy goin for em wherever they cood find em, and the next day, ez I saw em at the ralerode stashens, they hed, generally speekin, ther heds bandaged. It wuz cheerin to me, and I gloated over it.

Full of gladnis, I entered Kentucky, and joyfully I wendid my way to the Corners. I wuz the bearer uv tidins uv great joy, and my feet wuz pleasant onto the mountains. Ez I walked into Bascom's, they all saw in my face suthin uv importance.

"Wat is it?" sed Deekin Pogram. "Is it weal or woe?"

"Is the proud Caucashen still in the ascendant in Ohio, or hez the grovelin Afrikin ground him into the dust?" askt Issaker Gavitt.

"My friend," sed I, takin up the Deekin's whisky, wich, in the eggscitement uv the moment, he didn't observe, "the Constitooshnel Amendment, givin the nigger ekal rites, hez bin voted down by the liberty-lovin freemen uv Ohio. Three cheers for Ohio."

They wuz given with a will. The wildest enthoosiasm wuz awakened. Bascom put a spigot in a fresh barl, and the church bells wuz set a ringin. The niggers wore a dismayed look, and got out uv the way ez soon ez possible. A meetin wuz towunst organized. Deekin Pogram spoke. He felt that this wuz a proud day. Light wuz breakin. The dark clouds uv fanaticism wuz breakin away. We hed now the Afrikin under our feet. We hev got him in his normal posishen in Ohio, and, please God, we will soon hev him likewise in Kentucky. He moved the adopshen uv the follerin resolooshens:—

> WAREAS, Noer cust Canan, and condemned him to be a servant unto his brethren, thereby cleerly indikatin the status uv the race for all time to come to be one uv inferiority; and,
>
> WAREAS, To further show to the eyes uv the most obtoose that a diffrence wuz intended, the Almighty gave the nigger a diffrent anatomicle struckter, for full partikelars uv wich see the speeches uv the Demokratic stumpers doorin the late campaign; and,

WAREAS, The attempt to place the nigger on an ekality with the white in votin ez well ez taxashun, we consider the sappin uv the very foundashun uv civil liberty, ez well ez uv the Crischen religion; therefore,

RESOLVED, That the Constooshnel and Biblikle Democracy uv Kentucky send greetin to their brethren uv Ohio, with thanks for their prompt and effectooal squelchin uv the idea uv nigger superority.

RESOLVED, That to the Republikins uv Ohio, who, risin above party considerashuns, voted agin suffrage, our thanks is due, and we congratulate em that now they, ez well ez us, are saved from the danger uv marryin niggers; and likewise do we asshoor em, that in a spirit uv mutual forbearance, we care not wat particular creed they perfess, so long ez they vote our principles.

RESOLVED, That the will uv the people havin bin cleerly indikated, we demand the insershun uv the word 'white' in the Coonstitooshun uv the Yoonited States.

RESOLVED, That we ask the colored voters uv Tennessee, and other States where colored men hev votes, to observe how they are treated in Ohio, where the Ablishnists don't need em. In them States we extend to em a corjel invitashun to act with us.

RESOLVED, That a copy uv these resolooshens be sent to President Johnson, with an ashoorance uv our unabated confidence in his integrity, patriotism, and modisty.

The meetin broke up with three cheers for the Dimocracy uv Ohio, nine for the Republikins uv that State, and one for the State at large.

The Fakulty uv the Institoot met next mornin, for the purpus uv revisin the Scripters. It wuz desided that the word "white" should be insertid wherever necessary, and that that edishen only be yoosed by the Dimocracy and Conservativ Republikins. We made progress, the follerin bein a few uv the changes:—

"So God creatid a *white* man in his own image."

"Whosoever, therefore, shell confess me before *white* men," &c.

"Suffer little *white* children to come unto me, for uv sich is the kingdom uv Heaven."

Wich last is comfortin, ez it shows that the distincshen is kept up through all eternity. I give these merely ez samples. We shel hev it finisht in a few days, and, ef funds kin be raised, shel publish it. Sich a vershun uv the Skripters is needid.

I find the Demekratic mind is exercised over the question uv the succession to Wade. My voice is for Vallandygum. Never wuz there sich a saint, never wuz ther a man so abused by the tyranikel minions of irresponsible power. He hez suffered for us, and now he must hev his reward. It hez bin urged that the ten cent colleckshun in 1863 was suffishent pay for his marterdom. I deny it. I know all about it. He got nothin uv it. Every Demekrat in Ohio who hed taxes to pay, or who wanted a new pare uv pants, or whose boots needed half solin, took up a colleckshun for Vallandygum. I know that's so, for I wuz a Demekrat in Ohio, laborin under pekooniary embarasments in them days myself. Let Vallandygum hev the place he so well earned.

PETROLEUM V. NASBY, P. M.

(Wich is Postmaster).

FINLEY PETER DUNNE

The Negro Problem

1900

"What's goin' to happen to th' naygur?" asked Mr. Hennessy.

"Well," said Mr. Dooley, "he'll ayther have to go to th' north an' be a subjick race, or stay in th' south an' be an objick lesson. 'Tis a har-rd time he'll have, annyhow. I'm not sure that I'd not as lave be gently lynched in Mississippi as baten to death in New York. If I was a black man, I'd choose th' cotton belt in prifrince to th' belt on th' neck fr'm th' polisman's club. I wud so.

"I'm not so much throubled about th' naygur whin he lives among his opprissors as I am whin he falls into th' hands iv his liberators. Whin he's in th' south he can make up his mind to be lynched soon or late an' give his attintion to his other pleasures iv composin' rag-time music on a banjo, an' wurrukin' f'r th' man that used to own him an' now on'y owes him his wages. But 'tis th' divvle's own hardship f'r a coon to step out iv th' rooms iv th' S'ciety f'r th' Brotherhood iv Ma-an where he's been r-readin' a pome on th' 'Future of th' Moke' an' be pursooed be a mob iv abolitionists till he's dhriven to seek polis protection, which, Hinnissy, is th' polite name f'r fracture iv th' skull.

"I was f'r sthrikin' off th' shackles iv th' slave, me la-ad. 'Twas thrue I didn't vote f'r it, bein' that I heerd Stephen A. Douglas say 'twas onconstitootional, an' in thim days I wud go to th' flure with anny man f'r th' constitootion. I'm still with it, but not sthrong. It's movin' too fast f'r me. But no matther. Annyhow I was f'r makin' th' black man free, an' though I shtud be th' south as a spoortin' proposition I was kind iv glad in me heart whin Gin'ral Ulyss S. Grant bate Gin'ral Lee an' the rest iv th' Union officers captured Jeff Davis. I says to mesilf, 'Now,' I says, 'th' coon 'll have a chanst f'r his life,' says I, 'an' in due time we may injye him,' I says.

"An' sure enough it looked good f'r awhile, an' th' time come whin th' occas'nal dollar bill that wint acrost this bar on pay night wasn't good money onless it had th' name iv th' naygur on it. In thim days they was a young la-ad—a frind iv wan iv th' Donohue boys—that wint to th' public school up beyant, an' he was as bright a la-ad as ye'd want to see in a day's walk. Th' larnin' iv him wud sind Father Kelly back to his grammar. He cud spell to make a hare iv th' hedge schoolmasther, he was as quick at figures as th' iddycated pig they showed in th' tint las' week in Haley's vacant lot, and in joggerphy, asthronomy, algybbera, jommethry, chimisthry, physiojnomy, bassoophly an' fractions, I was often har-rd put mesilf to puzzle him. I heerd him gradyooate an' his composition was so fine very few cud make out what he meant.

"I met him on th' sthreet wan day afther he got out iv school. 'What ar-re ye goin' to do f'r ye'ersilf, Snowball,' says I—his name was Andhrew Jackson George Wash'n'ton Americus Caslateras Beresford Vanilla Hicks, but I called him 'Snowball,' him bein' as black as coal, d'ye see —I says to him: 'What ar're ye goin' to do f'r ye'ersilf?' I says. 'I'm goin to enther th' profession iv law,' he says, 'where be me acooman an' industhry I hope,' he says, 'f'r to rise to be a judge,' he says, 'a congrissman,' he says, 'a sinator,' he says, 'an p'rhaps,' he says, 'a prisidint iv th' United States,' he says. 'Theyse nawthin to prevint,' he says. 'Divvle a thing,' says I. 'Whin we made ye free,' says I, 'we opened up all these opporchunities to ye,' says I. 'Go on,' says I, 'an' enjye th' wealth an' position conferred on ye be th' constitootion,' I says. 'On'y,' I says, 'don't be too free,' I says. 'Th' freedom iv th' likes iv ye is a good thing an' a little iv it goes a long way,' I says, 'an' if I ever hear iv ye bein' presidint iv th' United States,' I says, 'I'll take me white-washin' away fr'm ye'er father, ye excelsior hair, poached-egg eyed, projiny iv tar,' I says, f'r me Anglo-Saxon feelin' was sthrong in thim days.

"Well, I used to hear iv him afther that defindin' coons in th' polis coort, an' now an' thin bein' mintioned among th' scatthrin' in raypublican county con-vintions, an' thin he dhropped out iv sight. 'Twas years befure I see him again. Wan day I was walkin' up th' levee smokin' a good tin cint seegar whin a coon wearin' a suit iv clothes that looked like a stained glass window in th' house iv a Dutch brewer an' a pop bottle in th' fr-ront iv his shirt, steps up to me an' he says: 'How dy'e do, Mistah Dooley,' says he. 'Don't ye know me—Mistah Hicks?' he says. 'Snowball,' says I. 'Step inside this dureway,' says I, 'less Clancy, th' polisman on th' corner, takes me f'r an octoroon,' I says. 'What ar-re ye do-in'?' says I. 'How did ye enjye th' prisidincy?' says I. He laughed an' told me th' story iv his life. He wint to practisin' law an' found his on'y clients was coons, an' they had no assets but their vote at th' prim'ry. Besides a warrant f'r a moke was the same as a letther iv inthroduction to th' warden iv th' pinitinchry. Th' on'y thing left f'r th' lawyer to do was to move f'r a new thrile an' afther he'd got two or three he thought ol' things was th' best an' ye do well to lave bad enough alone. He got so sick iv chicken he cudden't live on his fees an' he quit th' law an' wint into journalism. He r-run 'Th' Colored Supplimint,' but it was a failure, th' taste iv th' public lanin' more to quadhroon publications, an' no man that owned a resthrant or theaytre or dhrygoods store'd put in an adver-tisemint f'r fear th' subscribers'd see it an' come arround. Thin he attimpted to go into pollytics, an' th' best he cud get was carryin' a bucket iv wather f'r a Lincoln Club. He thried to larn a thrade an' found th' on'y place a naygur can larn a thrade is in prison an' he can't wurruk at that without committin' burglary. He started to take up subscriptions f'r a sthrugglin' church an' found th' profission was over-crowded. 'Fin'ly,' says he, ' 'twas up to me to be a porther in a saloon or go into th' on'y business,' he says, 'in which me race has a chanst,' he says. 'What's that?' says I. 'Craps,' says he. 'I've opened a palachal imporyium,' he says, 'where,' he says, ' 'twud please me very much,' he says, 'me ol' abolitionist frind,' he says, 'if ye'd dhrop in some day,' he says, 'an' I'll roll th' sweet, white bones f'r ye,' he says. ' 'Tis th' hope iv me people,' he says. 'We have an even chanst at ivry other pursoot,' he says, 'but 'tis on'y in craps we have a shade th' best iv it,' he says.

"So there ye ar-re, Hinnissy. An' what's it goin' to come to, says ye? Faith, I don't know an' th' naygurs don't know, an' be hivins, I think if th' lady that wrote th' piece we used to see at th' Halsted Sthreet Opry House come back to earth, she wudden't know. I used to be all broke up about Uncle Tom, but cud I give him a job tindin' bar in this here liquor store? I freed th' slave, Hinnissy, but, faith, I think 'twas like turrnin' him out iv a panthry into a cellar."

"Well, they got to take their chances," said Mr. Hennessy. "Ye can't do annything more f'r thim than make thim free."

"Ye can't," said Mr. Dooley; "on'y whin ye tell thim they're free they know we're on'y sthringin' thim."

LANGSTON HUGHES

There Ought To Be a Law

1950

"I have been up North a long time, but it looks like I just cannot learn to like white folks."

"I don't care to hear you say that," I said, "because there are a lot of good white people in this world."

"Not enough of them," said Simple, waving his evening paper. "If there was, they would make this American country good. But just look at what this paper is full of."

"You cannot dislike *all* white people for what the bad ones do," I said. "And I'm certain you don't dislike them all because once you told me yourself that you wouldn't wish any harm to befall Mrs. Roosevelt."

"Mrs. Roosevelt is different," said Simple.

"There now! You see, you are talking just as some white people talk about the Negroes they *happen* to like. They are always 'different.' That is a provincial way to think. You need to get around more."

"You mean among white folks?" asked Simple. "How can I make friends with white folks when they got Jim Crow all over the place?"

"Then you need to open your mind."

"I have near about *lost* my mind worrying with them," said Simple. "In fact, they have hurt my soul."

"You certainly feel bad tonight," I said. "Maybe you need a drink."

"Nothing in a bottle will help my soul," said Simple, "but I will take a drink."

"Maybe it will help your mind," I said. "Beer?"

"Yes."

"Glass or bottle?"

"A bottle because it contains two glasses," said Simple, spreading his paper out on the bar. "Look here at these headlines, man, where Congress is busy passing laws. While they're making all these laws, it looks like to me they ought to make one setting up a few Game Preserves for Negroes."

"What ever gave you that fantastic idea?" I asked.

"A movie short I saw the other night," said Simple, "about how the government is protecting wild life, preserving fish and game, and setting aside big tracts of land where nobody can fish, shoot, hunt, nor harm a single living creature with furs, fins, or feathers. But it did not show a thing about Negroes."

"I thought you said the picture was about 'wild life.' Negroes are not wild."

"No," said Simple, "but we need protection. This film showed how they put aside a thousand acres out West where the buffaloes roam and nobody can shoot a single one of them. If they do, they get in jail. It also showed some big National Park with government airplanes dropping food down to the deers when they got snowed under and had nothing to eat. The government protects and takes care of buffaloes and deers—which is more than the government does for me or my kinfolks down South. Last month they lynched a man in Georgia and just today I see where the Klan has whipped a Negro within a inch of his life in Alabama. And right up North here in New York a actor is suing a apartment house that won't even let a Negro go up on the elevator to see his producer. That is what I mean by Game Preserves for Negroes—Congress ought to set aside some place where we can go and nobody can jump on us and beat us, neither lynch us nor Jim Crow us every day. Colored folks rate as much protection as a buffalo, or a deer."

"You have a point there," I said.

"This here movie showed great big beautiful lakes with signs up all around:

NO FISHING—STATE GAME PRESERVE

But it did not show a single place with a sign up:

NO LYNCHING

It also showed flocks of wild ducks settling down in a nice green meadow behind a government sign that said:

NO HUNTING

It were nice and peaceful for them fish and ducks. There ought to be some place where it is nice and peaceful for me, too, even if I am not a fish or a duck.

"They showed one scene with two great big old longhorn elks locking horns on a Game Preserve somewhere out in Wyoming, fighting like mad. Nobody bothered them elks or tried to stop them from fighting. But just let me get in a little old fist fight here in this bar, they will lock me up and the Desk Sergeant will say, 'What are you colored boys doing, disturbing the peace?' Then they will give me thirty days and fine me twice as much as they would a white man for doing the same thing. There ought to be some place where I can fight in peace and not get fined them high fines."

"You disgust me," I said. "I thought you were talking about a place where you could be quiet and compose your mind. Instead, you are talking about fighting."

"I would like a place where I could do both," said Simple. "If the government can set aside some spot for a elk *to be a elk* without being bothered, or a fish *to be a fish* without getting hooked, or a buffalo *to be a buffalo* without being shot down, there ought to be some place in this American country where a Negro can be a Negro without being Jim Crowed. There ought to be a law. The next time I see my congressman, I am going to tell him to introduce a bill for Game Preserves for Negroes."

"The Southerners would filibuster it to death," I said.

"If we are such a problem to them Southerners," said Simple, "I should think they would want some place to preserve us out of their sight. But then, of course, you have to take into consideration that if the Negroes was taken out of the South, who would they lynch? What would they do for sport? A Game Preserve is for to keep people from bothering anything that is living.

"When that movie finished, it were sunset in Virginia and it showed a little deer and its mama laying down to sleep. Didn't nobody say, 'Get up, deer, you can't sleep here,' like they would to me if I was to go to the White Sulphur Springs Hotel."

" 'The foxes have holes, and the birds of the air have nests; but the Son of man hath not where to lay his head.' "

"That is why I want a Game Preserve for Negroes," said Simple.

HARRY GOLDEN

The Vertical Negro Plan

1956

Those who love North Carolina will jump at the chance to share in the great responsibility confronting our Governor and the State Legislature. A special session of the Legislature (July 25–28, 1956) passed a series of amendments to the State Constitution. These proposals submitted by the Governor and his Advisory Education Committee included the following:

(A) The elimination of the compulsory attendance law, "to prevent any child from being forced to attend a school with a child of another race."

(B) The establishment of "Education Expense Grants" for education in a private school, "in the case of a child assigned to a public school attended by a child of another race."

(C) A "uniform system of local option" whereby a majority of the folks in a school district may suspend or close a school if the situation becomes "intolerable."

But suppose a Negro child applies for this "Education Expense Grant" and says he wants to go to the private school too? There are fourteen Supreme Court decisions involving the use of public funds; there are only two "decisions" involving the elimination of racial discrimination in the public schools.

The Governor has said that critics of these proposals have not offered any constructive advice or alternatives. Permit me, therefore, to offer an idea for the consideration of the members of the regular sessions. A careful study of my plan, I believe, will show that it will save millions of dollars in tax funds and eliminate forever the danger to our public education system. Before I outline my plan, I would like to give you a little background.

One of the factors involved in our tremendous industrial growth and economic prosperity is the fact that the South, voluntarily, has all but eliminated VERTICAL SEGREGATION. The tremendous buying power of the twelve million Negroes in the South has been based wholly on the absence of racial segregation. The white and Negro stand at the same grocery and supermarket counters; deposit money at the same bank teller's window; pay phone and light bills to the same clerk; walk through the same dime and department stores, and stand at the same drugstore counters.

It is only when the Negro "sets" that the fur begins to fly.

Now, since we are not even thinking about restoring VERTICAL SEGREGATION, I think my plan would not only comply with the Supreme Court decisions, but would maintain "sitting-down" segregation. Now here is the GOLDEN VERTICAL NEGRO PLAN. Instead of all those complicated proposals, all the next session needs to do is pass one small amendment which would provide *only* desks in all the public schools of our state—*no seats*.

The desks should be those standing-up jobs, like the old-fashioned bookkeeping desk. Since no one in the South pays the slightest attention to a VERTICAL NEGRO, this will completely solve our problem. And it is not such a terrible inconvenience for young people to stand up during their classroom studies. In fact, this may be a blessing in disguise. They are not learning to read sitting down, anyway; maybe standing up will help. This will save more millions of dollars in the cost of our remedial English course when the kids enter college. In whatever direction you look, with the GOLDEN VERTICAL NEGRO PLAN you save millions of dollars, to say nothing of eliminating forever any danger to our public education system upon which rests the destiny, hopes, and happiness of this society.

MY WHITE BABY PLAN offers another possible solution to the segregation problem—this time in a field other than education.

Here is an actual case history of the "White Baby Plan to End Racial Segregation":

Some months ago there was a revival of the Laurence Olivier movie, *Hamlet*, and several Negro schoolteachers were eager to see it. One Saturday afternoon they asked some white friends to lend them two of their little children, a three-year-old girl and a six-year-old boy, and, holding these white children by the hands, they obtained tickets from the movie-house cashier without a moment's hesitation. They were in like Flynn.

This would also solve the baby-sitting problem for thousands and thousands of white working mothers. There can be a mutual exchange of references, then the people can sort of pool their children at a central point in each neighborhood, and every time a Negro wants to go to the movies all she need do is pick up a white child—and go.

Eventually the Negro community can set up a factory and manufacture white babies made of plastic, and when they want to go to the opera or to a concert, all they need do is carry that plastic doll in their arms. The dolls, of course, should all have blond curls and blue eyes, which would go even further; it would give the Negro woman and her husband priority over the whites for the very best seats in the house.

While I still have faith in the WHITE BABY PLAN, my final proposal may prove to be the most practical of all.

Only after a successful test was I ready to announce formally the GOLDEN "OUT-OF-ORDER" PLAN.

I tried my plan in a city of North Carolina, where the Negroes represent 39 percent of the population.

I prevailed upon the manager of a department store to shut the water off in his "white" water fountain and put up a sign, "Out-of-Order." For the first day or two the whites were hesitant, but little by little they began to drink out of the water fountain belonging to the "coloreds"— and by the end of the third week everybody was drinking the "segregated" water; with not a single solitary complaint to date.

I believe the test is of such sociological significance that the Governor should appoint a special committee of two members of the House and two Senators to investigate the GOLDEN "OUT-OF-ORDER" PLAN. We kept daily reports on the use of the unsegregated water fountain which should be of great value to this committee. This may be the answer to the necessary uplifting of the white morale. It is possible that the whites may accept desegregation if they are assured that the facilities are still "separate," albeit "Out-of-Order."

As I see it now, the key to my Plan is to keep the "Out-of-Order" sign up for at least two years. We must do this thing gradually.

ARTHUR HOPPE

White Moderates Are a Bit Limited

1963

Down in Alabama the Ku Klux Klan, which is fighting for all-out racial segregation, says "the most deadly and dangerous organization in the country today" is the Black Muslim Society. Which is fighting for all-out racial segregation.

In hopes of clarifying the split between these extremists, here is an exclusive interview with a middle-of-the-roader. Colonel Jefferson Davis Stonewall, president of The Southern Forces of Moderation. A group often quoted in the press these days.

Q: Colonel, what exactly is the stand of the Southern Moderate on the question of integration?

A: Well, son, we're for it and always have been. Within limits.

Q: Within limits?

A: That's right, boy. We favor taking colored folks into our homes, our theaters, our buses and our hearts. Within limits.

Q: Like?

A: Like the kitchens of our homes, the balconies of our theaters and the last three rows of our buses. But in our hearts, son, we go all the way.

Q: But the fight today, Colonel, seems more over integrating schools and lunch counters.

A: A lot of poppycock. We always allowed our darkies in our schools. Why, some of my fondest memories are of the colored folk I met in my schooling days at Ole Miss. There was Sam, who used to shine our shoes. And Old Homer, a-scrubbing the halls and—I don't know what we all would've done without them.

Q: I assume the same applies to lunch counters?

A: They been integrated down here for years. I ask you, a man's sitting on a stool on one side and a man's a-stacking dirty dishes on the other —they're both at the same lunch counter, aren't they?

Q: I think I see, Colonel. You're for integration within limits. But you're also for segregation.

A: That's why they call us Moderates, boy. You might say we stand for segregated integration. And gradualism.

Q: Gradualism?

A: Yep. We see things has got to change. But with effort and sacrifice on both sides it's our real hope that over the years things will gradually stay the way they are.

Q: Now about the Klan, Colonel—

A: Well, don't quote me, but we don't allow none of them in our Southern Forces of Moderation. Some of my best friends are Klansmen, mind you. But I say you let 'em in and they're going to give the place a bad name.

Q: But what about the Black Muslims? They're—

A: Radical, Red, rabble-rousing, racial agitators! Horsewhipping's too good for the likes of them!

Q: But, Colonel, they're for segregation, too. I mean they want all Negroes everywhere to pack up and move out to an all-Negro State.

A: That's going too far!

Q: But that would be real segregation, Colonel.

A: Son, when I look around at all our happy colored folk a-shining our shoes and a-mopping our floors and a-cleaning our lunch counters, I tell you from the bottom of my heart that us Southern Moderates are for segregation just like we're for integration.

Q: You mean?

A: Within limits.

GERALD WALKER

The Racial Inferiority of the White Southerner

1963

Some of my best friends are White Southerners, and I regret beyond words the necessity for raising questions which may sorely vex them. Yet the White Southerner Problem will never be solved if we continue to gloss over certain hard facts out of a shortsighted desire to spare a minority group's feelings. They—as well as we White Northerners—will be far better off if at last these troublesome matters are discussed openly.

Personally, I feel only the greatest affection and respect for the White Southerner, in his place. The trouble is, however, that lately the White Southerner has shown all too little awareness of what and where his proper place is. I refer, of course, to his precipitous turning away from his traditional agrarian way of life and his rather pushy efforts in recent years to attract new industry below the Mason-Dixon Line.

Now, generally speaking, it is certainly commendable for a backward region to try to raise itself. But I must add in all candor that the impatient, not to say aggressive, manner in which a handful of White Southerner agitators has gone about this task has sown the seeds of suspicion and competition between our two regions where previously there had been only harmony and understanding; indeed, inter-regional relations have deteriorated badly. Moreover, my concern goes far beyond the somewhat narrow consideration that a number of White Northerners have already lost their jobs as a result of their factories closing and moving South.

Rather, it seems to me that the real point is that perhaps it is time for the rest of the country to ask: Is the White Southerner really *ready* for progress? Is he trying to come too far too fast?

After all, the White Southerner is but one hundred years removed from practicing slavery. And while, admittedly, he had made rapid strides and come a long way since losing the Civil War to an adversary battle-proved to be his superior, has he yet *earned* the right of full participation in the industrialized mainstream of contemporary American life? Would it not be better for all concerned for the White Northerner to continue his stewardship of the South until such a time as there was not a shred of a doubt of the White Southerner's capacity to fend for himself?

For the plain fact of the matter is that there are vast areas of difference between the White Southerner and the White Northerner. These differences first became apparent to me when I was a carpetbagging freshman at the University of Georgia in 1945. At that time, though, I was still naive and inexperienced enough unquestioningly to accept the prevailing theory that regional differences stemmed from socioeconomic conditions.

Since then I have gotten to know the White Southerner well. I have lived in close proximity to these people for extended periods, visited their homes, broken bread with them, observed their customs, and gone

to their social functions. Making due allowance for the White Southerners' good qualities—humor, hospitality, charm, chattiness—I soon
came to realize that he was, in fact, a totally different and essentially
inferior breed when measured against his neighbor, the White Northerner.

These first-hand observations on my part have lately been substan-
tiated by the impartial findings of modern science, as set forth most
effectively by Carlton Putnam in his eye-opening work, *Race and Reason*. Mr. Putnam, whose extensive background as an airlines executive
led him directly into becoming a noted amateur authority in the fields of
anthropology, biology, psychology, and anatomy, is primarily concerned
with demonstrating the innate, hereditary factors which account for the
observable inferiority of the average Negro to the average White. (Some
indication of the brilliance with which he succeeded may be gathered
from the wide circulation—over 100,000 copies sold—and enthusiastic
reception that his book has enjoyed in Southern states since its publication in 1961: for example, Mississippi Governor Ross Barnett pro-
claimed October 26, 1961 as "Race And Reason Day," capped by a
$25-a-plate dinner in Putnam's honor. . . .

Valid scientific procedures are applicable to more than one set of
data. Thus, a yardstick may be used to measure the length of an eel as
well as a snake. It is only further proof of the usefulness of the anthropo-
logical and cultural criteria developed by Mr. Putnam and his school if
I now employ them in a painstaking, scientific comparison of the average WS[1] and the average WN.[2] As Mr. Putnam and similarly objective
researchers might say, let the chips fall where they may, it is only the
truth that we are after.

Let us begin with a few nineteenth-century observations.

Frederick Law Olmstead, the distinguished 19th-Century WN landscape architect, traveled throughout the entire Old South and in 1861,
in *The Cotton Kingdom*, he reported on his interviews with 500 WS
men in their own homes and across their own tables.

". . . Their destitution is not material only; it is intellectual and it is
moral. I know not what virtues they have that rude men everywhere have
not; but those which are commonly attributed to them, I am sure that
they lack; they are not generous or hospitable; and, to be plain, I must
say that their talk is not the talk of even courageous men elsewhere. They

[1] White Southerner.
[2] White Northerner.

boast and lack self-restraint, yet, when not excited, are habitually reserved and guarded in expressions of opinion very much like cowardly men elsewhere."

The WS may attempt to discount Olmstead's careful observations as the biased judgment of a Yankee. But it is impossible to explain away a strikingly similar description penned by Hinton Rowan Helper, a WS born in North Carolina, in 1857 in his book, *The Impending Crisis:*

"Poverty, ignorance, and superstition"—mind you, this is Helper talking about his fellow-WS's—"are the three leading characteristics of the non-slaveholding white of the South. Many of them grow up to the age of maturity, and pass through life without ever owning as much as five dollars at any one time. Thousands of them die at an advanced age, as ignorant of the common alphabet as if it had never been invented. All are more or less impressed with a belief in witches, ghosts, and supernatural signs. Few are exempt from habits of sensuality and intemperance. None have anything like adequate ideas of the duties which they owe either to their God, to themselves, or to their fellow-men. . . ."

Some might object that this is hardly a balanced portrait of WS society. What about, they might interject, the Southern Aristocrat? Aren't we distorting things by not including the finest flowering of Dixie's plantation civilization?

Here, then, is what historian Henry Adams had to say . . . about Rooney Lee, son of Robert E. Lee, and the other young Southern Bourbons whom he knew at Harvard from 1854 to 1858:

"Tall, largely built, handsome, genial," noted Adams, "with Liberal Virginia openness toward all he liked, he (Rooney Lee) had also the Virginian habit of command. . . . For a year, at least . . . was the most popular and prominent man in his class, but then seemed slowly to drop into the background. The habit of command was not enough, and the Virginian had little else. He was simple beyond analysis; so simple that even the simple New England student could not realize him. No one knew enough to know how ignorant he was; how childlike; how helpless. . . . As an animal the Southerner seemed to have every advantage, but even as an animal he steadily lost ground. . . . Strictly, the Southerner had no mind; he had temperament. He was not a scholar; he had no intellectual training; he could not analyze an idea, and he could not even conceive of admitting two. . . ."

Of course, it may be objected that [these] are but isolated impressions, albeit perceptive ones based on careful observation and investigation. What is needed, it might be said, is large-scale, objective, *up-to-date* evidence concerning the physical and mental makeup of the WS. For precisely this sort of data, let us now examine some highly revealing selective service statistics from World Wars I and II.

In 1917 army psychologists devised what they called the Beta intelligence test to which inductees were subjected. A leading segregationist intellectual spokesman, *Richmond News Leader* editor James Jackson Kilpatrick, cited a sampling of the Beta test results in his recent book, *The Southern Case for School Segregation*. Even the figures selected by him show the WS running a poor second to the WN, as can be seen from the following:

WHITE SOUTHERNERS AND WHITE NORTHERNERS ARMY INTELLIGENCE TESTS, 1918

WS		WN	
State	*Median Score*	*State*	*Median Score*
Mississippi	41.25	Pennsylvania	64.6
Kentucky	41.50	New York	64.0
Arkansas	41.55	Illinois	63.0
Georgia	42.12	Ohio	66.7

Oddly enough, although Mr. Kilpatrick used a similar differential between White Southerners and Negro Southerners as the basis for arguing the latter's inferiority and for justifying segregation, he did not feel logically impelled to draw the same conclusions about the WS in relation to the WN. This is a contemporary example of the WS's inability to conceive of admitting two ideas at once, first pointed out by Henry Adams a century ago.

In the three and a half decades between World Wars I and II, the WS—thanks to prodigious efforts by the Federal government and private foundations—experienced notable increases in educational, cultural, economic, health, and social opportunities. Surely, it might be supposed, these gains would have been reflected in some significant improvement in his showing when tested for military service. No such improvement can be discerned.

Illuminating also are the statistics showing the prevalence of certain specific defects per 1,000 white registrants from November, 1940 to December, 1943:

Region I (The North)
Syphilis—9.0

Gonorrhea and other venereal diseases—1.6
Educational and mental deficiency—21.5
Region IV (The South)
Syphilis—20.7
Gonorrhea, etc.—3.2
Educational and mental deficiency—69.2

The WS's poor showing physically and mentally is matched only by his moral deficiencies and criminal inclinations. . . . In particular, crimes of violence are an old Southern custom. Charlotte, N.C. was once known as "The Murder Capital of America." Writing in 1941, WS historian W. J. Cash said, ". . . long before hatred for the black man had begun to play any direct part in the pattern (of more than three hundred persons said to have been hanged or burned by mobs in the South between 1840 and 1860, less than ten percent were Negroes) the South had become peculiarly the home of lynching." . . .

Cash also pointed out that FBI official murder rates showed that ". . . the Southern cities were over five times as murderous as those of either the North Central area or the Far West, over six times as those of the Middle Atlantic country, and over eighteen times as those of New England!" True, slum Negroes did account for many of these Southern murders. But since the WS was the dominant majority in the South, it cannot escape the responsibility for having set the moral tone of the region, of which the over-all murder rate is but a reflection.

Still another peculiarly Southern crime is the deliberate setting of forest fires, folksily called "fire-strolling" by WS's. The region has one-fourth of the nation's forest acreage, but it is annually the scene of over 80 percent of U.S. forest fires. No less than 35 percent of Southern forest fires during 1956, according to an authoritative estimate, were the work of deliberate woods burners. In Louisiana, Mississippi, and Florida the percentage ran to 50 percent. . . .

Not only does the WS law-*breaker* show disproportionate violence and criminality, but there is a similar tendency operating among WS law *enforcers*. This blood-lust is particularly irresistible to WS judges and juries. For although the South holds less than one-third of the country's total population, year after year no less than two-thirds of American executions take place there.

In an attempt to escape the crime, violence, and primitive living standards which pervade their native region, over 4,000,000 Southerners

—White and Negro—left Dixie during the 1950s, somewhat more than the number of persons who fled East Germany during a comparable period. . . .

Albert N. Votaw, in the February, 1958 *Harper's*, described the prickly integration problem the WS presented to a typical Northern city. At that time there were 70,000 WS recent arrivals in Chicago. Settling together in one South Side neighborhood, they presented the authorities with a number of difficulties. A police captain was quoted as saying, "They are vicious and knife-happy. They are involved in 75 percent of our arrests in this district." Observed a municipal court judge, ". . . you'll never improve the neighborhood until you get rid of them."

The Chicago Sunday Tribune summed things up this way: "The Southern hillbilly migrants, who have descended like a plague of locusts in the last few years, have the lowest standard of living and moral code (if any), the biggest capacity for liquor, and the most savage tactics when drunk, which is most of the time."

Obviously, the WS isn't the same kind of person as the WN. He just isn't accustomed to or perhaps capable of living the same way the rest of us do, and we should make allowances for that fact. However, at the same time, we should put some sensible limit on the extent of the WS's participation in business, national affairs, and inter-regional social contact. After all, as Harry Golden has said, would you want your sister to marry a Governor Faubus?

The WS may very well represent an insoluble problem. In any event it is a problem that will take time—a great deal of time, perhaps centuries—to even approach solving. No one denies the economic disparity between WS and WN, but this is only a reflection of genetic facts. Hereditary equality and total, massive integration of the WS into the national economy are things that can neither be rushed nor legislated. We must maintain perspective and not plunge headlong into a dubious social experiment for the sake of some vague, abstract idea of justice. Our system may not be perfect, but it approaches true justice for all more closely than any other.

WS and WN should each stick to their own kind, moving forward separately and harmoniously as in the past. The WS should have enough regional and racial pride to want to develop in his own way and at his own natural pace, not force himself in when and where he isn't wanted. Besides, geographical separation is a basic law of nature. If the good Lord had intended WS's and WN's to work and live in the same way and locale, He would not have created a North and a South in the first place.

What, after all, has the WS contributed to American civilization? It is an extraordinary catalogue: hookworm, slavery, the filibuster, hominy grits, the Ku Klux Klan, pellagra, Mint Juleps, lynching, the University of Mississippi, and high treason in seceding from the Union. *Sic transit gloria* moonshine. . . .

It would be patently unfair to leave the impression that *all* WS's are naturally primitive, violent, criminal, shiftless, promiscuous, uncultured, and undistinguished. There have been a number, perhaps a hundred over the past three and a half centuries, who do not fall into those categories—but many of these *had Northern blood.* . . .

It only needs to be said that the average rank-and-file WS today is well satisfied with things as they are, but is being goaded on by a handful of agitators and fomentors into making more demands than the country can safely meet, or than WS's as a whole could handle in their present stage of development. . . .

JULES FEIFFER

The Dogs

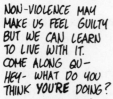

CHARLES ALVERSON

Every Neighborhood Needs One

1963

The Northern neighborhood that wants to avoid the stigma of being labeled lilywhite and the nuisance of being the target of pickets, sit-ins, lie-ins and just plain hang-around-ins cannot afford to be without an emergency Negro family in a glass case.

The beauty of this Negro family is that it ends forever accusations of *de facto* segregation without actually entailing any risk to the neighborhood.

Here's how it works. There you are; in a fine, upstanding American community. Not a boy in the neighborhood you wouldn't want to marry your daughter. But one Tuesday morning, suddenly something is different, disturbing. The NAACP has thrown a picket line across Elm Street, and you've got trouble.

But do you panic? Not with this handy, easy-to-get-at Negro family all ready for action. You just go out to the picket line, take Roy Wilkins by the hand to 42½D Watkins Lane and show him *your* colored family. Then watch those pickets pack up their signs, get in their buses and leave.

But now some of the advantages of the glass-enclosed Negro family that make it vastly superior to actual integration. The average unit consists of a father, a mother, and 2.5 children. The father in the unit is around 35, dark in complexion, but not *too* dark. Once integration threatens and you break the glass, he works as an assistant letter sorter at the Post Office. This job manages to support his family but just barely, thus preventing unseemly keeping up with the Joneses.

His job also provides the family with a car at least a year older than that of anyone else on the block—not a flashy Cadillac, but a serviceable 1953 Hudson. The father—whose name in Andrew Jackson Brown —call him Andy—keeps his yard tidy and takes a quiet pride in the feats of Willie Mays, Wilma Rudolph, and Louis Armstrong but not those of Sonny Liston. There is something he finds unseemly about a Negro fighting—and beating—white men. He quietly disapproves of the NAACP and CORE and is shocked by the Black Muslims.

The mother in the Negro family unit is a shade darker than her husband and not attractive. She did not finish high school but is quite obviously the strongest member of the family. Often she will have to work, and when she does she makes slightly more than her husband. Alma, as the mother is named, is a teetotaller and reproves Andy humorously when he drinks one of the five beers he is allowed per month. Alma is far too busy to take part in neighborhood clubs or activities but can always be counted on for the bare minimum contribution to a fund drive.

The son in the unit, Andy, Jr., gets average or slightly below average grades and is content to be a guard on the football team. Always slightly respectful toward white girls, he has too much "racial pride" to think of dating one. He has a boyish reverence for Abraham Lincoln. After high school he will attend a college nobody ever heard of where he will study pharmacy. He will then move far away. This is in itself a plus factor.

The daughter in your neighborhood's emergency Negro family, Francine, takes after her mother. She is very dark and wears braces but is bright—but not too bright—in school and wants to "better the lot of her people." She is very helpful in coaching other students and works backstage on the senior play. When a renegade white boy asks her to go to the senior prom she refuses, making it clear that it "just would not be right." Instead she helps out in the checkroom. She will go to college to study to become a social worker but will become pregnant in her junior year and disappear, probably to Chicago where she will turn to a life of sin.

Every other unit has a small baby. He will look "exactly like a little monkey." The baby will be sickly, walk and talk later than your own children, and will die of "weak blood" at the age of four. Everyone will be very sorry.

This glass-encased emergency Negro family has many added advantages that will more than make up for its moderate cost. The family has absolutely no friends or relatives, so there is no danger of a house and yard full of Negroes over the week-end. You can safely invite them to parties and barbecues without fear that they will accept. And if you ever need someone to play a Negro in a play, parade or pageant, you needn't resort to blackface.

All these and many more features make this Negro family something your neighborhood must have. Act now. With the recently accelerated demand you may wait too long and end up with a house full of uppity niggers.

RALPH ELLISON

*The Political Nigra**

". . . Gentlemen, I'm going to tell you once and for all, I'm going to impress upon you once and for all, the fact that everything the Nigra does is political. I don't like to take up so sobering a matter so early in the evening but some of us here are getting too drunk too soon—"

"Do you mean 'everything' literally?" Wiggins said.

"I mean *everything*," McGowan said. "And especially things which you Yankees would pass over as insignificant. We can start at random. Listen: If you catch a Nigra in the wrong section of town after dark— he's being political because he knows he's got no business being there. If he brushes against a white man on the street or on a stairway, that's very political. Because every once in a while the Nigras get together and organize these 'bumping campaigns' against the white folks. They'll try to knock you off the sidewalk and break your ribs and then they'll beg your pardon as though it was an accident, when we know damn well that it was politics.

"So watch the Nigra's face. If a Nigra rolls his eyes and pokes out his mouth at you—that's downright subversive. If he puts on aristocratic airs—watch him! If he talks about moving up North, he's being political again. Because we know for a fact that the Nigras are moving North in keeping with a long-range plan to seize control of the American government. If he talks too loud on the street or talks about sending his kids up North to college in your presence, or if he buys a tractor—all this is political. Be especially wary of the Nigra who tries to buy himself

* from a forthcoming novel.

a bulldozer so he can compete against white men because that is one of the most dangerous political acts of all. A Nigra like that is out to knock down Southern tradition and bury it, lock stock and barrel. He's worse than a whole herd of carpetbaggers or seven lean years of bollweevils. Waiter," he called to Sam, "bring us another round!" and then to us, "There's absolutely nothing to dry a man out like trying to educate a bunch of Yankees."

As I watched Sam approach, I became uneasy that McGowan in his excitement would offend him. After all, I had learned during the Thirties to respect the sensibilities of his people and to avoid all anti-minority stereotypes and clichés. One simply didn't laugh at unfortunates—within their hearing. But if Sam was aware of our conversation his face revealed nothing.

"Hy ya, Sam," McGowan said.

"Fine, Mr. McGowan," Sam said, and looking around the table, "Gentlemen?"

And we ordered, after which Sam slipped away.

"Let me tell y'all something else," McGowan went on. "If you catch a Nigra buying his food and clothing from the wrong dealer—or worse, if he goes to another town to trade, that's Nigra politics *pretending* to be Nigra economics. That's something for you to think about, Wiggins. If a Nigra owns more than one shotgun, rifle, or pistol, it's political. If he forgets to say 'sir' to a white man or tries to talk Yankee talk or if he drives too doggone slow or too doggone fast, or if he comes up with one of these little bug-eyed foreign cars—all these things are political and don't you forget it!"

McGowan paused. Sam was crossing the floor with a tray of drinks, which he placed before us and left.

"Come on, educate us some more," Thompson said. "Then we can talk seriously."

McGowan's eyes twinkled. "I'd be glad to. But if you think this isn't serious, study history. For instance, if a Nigra buys his woman a washing machine—watch him, he's dangerous! And if he gets her a clothes dryer and a dishwasher—put that Nigra under the jail for trying to undercut our American way of life. You all can smile if you want to but things like that are most political. In fact, there are few things in this world as political as a black Nigra woman owning her own washing machine.

"Now don't laugh about it. You Yankees must remember that the Industrial Revolution was *revolutionary*, because if y'all don't the Nigra does, and he never stops scheming to make it more so. So verily verily I say unto you Yankees: Watch the Nigra who owns more than one TV because he's getting too ambitious and that's bound to lead him into politics. What's more, if you allow the Nigra to see Indians killing white folks week after week—which is another Yankee mistake—he's apt to go bad and the next thing you know he's learning about that Nehru, Nasser, and those Mau-Maus and that's most politically unwise. It doesn't matter that the Indians are always defeated because the Nigra has the feeling deep down that *he* can win. After all, Nigras are Southern too.

"And I'll tell you something else: If his woman or his gal chillin come up wearing blonde wigs, or if they dye their kinky Nigra hair red, you might think it amusing but I know that those Nigra women are being defiantly political. On the other hand, if they *stop* straightening their hair in the old Southern darky tradition and start wearing it short and natural like those African Nigras—right there you have you a bunch of homegrown Nigras who're on the way to being hopelessly contaminated. Those Nigras are sweating and breathing politics. Call Edgar Hoover!

.   .   .   .

"If a Nigra joins the Book-of-the-Month Club or the Great Books program—investigate him. Because when a Nigra gets hold to such deals they become more political than *Das Kapital* and the Communist Manifesto put together. There was a time when everybody thought that the Bible was the only book that a Nigra should be allowed to read, but now I be damned if he hasn't even made the Good Book political. . . .

"But now let's look into another area. You want to watch what the Nigra eats because it has been established that some Nigra foods are political while others are not. And it's a proven fact that the moment the Nigra changes his diet he gets dissatisfied and restless. So watch what he eats. Fat meat, cornbread, lima beans, ham hocks, chitterlings, watermelon, blackeyed peas, molasses, collard greens, buttermilk and clabber, neckbones and red beans and rice, hominy, both grit and lye hominy— these are traditional foods and healthy for the Nigra and *usually*—and I stress the *usually*—not political—"

"What about chicken," Larkin said, "you overlooked chicken."

"Chicken is no problem," McGowan said. "It's traditional and harmless in the political sense—unless, of course, a wrong-headed political Nigra is caught stealing one. And even so, there's nothing necessarily political about a Nigra stealing a chicken. In fact, down South we agree that a Nigra's suppose to steal him a chicken every now and then and the only crime involved is in his getting caught.

"But," McGowan said, holding up his hand and allowing it to slap the table, *Pow! "lobster* is out!"

Wiggins sputtered over his drink. "Oh Lord," he said. "Oh Lord protect us!"

"Gentlemen, I tell you truly, lobster on a Nigra's table is political as hell. Lobster gives him false courage. It puts rocks in his Nigra jaws and wild ideas in his Nigra brain. In short, lobster, any kind of lobster, broiled, boiled, fried, fradiavalloed—serve it anyway you damn please— lobster simply messes a Nigra *up*. If the price of lobster ever hits bottom this country will have bad trouble. . . .

"Now Thompson, here was talking about our not having any 'forms' through which we can see what the Nigra is up to politically and I've been demonstrating that he's mistaken. But he's right to the extent that the Nigra hasn't developed any forms of his own. He's just copied the white man and twisted what he copied to fit the Nigra taste. But he does have his own Nigra church, and his own Nigra religion, and the point I want to make is that he gets *political* according to his religion. Did you ever hear that explained before?"

"*I* haven't," I said.

"I know it. None of you have; so I'll go on and tell you. Baptist Nigras and Methodist Nigras and Holy Roller Nigras are O.K. Even Seven Day Adventist Nigras are all right—even though they're a bit strange even to other Nigras. All these Nigra religions are O.K. But you have got to watch the Nigra who changes *from* Baptist *to* Episcopalian *or* Catholic. Because that is a Nigra who has gone ambitious and turned his back on the South. And make no mistake, that Nigra isn't searching for God, no siree; he's looking for a political scantling to head-whip you with. . . .

"Here are some other forms of Nigra politics which y'all have overlooked: these young buck Nigras going around wearing berets, beards and tennis shoes in the wintertime and whose britches are so doggone tight that they look like they're 'bout to bust out of them. They're not the same as the white boys who dress that way, they're politically dangerous and it's worse, in the long run, than letting a bunch of Nigras run around the Capital carrying loaded pistols. A law ought to be passed before something serious occurs.

"And be on watch for your quiet Nigra. Be very careful of the Nigra who's too quiet when other loud-mouthed Nigras—who are safe Nigras

—are out sassing white folks on the street corners and in the Yankee press and over the Yankee radio and TV. Never mind the loudmouths, they're like the little fyce dogs that bark at you when you approach the big gate and then, when you walk into the yard they run to lick your hand. Throw them a bone. But keep your eye on the quiet Nigra who watches every move the white man makes and studies it, because he's probably trying to think up a theory and a strategy and tactic to subvert something—" . . .

"And pay close attention to the Nigra who has the money to buy [a Cadillac] but picks an Imperial instead. Likewise the Nigras who love English autos. Watch all Nigras who pick Jaguars, Humbers, and if you ever hear of one, Rolls Royces. Likewise those who go around bragging about the Nigra vote electing the president of the United States. Such Nigras are playing dirty politics even though they might not be able to vote themselves. Yes, and watch the Nigra who comes telling a white man about the Nigra's 'gross yearly income,' because there you have an arrogant, biggety Nigra who is right up in your face talking open politics and who thinks you don't recognize it. Unless of course, you're convinced that the Nigra is really trying to tell you that he knows how you and him can make some quick money. In such a case the Nigra is just trying to make a little hustle for himself, so make a deal with him and don't worry about it because that Nigra doesn't give a damn about anybody or anything except himself—while the other type is trying to intimidate you.

"Then there's the Nigra who reads the Constitution and the law books and *broods* over them. That's one of the most political types there is. And like unto him is the Nigra who scratches his behind when he talks to a white man instead of scratching his head in the traditional Southern Nigra manner—because even where the Nigra *scratches* is political!" . . .

9 WAR AND PEACE

FROM THE AMERICAN REVOLUTION
TO THE FUTURE, IF ANY

The selections in this section deal with the kind of American politics that transcends borders—national and even terrestrial. War may be the ultimate expression of foreign policy, which in turn may be an extension of domestic politics, but the distinctions become increasingly difficult to make. And deliberate satire can hardly hope to match the nightmare burlesque of learned men earnestly debating the finer points of nuclear holocaust.

Under these circumstances it seems unlikely that a political humorist could and would influence United States foreign policy to any important extent. But it has not always been a farfetched notion. The mordant writings of Finley Peter Dunne, for example, have been generally credited with substantial changes in American methods, if not objectives, in the Philippines at the beginning of the century. Dunne was probably the most effective political satirist this country has yet produced; in his prime, "Mr. Dooley" was read throughout the nation, and was discussed regularly at Cabinet meetings. Perhaps the time has come for a successor to his eminence.

THE OLD DAYS AND THE OLD WAYS

This version of the classic Revolutionary War song is attributed to Edward Bangs, a 1775 Minute Man who was an undergraduate at Harvard when he wrote it.

EDWARD BANGS

The Farmer and His Son's

Return From a Visit to the Camp
(Yankee Doodle)

Father and I went down to Camp,
    Along with Captain *Goodin,*
And there we see the Men and Boys,
    As thick as Hasty-pudding;

CHORUS

Yankey doodle, keep it up,
    Yankey doodle-dandy,
Mind the Musick and the Step,
    And with the Girls be handy.

And there we see a Thousand Men,
    As rich as 'Squire *David,*
And what they wasted every Day,
    I wish it could be saved.

The 'Lasses they eat every Day,
    Would keep an House a Winter;
They have as much that I'll be bound
    They eat it when they're a mind to.

And there we see a swamping Gun,
    Large as a Log of Maple,
Upon a ducid little Cart,
    A Load for Father's Cattle,

And every Time they shoot it off,
    It takes an Horn of Powder,
It makes a noise like Father's Gun,
    Only a Nation louder.

I went as nigh to one myself,
    As '*Siah's* Underpinning;
And Father went as nigh again,
    I tho't the Duce was in him.

Cousin *Simon* grew so bold
    I tho't he would have cock'd it;
It scar'd me so I shriek'd it off,
    And hung by Father's Pocket.

And Captain *Davis* had a Gun,
    He kind of clapt his Hand on't,
And stuck a crooked stabbing Iron
    Upon the little End on't.

And there I see a Pumkin-Shell
    As big as Mother's Bason,
And every Time they touch'd it off
    They scamper'd like the Nation.

I see a little Barrel too,
    The Heads were made of Leather,
They knock'd upon with little Clubs,
    And call'd the Folks together.

And there was Captain *Washington*,
    And Gentlefolks about him;
They say he's grown so tarnal proud
    He will not ride without them.

He got him on his Meeting-Clothes,
    Upon a Slapping Stallion,
He set the World along in Rows,
    In Hundreds and in Millions.

The flaming Ribbons in his Hat,
    They look'd so taring fine ah,
I wanted pockily to get,
    To give to my Jemimah.

I see another Snarl of Men,
    A digging Graves, they told me,
So tarnal long, so tarnal deep,
    They 'tended they should hold me.

It scar'd me so I hook'd it off,
    Nor stopt as I remember,
Nor turn'd about 'till I got Home,
    Lock'd up in Mother's Chamber.

Every schoolboy knows that the British used mercenaries at Valley Forge; what is not so well-known is that the German princes who supplied them were "reimbursed" for those who were killed, as if for damaged merchandise. Franklin's "letter," from one of these suppliers to his field commander, was circulated in Europe.

BENJAMIN FRANKLIN

The Sale of the Hessians

1777

Monsieur Le Baron:—On my return from Naples, I received at Rome your letter of the 27th December of last year. I have learned with unspeakable pleasure the courage our troops exhibited at Trenton, and you cannot imagine my joy on being told that of the 1,950 Hessians engaged in the fight, but 345 escaped. There were just 1,605 men killed, and I cannot sufficiently commend your prudence in sending an exact list of the dead to my minister in London. This precaution was the more necessary, as the report sent to the English ministry does not give but 1,455 dead. This would make 483,450 florins instead of 643,500 which I am entitled to demand under our convention. You will comprehend the prejudice which such an error would work in my finances, and I do not doubt you will take the necessary pains to prove that Lord North's list is false and yours correct.

The court of London objects that there were a hundred wounded who ought not to be included in the list, nor paid for as dead; but I trust you will not overlook my instructions to you on quitting Cassel, and that you will not have tried by human succor to recall the life of the unfortunates whose days could not be lengthened but by the loss of a leg or an arm. That would be making them a pernicious present, and I am sure they would rather die than live in a condition no longer fit for my service. I do not mean by this that you should assassinate them; we should be humane, my dear Baron, but you may insinuate to the surgeons with entire propriety that a crippled man is a reproach to their profession, and that there is no wiser course than to let every one of them die when he ceases to be fit to fight.

I am about to send to you some new recruits. Don't economize them. Remember glory before all things. Glory is true wealth. There is nothing degrades the soldier like the love of money. He must care only for honour and reputation, but this reputation must be acquired in the midst of dangers. A battle gained without costing the conqueror any blood is an inglorious success, while the conquered cover themselves with glory by perishing with their arms in their hands. Do you remember that of the 300 Lacedæmonians who defended the defile of Thermopylæ, not one returned? How happy should I be could I say the same of my brave Hessians!

It is true that their king, Leonidas, perished with them: but things have changed, and it is no longer the custom for princes of the empire to go and fight in America for a cause with which they have no concern. And besides, to whom should they pay the thirty guineas per man if I did not stay in Europe to receive them? Then, it is necessary also that I be ready to send recruits to replace the men you lose. For this purpose I must return to Hesse. It is true, grown men are becoming scarce there, but I will send you boys. Besides, the scarcer the commodity the higher the price. I am assured that the women and little girls have begun to till our lands, and they get on not badly. You did right to send back to Europe that Dr. Crumerus who was so successful in curing dysentery. Don't bother with a man who is subject to looseness of the bowels. That disease makes bad soldiers. One coward will do more mischief in an engagement than ten brave men will do good. Better that they burst in their barracks than fly in a battle, and tarnish the glory of our arms. Besides, you know that they pay me as killed for all who die from disease, and I don't get a farthing for runaways. My trip to Italy, which has cost me enormously, makes it desirable that there should be a great mortality among them. You will therefore promise promotion to all who expose themselves; you will exhort them to seek glory in the midst of dangers; you will say to Major Maundorff: that I am not at all content with his saving the 345 men who escaped the massacre of Trenton. Through the whole campaign he has not had ten men killed in consequence of his orders. Finally, let it be your principal object to prolong the war and avoid a decisive engagement on either side, for I have made arrangements for a grand Italian opera, and I do not wish to be obliged to give it up. Meantime I pray God, my dear Baron de Hohendorf, to have you in his holy and gracious keeping.

Newell's "Orhpeus C. Kerr" (office-seeker, that is, which may not be as obvious now as it was a century ago), creator of the "Mackerel Brigade," was probably the funniest of the Civil War satirists, as well as the easiest to read today.

ORPHEUS C. KERR

(ROBERT HENRY NEWELL)

The Latest Improvements in Artillery

Washington, D.C., August—, 1861

By invitation of a well-known official, I visited the Navy-Yard yesterday, and witnessed the trial of some newly-invented rifled cannon. The trial was of short duration, and the jury brought in a verdict of "innocent of any intent to kill."

The first gun tried was similar to those used in the Revolution, except that it had a larger touch-hole, and the carriage was painted green, instead of blue. This novel and ingenious weapon was pointed at a target about sixty yards distant. It didn't hit it, and as nobody saw any ball, there was much perplexity expressed. A midshipman did say that he thought the ball must have run out of the touch-hole when they loaded up—for which he was instantly expelled from the service. After a long search without finding the ball, there was some thought of summoning the Naval Retiring Board to decide on the matter, when somebody happened to look into the mouth of the cannon, and discovered that the ball hadn't gone out at all. The inventor said this would happen sometimes, especially if you didn't put a brick over the touch-hole when you fired the gun. The Government was so pleased with this explanation, that it ordered forty of the guns on the spot, at two hundred thousand dollars apiece. The guns to be furnished as soon as the war is over.

The next weapon tried was Jink's double back-action revolving cannon for ferry-boats. It consists of a heavy bronze tube, revolving on a pivot, with both ends open, and a touch-hole in the middle. While one gunner puts a load in at one end, another puts in a load at the other end, and one touch-hole serves for both. Upon applying the match, the gun is whirled swiftly round on a pivot, and both balls fly out in circles, causing great slaughter on both sides. This terrible engine was aimed at the target with great accuracy; but as the gunner has a large family dependent on him for support, he refused to apply the match. The Government was satisfied without firing, and ordered six of the guns at a million dollars apiece. The guns to be furnished in time for our next war.

The last weapon subjected to trial was a mountain howitzer of a new pattern. The inventor explained that its great advantage was, that it required no powder. In battle it is placed on the top of a high mountain, and a ball slipped loosely into it. As the enemy passes the foot of the mountain, the gunner in charge tips over the howitzer, and the ball rolls down the side of the mountain into the midst of the doomed foe. The range of this terrible weapon depends greatly on the height of the mountain and the distance to its base. The Government ordered forty of these mountain howitzers at a hundred thousand dollars apiece, to be planted on the first mountains discovered in the enemy's country.

These are great times for gunsmiths, my boy; and if you find any old cannon around the junk-shops, just send them along.

There is much sensation in nautical circles arising from the immoral conduct of the rebel privateers; but public feeling has been somewhat easier since the invention of a craft for capturing the pirates, by an ingenious Connecticut chap. Yesterday he exhibited a small model of it at a cabinet meeting, and explained it thus:

"You will perceive," says he to the President, "that the machine itself will only be four times the size of the Great Eastern, and need not cost over a few millions of dollars. I have only got to discover one thing before I can make it perfect. You will observe that it has a steam-engine on board. This engine works a pair of immense iron clamps, which are let down into the water from the extreme end of a very lengthy horizontal spar. Upon approaching the pirate, the captain orders the engineer to put on steam. Instantly the clamps descend from the end of the spar and clutch the privateer athwartships. Then the engine is reversed, the privateer is lifted bodily out of the water, the spar swings around over the deck, and the pirate ship is let down into the hold by the run. Then shut your hatches, and you have ship and pirates safe and sound."

The President's gothic features lighted up beautifully at the words of the great inventor; but in a moment they assumed an expression of doubt, and says he:

"But how are you going to manage, if the privateer fires upon you while you are doing this?"

"My dear sir," says the inventor, "I told you I had only one thing to discover before I could make the machine perfect, and that's it."

So you see, my boy, there's a prospect of our doing something on the ocean next century, and there's only one thing in the way of our taking in pirates by the cargo.

Last evening a new brigadier-general, aged ninety-four years, made a speech to Regiment Five, Mackerel Brigade, and then furnished each man with a lead-pencil. He said that, as the Government was disappointed about receiving some provisions it had ordered for the troops, those pencils were intended to enable them to draw their rations as usual. I got a very big pencil, my boy, and have lived on a sheet of paper ever since.

Yours, pensively,
Orpheus C. Kerr

"Bill Arp" was the Confederacy's most popular wit.

BILL ARP

(CHARLES HENRY SMITH)

Letter to Mr. Abe Lincoln

April, 1861

Mr. Lincoln—

Sir: These are to inform you that we are all well, and hope these lines may find you in *statu quo*. We received your proclamation, and as you have put us on very short notice, a few of us boys have concluded to write you, and ask for a little more time. The fact is, we are most obliged to have a few more days, for the way things are happening, it is utterly impossible for us to disperse in twenty days. Old Virginia, and Tennessee, and North Carolina are continually aggravating us into tumults and carousments, and a body can't disperse until you put a stop to such unruly conduct on their part. I tried my darn'dst yesterday to disperse and retire, but it was no go; and besides, your marshal here ain't doing a darn'd thing—he don't read the riot-act, nor remonstrate, nor nothing, and ought to be turned out. If you conclude to do so, I am authorized to recommend to you Colonel Gibbons or Mr. McClung, who would attend to the business as well as most anybody.

The fact is, the boys around here want watching, or they'll take something. A few days ago I heard they surrounded two of our best citizens because they were named Fort and Sumter. Most of them are so hot that they fairly siz when you pour water on them, and that's the way they make up their military companies here now—when a man applies to join the volunteers, they sprinkle him, and if he sizzes they take him, and if he don't they don't.

Mr. Lincoln, sir, privately speaking, I'm afraid I'll get in a tight place here among these bloods, and have to slope out of it, and I would like much to have your Scotch cap and cloak that you travelled in to Washington. I suppose you wouldn't be likely to use the same disguise again when you left, and therefore I would propose to swap. I am five feet five, and could get my plough breeches and coat to you in eight or ten days if you can wait that long. I want you to write to me immediately about things generally, and let us know where you intend to do your fighting. Your proclamation says something about taking possession of all the private property at "All Hazards." We can't find no such a place on the map. I thought it must be about Charleston, or Savannah, or Harper's Ferry, but they say it ain't anywhere down South. One man said it was a little factory on an island in Lake Champlain, where they make sand-bags. My opinion is, that sand-bag business won't pay, and it is a great waste of money. Our boys here carry their sand in their gizzards, where it keeps better, and is always handy. I'm afraid your Government is giving you and your Kangaroo a great deal of unnecessary trouble, and my humble advice is, if things don't work better soon, you'd better grease it, or trade the darn'd old thing off. I'd take rails or any thing for it. If I could see you, I'd show you a sleight-of-hand trick that would change the whole concern into buttons quick. If you don't trade or do something else with it soon, it will spoil or die on your hands certain.

Give my respects to Bill Seward and the other members of the Kangaroo. What's Hannibal doing? I don't hear any thing from him now-a-days.

Yours, with care,
Bill Arp.

P.S.—If you can possibly extend that order to thirty days, do so. We have sent you a CHECK at Harper's Ferry (who keeps that darn'd old Ferry now? it's giving us a heap of trouble), but if you positively won't extend, we'll send you a check, drawn by Jeff. Davis, Beauregard endorser, payable on sight anywhere.

Yours,
B. A.

AMBROSE BIERCE

Jupiter Doke, Brigadier-General

From the Secretary of War to the Hon. Jupiter Doke, Hardpan Cross-roads, Posey County, Illinois.

Washington, November 3, 1861.

Having faith in your patriotism and ability, the President has been pleased to appoint you a brigadier-general of volunteers. Do you accept?

From the Hon. Jupiter Doke to the Secretary of War.

Hardpan, Illinois, November 9, 1861.

It is the proudest moment of my life. The office is one which should be neither sought nor declined. In times that try men's souls the patriot knows no North, no South, no East, no West. His motto should be: "My country, my whole country and nothing but my country." I accept the great trust confided in me by a free and intelligent people, and with a firm reliance on the principles of constitutional liberty, and invoking the guidance of an all-wise Providence, Ruler of Nations, shall labor so to discharge it as to leave no blot upon my political escutcheon. Say to his Excellency, the successor of the immortal Washington in the Seat of Power, that the patronage of my office will be bestowed with an eye single to securing the greatest good to the greatest number, the stability of republican institutions and the triumph of the party in all elections; and to this I pledge my life, my fortune and my sacred honor. I shall at once prepare an appropriate response to the speech of the chairman of the committee deputed to inform me of my appointment, and I trust the sentiments therein expressed will strike a sympathetic chord in the public heart, as well as command the Executive approval.

From the Secretary of War to Major-General Blount Wardorg, Commanding the Military Department of Eastern Kentucky.

Washington, November 14, 1861.

I have assigned to your department Brigadier-General Jupiter Doke, who will soon proceed to Distilleryville, on the Little Buttermilk River, and take command of the Illinois Brigade at that point, reporting to you by letter for orders. Is the route from Covington by way of Bluegrass, Opossum Corners and Horsecave still infested with bushwackers, as reported in your last dispatch? I have a plan for cleaning them out.

From Major-General Blount Wardorg to the Secretary of War.

Louisville, Kentucky, November 20, 1861.

The name and services of Brigadier-General Doke are unfamiliar to me, but I shall be pleased to have the advantage of his skill. The route from Covington to Distilleryville *via* Opossum Corners and Horsecave I have been compelled to abandon to the enemy, whose guerilla warfare made it impossible to keep it open without detaching too many troops from the front. The brigade at Distilleryville is supplied by steamboats up the Little Buttermilk.

From the Secretary of War to Brigadier-General Jupiter Doke, Hardpan, Illinois.

Washington, November 26 1861.

I deeply regret that your commission had been forwarded by mail before the receipt of your letter of acceptance; so we must dispense with the formality of official notification to you by a committee. The President is highly gratified by the noble and patriotic sentiments of your letter, and directs that you proceed at once to your command at Distilleryville, Kentucky, and there report by letter to Major-General Wardorg at Louisville, for orders. It is important that the strictest secrecy be observed regarding your movements until you have passed Covington, as it is desired to hold the enemy in front of Distilleryville until you are within three days of him. . . . Go by way of Bluegrass, Opossum Corners and Horsecave. All officers are expected to be in full uniform when *en route* to the front.

From Brigadier-General Jupiter Doke to the Secretary of War.

> *Covington, Kentucky, December 7, 1861.*

I arrived yesterday at this point, and have given my proxy to Joel Briller, Esq., my wife's cousin, and a staunch Republican, who will worthily represent Posey County in field and forum. He points with pride to a stainless record in the halls of legislation, which have often echoed to his soul-stirring eloquence on questions which lie at the very foundation of popular government. . . . Mr. Briller left for Distilleryville last evening, and the standard bearer of the Democratic host confronting that stronghold of freedom will find him a lion in his path. I have been asked to remain here and deliver some addresses to the people in a local contest involving issues of paramount importance. That duty being performed, I shall in person enter the arena of armed debate and move in the direction of the heaviest firing, burning my ships behind me. I forward by this mail to his Excellency the President a request for the appointment of my son, Jabez Leonidas Doke, as postmaster at Hardpan. I would take it, sir, as a great favor if you would give the application a strong oral indorsement, as the appointment is in the line of reform. Be kind enough to inform me what are the emoluments of the office I hold in the military arm, and if they are by salary or fees. Are there any perquisites? My mileage account will be transmitted monthly.

From Brigadier-General Jupiter Doke to Major-General Blount Wardorg.

> *Distilleryville, Kentucky, January 12, 1862.*

I arrived on the tented field yesterday by steamboat, the recent storms having inundated the landscape, covering, I understand, the greater part of a congressional district. I am pained to find that Joel Briller, Esq., a prominent citizen of Posey County, Illinois, and a far-seeing statesman who held my proxy, and who a month ago should have been thundering at the gates of Disunion, has not been heard from, and has doubtless been sacrificed upon the altar of his country. In him the American people lose a bulwark of freedom. I would respectfully move that you designate a committee to draw up resolutions of respect to his memory, and that the office holders and men under your command wear the usual badge of mourning for thirty days. I shall at once place myself at the head of affairs here, and am now ready to entertain any suggestions which you may make, looking to the better enforcement of the laws in this commonwealth. The militant Democrats on the other side of the river appear to be contemplating extreme measures. They have two large cannons facing this way, and yesterday morning, I am told, some of them came down to the water's edge and remained in session for some time, making infamous allegations.

From the Diary of Brigadier-General Jupiter Doke, at Distilleryville, Kentucky.

January 12, 1862.—On my arrival yesterday at the Henry Clay Hotel (named in honor of the late far-seeing statesman) I was waited on by a delegation consisting of the three colonels intrusted with the command of the regiments of my brigade. It was an occasion that will be memorable in the political annals of America. Forwarded copies of the speeches to the Posey *Maverick,* to be spread upon the record of the ages. The gentlemen composing the delegation unanimously reaffirmed their devotion to the principles of national unity and the Republican party. . . .

January 14, 1862.—Wrote to the President, asking for the contract to supply this command with firearms and regalia through my brother-in-law, prominently identified with the manufacturing interests of the country. Club of cannon soldiers arrived at Jayhawk, three miles back from here, on their way to join us in battle array. Marched my whole brigade to Jayhawk to escort them into town, but their chairman, mistaking us for the opposing party, opened fire on the head of the procession and by the extraordinary noise of the cannon balls (I had no conception of it!) so frightened my horse that I was unseated without a contest. The meeting adjourned in disorder and returning to camp I found that a deputation of the enemy had crossed the river in our absence and made a division of the loaves and fishes. Wrote to the President, applying for the Gubernatorial Chair of the Territory of Idaho.

From Editorial Article in the Posey, Illinois, Maverick, *January 20, 1862.*

Brigadier-General Doke's thrilling account, in another column, of the Battle of Distilleryville will make the heart of every loyal Illinoisian leap with exultation. The brilliant exploit marks an era in military history, and as General Doke says, "lays broad and deep the foundations of American prowess in arms." As none of the troops engaged, except the gallant author-chieftain (a host in himself) hails from Posey County, he justly considered that a list of the fallen would only occupy our valuable space to the exclusion of more important matter, but his account of the strategic ruse by which he apparently abandoned his camp and so inveigled a perfidious enemy into it for the purpose of murdering the sick, the unfortunate *countertempus* at Jayhawk, the subsequent dash upon a trapped enemy flushed with a supposed success, driving their terrified legions across an impassable river which precluded pursuit—all these "moving accidents by flood and field" are related with a pen of fire and have all the terrible interest of romance.

Verily, truth is stranger than fiction and the pen is mightier than the sword. When by the graphic power of the art preservative of all arts we are brought face to face with such glorious events as these, the *Maverick's* enterprise in securing for its thousands of readers the services so distinguished a contributor as the Great Captain who made the history as well as wrote it seems a matter of almost secondary importance. For President in 1864 (subject to the decision of the Republican National Convention) Brigadier-General Jupiter Doke, of Illinois!

From Major-General Blount Wardorg to Brigadier-General Jupiter Doke.

Louisville, January 22, 1862.

Your letter apprising me of your arrival at Distilleryville was delayed in transmission, having only just been received (open) through the courtesy of the Confederate department commander under a flag of truce. He begs me to assure you that he would consider it an act of cruelty to trouble you, and I think it would be. Maintain, however, a threatening attitude, but at the least pressure retire. Your position is simply an outpost which it is not intended to hold.

From Major-General Blount Wardorg to the Secretary of War.

Louisville, January 23, 1862.

I have certain information that the enemy has concentrated twenty thousand troops of all arms on the Little Buttermilk. According to your assignment, General Doke is in command of the small brigade of raw troops opposing them. It is no part of my plan to contest the enemy's advance at that point, but I cannot hold myself responsible for any reverses to the brigade mentioned, under its present commander. I think him a fool.

From the Secretary of War to Major-General Blount Wardorg.

Washington, February 1, 1862.

The President has great faith in General Doke. If your estimate of him is correct, however, he would seem to be singularly well placed where he now is, as your plans appear to contemplate a considerable sacrifice for whatever advantages you expect to gain.

From Brigadier-General Jupiter Doke to Major-General Blount Wardorg.

Distilleryville, February 1, 1862.

To-morrow I shall remove my headquarters to Jayhawk in order to point the way whenever my brigade retires from Distilleryville, as fore-shadowed by your letter of the 22d ult. I have appointed a Committee on Retreat, the minutes of whose first meeting I transmit to you. You will perceive that the committee having been duly organized by the election of a chairman and secretary, a resolution (prepared by myself) was adopted, to the effect that in case treason again raises her hideous head on this side of the river every man of the brigade is to mount a mule, the procession to move promptly in the direction of Louisville and the loyal North. In preparation for such an emergency I have for some time been collecting mules from the resident Democracy, and have on hand 2300 in a field at Jayhawk. Eternal vigilance is the price of liberty!

From Major-General Gibeon J. Buxter, C. S. A., to the Confederate Secretary of War.

Bung Station, Kentucky, February 4, 1862.

On the night of the 2d inst., our entire force, consisting of 25,000 men and thirty-two field pieces, under command of Major-General Simmons

B. Flood, crossed by a ford to the north side of Little Buttermilk River at a point three miles above Distilleryville and moved obliquely down and away from the stream, to strike the Covington turnpike at Jayhawk; the object being, as you know, to capture Covington, destroy Cincinnati and occupy the Ohio Valley. For some months there had been in our front only a small brigade of undisciplined troops, apparently without a commander, who were useful to us, for by not disturbing them we could create an impression of our weakness. But the movement on Jayhawk having isolated them, I was about to detach an Alabama regiment to bring them in, my division being the leading one, when an earth-shaking rumble was felt and heard, and suddenly the head-of-column was struck by one of the terrible tornadoes for which this region is famous, and utterly annihilated. The tornado, I believe, passed along the entire length of the road back to the ford, dispersing or destroying our entire army; but of this I cannot be sure, for I was lifted from the earth insensible and blown back to the south side of the river. Continuous firing all night on the north side and the reports of such of our men as have recrossed at the ford convince me that the Yankee brigade has exterminated the disabled survivors. Our loss has been uncommonly heavy. Of my own division of 15,000 infantry, the casualties—killed, wounded, captured, and missing—are 14,994. Of General Dolliver Billows' division, 11,200 strong, I can find but two officers and a nigger cook. Of the artillery, 800 men, none has reported on this side of the river. General Flood is dead. I have assumed command of the expeditionary force, but owing to the heavy losses have deemed it advisable to contract my line of supplies as rapidly as possible. I shall push southward to-morrow morning early. The purposes of the campaign have been as yet but partly accomplished.

From Major-General Dolliver Billows, C. S. A., to the Confederate Secretary of War.

Buhac, Kentucky, February 5, 1862.

. . . But during the 2d they had, unknown to us, been reinforced by fifty thousand cavalry, and being apprised of our movement by a spy, this vast body was drawn up in the darkness at Jayhawk, and as the head of our column reached that point at about 11 P.M., fell upon it with astonishing fury, destroying the division of General Buxter in an instant. . . .

Resolutions of Congress, February 15, 1862.

Resolved, That the thanks of Congress are due, and hereby tendered, to Brigadier-General Jupiter Doke and the gallant men under his command for their unparalleled feat of attacking—themselves only 2,000 strong—an army of 25,000 men and utterly overthrowing it, killing 5327, making prisoners of 19,003, of whom more than half were wounded, taking 32 guns, 20,000 stand of small arms and, in short, the enemy's entire equipment.

Resolved, That for this unexampled victory the President be requested to designate a day of thanksgiving and public celebration of religious rites in the various churches.

Resolved, That he be requested, in further commemoration of the great event, and in reward of the gallant spirits whose deeds have added such imperishable lustre to the American arms, to appoint, with the advice and consent of the Senate, the following officer:
One major-general.

Statement of Mr. Hannibal Alcazar Peyton, of Jayhawk, Kentucky.

Dat wus a almighty dark night, sho', and dese yere ole eyes aint wuf shuks, but I's got a year like a sque'l, an' w'en I cotch de mummer o' v'ices I knowed dat gang b'long on de far side o' de ribber. So I jes' runs in de house an' wakes Marse Doke an' tells him: "Skin outer dis fo' yo' life!" An' de Lo'd bress my soul! ef dat man didn' go right fru de winder in his shir' tail an' break for to cross de mule patch! An' dem twenty-free hunerd mules dey jes' t'ink it is de debble hese'f wid de brandin' iron, an' dey bu'st outen dat patch like a yarthquake, an' pile inter de upper ford road, an' flash down it five deep, an' it full o' Confed'rates from en' to en'! . . .

ABRAHAM LINCOLN

Wires to the Front

Telegram to General George B. McClellan

October 24, 1862

Major-General McClellan:

I have just read your despatch about sore-tongued and fatigued horses. Will you pardon me for asking what the horses of your army have done since the battle of Antietam that fatigues anything?

A. Lincoln

Telegram to General George B. McClellan

October 27, 1862

Major-General McClellan:

Yours of yesterday received. Most certainly I intend no injustice to any, and if I have done any I deeply regret it. To be told, after more than five weeks' total inaction of the army, and during which period we sent to the army every fresh horse we possibly could, amounting in the whole to 7,918, that the cavalry horses were too much fatigued to move, presents a very cheerless, almost hopeless, prospect for the future, and it may have forced something of impatience in my dispatch. If not recruited and rested then, when could they ever be? I suppose the river is rising, and I am glad to believe you are crossing.

A. Lincoln

Telegram to Governor John A. Andrew

Please say to these gentlemen that if they do not work quickly I will make quick work with them. In the name of all that is reasonable, how long does it take to pay a couple of regiments?

A. Lincoln

June 14, 1863

General Tyler, Martinsburg:

If you are besieged how do you despatch me? Why do you not leave before being besieged?

A. Lincoln

Telegrams to J. K. Dubois and O. M. Hatch

September 13, 1863

Hon. J. K. Dubois, Hon. O. M. Hatch:

What nation do you desire General Allen to be made quarter-master-general of? This nation already has a quarter-master-general.

A. Lincoln

September 22, 1863

Hon. O. M. Hatch, Hon. J. K. Dubois, Springfield, Ill.:

Your letter is just received. The particular form of my despatch was jocular, which I supposed you gentlemen knew me well enough to understand. General Allen is considered here as a very faithful and capable officer, and one who would be at least thought of for quarter-master-general if that office were vacant.

A. Lincoln

FINLEY PETER DUNNE

On War Preparations

1898

"Well," Mr. Hennessy asked, "how goes th' war?"

"Splendid, thank ye," said Mr. Dooley. "Fine, fine. It makes me heart throb with pride that I'm a citizen iv th' Sixth Wa-ard."

"Has th' ar-rmy started f'r Cuba yet?"

"Wan ar-rmy, says ye? Twinty! Las' Choosdah an advance ar-rmy iv wan hundherd an' twinty thousand men landed fr'm th' Gussie, with tin thousand cannons hurlin' projick-tyles weighin' eight hundherd pounds sivinteen miles. Winsdah night a second ar-rmy iv injineers, miners, plumbers, an' lawn tinnis experts, numberin' in all four hundherd an' eighty thousan' men, ar-rmed with death-dealin' canned goods, was hurried to Havana to storm th' city.

"Thursdah mornin' three thousand full rigimints acrost to Matoonzas, an' afther a spirited battle captured th' Rainy Christiny golf links, two up an' hell to play, an' will hold thim again all comers. Th' same afthernoon th' reg'lar cavalry, consistin' iv four hundherd an' eight thousan' well-mounted men, was loaded aboord th' tug *Lucy J.*, and departed on their earned iv death amidst th' cheers iv eight millyon sojers left behind at Chickamaha. These cav'lry'll co-operate with Commodore Schlow; an' whin he desthroys th' Spanish fleet, as he does ivry Sundah an' holy day except in Lent, an' finds out where they ar-re an' desthroys thim, afther batterin' down th' forts where they ar-re con-cealed so that he can't see thim, but thinks they ar-re on their way f'r to fight Cousin George Dooley, th' cav'lry will make a dash back to Tampa, where Gin'ral Miles is preparin' to desthroy th' Spanish at wan blow—an' he's th' boy to blow.

"The gin'ral arrived th' other day, fully prepared f'r th' bloody wurruk iv war. He had his intire fam'ly with him. He r-rode recklessly into camp, mounted on a superb specyal ca-ar. As himsilf an' Uncle Mike Miles, an' Cousin Hennery Miles, an' Master Miles, aged eight years, dismounted fr'm th' specyal train, they were received with wild cheers be eight millyon iv th' bravest sojers that iver give up their lives f'r their counthry. Th' press cinchorship is so pow'rful that no news is allowed to go out; but I have it fr'm th' specyal corryspondint iv Mesilf, Clancy th' Butcher, Mike Casey, an' th' City Direchtry that Gin'ral Miles instantly repaired himsilf to th' hotel, where he made his plans f'r cr-rushin' th' Spanyards at wan blow. He will equip th' ar-my with blow-guns at wanst. His uniforms ar-re comin' down in specyal steel protected bullyon trains fr'm th' mint, where they've been kept f'r a year. He has ordhered out th' gold resarve f'r to equip his staff, numberin' eight thousan' men, manny iv whom ar-re clubmen; an' as soon as he can have his pitchers took, he will cr-rush th' Spanish with wan blow. Th' pur-pose iv th' gin'ral is to permit no delay. Decisive action is demanded be th' people. An', whin th' hot air masheens has been sint to th' front, Gin'ral Miles will strike wan blow that'll be th' damdest blow since th' year iv th' big wind in Ireland.

"Iv coorse, they'se dissinsions in th' cabinet; but they don't amount to nawthin'. Th' Sicrety iv War is in favor iv sawin' th' Spanish ar-rmy into two-be-four joists. Th' Sicrety iv th' Threeasury has a scheme f'r roonin' thim be lindin' thim money. Th' Sicrety iv th' Navy wants to sue thim befure th' Mattsachusetts Supreme Coort. I've heerd that th' Prisi-dent is arrangin' a knee dhrill, with th' idee iv prayin' th' villyans to th' divvil. But these diff'rences don't count. We're all wan people, an' we look to Gin'ral Miles to desthroy th' Spanish with wan blow. Whin it comes, trees will be lifted out be th' roots. Morro Castle'll cave in, an' th' air'll be full iv Spanish whiskers. A long blow, a sthrong blow, an' a blow all together."

"We're a gr-reat people," said Mr. Hennessy, earnestly.

"We ar-re," said Mr. Dooley. "We ar-re that. An' th' best iv it is, we know we ar-re."

Expansion

1899

"Whin we plant what Hogan calls th' starry banner iv Freedom in th' Ph'lippeens," said Mr. Dooley, "an' give th' sacred blessin' iv liberty to the poor, down-trodden people iv thim unfortunate isles—dam thim!—we'll larn thim a lesson."

"Sure," said Mr. Hennessy, sadly, "we have a thing or two to larn oursilves."

"But it isn't f'r thim to larn us," said Mr. Dooley. " 'Tis not f'r thim wretched an' degraded crathers, without a mind or a shirt iv their own, f'r to give lessons in politeness an' liberty to a nation that mannyfacthers more dhressed beef than anny other imperyal nation in th' wurruld. We say to thim: 'Naygurs,' we say, 'poor, dissolute, uncovered wretches,' says we, 'whin th' crool hand iv Spain forged man'cles f'r ye'er limbs, as Hogan says, who was it crossed th' say an' sthruck off th' comealongs? We did—by dad, we did. An' now, ye mis'rable, childish-minded apes, we propose f'r to larn ye th' uses iv liberty. In ivry city in this unfair land we will erect school-houses an' packin' houses an' houses iv correction; an' we'll larn ye our language, because 'tis aisier to larn ye ours than to larn oursilves yours. An' we'll give ye clothes, if ye pay f'r thim; an', if ye don't, ye can go without. An', whin ye're hungry, ye can go to th' morgue—we mane th' resth'rant—an' ate a good square meal iv ar-rmy beef. An' we'll sind th' gr-reat Gin'ral Eagan over f'r to larn ye etiquette, an' Andhrew Carnegie to larn ye pathriteism with blow-holes into it, an' Gin'ral Alger to larn ye to hould onto a job; an', whin ye've become edycated an' have all th' blessin's iv civilization that we don't want, that'll count ye one. We can't give ye anny votes, because we haven't more thin enough to go round now; but we'll threat ye th' way a father shud threat his childher if we have to break ivry bone in ye'er bodies. So come to our ar-rms,' says we.

"But, glory be, 'tis more like a rasslin' match than a father's embrace. Up gets this little monkey iv an' Aggynaldoo, an' says he, 'Not for us,' he says. 'We thank ye kindly; but we believe,' he says, 'in pathronizin' home industhries,' he says. 'An,' he says, 'I have on hand,' he says, 'an' f'r sale,' he says, 'a very superyor brand iv home-made liberty, like ye'er mother used to make,' he says. ' 'Tis a long way fr'm ye'er plant to here,' he says, 'an' be th' time a cargo iv liberty,' he says, 'got out here an' was handled be th' middlemen,' he says, 'it might spoil,' he says. 'We don't want anny col' storage or embalmed liberty,' he says. 'What we want an' what th' ol' reliable house iv Aggynaldoo,' he says, 'supplies to th' thrade,' he says, 'is fr-esh liberty r-right off th' far-rm,' he says. 'I can't do annything with ye'er proposition,' he says. 'I can't give up,' he says, 'th' rights f'r which f'r five years I've fought an' bled ivry wan I cud reach,' he says. 'Onless,' he says, ye'd feel like buyin' out th' whole business,' he says. 'I'm a pathrite,' he says; 'but I'm no bigot,' he says.

"An' there it stands, Hinnissy, with th' indulgent parent kneelin' on th' stomach iv his adopted child, while a dillygation fr'm Boston bastes him with an umbrella. There it stands, an' how will it come out I din-naw. I'm not much iv an expansionist mesilf. F'r th' las' tin years I've been thryin' to decide whether 'twud be good policy an' thrue to me thraditions to make this here bar two or three feet longer, an manny's th' night I've laid awake tryin' to puzzle it out. But I don't know what to do with th' Ph'lippeens anny more thin I did las' summer, befure I heerd tell iv thim. We can't give thim to anny wan without makin' th' wan that gets thim feel th' way Doherty felt to Clancy whin Clancy med a frindly call an' give Doherty's childher th' measles. We can't sell thim, we can't ate thim, an' we can't throw thim into th' alley whin no wan is lookin'. An' 'twud be a disgrace f'r to lave befure we've pounded these frindless an' ongrateful people into insinsibility. So I suppose,

Hinnissy, we'll have to stay an' do th' best we can, an' lave Andhrew Carnegie secede fr'm th' Union. They'se wan consolation; an' that is, if th' American people can govern thimsilves, they can govern annything that walks."

"An' what 'd ye do with Aggy—what-d'ye-call-him?" asked Mr. Hennessy.

"Well," Mr. Dooley replied, with brightening eyes, "I know what they'd do with him in this ward. They'd give that pathrite what he asks, an' thin they'd throw him down an' take it away fr'm him."

MARK TWAIN

(SAMUEL L. CLEMENS)

To the Person Sitting in Darkness

(excerpts)

1901

. . . The following news from China appeared in the *Sun,* of New York, on Christmas Eve. The italics are mine:

> The Rev. Mr. Ament, of the American Board of Foreign Missions, has returned from a trip which he made for the purpose of collecting indemnities for damages done by Boxers. *Everywhere he went he compelled the Chinese to pay.* He says that all his native Christians are now provided for. He had 700 of them under his charge, and 300 were killed. He has *collected* 300 *taels for each* of these murders, and has *compelled full payment for all the property belonging to Christians* that was destroyed. He also assessed *fines* amounting to THIRTEEN TIMES the amount of the indemnity. *This money will be used for the propagation of the Gospel.*
>
> Mr. Ament declares that the compensation he has collected is *moderate* when compared with the amount secured by the Catholics, who demand, in addition to money, *head for head.* They collect 500 taels for each murder of a Catholic. In the Wenchiu country, 680 Catholics were

killed, and for this the European Catholics here demand 750,000 strings of cash and 680 *heads*.

In the course of a conversation, Mr. Ament referred to the attitude of the missionaries toward the Chinese. He said:

"I deny emphatically that the missionaries are *vindictive*, that they *generally* looted, or that they have done anything *since* the siege that *the circumstances did not demand*. I criticize the Americans. *The soft hand of the Americans is not as good as the mailed fist of the Germans*: —If you deal with the Chinese with a soft hand they will take advantage of it.

"The statement that the French government will return the loot taken by the French soldiers is the source of the greatest amusement here. The French soldiers were more systematic looters than the Germans, and it is a fact that today *Catholic Christians*, carrying French flags and armed with modern guns, *are looting villages* in the Province of Chili."

By happy luck, we get all these glad tidings on Christmas Eve. . . . Our spirits soar, and we find we can even make jokes: Taels, I win, Heads you lose.

Our Reverend Ament is the right man in the right place. What we want of our missionaries out there is, not that they shall merely represent in their acts and persons the grace and gentleness and charity and loving-kindness of our religion, but that they shall also represent the American spirit. The oldest Americans are the Pawnees. Macallum's History says:

When a white Boxer kills a Pawnee and destroys his property, the other Pawnees do not trouble to seek *him* out, they kill any white person that comes along; also, they make some white village pay deceased's heirs the full cash value of deceased, together with full cash value of the property destroyed; they also make the village pay, in addition, *thirteen times* the value of that property into a fund for the dissemination of the Pawnee religion, which they regard as the best of all religions for the softening and humanizing of the heart of man. It is their idea that it is only fair and right that the innocent should be made to suffer for the guilty, and that it is better that ninety and nine innocent should suffer than that one guilty person should escape.

Our Reverend Ament is justifiably jealous of those enterprising Catholics, who not only get big money for each lost convert, but get "head for head" besides. But he should soothe himself with the reflections that the entirety of their exactions are for their own pockets, whereas he, less selfishly, devotes only 300 taels per head to that service, and gives the whole vast thirteen repetitions of the property-indemnity to the service of propagating the Gospel. His magnanimity has won him the approval of his nation, and will get him a monument. Let him be content with these rewards. We all hold him dear for manfully defending his fellow missionaries from exaggerated charges which were beginning to distress us, but which his testimony has so considerably modified that we can now contemplate them without noticeable pain. For now we know that, even before the siege, the missionaries were not "generally" out looting, and that, "since the siege," they have acted quite handsomely, except when "circumstances" crowded them. I am arranging for the monument. Subscriptions for it can be sent to the American Board; designs for it can be sent to me. Designs must allegorically set forth the thirteen reduplications of the indemnity, and the object for which they were exacted; as ornaments, the designs must exhibit 680 heads, so disposed as to give a pleasing and pretty effect; for the Catholics have done nicely, and are entitled to notice in the monument. Mottoes may be suggested, if any shall be discovered that will satisfactorily cover the ground.

Mr. Ament's financial feat of squeezing a thirteenfold indemnity out of the pauper peasants to square other people's offenses, thus condemning them and their women and innocent little children to inevitable starvation and lingering death, in order that the blood money so acquired might be *used for the propagation of the Gospel,"* does not flutter my serenity; although the act and the words, taken together, concrete a blasphemy so hideous and so colossal that, without doubt, its mate is not findable in the history of this or of any other age. Yet, if a layman had done that thing and justified it with those words, I should have shuddered, I know. Or, if I had done the thing and said the words myself—However, the thought is unthinkable, irreverent as some imperfectly informed people think me. Sometimes an ordained minister sets out to be blasphemous. When this happens, the layman is out of the running; he stands no chance.

We have Mr. Ament's impassioned assurance that the missionaries are not "vindictive." Let us hope and pray that they will never become so, but will remain in the almost morbidly fair and just and gentle temper which is affording so much satisfaction to their brother and champion today.

· · · · · · · · · · · · · · · · · · · ·

Shall we go on conferring our civilization upon the peoples that sit in darkness, or shall we give those poor things a rest? Shall we bang right ahead in our old-time, loud, pious way, and commit the new century to the game; or shall we sober up and sit down and think it over first? Would it not be prudent to get our civilization tools together, and see how much stock is left on hand in the way of glass beads and theology, and maxim guns and hymn books, and trade gin and torches of progress and enlightenment (patent adjustable ones, good to fire villages with, upon occasion), and balance the books, and arrive at the profit and loss, so that we may intelligently decide whether to continue the business or sell out the property and start a new civilization scheme on the proceeds?

Extending the blessings of civilization to our brother who sits in darkness has been a good trade and has paid well, on the whole; and there is money in it yet, if carefully worked—but not enough, in my judgment, to make any considerable risk advisable. The people that sit in darkness are getting to be too scarce—too scarce and too shy. And such darkness as is now left is really of but an indifferent quality, and not dark enough for the game. The most of those people that sit in darkness have been furnished with more light than was good for them or profitable for us. We have been injudicious.

The blessings-of-civilization trust, wisely and cautiously administered, is a daisy. There is more money in it, more territory, more sovereignty, and other kinds of emolument, than there is in any other game that is played. But Christendom has been playing it badly of late years, and must certainly suffer by it, in my opinion. She has been so eager to get every stake that appeared on the green cloth, that the people who sit in darkness have noticed it—they have noticed it, and have begun to show alarm. They have become suspicious of the blessings of civilization. More—they have begun to examine them. This is not well. . . .

We all know that the business is being ruined. The reason is not far to seek. It is because our Mr. McKinley, and Mr. Chamberlain, and the Kaiser, and the Czar and the French have been exporting the actual thing *with the outside cover left off*. This is bad for the game. It shows that these new players of it are not sufficiently acquainted with it.

It is a distress to look on and note the mismoves, they are so strange and so awkward. Mr. Chamberlain manufactures a war out of materials so inadequate and so fanciful that they make the boxes grieve and the gallery laugh, and he tries hard to persuade himself that it isn't purely a private raid for cash, but has a sort of dim, vague respectability about it somewhere, if he could only find the spot; and that, by and by, he can scour the flag clean again after he has finished dragging it through the mud, and make it shine and flash in the vault of heaven once more as it had shone and flashed there a thousand years in the world's respect until he laid his unfaithful hand upon it. . . . Is *this* a case of magnanimity, forbearance, love, gentleness, mercy, protection of the weak—this strange and overshowy onslaught of an elephant upon a nest of field mice, on the pretext that the mice had squeaked an insolence at him—conduct which "no self-respecting government could allow to pass unavenged"? as Mr. Chamberlain said. . . .

Then they that sit in darkness are troubled, and shake their heads; and they read this extract from a letter of a British private, recounting his exploits in one of Methuen's victories, some days before the affair of Magersfontein, and they are troubled again:

> We tore up the hill and into the intrenchments, and the Boers saw we had them; so they dropped their guns and went down on their knees and put up their hands clasped, and begged for mercy. And we gave it to them—*with the long spoon.*

The long spoon is the bayonet. See *Lloyd's Weekly*, London, of those days. The same number—and the same column—contained some quite unconscious satire in the form of shocked and bitter upbraidings of the Boers for their brutalities and inhumanities!

Next, to our heavy damage, the Kaiser went to playing the game without first mastering it. He lost a couple of missionaries in a riot in Shantung, and in his account he made an overcharge for them. China had to pay a hundred thousand dollars apiece for them, in money; twelve miles of territory, containing several millions of inhabitants and worth twenty million dollars; and to build a monument, and also a Christian church; whereas the people of China could have been depended upon to remember the missionaries without the help of these expensive memorials. This was all bad play. Bad, because it would not, and could not, and will not now or ever, deceive the person sitting in darkness. He knows that it was an overcharge. . . .

And next Russia must go and play the game injudiciously. She affronts England once or twice—with the person sitting in darkness observing and noting; by moral assistance of France and Germany, she robs Japan of her hard-earned spoil, all swimming in Chinese blood—Port Arthur— with the person again observing and noting; then she seizes Manchuria, raids its villages, and chokes its great river with the swollen corpses of countless massacred peasants—that astonished person still observing and noting. And perhaps he is saying to himself: "It is yet *another* civilized power, with its banner of the Prince of Peace in one hand and its loot basket and its butcher knife in the other. Is there no salvation for us but to adopt civilization and lift ourselves down to its level?"

And by and by comes America, and our master of the game plays it badly—plays it as Mr. Chamberlain was playing it in South Africa. . . . Dewey could have gone about his affairs elsewhere, and left the competent Filipino army to starve out the little Spanish garrison and send it home, and the Filipino citizens to set up the form of government they might prefer. . . . But we played the Chamberlain game, and lost the chance to add another Cuba and another honorable deed to our good record. . . .

. . . Mr. Chamberlain has arranged England's opinion of the South African matter, and done it most cleverly and successfully. He presented the facts—some of the facts—and showed those confiding people what the facts meant. He did it statistically, which is a good way. He used the formula: "Twice 2 are 14, and 2 from 9 leaves 35." Figures are effective; figures will convince the elect.

Now, my plan is a still bolder one than Mr. Chamberlain's though apparently a copy of it. Let us be franker than Mr. Chamberlain; let us audaciously present the whole of the facts, shirking none, then explain them according to Mr. Chamberlain's formula. This daring truthfulness will astonish and dazzle the person sitting in darkness, and he will take the explanation down before his mental vision has had time to get back into focus. Let us say to him:

"Our case is simple. On the first of May, Dewey destroyed the Spanish fleet. This left the archipelago in the hands of its proper and rightful owners, the Filipino nation. . . . Our traditions required that Dewey should now set up his warning sign, and go away. But the master of the game happened to think of another plan—the European plan. He acted upon it. This was, to send out an army—ostensibly to help the native patriots put the finishing touch upon their long and plucky struggle for independence, but really to take their land away from them and keep it. . . ."

At this point in our frank statement of fact to the person sitting in darkness, we should throw in a little trade taffy about the blessings of civilization—for a change, and for the refreshment of his spirit—then go on with our tale:

"We and the patriots having captured Manila, Spain's ownership of

the archipelago and her sovereignty over it were at an end—obliterated
—annihilated—not a rag or shred of either remaining behind. It was
then that we conceived the divinely humorous idea of *buying* both of
these specters from Spain! (It is quite safe to confess this to the person
sitting in darkness, since neither he nor any other sane person will believe it.) In buying those ghosts for twenty millions, we also contracted
to take care of the friars and their accumulations. I think we also agreed
to propagate leprosy and smallpox, but as to this there is doubt. . . .

"With our treaty ratified, Manila subdued, and our ghosts secured,
we had no further use for Aguinaldo and the owners of the archipelago.
We forced a war, and we have been hunting America's guest and ally
through the woods and swamps ever since."

. . . .
.

Kitchener knows how to handle disagreeable people who are fighting
for their homes and their liberties, and we must let on that we are merely
imitating Kitchener, and have no national interest in the matter, further
than to get ourselves admired by the great family of nations, in
which august company our master of the game has bought a place for
us in the back row.

Of course, we must not venture to ignore our General MacArthur's
reports—oh, why do they keep on printing those embarrassing things?—
we must drop them trippingly from the tongue and take the chances:

> During the last ten months our losses have been 268 killed and 750
> wounded; Filipino loss, *three thousand two hundred and twenty-seven
> killed*, and 694 wounded.

We must stand ready to grab the person sitting in darkness, for he
will swoon away at this confession saying: "Good God! those 'niggers'
spare their wounded, and the Americans massacre theirs!" . . .

Having now laid all the historical facts before the person sitting in
darkness, we should bring him to again, and explain them to him. We
should say to him:

"They look doubtful, but in reality they are not. There have been
lies; yes, but they were told in a good cause. We have been treacherous;
but that was only in order that real good might come out of apparent
evil. . . . This world-girdling accumulation of trained morals, high principles, and justice cannot do an unright thing, an unfair thing, an ungenerous thing, an unclean thing. It knows what it is about. Give yourself no uneasiness; it is all right."

Now then, that will convince the person. You will see. It will restore the business. . . .

We cannot conceal from ourselves that, privately, we are a little troubled about our uniform. It is one of our prides; it is acquainted with honor; it is familiar with great deeds and noble; we love it, we revere it; and so this errand it is on makes us uneasy. And our flag—another pride of ours, our chiefest! We have worshiped it so; and when we have seen it in far lands—glimpsing it unexpectedly in that strange sky, waving its welcome and benediction to us—we have caught our breaths, and uncovered our heads, and couldn't speak, for a moment, for the thought of what it was to us and the great ideals it stood for. Indeed, we *must* do something about these things; it is easily managed. We can have a special one—our states do it: we can have just our usual flag, with the white stripes painted black and the stars replaced by the skull and cross-bones. . . .

WILL ROGERS

The War of Washington

1918

Want to speak about the training of these officers in this war of Washington, or how to get a higher Commission. In all my gags I like to take the part of the private against the officers as it is always more popular to uphold the few against the many.

First thing is to come to Washington. Thats the most essential thing. Then try to get a room, thats the hardest thing. No previous experience necessary to be an officer unless it is that you are in danger of being drafted as a private by your own board. Then pick out the branch of service whose office hours are the shortest. Then get your home senators address. Await your turn in line and if you draw only a Capt. dont feel discouraged. You may meet a cabinet officer and be promoted before night.

Next the most essential thing is your uniform. Without it you wouldent want the office. Then decide whether you want to take your savings of years and get an officers equipment or pay a weeks room rent with it. They both cost the same. Unfortunately, our uniforms are mostly alike. When we have had as many wars as the European countries we can remedy that to the satisfaction of our officers. Your only chance of ranking above your fellow officers is to get a more expensive grade of cloth. Now you wont have time to have this made to order AS Foch is holding up this war now waiting till you get in. Besides you have a date at the photographers at four o'clock so go to the best ready-made store. He will fit you till you can have a suit made and will show you what insignia to put on your shoulder and which end of your putees to go on top. If you decide as most of them do to get boots and spurs be sure to get spurs without the rowels or sharp things in them, as you may cut your boots up with them. Besides they are more apt to catch in your clutch and you cant shift your gears as well with them.

Now when you have found a coat that is uncomfortably tight and pants with the necessary bigness above the knees the clerk for a small extra fee will show you how to salute as you may in going out meet a cadet who has only been in West Point three years and you as a superior officer must return his humble salute. Now with the salute learned you are a full-fledged American Officer in the Great War of Washington, D.C.

Now try and think of some humble unpatriotic friend whom you used to know before you entered this awful conflict who is toiling trying to make enough to pay his taxes and meet his payments on his Liberty Bonds and ask him out to dinner with you. You cant afford to go in any but the best now as you may be humiliated by being next to a lot of non-com officers. Now be sure and tell your friend confidentially that you got it straight but he must not mention where it come from that Turkey was about through and that the only thing you are sore about is that it may end before you get across. Now the Follies are playing in town so you take your friend. Now its perfectly proper for an army Washington officer to admit that ignorance of the war but its gross negligence to admit he is not acquainted with at least five of the girls. When the usher comes back and says there is no answer, bawl him out before your friend and tell him you bet he give it to the wrong girl and was he sure he told her it was Captain Jasbo.

From now on you pan the show. Its the worst you've ever seen and you've seen them all.

Now its tomorrow morning and you are to start in as the deciding factor in this war. When you get to your office building your hardest war work is trying to find a place to park your car.

Now make sure of one thing and that is as to where you are to be located. The saddest case that has happened in this war was a fellow dident notice how his appointment read and he found he had been put with a regiment that was to go to the European War. But that was the only case.

You spend your first day being introduced to your typewriters. By night you will begin to realize what a tremendous war this is. Now its time to dress for dinner so you return to your rest billets. Brush your new suit, see that your shoulder tags are on straight and make for a café, get a table where you can get a good view of all these new officers who have only been appointed today.

Tonight you start in on your military training. You attend a school for twelve lessons to learn how to dance with a girl without catching your spurs in her dress.

Carry a French book in your pocket. You know you are not going to use it but it lends a certain amount of atmosphere.

You've now been in about long enough to commence figuring on a promotion. By this time you should be receiving the paper from home. That is one of the most anxious moments of your entire military career, wondering how the picture will turn out and if its on the front page.

You know one of the most unfortunate cases in this war was a boy after sacrificing a good home and all his social standing to enlist as a 2nd Lieutenant in this civil conflict returned home on a furlough and dident look well in his uniform. Well his people were just simply killed about it. Now they dont know whether to try and get him out of the army or get another Tailor. You know the ordinary person dont realize the chances these men take when they enlist in the service. Why I have seen them pouring out of those government buildings after a hard days struggle with three Austrian notes and the ink on their hands up to their wrists.

Why the casualty list in one day out of a million and a half officers in Washington was ten wounded getting in and out of Taxicabs. Two choked through their collars being too tight, 61 hurt through typewriters choking up, 500 prostrated when they heard war was over and they would have to go back to work.

It will take two years to muster all of them out of Willard Hotel Lobby. It will take all the Drawing Room space on McAdoos Railroad for years to get them home again.

Then people at home will have to listen for another year why they dident go over. The hardest part of it is trying to look like an officer, and how to act in the presence of someone who has been across. Also how to properly thank the staff officers for past performances and ask for future ones.

I met one officer here who could tell me what he was doing without explaining. Most of them had their hardest jobs trying to make their uniforms look worn somewhere else besides the trouser seat.

They are allowed to keep their uniforms to show their children and grand children the desk marks on them. One officer had been recommended for gallantry. He has only missed one show and no dances since the war started.

NOT SO LONG AGO

WILL ROGERS

Recognizing Russia

1933

Now everybody is saying, Will we recognize Russia? Sure we will if they will buy anything.

In the A.F.N. (absolutely financially nutty) days we wouldent recognize Russia, for they had defaulted on their debts, wouldent go to church and were socialists. In fact in those C.D. (Cuckoo days) we were so cocky rich that we wouldent hardly recognize each other. But, Brother, it's different now. We are just looking for something to recognize. And debts, my Lord, if we dident recognize nations that owed us and dident pay, we would be a Robinson Crusoe on a desert island.

Russia might have been aetheists when we had money, but now that we are broke we aint going to let religion interfere with business. Some nations can come over that worship a golden calf but we will recognize them as long as they will buy the bronze from us to keep the old calf golden. We sell to the Chinese and they are heatherns, just like the Republicans.

Yes, sir, we are going to recognize Russia. We would recognize the Devil with a false face on if he would contract for some pitchforks. The shape we are in right now we would be glad to receive a good will tour from Alababa and his Forty Thieves, if they needed enough tooth paste and radio tubes. So bring on your Russia. We will trade 'em cotton for caviar and Junius Facial Cream for Vodka.

Nothing will bring a Nation off its moral high horse like poverty. Poverty is a terrible handicap but a great humanizer.

Speaking of finances, I have heard of a nation being frightened to death of a war, of folks worried to distraction over the health of their loved ones, of people uneasy of a threatened pestilence, but we will go on record as being the first nation that is literally scared to death over what will happen to its dollar.

This nation needs a more equal distribution of wealth. That's one thing the dumb guy knew before the economist. And I will say one thing for this Administration. They may not get wealth equally divided among everybody. But they have done one thing:

It's the only time when the fellow with money is worrying more than the one without it.

JAMES THURBER

The Rabbits Who Caused All the Trouble

1939

Within the memory of the youngest child there was a family of rabbits who lived near a pack of wolves. The wolves announced that they did not like the way the rabbits were living. (The wolves were crazy about the way they themselves were living, because it was the only way to live.) One night several wolves were killed in an earthquake and this was blamed on the rabbits, for it is well-known that rabbits pound on the ground with their hind legs and cause earthquakes. On another night one of the wolves was killed by a bolt of lightning and this was also blamed on the rabbits, for it is well-known that lettuce-eaters cause lightning. The wolves threatened to civilize the rabbits if they didn't behave, and the rabbits decided to run away to a desert island. But the other animals, who lived at a great distance, shamed them, saying, "You must stay where you are and be brave. This is no world for escapists. If the wolves attack you, we will come to your aid, in all probability." So the rabbits continued to live near the wolves and one day there was a terrible flood which drowned a great many wolves. This was blamed on the rabbits, for it is well-known that carrot-nibblers with long ears cause floods. The wolves descended on the rabbits, for their own good, and imprisoned them in a dark cave, for their own protection.

When nothing was heard about the rabbits for some weeks, the other animals demanded to know what had happened to them. The wolves replied that the rabbits had been eaten and since they had been eaten the affair was a purely internal matter. But the other animals warned that they might possibly unite against the wolves unless some reason was given for the destruction of the rabbits. So the wolves gave them one. "They were trying to escape," said the wolves, "and, as you know, this is no world for escapists."

Moral: Run, don't walk, to the nearest desert island.

ART BUCHWALD

Conversation on a Plane

1960

Traveling the way I do, I'm always running into interesting people. The other day on my way up from Rome I met a white-haired German businessman. This was my end of the conversation.

"Yes, I speak English. . . . No, I'm not English, I'm American. Oh, you're German. . . . Thank you for your card. . . . Here's mine. . . . I see you're in the steel business. That must be a good business. . . . Oh, you once owned your own steel plant in Leipzig? Before the war? During the war. . . . The British and the Americans destroyed your plant? How? . . . With bombs. That's a shame. Were they big bombs? . . . Very big bombs. That really is a shame. . . . They destroyed your plant twice. You rebuilt it and then they destroyed it again. . . . That's terrible. They shouldn't have done it. I mean, after all it was your plant and . . . Were they high-flying planes or low-flying planes? . . . You couldn't tell because you were in a bomb shelter. . . . But the bombs made a lot of noise? . . . I can appreciate how you felt. . . .

"But isn't Leipzig in the Eastern zone? . . . Then you were captured by the Russians? Did they throw you in prison? . . . Only for a couple of weeks? That's too bad. I mean that's bad that they threw you in prison. . . . Did they mistreat you? They did. . . . Isn't that awful. I bet they tortured you. . . . They did! Isn't that wonderful. I mean isn't that wonderful that they didn't torture you more than two weeks. . . . Were you a member of the Nazi party? . . . Naturally, of course you weren't. . . . I'm sorry I asked. . . .

"I see. . . . All you did was make steel for the army. . . . You had to. Of course you did. . . . No, I wasn't in the Air Force. I was in the Marines. We were in the Pacific. We didn't bomb any German steel plants. . . . We wanted to . . . that is to say, we wanted to be in the European theater. Everybody during the war wanted to be some place else. . . . No, I'm not bitter about the war. I've got nothing against the Germans, particularly somebody who made steel. It isn't as if you were fighting us. . . . After all, you can make other things with steel besides guns . . . like Venetian blinds or air-conditioning units. I'll bet that's what your plant made. . . . You made steel hospital beds? There, what did I tell you! I knew you were the type of person that wouldn't make war equipment. . . . Tell me, did anyone else torture you besides the Russians? The East German Communists arrested you but didn't torture you? . . . What's wrong with them? . . . No, I mean what's their problem, I didn't mean what was wrong with them for not torturing you. . . . You'll have to excuse me, my English isn't so good.

"No, I don't speak German. I live in France. . . . Oh yes, I like it very much. . . . You had French workers working for you during the war? . . . Did they work well? . . . Not so good? . . . They work much better now. . . . I guess during the war they didn't like to work so much. . . . The French are funny that way. Put them in their own steel plant and they'll work like mad . . . but send them to a German steel plant and they'll goof off every time. . . .

"I see by your card you're still in the steel business. In West Germany. How's it going? . . . Very good. . . . That's too bad. I mean that's too bad that you can't be in the steel business in East Germany.

"I'll bet you're furious at the Americans and British for destroying your plant. . . . You're not any more because now they're among your best customers? And you say your business is even bigger than it was before the war? . . . That's wonderful, really, really wonderful. . . .

"No, stewardess, I don't want any lunch. For some reason I just lost my appetite."

JOSEPH HELLER

*Milo**

1961

April had been the best month of all for Milo. Lilacs bloomed in April and fruit ripened on the vine. Heartbeats quickened and old appetites were renewed. In April a livelier iris gleamed upon the burnished dove. April was spring, and in the spring Milo Minderbinder's fancy had lightly turned to thoughts of tangerines.

"Tangerines?"

"Yes, sir."

"My men would love tangerines," admitted the colonel in Sardinia who commanded four squadrons of B-26s.

"There'll be all the tangerines they can eat that you're able to pay for with money from your mess fund," Milo assured him.

"Casaba melons?"

"Are going for a song in Damascus."

"I have a weakness for casaba melons. I've always had a weakness for casaba melons."

"Just lend me one plane from each squadron, just one plane, and you'll have all the casabas you can eat that you've money to pay for."

"We buy from the syndicate?"

"And everybody has a share."

"It's amazing, positively amazing. How can you do it?"

"Mass purchasing power makes the big difference. For example, breaded veal cutlets."

"I'm not so crazy about breaded veal cutlets," grumbled the skeptical B-25 commander in the north of Corsica.

"Breaded veal cutlets are very nutritious," Milo admonished him piously. "They contain egg yolk and bread crumbs. And so are lamb chops."

* from *Catch-22.*

"Ah, lamb chops," echoed the B-25 commander. "Good lamb chops?"

"The best," said Milo, "that the black market has to offer."

"Baby lamb chops?"

"In the cutest little pink paper panties you ever saw. Are going for a song in Portugal."

"I can't send a plane to Portugal. I haven't the authority."

"I can, once you lend the plane to me. With a pilot to fly it. And don't forget—you'll get General Dreedle."

"Will General Dreedle eat in my mess hall again?"

"Like a pig, once you start feeding him my best white fresh eggs fried in my pure creamery butter. There'll be tangerines too, and casaba melons, honeydews, filet of Dover sole, baked Alaska, and cockles and mussels."

"And everybody has a share?"

"That," said Milo, "is the most beautiful part of it."

"I don't like it," growled the uncooperative fighter-plane commander, who didn't like Milo either.

"There's an uncooperative fighter-plane commander up north who's got it in for me," Milo complained to General Dreedle. "It takes just one person to ruin the whole thing, and then you wouldn't have your fresh eggs fried in my pure creamery butter any more."

General Dreedle had the uncooperative fighter-plane commander transferred to the Solomon Islands to dig graves and replaced him with a senile colonel with bursitis and a craving for litchi nuts who introduced Milo to the B-17 general on the mainland with a yearning for Polish sausage.

"Polish sausage is going for peanuts in Cracow," Milo informed him.

"Polish sausage," sighed the general nostalgically. "You know, I'd give just about anything for a good hunk of Polish sausage. Just about anything."

"You don't have to give *anything*. Just give me one plane for each mess hall and a pilot who will do what he's told. And a small down payment on your initial order as a token of good faith."

"But Cracow is hundreds of miles behind the enemy lines. How will you get to the sausage?"

"There's an international Polish sausage exchange in Geneva. I'll just fly the peanuts into Switzerland and exchange them for Polish sausage at the open market rate. They'll fly the peanuts back to Cracow and I'll fly the Polish sausage back to you. You buy only as much Polish sausage as you want through the syndicate. There'll be tangerines too, with only a little artificial coloring added. And eggs from Malta and Scotch from Sicily. You'll be paying the money to yourself when you buy from the syndicate, since you'll own a share, so you'll really be getting everything you buy for nothing. Doesn't that make sense?"

"Sheer genius. How in the world did you ever think of it?"

"My name is Milo Minderbinder. I am twenty-seven years old."

Milo Minderbinder's planes flew in from everywhere, the pursuit planes, bombers, and cargo ships streaming into Colonel Cathcart's field with pilots at the controls who would do what they were told. The planes were decorated with flamboyant squadron emblems illustrating such laudable ideals as Courage, Might, Justice, Truth, Liberty, Love, Honor and Patriotism that were painted out at once by Milo's mechanics with a double coat of flat white and replaced in garish purple with the stenciled name M & M ENTERPRISES, FINE FRUITS AND PRODUCE. The "M & M" in "M & M ENTERPRISES" stood for Milo & Minderbinder, and the & was inserted, Milo revealed candidly, to nullify any impression that the syndicate was a one-man operation. Planes arrived for Milo from airfields in Italy, North Africa and England, and from Air Transport Command stations in Liberia, Ascension Island, Cairo and Karachi. Pursuit planes were traded for additional cargo ships or retained for emergency invoice duty and small-parcel service; trucks and tanks were procured from the ground forces and used for short-distance road hauling. Everybody had a share, and men got fat and moved about tamely with toothpicks in their greasy lips. Milo supervised the whole expanding operation by himself. Deep otter-brown lines of preoccupation etched themselves permanently into his careworn face and gave him a harried look of sobriety and mistrust. Everybody but Yossarian thought Milo was a jerk, first for volunteering for the job of mess officer and next for taking it so seriously. Yossarian also thought that Milo was a jerk; but he also knew that Milo was a genius.

One day Milo flew away to England to pick up a load of Turkish halvah and came flying back from Madagascar leading four German bombers filled with yams, collards, mustard greens and black-eyed Georgia peas. Milo was dumfounded when he stepped down to the ground and found a contingent of armed M.P.s waiting to imprison the German pilots and confiscate their planes. *Confiscate!* The mere word was anathema to him, and he stormed back and forth in excoriating condemnation, shaking a piercing finger of rebuke in the guilt-ridden faces of Colonel Cathcart, Colonel Korn and the poor battle-scarred captain with the submachine gun who commanded the M.P.s.

"Is this Russia?" Milo assailed them incredulously at the top of his voice. "*Confiscate?*" he shrieked, as though he could not believe his own ears. "Since when is it the policy of the American government to confiscate the private property of its citizens? Shame on you! Shame on all of you for even thinking such a horrible thought."

"But Milo," Major Danby interrupted timidly, "we're at war with Germany, and those are German planes."

"They are no such thing!" Milo retorted furiously. "Those planes belong to the syndicate, and everybody has a share. *Confiscate?* How can you possibly confiscate your own private property? *Confiscate*, indeed! I've never heard anything so depraved in my whole life."

And sure enough, Milo was right, for when they looked, his mechanics had painted out the German swastikas on the wings, tails and fuselages with double coats of flat white and stenciled in the words M & M ENTER-PRISES, FINE FRUITS AND PRODUCE. Right before their eyes he had transformed his syndicate into an international cartel.

Milo's argosies of plenty now filled the air. Planes poured in from Norway, Denmark, France, Germany, Austria, Italy, Yugoslavia, Romania, Bulgaria, Sweden, Finland, Poland—from everywhere in Europe, in fact, but Russia, with whom Milo refused to do business. When everybody who was going to had signed up with M & M Enterprises, Fine Fruits and Produce, Milo created a wholly owned subsidiary, M & M Enterprises, Fancy Pastry, and obtained more airplanes and more money from the mess funds for scones and crumpets from the British Isles, prune and cheese Danish from Copenhagen, éclairs, cream puffs, Napoleons and *petits fours* from Paris, Reims and Grenoble, *Kugelhopf*, pumpernickel and *Pfefferkuchen* from Berlin, *Linzer* and *Dobos Torten* from Vienna, *Strudel* from Hungary and *baklava* from Ankara. Each morning Milo sent planes aloft all over Europe and North Africa hauling long red tow signs advertising the day's specials in large square letters: "EYE ROUND, 79¢ . . . WHITING, 21¢." He boosted cash income for the syndicate by leasing tow signs to Pet Milk, Gaines Dog Food, and Noxzema. In a spirit of civic enterprise, he regularly allotted a certain amount of free aerial advertising space to General Peckem for the propagation of such messages in the public interest as NEATNESS COUNTS, HASTE MAKES WASTE, and THE FAMILY THAT PRAYS TOGETHER STAYS TOGETHER. Milo purchased spot radio announcements on Axis Sally's and Lord Haw Haw's daily propaganda broadcasts from Berlin to keep things moving. Business boomed on every battlefront.

Milo's planes were a familiar sight. They had freedom of passage everywhere, and one day Milo contracted with the American military authorities to bomb the German-held highway bridge at Orvieto and with the German military authorities to defend the highway bridge at at Orvieto with antiaircraft fire against his own attack. His fee for attacking the bridge for America was the total cost of the operation plus six percent, and his fee from Germany for defending the bridge was the same cost-plus-six agreement augmented by a merit bonus of a thousand dollars for every American plane he shot down. The consummation of these deals represented an important victory for private enterprise, he pointed out, since the armies of both countries were socialized institutions. Once the contracts were signed, there seemed to be no point in using the resources of the syndicate to bomb and defend the bridge, inasmuch as both governments had ample men and material right there to do so and were perfectly happy to contribute them, and in the end Milo realized a fantastic profit from both halves of his project for doing nothing more than signing his name twice.

The arrangements were fair to both sides. Since Milo did have freedom of passage everywhere, his planes were able to steal over in a sneak attack without alerting the German antiaircraft gunners; and since Milo knew about the attack, he was able to alert the German antiaircraft gunners in sufficient time for them to begin firing accurately the moment the planes came into range. It was an ideal arrangement for everyone but the dead man in Yossarian's tent, who was killed over the target the day he arrived.

"I didn't kill him!" Milo kept replying passionately to Yossarian's angry protest. "I wasn't even there that day, I tell you. Do you think I was down there on the ground firing an antiaircraft gun when the planes came over?

"But you organized the whole thing, didn't you?" Yossarian shouted back at him in the velvet darkness cloaking the path leading past the still vehicles of the motor pool to the open-air movie theater.

"And I didn't organize anything," Milo answered indignantly, drawing great agitated sniffs of air in through his hissing, pale, twitching nose. "The Germans have the bridge, and we were going to bomb it, whether I stepped into the picture or not. I just saw a wonderful opportunity to make some profit out of the mission, and I took it. What's so terrible about that?"

"What's so terrible about it? Milo, a man in my tent was killed on that mission before he could even unpack his bags."

"But I didn't kill him."

"You got a thousand dollars extra for it."

"But I didn't kill him. I wasn't even there, I tell you. I was in Barcelona buying olive oil and skinless and boneless sardines, and I've got the purchase orders to prove it. And I didn't get the thousand dollars. That thousand dollars went to the syndicate, and everybody got a share, even you." Milo was appealing to Yossarian from the bottom of his soul. "Look, I didn't start this war, Yossarian, no matter what that lousy Wintergreen is saying. I'm just trying to put it on a businesslike basis. Is anything wrong with that? You know, a thousand dollars ain't such a bad price for a medium bomber and a crew. If I can persuade the Germans to pay me a thousand dollars for every plane they shoot down, why shouldn't I take it?"

"Because you're dealing with the enemy, that's why. Can't you understand that we're fighting a war? People are dying. Look around you, for Christ's sake!"

Milo shook his head with weary forbearance. "And the Germans are not our enemies," he declared. "Oh, I know what you're going to say. Sure, we're at war with them. But the Germans are also members in good standing of the syndicate, and it's my job to protect their rights as shareholders. Maybe they did start the war, and maybe they are killing millions of people, but they pay their bills a lot more promptly than some allies of ours I could name. Don't you understand that I have to respect the sanctity of my contract with Germany? Can't you see it from my point of view? . . .

TERRY SOUTHERN

*Cuba Libre**

. . . It was, in fact, true: this man *had* participated in the Cuban fiasco, of April 17, 1961, right up to the eleventh-hour moment. . . . I invited him over to my place for some drinks and a couple of hours tape-record-

* Excerpts from an interview published in *Esquire*, June, 1963.

ing of his curious tale. Here then is the story of Boris Grgurevich, thirty-three, born and raised in New York City; it is a verbatim transcript of the recorded interview:

Well, now let me ask you this, how did you get involved in this Cuban fiasco?

It was *cold,* man . . . you know, like January. You remember that big snowstorm? When they pulled all the cars off the street? Yeah, well that was it. . . . *Cold.* And this friend of mine, Ramón, comes by. I know him ten, fifteen years, but you know, haven't seen him for a while, so there's a big bla-bla hello scene . . . and he was running from something, I mean that was pretty obvious, but he was always very high-strung, moving around a lot—Miami, L.A., Mexico—and right away he says, "Man, let's got to *Miami,* where it's WARM." . . .

Had he mentioned anything about Cuba before you left for Miami?

No, man, he didn't say anything about *Cuba*—or maybe he *did* mention it, you know, fleetingly . . . like "bla-bla-bla the Cuban situation," or some crap like that, but we were just going to *Miami.* I mean he probably *did* mention it, because he was *born* in Cuba, you dig, and speaks Spanish and so on—but Castro was all right with me . . . I mean he had that *beard,* you know, and he seemed pretty interesting. No, we didn't talk about that, we get down to Miami, and we have three great days at the track, and then we have four terrible ones. . . . And so Ramón's taking me around—I mean, he knows Miami, see, and there's a *liquor* store in the neighborhood and he introduces me to this guy owns the liquor store—nice guy to know, owns a liquor store, and we get very friendly, you know, and he's giving us bottles of *rum.* Well, he's *Cuban,* dig, and he and Ramón start yakking it up about *Cuba* and "bla-bla Castro" and so on, and now he's talking about the "*invasion*" and how he's going to get back what they *took* from him and all that jive. And naturally I'm *agreeing* with him—well I mean he keeps laying this *rum* on us, about three bottles a day . . . but he's, well he was obviously full of crap, a kind of middle-aged hustler businessman . . . and all these cats hanging around the liquor store all looked like *hoods,* but sort of *failing,* you know? Anyway, we were meeting all these hood-faces hanging around this liquor store, mostly Cubans, or born in Cuba, and one of them took us to this . . . well, they had this recruiting station, you know, where they're all signing up for the *invasion,* and Ramón, well he's getting more and more excited about this—he's a *salesman* actually, I mean that's what he does, you know, in real life, sell things, and so he's selling himself on this idea, invading Cuba . . . and of course he was selling me on it too.

Well, now this recruiting—this station—was this being done quite openly?

Openly? Well, man, it was open twenty-four hours a day. You know, like in the middle of town.

. . . .

All right, now let me ask you this, what was Ramón's idea exactly—I mean, if the invasion was successful, did he think he would get something out of it?

Well, Ramón's what you might call an *essentialist*—and he just more or less figures that the man with the gun is, you know, *the man with the gun.*

And how did you feel about it?

The money was the thing that interested me—I mean we'd had these four very bad days at the track, and I had no *money.* Well, they were offering two-fifty a month and, you know, room and board, and . . . let's see, what else . . . yeah, *a trip to Guatemala.* But I guess the main thing was these cats at the recruiting station, giving this big spiel about "bla-bla-bla the American Government, the C.I.A., the U.S. Army," and so on. I mean the picture *they* were painting had *battleships* in it, Dad —you know, rockets against pitchforks. Well man, I mean how could we lose? Cuba versus America—are you kidding?

So it was pretty obvious even then that it was an American project?

Well *of course*, man—that was the whole pitch. You don't think they could have got these guys in there any other way, do you? I mean most of *these* guys were just sort of tired, middle-aged businessmen, or young hustlers . . . *they* weren't going to do anything, anybody could see that. It was like they were recruiting for the *parade*, you know, to march through Havana—and these guys were joining up to be *in* the parade, that's all. . . .

Did you meet other Americans who wanted to go?

Well, they didn't want Americans, you see, they wanted *Cubans*—for the big parade, dig? So you had to be Cuban, or if you were American, like Ramón, you had to be born in Cuba. But yeah, there were some other Americans down there, trying to get in—guys from the South mostly, these real . . . you know, anything-is-better-than-home types.

Most of them had been in the Army or something like that. But they didn't want them—they wanted Cubans.

So how did you get in?

Well, man, I mean they didn't make an *issue* of it or anything like that, not as far as *I* was concerned, because we had gotten sort of friendly with them, these C.I.A. cats . . . and they weren't bad guys really—I mean they thought *they* were doing the right thing and they thought *we* were doing the right thing, so we had a pretty good relationship with them. They were nice guys actually—just sort of goofy. . . .

How did you get to the airport?

Well, one night about a week after we signed up and had finished taking these physicals they said, "Okay, this is it"—you know, very dramatic—and they picked us up, there were about ninety of us altogether, in these trucks . . . sort of like moving vans, and, well, went to the airport. . . .

Then we get on the plane . . . C-47 . . . with the windows taped up, you know, no light, very cloak-and-dagger. And the trip . . . well, we took off that night and landed the next morning. Guatemala. And it was *hot*, man . . . wow, was it *hot*. Cats falling out all over the place —I mean, *these* guys were in no shape to start with, and then this *heat*. . . . First we pass a Guatemalan outpost, then a Cuban one. And it's all *lava*—the campsite was all lava . . . cut right out of the side of this mountain about 8,000 feet up. It was laid out in three levels, you dig, like huge terraces. The first level had the firing range, parade ground, the second had the barracks, mess hall, and so on, and then at the top was where the C.I.A. lived. . . . And it was supposed to be a secret camp, but of course everyone knew about it—I mean they were fifteen hundred guys up there eventually, blasting away all day with rifles, machine guns, mortars. And it was written up in all the newspapers and magazines—including *Bohemia Libre*. Know that one? It's the big anti-Communist magazine there.

. . . .

Did you start your training right away?

Yeah, you started off as a group. . . . They would keep all the guys who arrived together as a group, right through Basic Training—you know, marching, calisthenics, rifle range, and so on. And then they would train you for some specialty—like mortar, machine gun, or something. But we didn't get started until the next day. I mean there was a

When did you learn that you weren't going to take part in the invasion itself?

Not until the very last minute. We had *no idea* we weren't going, and it was a big drag man—I mean we'd been there *three months*, dig, and we wanted to *go*. We bugged the hell out of the Americans, Ramón and I, trying to get on that ship—but they wouldn't crack. "There's nothing we can do, your names weren't on the list," was all they would say. There were fourteen of us who didn't go. . . . We were all sore as hell about it. . . .

LIVING DANGEROUSLY IN THE AGE OF OVERKILL

FRANK SULLIVAN

The Cliché Expert Testifies on the Atom

1945

Q.: Mr. Arbuthnot, you're the very man I want to see. I've been longing to examine you on atomic energy.

A.: Well, my boy, you've come to the right party. I believe I can say that I know all the clichés on the subject.

Q.: How can you say that?

A.: Without fear of successful contradiction.

Q.: I'm glad to hear it. I suspected you would be making a study of the atomic cliché.

A.: A study! Why I've been doing nothing since V-J Day but listen to the experts explain atomic energy and the bomb on the air, or editorialize about them in the newspapers. Indeed I *am* the cliché expert of the atom. You realize of course what the dropping of that test bomb in the stillness of the New Mexico night did.

Q.: What did it do?

A.: It ushered in the atomic age, that's what it did. You know what kind of discovery this is?

Q.: What kind?

A.: A tremendous scientific discovery.

Q.: Could the atomic age have arrived by means of any other verb than "usher"?

A.: No. "Usher" has the priority.

Q.: Mr. Arbuthnot, what will never be the same?

A.: The world.

Q.: Are you pleased?

A.: I don't know. The splitting of the atom could prove a boon to mankind. It could pave the way for a bright new world. On the other hand it may spell the doom of civilization as we know it.

Q.: You mean that it has—

A.: Vast possibilities for good or evil.

Q.: At any rate, Mr. Arbuthnot, as long as the bomb had to be discovered, I'm glad we got it first.

A.: If you don't mind, I will be the one to recite the clichés here. You asked me to, you know.

Q.: I'm sorry.

A.: Quite all right. I shudder to think.

Q.: What?

A.: Of what might have happened if Germany or Japan had got the bomb first.

Q.: What kind of race was it between the Allied and German scientists?

A.: A close race.

Q.: What pressed?

A.: Time pressed.

Q.: With what kind of energy did the scientists work in their race to get the bomb?

A.: Feverish energy. Had the war lasted another six months the Germans might have had the bomb. It boggles.

Q.: What boggles?

A.: This tremendous scientific discovery boggles the imagination. Also stirs same.

Q.: Where do we stand, Mr. Arbuthnot?

A.: At the threshold of a new era.

Q.: And humanity is where?

A.: At the crossroads. Will civilization survive? Harness.

Q.: Harness, Mr. Arbuthnot? What about it?

A.: Harness and unleash. You had better learn to use those two words, my boy, if you expect to talk about the atom, or write about it, either. They are two words very frequently used. With pea, of course.

Q.: Why pea?

A.: Oh, everything is in terms of the pea. You know how much U-235 it would take to drive a car to the moon and back ?

Q.: No, sir. How much?

A.: A lump the size of a pea. Know how much U-235 it would take to ring your electric doorbell for twenty million years?

Q.: How much, God forbid?

A.: A lump the size of a pea. Know how much it would take to lift the Empire Building twelve miles into the air?

Q.: I wish you would let the Empire State Building alone, Mr. Arbuthnot. It is all right where it is.

A.: Sorry. It must be lifted twelve miles into the air. Otherwise, do you know who would not be able to understand the practical application, or meaning, of atomic energy?

Q.: No. Who?

A.: The average layman.

Q.: I see. Well, in that case, up she goes. I gather that a lump the size of a pea would do it.

A.: Exactly.

Q.: You wouldn't settle for a lump the size of a radish, or a bean?

A.: Sorry. The pea is the accepted vegetable in these explanations. Do you know what the atomic energy in the lobe of your left ear could do?

Q.: What?

A.: If harnessed, it could propel a B-29 from Tokyo to San Francisco.

Q.: It *could!*

A.: Do you know that the energy in every breath you take could send the Twentieth Century Limited from New York to Chicago?

Q.: Mercy on us, Mr. Arbuthnot!

A.: And the atomic energy in your thumbnail could, if unleashed, destroy a city twice the size of three Seattles. Likewise, the energy in your . . .

Q.: For God's sake, stop, Mr. Arbuthnot! You make me feel like a menace to world security in dire need of control by international authority in the interests of world peace. Kindly leave off explaining atomic energy to me in terms so simple a layman can understand. Explain it to me in scientific terms, and the more abstruse the better.

A.: Well, listen carefully and I'll give you a highly technical explanation. In the first place the existence of the atom was only suspected. Then Einstein . . . equation . . . nucleus . . . electron . . . bombard . . . proton . . . deuteron . . . radioactive . . . neutron . . . atomic weight . . . beta rays . . . matter . . . split . . . chain reaction . . . gamma rays . . . alpha particles . . . Mme. Curie . . . break down . . . energy . . . end products . . . control . . . impact . . . uranium . . . Dr. Niels Bohr . . . barium . . . orbit . . . Dr. Lise Meitner . . . knowledge pooled . . . Dr. Enrico Fermi . . . military possibilities . . . Dr. Vannevar Bush . . . U-235 . . . isotopes . . .

U-238 . . . autocatalytic . . . heavy water . . . New Mexico . . . mushroom-shaped cloud . . . awesome sight . . . fission . . . William L. Laurence . . . and there you had a weapon potentially destructive beyond the wildest nightmares of science. Do I make myself clear?

Q.: Perfectly. Now, Mr. Arbuthnot, what is nuclear energy the greatest discovery since?

A.: It is the greatest discovery since the discovery of fire. You will find that "Promethean" is the correct adjective to use here.

Q.: What does this tremendous scientific discovery do to large armies?

A.: It spells the doom of large armies. It also spells the doom of large navies. Likewise, it spells the doom of large air forces. Similarly, as I mentioned earlier, it may spell the doom of civilization. I doubt if so many dooms have been spelled by anything since the phrase was first coined.

Q.: When was that, sir?

A.: I should imagine at the time gunpowder spelled the doom of the bow and arrow.

Q.: What is the atomic bomb a menace to?

A.: World order, world peace, and world security.

Q.: What must be done to it?

A.: It must be controlled by an international authority. The San Francisco Charter must be revised to fit the Atomic Age.

Q.: What does the bomb make essential?

A.: It makes world unity essential. It makes an international league for peace essential if the world is not to be plunged into a third war which will destroy civilization.

Q.: In short, its use must be—

A.: Banned.

Q.: What kind of plaything is the bomb?

A.: A dangerous plaything. A dangerous toy.

Q.: What kind of boomerang is it?

A.: A potential boomerang.

Q.: What else is it?

A.: It is the greatest challenge mankind has yet faced. It is also the greatest destructive force in history. It has revolutionary possibilities and enormous significance and its discovery caused international repercussions.

Q.: What does the splitting of the atom unleash?

A.: The hidden forces of the universe. Vast.

Q.: Vast?

A.: That's another word you'd better keep at hand if you expect to talk or write about this tremendous scientific discovery. Vast energy, you know. Vast possibilities. Vast implications. Vast prospects; it opens them.

Q.: I see. What cannot grasp the full significance of the tremendous scientific discovery?

A.: The human mind.

Q.: Whose stone is it?

A.: The philosopher's stone.

Q.: Whose dream?

A.: The alchemist's dream.

Q.: And whose monster?

A.: Frankenstein's monster.

Q.: What does it transcend?

A.: It transcends the wildest imaginings of Jules Verne.

Q.: And of whom else?

A.: H. G. Wells.

Q.: The fantastic prophecies of these gentlemen have become what?

A.: Stern reality.

Q.: What does it make seem tame?

A.: The adventures of Superman and Flash Gordon.

Q.: Very good, Mr. Arbuthnot. Now, then, in addition to ushering in the Atomic Age, what else does this T.S.D. do?

A.: It brightens the prospect for the abolition of war but increases the possibility of another war. It adds to the store of human knowledge. It unlocks the door to the mysteries of the universe. It makes flights into interstellar space a possibility. It endangers our security and makes future aggression a temptation.

Q.: What has it done to warfare?

A.: It has revolutionized warfare, and outmoded it, and may outlaw it. It has changed all existing concepts of military power. It has made current weapons of war obsolete.

Q.: And what may it do to cities?

A.: It may drive cities underground.

Q.: Mr. Arbuthnot, in the happy event that atomic energy is not used destructively, what kind of role will it play?

A.: A peacetime role.

Q.: Meaning?

A.: Meaning cheap power, cheap fuel. A lump of U-235—

Q.: The size of a pea?

A.: No, not this time—the size of forty pounds of coal would run the entire nation's heating plants all winter.

Q.: What would that result in?

A.: Sweeping changes in our daily life and unemployment on a hitherto unheard-of scale.

Q.: Bringing about what kind of revolution?

A.: An industrial revolution.

Q.: Mr. Arbuthnot, should we share the secret with other nations?

A.: Yes and no.

Q.: If the latter, why?

A.: Because we can be trusted with it.

Q.: Why can we be trusted with it?

A.: Because we would use it only in self-defense and as a last resort.

Q.: Who could not be trusted with it?

A.: Some future Hitler. Some gangster nation. Some future aggressor.

Q.: If we should share it, why that?

A.: As a gesture of confidence in other nations.

Q.: And anyhow—

A.: Anyhow, every nation will possess the secret within five years.

Q.: Now, Mr. Arbuthnot, can you tell us what is ironic?

A.: It is ironic that several of the major contributions to the bomb were made by scientists whom Hitler and Mussolini had exiled.

Q.: In other words, Hitler cooked—

A.: His own goose.

Q.: What else is ironic?

A.: The spending of two billions on the bomb, in contrast to the amounts spent on education, public health, slum clearance, and research on cancer and other diseases.

Q.: What kind of commentary is that?

A.: A sad commentary on our so-called, or vaunted, civilization.

Q.: Mr. Arbuthnot, how ready is man for the Atomic Age?

A.: As ready as a child is to handle dynamite.

Q.: What kind of little boys do the atomic scientists remind you of?

A.: Of little boys playing with matches.

Q.: What is a possibility of the future?

A.: Atomic bombs a hundred times more destructive than the one dropped on Nagasaki.

Q.: What is such a discovery known as?

A.: It is known as man's conquest of natural forces.

Q.: What does such a discovery advance?

A.: It advances the frontiers of science.

Q.: And what does the invention of this key to world suicide constitute?

A.: It constitutes scientific progress.

MARYA MANNES

You're a Big Boy Now

1954

Once (we thought) where'er we went,
We were viewed as heaven-sent;
From Bonn to Barein, Rome to Rio;
People welcomed us *con brio*,
            but now they do not love us any more.

When now we visit foreign places
We find a sea of stony faces
Instinct with doubt and with suspicion
However innocent our mission,
            for now they do not love us any more.

Such is the sorry price of power
That minds of other men turn sour,
Seeing in the wagging of our tail
Only a newer, bigger flail,
            for now they do not love us any more.

GEORGE G. KIRSTEIN

Non-Survivability Plus

1960

The way to disarm is to arm. A country has to have more arms than its potential enemy in order to negotiate disarmament from a position of strength. Once we have arms superiority, the Russians will presumably be forced to disarm. One odd thing about this prevailing current doctrine is that it is not expected to work in reverse. If the Russians gain arms superiority over us, we will not begin to disarm—we will "close the gap." Another curious thing about it is that when we did have arms superiority—when we had the A-bomb and the Russians didn't—neither they nor we disarmed. They closed the gap.

But just because the theory has not worked so far in either direction is no reason to abandon it. The task before us is to compose a logic to justify our immutable theory, and for this purpose we need a new language. Fortunately such an instrument is already at hand, for both the armed services and the research centers of the great universities have men trained in the manufacture of a new jargon which will serve as a framework for the new logic. For simplicity's sake and to differentiate it from English, this language may be called Desperanto.

For example, all reasonable men know that the way to stop an enemy from attacking us is to have the capacity to destroy him if he makes the first move. This ability for "instant and massive" retaliation is labeled "deterrence" and for it to be effective we must have overwhelming "deterrent capability." General Power points out that if we have sufficient "deterrent capability," it will be impossible for an aggressor to develop a "confidence factor." "Deterrent capability," the very keystone of the new logic, has several synonyms, of which the one most frequently used is "kill" power. Fortunately, we are told that at the present time our "kill" power—take it for all in all—is superior to the Russians'. However, we are still in danger because of the "missile gap." It is not enough to have over-all superior "kill" power; paradoxically, we must have a surplus of it in order to guarantee our survival. A surplus of "kill" power is called "over-kill" and the key equation of the new theory is, "Over-kill equals total non-survivability plus." In this equation, of course, we have the "over-kill" and the enemy has the "non-survivability plus."

Unfortunately, we do not have enough "deterrent capability" even when we have lots of "over-kill," as we now have. "Over-kill" doesn't take care of "limited aggression" in what Representative Walter calls "fourth-dimensional" war. In order to stop this "limited aggression" threat, we must have "limited deterrents" or clearly there will be a "deterrent gap." We must have an over-all military "posture" capable of defending ourselves by every means from launching "preventive war" (this used to be called "attack" in the old language) to repelling invaders armed with slingshots. I feel myself that the military is guilty of overlooking our slingshot "capability," but perhaps we should not be too harsh, for they have overlooked little else. None the less, the Democratic candidates, particularly Senator Symington, may have a real campaign issue in this slingshot "gap." Fortunately, there is not a correlative "bow and arrow" gap, because we have a ready reserve or "militia" of sportsmen skilled with this weapon.

The logicians of "deterrence" may at last be satisfied when we perfect, as we are sure to do soon, the "Domesday bomb." This weapon, when hitched up to an electronic brain, will be able to destroy the remainder of mankind even if no survivors are left in the attacked country to set it off. This is what spokesmen of the new logic call an "invulnerable deterrent." Apparently this cobalt-coated hydrogen bomb creates a radioactive fallout so excessive that *On the Beach* can become fact—not fiction. This is total "over-kill," or the end of the line. Indeed, the "Domesday bomb" may be the "fantastic new weapon" about which Mr. Khrushchev recently bragged. So the "Domesday bomb gap" may be already upon us, although, due to the "intelligence gap and a reappraisal of Soviet "intentions" as contrasted with "capabilities," it may be some time before we can know whether we are in this jeopardy. Unless a "Domesday bomb" can be set up in each "free" country the potential enemy's "confidence factor" may become absolutely overwhelming, because according to the experts only a weapon guaranteeing "unacceptable damage" will deter all rational rulers from aggression.

But I foresee a future gap even after we announce that we and all our friends, great and small, also have the "Domesday bomb." Let us suppose that the Russians beat us to the moon. Suppose then that there are two Russians or even a couple of Russian dogs on that satellite when the "Domesday bomb" goes off. Clearly we have failed to reduce "survivability" to zero. We need a "Domesday moon bomb"—one capable not only of destroying mankind on earth but on the moon as well, preferably simultaneously. Without such a deterrent we are at the absolute mercy of the enemy. Let's have no spiritual flabbiness nor lack of zeal in perfecting this weapon. Let us have a "crash" program to meet this problem. Here is a gap which can be foreseen and "definitized." With the possession of this super-massive retaliatory defense deterrent, we can "finalize" our future.

ART BUCHWALD

Talk, Talk, Talk, Talk

1962

I've been watching the disarmament talks now being held in Geneva with a great deal of interest. They seem to be taking on a pattern and they will probably be going on for a long time.

One has only to look into the future. The setting is the same but Ambassador Zorin of the Soviet Union has been replaced by Ambassador Groanyko and Ambassador Dean has been replaced by Ambassador Stone.

I take you to the 12,654th plenary session of the 17-nation disarmament conference in Geneva, in the year 1994.

Ambassador Stone is about to make a statement, but he sneezes instead.

AMBASSADOR GROANYKO: Your proposal is entirely unacceptable to the Soviet Socialist Republics.

STONE: But I didn't make a proposal, I just sneezed.

GROANYKO: I ask for a five-minute recess to confer with my staff.

(*The recess is granted and* GROANYKO *huddles with Soviet experts.*)

GROANYKO: What should our response be?

SOVIET ADVISER: We could say *Gesundheit.*

GROANYKO: Yes, but how do we know the sneeze wasn't a trap to make us say *Gesundheit?*

2D SOVIET ADVISER: But if we don't say *Gesundheit,* and he really sneezed, it could be a big propaganda victory for the West.

GROANYKO: Should we ask time to get instructions from Moscow?

SOVIET ADVISER: No. It would look like we don't have authority to make decisions on our own.

GROANYKO: I think the best thing is to say *Gesundheit* with reservations. If it's a trap we can always renounce it.

(*The session is called back to order.*)

GROANYKO: Mr. Chairman, I wish to address a word to the Ambassador from the United States.

CHAIRMAN: Does the American Ambassador yield?

STONE: I do.

GROANYKO: *Gesundheit.*

STONE: I object to the Soviet proposal. They are not dealing in good faith and my government cannot accept their proposal.

GROANYKO: But all I said was *Gesundheit* in answer to your sneeze.

STONE: I request a five-minute recess to discuss this with my British colleagues.

(*The recess is granted and* STONE *huddles with the* BRITISH AMBASSADOR.)

STONE: What do you make of it?

BRITISH AMBASSADOR: I don't like it.

STONE: Neither do I. I've sneezed before and they've never said *Gesundheit.*

BRITISH AMBASSADOR: If we accept it, and then he sneezes, we'll have to say *Gesundheit* to him.

STONE: If we give in on this, we may have to give in on other things.

BRITISH AMBASSADOR: At the same time it might be the opening we need.

STONE: I wish we knew. I could sneeze again and see what they do.

BRITISH AMBASSADOR: Or I could sneeze and see if they'll say it to me as well as to you.

STONE: Why do you think they spoke in German?

BRITISH AMBASSADOR: That's what I've been wondering. They've got something up their sleeves.

STONE: Suppose I say "thank you" on the provision that if they accept the rest of our proposals, we will accept their *Gesundheit*.

BRITISH AMBASSADOR: Good idea. It could be the first real indication of their intentions that we've had.

(*The session is called back to order.*)

STONE: I wish to thank the Soviet Ambassador for saying *Gesundheit*.

GROANYKO: I wish to object to the American Ambassador's statement and cannot see any significant change in the American warlike attitude toward these talks.

STONE: All I said was, Thank you for saying *Gesundheit*.

GROANYKO: I demand a two-hour recess to discuss this new proposal with my government, but I want to point out that unless something more concrete comes of these negotiations, they will have to be terminated.

CHAIRMAN: The meeting is adjourned until tomorrow morning at ten o'clock.

JULES FEIFFER
Civil Defense

FOR YEARS THOSE OF US WHO
HAVE TOILED IN THE VINEYARDS
OF SUBURBAN CIVIL DEFENSE
HAVE BEEN CONCERNED WITH
THE PROBLEM OF HOW TO
MAINTAIN LAW AND ORDER
FOLLOWING A NUCLEAR ASSAULT.

THE BIG CITIES WOULD, OF COURSE,
BE ANNIHILATED THEREBY
SIMPLIFYING **THEIR** CIVIL
DEFENSE PROBLEMS
IMMEASURABLY. HOWEVER,
FOR THOSE OF US IN **SUBURBIA**
THERE ARE **BOUND** TO BE
COMPLICATIONS.

WE WOULD BE SUBJECT TO
MASS ONSLAUGHTS OF
REFUGEES FROM THE CITY.
WHILE OUR HEARTS, AS
ALL HEARTS MUST, GO OUT
TO THESE VICTIMS THEY
DO POSE A THREAT TO
OUR CAREFULLY PLANNED
PROGRAM.

HOW CAN ONE TELL A RADIO-ACTIVE MOB THAT THEY WOULDN'T BE HAPPY IN OUR TOWN? NO, WE CAN ONLY PRESERVE OUR WAY OF LIFE BY BARRICADING OUR STREETS AND RE-DIRECTING ALL MIGRANT TRAFFIC TO THE PUBLIC HIGH-WAYS, AIDING THEM PERHAPS, WITH IMPROVED DIRECTIONAL SIGNS AND FREE ROAD MAPS.

BUT WHEN MAN'S SURVIVAL IS AT STAKE HE MAY WELL SURRENDER TO THE **BASER** INSTINCTS. OUR BARRICADES MIGHT HAVE TO BE DEFENDED BY **FORCE OF ARMS.** BUT JUST AS WE ARE WILLING TO GO TO WAR TO DEFEND OUR FREEDOM SO WE SHALL BE WILLING TO DEFEND WHAT'S LEFT OF IT BY MANNING THE SUBURBAN BARRICADES !

IN SUBURBAN CIVIL DEFENSE OUR MOTTO IS: IF YOU CAN'T GET YOURSELF A RUSSIAN, SETTLE FOR AN AMERICAN.

JOHN FRANCIS PUTNAM

A Plan for Surrender

1962

A request for funds was made to Congress recently to implement a study on how to go about a "possible surrender" of the United States to a foreign power.

Journalistic war horses immediately began to whinny and snort. The Hearst papers plated forty columns of vehemence and called in their Sports Cartoonists to lend a little extra color to the editorial page. (When you want to get across the idea to *Journal-American* readers that *Uncle Sam is no Quitter!*—it has to be done with a view from the bleachers.)

Congressmen went all out in a revel of true bipartisan indignation, and those Washington columnists who are largely syndicated in rural areas began dusting off such phrases as "irresponsible boondoggling" and "budgetary frills."

Since this dangerous idea has not gone beyond the proposal stage, no attempt has been made to blame and prosecute anybody and the project has been quietly dropped. It is distressing to think that we must abandon this serious investigation into the mechanics and protocol of a surrender. It is an adventurous and imaginative idea and quite in accord with any long view of history.

Therefore, in the interests of patriotism, history, and greater economy in government, the following Surrender Plan is offered, absolutely without cost, to the War Plans Division of the Department of Defense.

First there is the semantic problem: that word *surrender*. Like *masturbation* and *whiskey priest* it has to disappear from public utterance, and something quiet and eloquent must take its place. We suggest the word *adjustment*. Americans, as is well-known, are constantly adjusting themselves to everything from environment to posture chairs—and besides, the word *adjustment* has comfortable chiropractic overtones. With our big, rich nation suddenly forced to throw in the sponge, it becomes a matter of "now or never" with that old backbone!

The "adjustment" ceremony and proceedings should be in good taste, even if it no longer is expected of us. We must maintain a Jeffersonian simplicity at all costs and see to it that it evolves as a strictly *civilian* affair. Everybody on our side will show up in slacks and sports shirts. (No ties.) We'll work to achieve that relaxed, back-yard-cook-out kind of informality that's never failed to win us friends. If we play our cards right, this can be the first surrender between two major powers to be conducted on a "first-name basis."

Location of the Adjustment Meeting is very important. It should not only offer all possible amenities, but it also ought to be spacious enough to house a provisional U.S. Government once the ceremonies are over. White Sulphur Springs would be ideal. The supply of good Bourbon is ample, and the location is remote enough to establish the validity of an Administration which, due to the new imperatives, would be much less accountable to popular will than any previous ones.

A sword is usually offered up to the successful opponent as a part of the ritual of surrender. In this case, an Honor Scout might give up his six-blade "official" knife on behalf of the United States of America. Show us the Field Marshal with kids of his own who would ever dream of keeping *that* knife. His impulsive return of the six-blader to the big-eyed boy scout would do more for reconciliation among nations than a mass repatriation of enemy-held prisoners.

As for the activation of the ceremony itself, a Joint Staging Committee from the major television networks would put through a crash program to "showcase" the event, complete with background choral group, ballet, and an augmented symphony orchestra. The actual event must be timed so that television coverage will reach the entire country at once, regardless of time-lapse: for, a repeat performance for the West Coast might well cause an exasperated enemy delegation to impose more stringent terms on the second go-round.

The production and artistic staff of the TV Spectacular—entitled *Make The Best Of It, U.S.A.!*—would be wise to forego the usual list of credits. Identification with *this* show is bound, in years to come, to land them in the files of some future equivalent of the Attorney General's List.

Practical thinking would of course present the entire event on a closed-circuit pay-TV basis with the proceeds contributed as a first in-stallment on our War Reparations Bill.

The choice of suitable delegates to the Adjustment Meeting will be a delicate matter. They must be persons of real stature totally divorced from politics—persons who could later on survive the taint and stink of having been in on the "give up!" Figures identified with Sports but not necessarily athletes, like Dan Topping; men identified with the enter-tainment world but not necessarily actors, like Jerry Geisler; champions of religion without official clerical status, like Godfrey P. Schmidt. In short, *Celebrity*—as truly representing the New American Virtue—should confront (and perhaps even dazzle) our opponents across the green baize-covered table.

In any event, if our America is brought to this melancholy pass, we can always draw upon our cultural heritage for strength and wisdom, remembering that it is really *we* who are the good guys, cheerful even when the ammo runs out, and having faith that forever and ever, just over the rim of the hill, some epic troop of cavalry is waiting for the cue so we can say at the end, "Golly, fellows, we thought you'd never get here!"

CONGRESSMAN JIM WRIGHT

Hot Line

1963

They have just finished installing the direct line from the White House to the Kremlin, and somebody goofed.

The mistake, as I see it, was in equipping the circuit with teletype machines rather than telephones.

This will reduce the margin for error in handling high-priority mes-sages in times of world crisis, so I suppose it's all for the best.

But I was sort of hoping that we might be able to subject Khrushchev to America's ultimate war-of-nerves weapon—the telephone.

Unless I miss my guess, we could reduce him to a jabbering, helpless psychological wreck in certainly no more than a week.

A 100-megaton bomb can do nothing more than destroy and set fire to an area the size of Delaware, and there is always a chance it might not hit within range. From the telephone, on the other hand, there is no escape. It will seek you out wherever you are. Ask any businessman.

To those who protest that this would be too inhumane, I offer the following. We wouldn't have to telephonize Khrushchev to a point of complete insensibility. Just before he showed signs of cracking, we could offer to disconnect his telephone as soon as he junked all his missiles and guns and stopped trying to make us all Communists.

Of course my idea wouldn't work if use of the telephone line were limited only to President Kennedy and Khrushchev. It would be improper for Mr. Kennedy, as our head of state, to wage an electronic war of nerves against Khrushchev.

American taxpayers, on the other hand, would be under no such restrictions. We could call up Khrushchev at any hour of the day or night, just as we do each other.

One of the first such calls, undoubtedly, would come from the telephone company itself. As a new subscriber, Khrushchev would be asked to give the exact number of rooms in the Kremlin, together with a brief description of the decor in each.

Presuming that Khrushchev's mind was still sound after the telephone company's genteel inquisition, he would then be ready to receive other calls. An important factor would be the difference in time between here and Moscow.

There are, for instance, those throaty-voiced young ladies whose job it is to call up gentlemen at random and inquire suggestively if you know how much fun you could have taking dancing lessons. These calls usually come early in the evening.

"Is dancing lessons, you say?" Khrushchev would sputter. "You are knowing it is 2 o'clock in the morning in Moscow? I am being in bed, please."

If one of these calls happened to be answered by Mrs. Khrushchev, so much the better.

Comrade Khrushchev then could be called, in this order, by people selling:

1) The *Washington Post*, your morning newspaper.
2) *Life* magazine (with a special introductory offer).
3) Cemetery lots.

Of these possibilities, the third is the most intriguing. Imagine Khrushchev trying to talk faster than a cemetery-lot salesman.

"*Nyet! Nyet! Nyet!* It is *I* who am supposed to bury *YOU!*"

Another possibility is a series of calls from television rating services: "Hello, Chairman Khrushchev? This is Video Poll, Inc. Is your television on, sir?"

"*Da.*"

"Would you mind telling me what program you are watching, please?"

"Is watching me, it is!"

Of course I'm only spoofing about all this. The telephone is a magnificent instrument. Through its electronic magic, distance evaporates and friend is linked with friend, doctor with patient, businessman with customer, wife with husband, mother with son. It serves a truly noble and —Excuse me a moment, please. It's ringing again.

You can't say civilization don't advance, however, for in every war they kill you a new way.—*Will Rogers*

JAMES THURBER

The Tiger Who Would Be King

One morning the tiger woke up in the jungle and told his mate that he was king of beasts.

"Leo, the lion, is king of beasts," she said.

"We need a change," said the tiger. "The creatures are crying for a change."

The tigress listened but she could hear no crying, except that of her cubs.

"I'll be king of beasts by the time the moon rises," said the tiger. "It will be a yellow moon with black stripes, in my honor."

"Oh, sure," said the tigress as she went to look after her young, one of whom, a male, very like his father, had got an imaginary thorn in his paw.

The tiger prowled through the jungle till he came to the lion's den. "Come out," he roared, "and greet the king of beasts! The king is dead, long live the king!"

Inside the den, the lioness woke her mate. "The king is here to see you," she said.

"What king?" he inquired, sleepily.

"The king of beasts," she said.

"I am the king of beasts," roared Leo, and he charged out of the den to defend his crown against the pretender.

It was a terrible fight, and it lasted until the setting of the sun. All the animals of the jungle joined in, some taking the side of the tiger and others the side of the lion. Every creature from the aardvark to the zebra took part in the struggle to overthrow the lion or to repulse the tiger, and some did not know which they were fighting for, and some fought for both, and some fought whoever was nearest, and some fought for the sake of fighting.

"What are we fighting for?" someone asked the aardvark.

"The old order," said the aardvark.

"What are we dying for?" someone asked the zebra.

"The new order," said the zebra.

When the moon rose, fevered and gibbous, it shone upon a jungle in which nothing stirred except a macaw and a cockatoo, screaming in horror. All the beasts were dead except the tiger, and his days were numbered and his time was ticking away. He was monarch of all he surveyed, but it didn't seem to mean anything.

MORAL: *You can't very well be king of beasts if there aren't any.*

OUTER SPACE—THE NEW FRONTIER?

ARTHUR HOPPE

Everybody Loves a Party

1961

In those early days we may have been way behind the Russians in space. And they may have scored one propaganda victory after another. While I didn't wish to sound sour grapes, I always felt we could write better dialogue than those new-wave scenarios Tass put out whenever Mr. Khrushchev greeted a new hero astronaut on the telephone.

The way I saw it, our own hero astronaut, Mr. Tab Hunter, lands safely after orbiting the earth a hundred and forty-two times, and he hits the nearest phone booth, script in hand:

THE PRESIDENT: I am listening to you, Mr. Hunter, and cordial congratulations.

MR. HUNTER: Mr. President, I report that the task set by the Democratic Party and the government has been fulfilled.

THE PRESIDENT: Wonderful. This is a happy time for the whole of mankind. I kiss you on both cheeks. We are proud that you, an American man, a Democrat, have done this. By the way, how was the trip?

MR. HUNTER: Wonderful, John Fitzgerald. While flying over Kansas I could look down and see the free-enterprise farms made prosperous by our party's imaginative flexible-parity, acreage-allotment, and soil-bank programs.

THE PRESIDENT: Wonderful.

MR. HUNTER: Thank you. I also flew over cities and towns where I could look down and see people smiling joyfully because they were the happy beneficiaries of our party's imaginative social-security, indigent-welfare and aid-to-needy-children programs.

THE PRESIDENT: Wonderful. You have shown that you are a good Democrat and can hold high the banner of Thomas Jefferson. And how's the wife? We all know how wives are. Ho, ho, ho.

MR. HUNTER: Ho, ho, ho. Wonderful, John Fitzgerald. She has been home doing calisthenics during my flight. She is a loyal Democrat and a true American woman. She works eighteen hours a day in a boiler-plate factory and reads the *Collected Works of Grover Cleveland* to me aloud at night.

THE PRESIDENT: Wonderful. And now go home to your wife and get some rest. You have earned it. Only a true Democratic Party man could have performed your feat.

MR. HUNTER: Thank you from the bottom of my heart, John Fitzgerald. I promise to continue to fulfill the lofty duties of a Democrat as I have fulfilled them today. *Au revoir*.

That would give the Russians a thing or two to think about. But on second thought, I bet we couldn't bring it off. The trouble is, a totalitarian society has even more unfair advantages in a propaganda war than in a space race. We set up one of our hero astronauts with a script like that and the odds are fifty-fifty he'll turn out to be a Republican who wants to talk about the do-nothing Truman years.

Well, democracy may not be as efficient. But it's a hell of a lot more believable.

M. J. ARLEN

The Space Race

(*A Bemused Glimpse Ahead*)

1962

The recent Russian space feat, consisting of the rendezvous in orbit of the entire company of the Leningrad Symphony Orchestra, their lunar flight, their descent to the surface of the moon, their exceptionally sensitive rendering of Prokofieff's Fifth Symphony, their safe return to the mother ship, and their subsequent landing in a cornfield outside Odessa, has elicited the admiration of the world and the keen interest of U.S. scientists. The official United States position was stated in a cable dispatched by the President to Premier Khrushchev three hours after word had been received in Washington of the epochal accomplishment. "I congratulate you all on this adventurous and exciting space flight," telegraphed the President. "I know the American people join with me in applauding the success of this latest achievement."

Privately, however, many U.S. scientists feel that the new Russian feat, while exciting in itself, has not necessarily demonstrated that the Russians have made any significantly new strides in the technology of space flight. "We knew they had the booster power," said Dr. Hans Moriarty, Program Director for the U.S. Space Commission. "We knew they could rendezvous men. We knew they could send them down to the moon and bring them back. We knew the Leningrad Symphony could play Prokofieff. We're maintaining a wait-and-see attitude."

The United States meanwhile announced a "crash" approach to the launching of the Excalibur XVIII rocket, designed to carry a Polaroid camera and a payload of extraordinarily precise geologic instruments to the surface of Saturn. U.S. scientists have pointed out with quiet pride that the Russians are at least "five years behind us" in the development of Polaroid cameras and extraordinarily precise geologic instruments. Possibly, admitted Dr. Moriarty, the United States is lagging, too, in the sense of not yet having achieved orbital rendezvous—*successful* orbital rendezvous, that is—descent to the surface of the moon, and, naturally, return from the surface of the moon. But it is in the "broad base" of the U.S. space program, said Dr. Moriarty, that this country's ultimate advantage lies.

Last week, Dr. Norman Wilking, director of Project Titania, told a packed and cheering Senate hearing room that the United States is "second to none" in the variety and sophistication of its space scientific explorations. Dr. Wilking called attention to the flight of the Janus III last month, which carried a payload of exceptionally sensitive medical instruments to the surface of Venus, the Sabre IV two weeks ago, which carried a payload of unusually accurate dental equipment to the surface of Mars, and the Hamadryad V, launched three days before the Russian feat and carrying the most elaborate payload of rainfall-measuring instruments yet designed, which scored a heartbreaking near-hit on Pluto. Dr. Wilking also mentioned the fact, forgotten by many now in the afterglow of the Russian propaganda triumph, that the United States is currently orbiting no less than 4,655 objects in space (not counting the "lost" package of needles), many of which are still reporting back virtually priceless scientific data, as compared with the Russian total of 35.

The United States' man-in-space program also took important strides forward with the successful mediation by Secretary of Labor Presswell of the forty-seven-day-long strike of cafeteria workers at Cape Canaveral. The walk-out, which had been sympathetically joined by electrical workers, machinists, carpenters, plumbers, and teamsters, was resolved after an all-night session involving Secretary Presswell; Senator Spaulding; Dr. Fielding Felspar, Executive Director of Project Albatross; Admiral Otis Macomber, Chairman of the Joint Chiefs of Staff; and Mrs. Amelia Quinn, President of Local 745, Cafeteria Workers of Southern Florida. The solution of the dispute, which had originally developed over a contract demand by Local 745 that an "extra man" be allowed aboard each space capsule for "in-flight feeding," should shortly permit countdown to be resumed on the two giant Baal rockets, which are to loft Astronauts Waldo Perkins and O. Lucien Moore into what U.S. spacemen confidently expect will be a record total of 425 orbits around the earth.

U.S. space authorities, in fact, remark that although the Russians have achieved a certain technical distinction in having sent men around the moon, onto the moon, and back from the moon, they still lag "significantly" behind us in the number of earth orbital flights, where the U.S. now leads with a total of 127 individual flights, for a total of 1,562 orbits, compared with 37 individual flights and a total of 570 orbits for the Russians.

"The scientific importance of these earth orbital flights cannot be stressed too highly," said the ruggedly handsome Dr. Felspar recently. "Last month, 'Wash' Dickerson brought back a great deal of very interesting data on a flight of 360 orbits' duration, including his report of sighting, just before dawn over Perth, Australia, something that very much resembled a flight of green horseflies. We expect that Perkins and O. Lucien Moore will bring back a lot of very interesting data on a flight of at least 450 orbits' duration. We are learning something all the time."

By the end of the year, the U.S. expects to be able to rendezvous two astronauts in earth orbit. Within the next three to four years, we expect to be able not only to rendezvous two astronauts in earth orbit but to lower them simultaneously, in Albatross capsules, now in the design stage, to the surface of Zion National Park, where the Space Commission is currently constructing a replica of the moon as an aid in training. "We are perhaps behind the Russians for the short term," admits Dr. Felspar, "but I have no doubt whatsoever that this country's steady accumulation of priceless scientific information is going to pay off handsomely in the long run, or possibly later."

RICHARD R. LINGEMAN

Moon Shot Eclipsed by Sun

1963

NASA announced today that it has decided to scrap its program to land a manned space vehicle on the moon because the Russians' space program is so far ahead they are certain to win the race. Instead, a crash program will be initiated to land a man on the sun. "We have seized the initiative," said a spokesman for the agency. "I doubt that the Russians have even thought of it yet." NASA's overall strategy is to concede the moon, Mars, Venus, and the other planets to Russia, and concentrate on a multi-billion program which will get us to the sun first. A Pentagon strategist heartily endorsed the program. "Whoever controls the sun, controls the solar system," he said.

The program has been dubbed "Operation Mantan" by NASA, and Miami Beach was designated as the launching site, after the Miami Chamber of Commerce convinced NASA meteorologists that the resort had more sun than any other city in the U.S.

A NASA spokesman denied that the sun's intense heat, capable of incinerating any substance now known to man, would be an obstacle to a sun-shoot. "These technical matters can be worked out at a later date," he said. "The important thing is to get going, to beat the Russians to the draw. Why do we want to spend billions of dollars to land a man on the sun? I'll tell you why. It's not just a matter of beating the Russians or even giving a boost to the Florida economy. Above all, it's because it is there!"

RUSSELL BAKER

The Enemy Moon

1964

It is gray and windy here and at night there is an evil white moon which laughs at the F.B.I.

Recently a crew from the state projectile factory sent a camera to the moon to take pictures. The National Security Council was curious to know why the moon was laughing and whose side it was on in the struggle for men's minds. The camera never came back.

Men in ten-gallon hats and three-button suits are standing on marble steps throughout the city trying to reassure passersby. They are certain to get to the bottom of this moon affair before 1970, they insist. The people, for the most part, hurry past them with eyes averted.

A short time ago, a man had his name taken down for arguing. "Why are you so sure we will win the race for space and therefore beat Communism in the struggle for men's minds?" the man asked. "Because we are able to put more sand into space than any other great power," came the reply. "Right now, for example, we are orbiting 50 percent more sand than any other washday product."

"You talk like a soap salesman," said the skeptic. "My advice to all of you is, Leave that moon alone." Whereupon the man's name was taken down by the police and circulated among his neighbors, who, fortunately for him, reported that he kept regular hours, drank little and always spoke well of Chiang Kai-shek.

The big house of the Leader here is dark and eerie under the bone-white moonlight. The Leader treads through the big house at night snapping out lights. There are rumors that he is quite gone on the subject. He has been telling people he must hold down the light bill so there will be enough money left to go to the moon and win the struggle for men's minds.

The townspeople say that the Leader is entitled to a few idiosyncrasies, considering the problems he has. For one thing the Inspired Man from over the sea has been going around saying that the Generalissimo has no clothes on. This had been whispered around town for several years, but everybody had agreed not to say it aloud because of the general understanding that two or three Congressional committees were ready to ruin anyone who did.

The Leader may also be distracted by the vulpine barking of his enemies who hope to put him out of the big dark house. The townspeople dread these marauders, who fly through the air and alight without warning to deliver their fearful boring attack.

They come in many guises. Some stand on street corners showing their teeth. It is best to go around the block to avoid this kind. He seizes his victim by the hand, shows his teeth and says, "As I can display more teeth than any other borer, I am clearly the nicest fellow around and should therefore be made the Leader."

Others take the opposite tack, seizing the victim's hand and urging him to let his old mother pay her own hospital bills and saying, "I am clearly the meanest fellow around and should therefore be made the Leader." Others seize the townspeople by the ears and shout things like, "Since you insist that I sacrifice myself to become the Leader, my inner nobility constrains me to give in."

These borers rarely talk about anything that is uppermost in the minds of the townspeople. They are given to tedious explanations of why the Generalissimo really does have clothes on even though he looks naked and how the struggle for men's minds can be won by putting sand into orbit with more imagination. On more vital questions, they are intellectually limp.

Ask, "What will you do to restore my enthusiasm?" and they tell you about Social Security. Ask, "What will you do for peace of mind?" and they tell you about the struggle for men's minds. Ask, "Why is that evil moon laughing at the F.B.I.?" and they tell you that if they are elected they will wipe that smirk off the moon's face.

Tell them, "Let that moon alone," and they will signal for policemen to take your name.

SPECIAL
ACKNOWLEDGMENTS

I am indebted to many people for suggestions, for making otherwise inaccessible material available to me, and for other kinds of assistance, and I very much regret that it appears impracticable to credit them properly by name. They include editors· and publishers, librarians and scholars, journalists and politicians, and quite a few of the writers whose work is represented here. Some of these people are old friends, others I know only through correspondence or telephone conversations. I am most grateful for their help, and I hope that the difference between what they find in this book and what they had expected to find, however great, does not constitute a net loss.

Anthologists are necessarily indebted to their predecessors as well; I list below some of the earlier collections I think most likely to interest readers of this book. Arthur P. Dudden's *Assault of Laughter*, published in 1962, is the only one I've seen that also deals particularly with American political humor; its emphasis is on older writings. Henry C. Carlisle, Jr.'s equally recent *American Satire in Prose and Verse* is a wide-ranging and sprightly collection. James R. Aswell's *Native American Humor*, Walter Blair's *Horse Sense in American Humor* (and other books), Edward Boykin's *The Wit and Wisdom of Congress* (from the Congressional Record), and Kenneth S. Lynn's *The Comic Tradition in America* are useful historical anthologies. There are many good general collections of humor and Americana, such as those edited by E. B. and Katharine S. White, B. A. Botkin, Edwin Seaver, Louis Untermeyer, Bennett Cerf, and Clifton Fadiman, and such engaging specialized anthologies as Dwight Macdonald's *Parodies*.